Tom Aitken

ONE HUNDRED *&* ONE
Beautiful TOWNS *in Great Britain*

RIZZOLI
NEW YORK

HIGHLANDS

SCOTTISH LOWLANDS

NOTHERN IRELAND

ISLANDS

NORTHEAST

YORKSHIRE

LAKE DISTRICT & NORTHWEST

MIDLANDS

WALES

WELSH BORDERS

EAST ANGLIA

COTSWOLDS

SOUTHEAST

WEST COUNTRY

ISLE OF WIGHT

REGIONAL CONTENTS

ALPHABETICAL CONTENTS

PREFACE

There are many more than 101 beautiful places in Great Britain and they are beautiful in many different ways. Britain is not large but its cultural, social, and historical variety is vast. Its four constituent parts differ from each other and within themselves. Landscapes vary dramatically. Moorland, seaside cliffs, river valleys, rolling hills, lakes and mountains, fenland flats, and windswept plateaus promote different ways and paces of life. Building materials and architectural styles differ. Towns built in stone and slate look very unlike towns built in brick and tile. Beauty for eye and mind may be found in both.

Striking differences of speech may add enjoyment as well as mystery to your visit. I, a Londoner, once waited for friends in a pub near the sea in Lincolnshire, listening to people talking. It was like being somewhere in Europe where I half-knew the language. I could identify most of the words in any sentence, but some—usually important ones—were unrecognizable. In parts of North Wales, business, domestic life, and education are conducted in Welsh. In western and highland Scotland many people still use Gaelic. These differences derive from many causes, not least from more than 2,000 years of history. You will read in these pages of the effects—on towns, their buildings, and the lives lived in them—of wool, fish, coal, clay, seas and rivers, churches, schools, and mineral springs; and of upheavals brought about by wars, invasions, and weather. You cannot sensibly generalize about either British towns or British people.

Change often brings with it rebuilding and development. The effects may be good, bad, or mixed. As has happened to some degree almost everywhere in postwar Europe, some new building has been done with willful disregard of the past and of the surroundings. In a typically sweeping utterance, Prince Charles asserted that architects have done more harm to London than did the Luftwaffe. Similar concerns are voiced elsewhere. (In many High Streets a glance at facades above banal shop fronts at ground level will induce a sharp pang of regret.) But if some towns are not so wholly beautiful as they were a few generations ago, change has revealed long-obscured beauty in others. In Hull, for example, the restored eighteenth-century port is a refreshing enclave in the heart of an otherwise not entirely attractive urban spread. Beauty is close at hand in most parts of Britain—within a short walk or, at worst, within a short drive. Great Britain has twenty-four UNESCO World Heritage Sites—in comparison with Italy's thirty-seven, a far from disgraceful figure.

Come once, return often. Great Britain is complicated, fascinating—and beautiful.

CANTERBURY

MURDER IN THE CATHEDRAL

CANTERBURY IS THE FIRST SUBSTANTIAL INLAND TOWN ON THE ROAD from Dover to London. Its situation—at a ford where the river Stour could be crossed—made it from Roman times an important center of communications and a fortified defensive position. The name "Canterbury" derives from Cantawarabyrig—the fortress of the people of Kent. Shallow-keeled boats could sail as far as the city, so invaders often came across the sea. The Romans themselves had done so, and they were followed by Saxons, Vikings, Danes, and Normans. In spring 597 a different sort of invader arrived: Augustine, sent by Pope Gregory the Great to refound the Church in England. There had been churches there, earlier. One of them, St Martin's, claimed to be "the oldest parish church in England," is still standing, incorporating remains from Roman times onward. The city's attraction for visitors and pilgrims was greatly increased in 1170 when the archbishop, Thomas Beckett, was murdered in the cathedral in the darkness of a midwinter dusk. This may have been instigated by King Henry II, who was reported to have said, in self-pitying rage, "Who will free me from this turbulent priest?" Vast pilgrimages followed. Geoffrey Chaucer (c. 1345-1400) gives an account, in his most famous long poem, *The Canterbury Tales*, of pilgrims on horseback traveling the pilgrim road from London to Canterbury.

The cathedral is the result of many rebuildings and extensions. It is unified as a building by the tall, slender central tower, popularly known as "Bell Harry." Of the many magnificent features of the interior, perhaps the most striking is the ascent from the nave—itself a gracefully tall and narrow space—to the Shrine of St Thomas. You can imagine crowds of excited pilgrims streaming up it as they reached the end of their journey.

Elsewhere in the town, charming cobbled lanes will take you to the Westgate Museum, built into the round towers of the city's medieval walls, which continue to define the city center. The Museum of Canterbury occupies part of the Poor Priests' Hospital, another richly textured medieval stone building. Next to St Martin's Church are the ruins of St Augustine's Abbey, which was destroyed when, in the 1530s, Henry VIII dissolved all the monasteries in England and used their wealth for his own purposes. The City Council meets under the elaborate rafters and roof of the former Church of the Holy Cross, presented to the city in 1978.

The Old Weavers' House has stood here since c. 1500.

facing page
Vaults supporting the roof of the cathedral fan out from the compound piers.

From Canterbury it is possible to visit many interesting and attractive places in Kent. There are picture-book villages. Of the coastal towns, Whitstable is associated with oysters, yachting, and windsurfing. Margate and Ramsgate ("gate" here refers to a gap in the cliffs) will tell you much about the British holiday maker before the age of cheap air travel. Margate is downmarket (T.S. Eliot, on Margate sands, found that he could connect "nothing with nothing"); Ramsgate is slightly grander. Sandwich, once an important port, is now a mile inland. It is a jewel in Kent's crown. P. G. Wodehouse, on the golf course, claimed to have been put off his game by "the uproar of the butterflies in the adjoining meadows."

If you want to hear choral evensong in Canterbury Cathedral you should check the times. In 1970 the service was at 4:30 P.M. on weekdays and 2:30 P.M. at the weekends. Afterward you may like to stroll through the many attractive gardens, dropping in eventually for a drink at The Old Weavers' House. You may also like to eat there, although the interior has been clumsily restored.

The playwright Christopher Marlowe was born in Canterbury and you can see the church where he was baptized and the school where he was educated, and attend a performance in the theater that bears his name. Because Marlowe wrote only seven plays before his early death you are unlikely to see one by him.

left
The chapel of the Infirmary by the cloisters of Canterbury Cathedral.

right
Canterbury's West Gate marks the high road to London.

below
The river Stour flows serenely through Canterbury.

For a few months at the beginning of 2005 Kent County Cricket Ground was without an unusual feature that was famed in all those parts of the world where cricket is played. It had a lime growing actually on the field of play. It is a symbol of cricket's infinite eccentricity that instead of tearing it down, the club simply changed the rules for matches played on the grounds to accommodate its presence. If a batsman managed to strike it, he was awarded four runs. If he hit the ball over it, he got six. Best of all, you could not be caught out if the ball had hit the tree first. Loss of the tree provoked many terrible puns. A new tree, grown in anticipation, replaced the old before the 2005 cricket season began.

CHICHESTER

SOUTHEAST   LANDSCAPE WITH SPIRE

CHICHESTER CATHEDRAL SPIRE IS SAID TO BE THE ONLY ONE in England that is visible from out at sea. It's worth seeing close up as well. Chichester was once a small market town and its center is wonderfully preserved. There are many styles of architecture represented in its buildings, but because most are domestic in scale they stand harmoniously together. The four principal streets—named after the points of the compass—intersect in the center at the Market Cross. An elaborately decorated octagonal structure in stone built in 1501, this combines the functions of landmark, shelter, and clocktower—but is also a marvelous Gothic fantasy. As with so many British towns, you should walk through the lanes and back alleys to see what is really there, because many street-front facades have been modernized.

Chichester Cathedral was built during roughly two centuries between about 1091 and 1305. It incorporates various architectural styles from that period. It is of medium size, and is thought of as the most typical English cathedral and one of the most lovable. One most attractive stained glass window is by Marc Chagall (1887-1985). The bell tower, unusually, is separate from the main structure. It provides a fitting focus for its town and the surrounding landscape.

The surrounding areas offer peace and tranquillity and many and varied treasures. At Petworth Park, a magnificent country house set in a deer park landscaped by "Capability" Brown, there is a "state of the art" Victorian kitchen and a large art collection, including a number of paintings by J.M.W. Turner, one of the great figures in the history of landscape painting, who had a studio there. Chichester Harbor, a largely enclosed inlet of the English Channel stretching as far as Havant and Portsmouth, provides water trips and many fascinating and beautiful walks. At Fishbourne Roman Palace you will find the largest Roman villa in England. It was destroyed by fire in 285 BCE—and rediscovered by a workman digging a water main in 1960. The remains of its north wing contain a fine and large collection of in situ mosaics, including that of Cupid riding on a dolphin. At Bosham there is Holy Trinity Church, thought to have been used by King Canute—and some people believe that this is where, by proving that he could not stop the tide coming in, he demonstrated to his courtiers that his powers were limited. Sadly, it appears that the story was invented by a twelfth-century historian bent on moralizing about human weakness and the power of God.

Chichester Canal Wharf, starting point of an attractive walk.

facing page
Spires of the Cathedral and Market Cross are landmarks in this small city.

If you have time during your visit, go also to Arundel (ten miles) where there is a large hilltop castle that since the sixteenth century has been owned by the dukes of Norfolk, a line with various claims to fame. They are the heads of England's most prominent Roman Catholic family. One of their responsibilities is the staging of coronations of new monarchs. It is believed by some that the first duke, who was constable of the Tower of London when two princes were (probably) murdered there in 1483, was complicit in their deaths. Be that as it may, the rooms at Arundel are magnificent and the collections—paintings and furniture, tapestries and stained glass, china and clocks, sculpture and carving, heraldry and armor—are fascinating.

If you are in Chichester between April and September you can see the Chichester Festival productions at the theatre, which was founded by Sir Laurence Olivier. These are mainly mainstream plays with, these days, a one-per-season neglected American musical. At other times of year other companies visit the theatre. In the streets of the town, too, you may, on special occasions, come across the Town Crier making announcements in early nineteenth-century costume and at other times various forms of street theatre and entertainment.

EASTBOURNE

DEBUSSY AND THE WHITE PALACE

EASTBOURNE IS THOUGHT OF ELSEWHERE IN ENGLAND AS A PLACE you go to retire—and since it is a seaside resort with a good climate, that makes sense—but it has much to offer to those who are younger. It is an excellent center for touring the South Downs, a range of low, rolling, mainly treeless chalk hills, described by Rudyard Kipling, who lived not far away, as "blunt, bow-headed, whalebacked" and by T. H. Huxley as "a well-dressed carcase of mutton." The grass on the downs is traditionally kept short by flocks of sheep. We can sample some of the delights of the downs by going about three miles southwest from Eastbourne to Beachy Head, a spectacular and beautiful chalk headland. Below this 500-foot vertical drop there is a red-and-white lighthouse. Farther west from Beachy Head, a series of cliffs known as the Seven Sisters gives its name to a beautiful and popular 700-acre country park. Great care is necessary when walking on the cliffs. Further inland there is pleasant walking to be enjoyed in Friston Forest. On the seafront at Eastbourne itself stands Wish Tower, one of the few survivors of seventy-four Martello towers built along the South Coast when it was feared that Napoleon would invade. As it was, he never tried. However, five miles farther along the coast to the northeast is Pevensey Bay where, in 1066, William of Normandy landed with 5,000 men to begin his conquest of England.

The chalk cliffs of Beachy Head tower over a tiny lighthouse.

facing page
Eastbourne Pier recalls seaside life in the Victorian and Edwardian eras.

Eastbourne's beaches are famous. Falling Sands Beach at the foot of Beachy Head is quieter than the popular stretch between the pier and the Wish Tower. A five-mile promenade along this stretch of shoreline takes you past the Carpet Gardens, the famous 1930s bandstand, and the smartly restored Victorian Pier. The bandstand mounts nine performances per week during the summer months. It also exhibits a plaque in memory of John Wesley Woodward, a local bandsman who, in 1912, was one of the musicians who continued to play on the *Titanic* while it was sinking. The town's stately seafront is dominated by the Grand (very grand) Hotel, built in 1875 and known locally as the White Palace. The French composer Claude Debussy stayed at the Grand Hotel for two months in 1905 (on the run from marital complications in Paris) while he finished scoring his orchestral work *La Mer*. One of his later preludes for piano, *Minstrels*, recalled some musicians—apparently a banjo player and a drummer—he had heard playing outside the hotel. It is still a luxurious, if expensive, place to stay.

At Bexhill, ten miles along the coast, you will find a remarkable modern building, the De La Warr Pavilion. Another six miles will take you to Hastings. Inland from these is the town of Battle, where King Harold died in 1066. (See under HASTINGS). The South Downs Way, one of the most popular walking trails in Southern England, extends from Beachy Head along the ridge of the downs for about eighty miles towards Winchester, a small cathedral city well worth a visit. Most walkers, however, start at the Winchester end. You need about a week to walk the whole distance. Remember to be prepared for changes in the weather.

At Herstmonceux, ten miles inland from Eastbourne, stands Herstmonceux Castle, a fortified manor house. Begun in 1441, it is the oldest brick building of any importance left standing in England. Every year, on the last weekend in August, a three-day medieval festival is staged there. More than 1,000 knights, bowmen, and men-at-arms lay siege to the castle with full cannon support. Activities and entertainments for the whole family include mounted skill-at-arms tournaments, falconry displays, longbow competition, Have-A-Go-Archery, archery displays, puppeteers, jesters, strolling minstrels, Europe's largest medieval-traders' row, fabulous craft stalls, Living History encampments, kids' kingdom, hog roast, and historic walled gardens. Brightly colored costumes and tents contribute to the gaiety of the occasion.

GUILDFORD

A MASSACRE AND A MODERN CATHEDRAL

GUILDFORD, THE COUNTY SEAT OF SURREY, IS SET IN A GAP IN THE NORTH DOWNS where the river Wey breaks through the hills. Its situation has made it an important transport staging post between London and the naval cities of the South Coast, contributing to its long-standing prosperity. Its name means "place with the golden ford." There have been dramatic moments in its history. During the turbulent period following the death of King Canute in 1042, a claimant to the throne was captured at Guildford. He died after his eyes were cut out; meanwhile his supporters were massacred.

Jane Austen wrote her most famous novels in this house at Chawton.

facing page
Guildford Castle was a royal residence for three centuries.

The oldest surviving building in Guildford is St Mary's Church. It probably replaced an even earlier, wooden church built during the seventh century, when the Saxons became Christians. The existing stone tower was built around 1050 and other parts were rebuilt during the eleventh to thirteenth centuries. Guildford has fortunately been able to preserve many other buildings from past eras. The Great Tower of a castle erected in c. 1300 survives, while High Street boasts many Tudor structures, including the elegant Guildhall, which features a magnificent bracket clock extending outward from its facade. Next to the castle stands a beautiful seventeenth-century building housing the town museum, which traces the archaeological history of the area and its crafts (including a fine collection of needlework) and industries. On High Street stands an imposing almshouse, founded in 1619 to provide accommodations for twelve single men and eight single women. It is still in use and since 1984 has accommodated couples in an additional new building. In the hall there is furniture dating from 1622 and the chapel has some very striking stained glass. On Stag's Hill, dominating Guildford's skyline, stands the dignified, somewhat unadventurous, modern cathedral, built between 1936 and 1966. Its interior, however, is impressively spacious and light. A number of free guided tours of the town or particular aspects of it are available. In the Surrey and Hampshire countryside nearby are many places of interest. The closest is Clandon Park, built by the Venetian architect Giacomo Leoni in the 1730s.

The rooms include a two-storied marble hall, one of the finest in Europe, and a room displaying large,

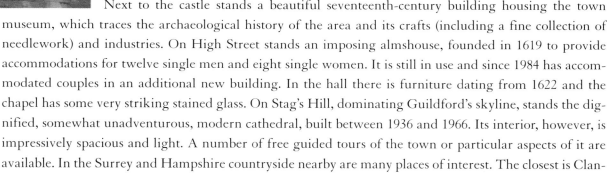

The Great Barn at Wanborough is one of the most important medieval barns in southeast England. It is one of the finest examples of ancient timber building and was built in 1388 for the Cistercian monks of Waverley Abbey, five miles away. It was part of a "grange"—a farm supplying the abbey's needs. The Great Barn holds a permanent display of local and historic interest as well as special events and exhibitions throughout the summer. The local church dates from c. 1100 and is the smallest in Surrey. It is a short distance from the Great Barn and is well worth a visit.

framed tapestries. The gardens are splendidly maintained and feature a Maori meeting house and a grotto. In the village of Compton is an art gallery devoted to the paintings of G. F. Watts, who lived there. His portraits of his eminent Victorian contemporaries are well regarded. His wife, Mary, designed a funeral chapel for a new village graveyard, which combines Art Nouveau, Celtic, Romanesque, and Egyptian influences in a unique way.

At Tilford you will find the Rural Life Centre. This has a number of reconstructed buildings and displays of local crafts and trades. There is an aboretum with more than 100 species of trees from around the world and a narrow-gauge light railway. If you are able, it is worth taking a longer trip to Chawton to see the small house in which Jane Austen lived and wrote her celebrated novels, covering her manuscript when visitors called. Not far away is Selborne, where the eighteenth-century naturalist Gilbert White lived and wrote his great work *The Natural History of Selborne*. Captain Oates, of Captain Scott's ill-fated Antarctic expedition of 1912 also lived and is commemorated there.

HASTINGS

1066, A COUNTRY PARK, AND KIPLING

ONE OF THE DATES EVERY BRITISH SCHOOL CHILD WAS ONCE ASSUMED TO KNOW was the year of the Norman Conquest of England, 1066. The battle that took place shortly after the Normans landed and proved that they intended to stay, takes its name from Hastings but was actually fought at Battle, six miles inland. William the Conqueror built Battle Abbey (1070-94) as a penance, ordered by Pope Alexander II, for the loss of life incurred by the battle and earlier raids. (Alexander, however, supported William, who was more interested in ecclesiastical reform than was Harold, the English king.)

At the time of the battle, Hastings was a fishing village. Today it is still home to Europe's largest beach-launched fishing fleet. The boats are pulled up the shingle beach by winches and the tall, narrow, wooden net shops, where nets are dried and stored, are a distinctive part of the scene. The narrow streets of the Stade (fisherman's quarter) are picturesque and characterful. The Fisherman's Museum is there, in what used to be the fishermen's church and contains the town's last lugger (a small fishing boat with an obliquely hung sail). The town stands where the High Weald—a ridge of sands and clay deposited long ago by rivers, then raised by movements of the earth's crust—meets the sea. West Hill offers Hastings Castle, the Smugglers' Caves (where contraband used to be stored), the most extensive cave system in southeast England, and spectacular views over town and sea, and is reached by a elevator (1891) from the town center. To the east lie cliffs where black redstar, fulmar peregrine, and rock pipit nest and breed and the habitat favors many varieties of insects and spiders. Above the cliffs is the Hastings Country Park, a Site of Special Scientific Interest, where you can wander for hours or days through grassland and heath (keep alert for Dartford warblers, stonechats, and yellowhammers), the wetlands of Combe Haven Valley (containing Filsham Reedbed, grazing marsh, willow carr, and sedge fen) and woodlands (look out for dormice, stoats, and weasels). These last are often "gil" woodlands, gils being steep-sided ravines cut out of the sandstone by streams. Woods and gardens are also a feature of Hastings itself, giving it a pleasantly green and welcoming appearance. In Queen's Road you will see a plaque to John Logie Baird, who experimented with the transmission of television images here during the 1920s. Sophia Jex-Blake, one of the leaders of women who campaigned to be allowed to train and practice as doctors, was born in Hastings in 1840.

The Hastings fishing fleet at rest on the beach.

facing page
Warrior Square, presided over by Queen Victoria, is one of many fine public gardens.

Five miles from Hastings, along the coast to the west, you will find the recently refurbished De La Warr Pavilion, a supremely elegant modernist-style culture center, designed by Mendelsohn and Chermayeff and built in the 1930s. Don't miss the spiral staircase. At Battle, visit the abbey, see the spot where King Harold died, stroll past Georgian and medieval houses, and visit Yesterday's World. This re-creates the settings of English life from Victorian times onward and is highly praised as a family attraction. A good day out can be spent by going to Bodiam Castle, an almost perfectly preserved moated fortress, then taking the Kent and East Sussex Steam Railway to Tenterden, an attractive market town. (But be sure you know how you will return to Hastings.)

Should you be interested in Rudyard Kipling, who wrote many novels and short stories set in India, as well as the Jungle Books and *Puck of Pook's Hill*, you can visit his beautiful house, Bateman's (built 1603) at Burwash, about fifteen miles away. Kipling loved the county of Sussex, and in 1902 wrote this: "God gave to men all earth to love, / But, since our hearts are small, / Ordained for each one spot should prove / Beloved over all...." He, however, was not a narrow-minded patriot, asking as he did, in another connection, this question: "...what should they know of England who only England know?"

ROCHESTER

A SHIP IN THE SKY AND A BOY'S DREAM

IF YOU CHOOSE TO STAY AT THE BULL AND ROYAL VICTORIA HOTEL IN ROCHESTER, a former coaching inn, over 400 years old, you will share a roof, at some distance of time, with the then Princess Victoria, who stayed there in 1836. That same year, Charles Dickens, one of England's great Victorian novelists, published his first big success, *The Pickwick Papers*, in which the Bull appears under its own name. Much later, in *Great Expectations*, it appears as the Blue Boar. Dickens had lived as a boy in disreputable Chatham on the river Medway, and loved to visit its pleasanter neighbor. During these visits and walks into the countryside beyond he became fascinated by a house called Gad's Hill Place. It seems that his father told him that he might be a success and be able to buy it someday. So indeed it turned out, and Dickens lived there from 1857 until his death in 1870. When he died he left an unfinished novel, *Edwin Drood*. Blending the low life of Chatham and London with the respectability of Rochester, it begins: "An ancient English Cathedral Tower? How can the ancient English Cathedral Tower be here?" We learn that the man whose confused thoughts we are reading is in an opium den.

Apart from the Bull Inn, much that Princess Victoria and Dickens would have seen survives from nineteenth-century Rochester. The quaint narrow High Street has kept some shops of the time. Much earlier, Rochester had been a Roman fortified town, then a small Saxon village. Like Canterbury, it was situated at an important defensive position on the road between Dover and London. Parts of the early town walls still circle the inner center. In 1088, following the Norman conquest, the old Roman fort was replaced by a castle, a well-preserved stone keep set in attractive grounds. Restoration House and Gardens is an Elizabethan city mansion, believed to have been Dickens's model for the house of jilted, reclusive, and vengeful Miss Havisham in *Great Expectations*. Presumably, however, no one who lived in the real house was remotely like Miss Havisham: "…dressed in rich materials—satins, and lace, and silks—all of white. Her shoes were white… she had bridal flowers in her hair, but her hair was white."

The former Guildhall, with its astonishing rooftop weather vane—a fully rigged eighteenth-century warship—houses a museum that exhibits a full-scale re-creation of part of a Medway prison ship and, in stark contrast, a Victorian drawing room and kitchen, along with eighteenth-century cabinetmakers' tools and a 200,000-year-old axe, which you are permitted to touch.

Much of the city's past is preserved in the town centre.

facing page
The well-preserved Norman Keep dominates the city's skyline.

The building which, along with the Norman castle, represents the longest preserved enclosed buildings in Rochester is Dickens's "ancient English Cathedral"—the country's second oldest after its neighbour at Canterbury. Augustine ordained Justus as first bishop in 604. There was a church on the present site that has now disappeared. Of its successor, built by Bishop Gundulf (1076-1108), a detached tower and part of the crypt remain. The rest was reconstructed during the following two centuries. Whereas the castle impresses us as a tall building (it is the tallest Norman Keep in England and is worth climbing for the views over the River Medway) the cathedral looks stocky and solid, sheltering beneath the castle on the hill above it.

Guided walking tours and ghost tours of Rochester are available. You may wish to reverse Dicken's footsteps and go to Chatham to visit the historic dockyard, which is now a museum of shipbuilding and nautical crafts. Next door to the dockyard is Fort Amherst, built in the eighteenth century and considerably enlarged in Napoleonic times. Napoleonic prisoners of war were made to dig more than a mile of tunnels, which were used to move ammunition from one part of the fortress to another. Rochester also has convenient direct-rail links to London, Canterbury, and numerous Kent Coast destinations.

R Y E

NOVELISTS AND SMUGGLERS

RYE, DESPITE BEING A HILLTOP TOWN, WAS ONCE A SEAPORT, one of the Cinque Ports, which were charged with the provision of ships to defend the coast of southeast England. At that time it was virtually an island. The estuaries of two rivers, the Tillingham and Rother, flowed into the sea on either side and it was linked to the mainland only by an easily defensible strip of land. Even the immediate mainland, however, consist-ed of marshland, one-hundred square miles of marshland (which until Roman times had been largely under the sea) now called Romney Marsh. As the sea level between Britain and the Continent gradually sank, the Romans and their successors tried to drain it. The eventual success of these attempts caused the silting-up of the rivers and a seaward exten-sion of dry land. Rye, consequently, is now over a mile from the sea, although its fishing fleet can still sail up the Rother and dock just east of the town.

An interesting variety of people have practiced their professions, trades, and criminal activities in Rye. In the eighteenth century the Hawkhurst Gang of smugglers could be seen drinking in the inglenooks of the Mermaid Inn, their loaded pistols lying on the table ready for any emergency. (Look out for the fetching sign above the door, in a street of houses still much as it was when rebuilt in the fourteenth century.) Like most smug-glers on England's south coast, the gang was useful to many otherwise more law-abiding residents, but a series of horrific murders put an end to its popularity. Another group, novelists, is associated with Lamb House. This is Rye's grandest mansion, although its front door opens directly onto the street. Its secluded garden is concealed from the town but encapsulates its serenity. Henry James lived there for the last nine-teen years of his life (1897-1916) and wrote, or rather dictated, *The Ambassadors* and *The Wings of the Dove* in the house. He was followed by E. F. Benson, whose well-known Mapp and Lucia stories are set in "Tilling," a fictional town easily recognizable as Rye. A later tenant, Rumer Godden, set her novel *This House of Brede* in the area. Another of her novels, *Black Narcissus*, was turned into a well-known film, admired by many but, sadly, not by Godden herself. It is strange to think of these rooms and this garden giving inspiration to three such different writers: James, in his last period, composing long sentences drawing subtle distinc-tions between fine shades of emotion; Benson, writing light satires about two *grandes dames* in a small provincial town; and Godden exploring the minds of foreigners in Eastern settings, children, and religious people. Unsurprisingly, Rye hosts an annual literary festival.

The Land Gate Tower defended Rye against overland invaders.

facing page
This medieval house faces St Mary's Church.

There is surely no more picturesque small town in England than Rye. Narrow, steep cobbled streets; Tudor-style houses; views over Romney Marsh and toward the sea; an unexpected golden cherub supporting a balcony; autumnally colored rooftops, pretty gardens and greenery; the occasional stone pinnacle or rooftop gazebo; stone buildings facing, across narrow lanes, tile-hung cottages; a house with a leaning chimney: Rye is crammed with visual curiosities and delights. The Ypres Tower and the Landgate (the only survivor of four) were built about 800 years ago at a time when French raiders often attacked the town.

A pleasant walk starts and ends at Rye Harbor. Walk to the sea, past the information center, then westward above the beach, with views of Turnery Pool and the Nature Reserve—which we are not permitted to enter. In early summer the shingle here becomes a colorful flower bed and the gravel pits play host to nesting terns, gulls, ducks, and waders. Camber Castle can be seen some way inland. Take the right turn inland when you reach it and another at the first of several lakes. Follow the path alongside them back to Rye Harbor. (The length of this walk is a little over four miles).

Nearby Winchelsea, another hilltop town, was rebuilt after a great storm in 1288 as a port to serve the Gascon wine trade. Its original grid pattern survives, but the houses are mainly Georgian and modern, not medieval. The Old Court Hall Museum gives an account of its history. Camber Sands is an attractive stretch of beach where at low tide the sea retreats half a mile. Quite different—and very dangerous to swim from—is the gravel beach at Dungeness, and the two looming nuclear power stations give the area a somewhat sinister feeling. The film director Derek Jarman, however, loved its bleak landscape and lived in Prospect Cottage there, creating a celebrated "garden" out of beach debris and gravel.

ST ALBANS

PERSECUTION, MARTYRDOM, AND A PLAYWRIGHT SUNNING HIMSELF

WHEN THE ROMANS ARRIVED ON THE WESTERN BANK OF THE RIVER VER in 43 they found the capital city of the Catuvellauni tribe. They established a settlement of their own there, adopting the old name to Latin spellings as Verulamium. When Boudicca, queen of the Iceni of East Anglia rebelled against Roman rule in 60, she destroyed the city. Boudicca was defeated and killed and Verulamium was rebuilt, this time with a forum, public baths, theater, temple complex, covered market and monumental arches. During the next two centuries a ring of defenses was constructed, first as earthworks, later in stone.

The city flourished until the end of Roman rule in 409. Traces of the Roman buildings remain and may be seen during the course of a pleasant stroll. Look through the Verulamium Museum, with its vivid evocations of life in the city, before jumping briefly forward in time by visiting St Michael's Church, built probably in 948, in part using bricks from the city. There is a monument to the essayist and statesman Sir Francis Bacon, a local boy. Leaving the church, we return to Roman times by visiting the remains of the theater, unique among Roman theaters in Britain in that it has a stage.

The remains of St Albans's Roman Theater

facing page
The cathedral's Gothic Revival altar screen.

During a lakeside walk across the park we pass other Roman sites. Perhaps we drop in at the equally unique Ye Olde Fighting Cocks pub for lunch. This octagonal building, originally the dovecote of St Albans Abbey, was removed from there in the 1530s, when abbeys and monasteries were dissolved by Henry VIII. It claims to be the oldest pub in Britain, but the claim has been disputed.

By now we are in present-day St Albans—but history still surrounds us. Bede, the first historian of the English Church, tells us that Alban was a Roman living in Verulamium during the persecution of Christians unleashed throughout the empire by Diocletian in 303. Alban gave sanctuary to a fleeing priest, was converted by him to Christianity and, when soldiers were sent to investigate rumors, gave himself up wearing the priest's cloak. He proclaimed his new faith before a judge and was executed. Miracles attended his death. After the persecution ended, a church was built in his honor. In 1213 many English barons met there to discuss the ideas that emerged as the Magna Carta, which King John was forced to sign in 1215. After the dissolution of the monastery endowed in c. 794 by King Offa, the abbey church was bought from the king by the parish. The price they paid was, apparently, 400 British pounds.

In 1877, the very large parish church became the cathedral of a new diocese. Almost every medieval architectural style can be found in it somewhere. The varying shapes of the different sets of windows provide the key to the styles. A few medieval wall paintings survive. The nave is 550 feet long, the second longest in Europe, but its square Norman tower looks stumpy, a planned spire never having been added. Nineteenth-century additions to the west front (by a wealthy, opinionated patron, Lord Grimethorpe) are sometimes thought inapt. Although the overall effect of the building can seem rather somber, there are many good things in it—even if they do not always fit well together.

Outside St Albans the Gardens of the Rose at Chiswell Green are a mecca for rose devotees. Its twelve acres grow more than 30,000 rose bushes in 1,750 varieties, together with 600 unnamed novelties in the trial grounds. At Ayot St Lawrence is Shaw's Corner, the house in which George Bernard Shaw, author of *Pygmalion*, *St Joan*, and many other plays, lived for the last forty-four years of his life. One of the most fascinating exhibits is the summerhouse in the garden, where he wrote, which can be turned so as to face always the direct light of the sun. The villagers, initially rather suspicious, warmed to him somewhat when he appeared, helmeted, to help chop up and remove trees blown down in the roads by a storm.

TUNBRIDGE WELLS

WATERS AND "SPLENITICK DISTEMPERS"

TUNBRIDGE WELLS IS ONE OF THE JEWELS OF THE KENTISH WEALD, an area between the North and South Downs, once heavily wooded. From the Middle Ages onward much of the forest was felled, to be used in smelting the plentiful iron ore and building ships for the Royal Navy. After 1606, when young Lord North happened upon the Chalybeate spring and was cured of an illness by drinking its water, the town came into being as a kind of health farm, much easier for Londoners to reach than Bath, where overindulgent courtiers could recuperate. In 1662 the waters were praised as being "good for splenitick distempers" by Thomas Fuller, in his wonderfully named book *The History of the Worthies of England*. After Princess (later Queen) Anne's son slipped and fell in 1697, she ordered that the area around the spring be paved. When she returned the following year it had not been done; she left and never returned. Today, paved with stone—although some of the red tiles (laid too late to appease the royal wrath) are incorporated—the street is still known as "the Pantiles"and, with its colonnades, wrought-iron balconies, trees, and specialist boutiques, has an almost Parisian chic.

The Pantiles has been a fashionable promenade since the 1700s.

In the 1830s Princess (later Queen) Victoria often holidayed nearby at the Claverly Hotel (now the Hotel du Vin) and a brass plaque marks the pew in the Church of King Charles-the-Martyr where she sat. Modest outside, the building has an extraordinary Baroque plaster ceiling by Christopher Wren's chief plasterer. In the nineteenth century Decimus Burton built an estate of mansions and villas, some of which survive. There are plenty of green areas within the town, including a cricket ground surrounded by rhododendrons. At the beginning of the nineteenth century, as Brighton became ever more popular with the smart set, Tunbridge Wells declined, becoming known as the home of a mythological creature, "Disgusted of Tunbridge Wells," who fulminated anonymously in newspaper correspondence columns on subjects of scandal and concern. Nobility and celebrities are perhaps relatively seldom seen there nowadays, but the elegance of the shops in the principal streets still draws a healthy influx of visitors. No fewer than thirty-seven businesses dealing in antiques and collectables are listed; twenty-six deal in arts and crafts, twenty-three in books, nine in fine art, and twenty-three in frames and prints. Even allowing for some overlap in listings and for one or two suspect entries, that is a great many shops.

Near Tunbridge Wells there is a wealth of gardens, walks over open areas or through woodlands. At High Rocks, outcrops of sandstone linked by bridges provide tranquil woodland scenic walks. In the River Tiese Valley are the ruins of Old Bayham Abbey, set in an eighteenth-century landscape designed by Humphry Repton. The national collections of hellebores and Japanese anemones are at Broadview Gardens, Hadlow. Bedgebury National Pinetum, near Goudhurst, has a collection of conifers and unusual deciduous trees set amongst parkland with lakes, streams, and rolling hills. Finchcocks has herbaceous borders, shrubs, woodland walks, and a walled kitchen garden. As a bonus, the fine Georgian manor house holds collections of pictures, costumes, and over one-hundred period keyboard instruments, which you can hear being played by professional musicians. At Marle Place we find an extensive Italianate scented garden with a rockery, gazebo, and mosaic terrace, and, within the yew-hedged kitchen garden, a restored Victorian greenhouse holding a display of orchids.

At Cranbrook there is a museum of local history and a splendid working windmill. Not far away is Sissinghurst, where the remains of an Elizabethan mansion were restored by the writer Vita Sackville-West and her diplomat husband, Harold Nicolson, who laid out one of the world's most celebrated gardens, conceived as a series of intimate, open-air rooms. Finally, at Bewl Water, a cruise, sailing, canoeing, rowing, and windsurfing are all possible, or you can walk or cycle the thirteen-mile "Round Water Route."

facing page
Bodiam Castle and its broad moat were constructed in the 1380s.

WINCHESTER

TWO KINGS AND JANE AUSTEN

facing page
Winchester's comfortably bustling High Street.

below
Parts of the Anglo-Saxon Old Minster survive near the cathedral.

FOR A TIME IN THE MEDIEVAL PERIOD WINCHESTER WAS THE ENGLISH CAPITAL. This was because in the 880s, Alfred, King of Wessex, declared himself king of that part of England not ruled by the Danes. He and his successors labored mightily and ruthlessly to bring all small kingdoms in England under their control, particularly that of Mercia, which, during the eighth and early ninth centuries, had been leader among the seven kingdoms. After 1066 there was a period when William treated it and London as joint capitals. He had himself crowned in both cities and even kept the Domesday Book in Winchester. But, inevitably, it eventually became merely a quiet provincial town, as it had been under the Romans (70-410).

A statue in High Street commemorates Winchester's association with King Alfred—a real figure, although also the subject of legend. The legendary King Arthur is remembered too: the top of what was once believed to be his original Round Table is displayed in Winchester Castle. This is now regarded as a pious medieval reconstruction of that imaginary piece of furniture. Winchester was also of ecclesiastical importance, having been made a bishopric in 662. After the Conquest, in 1079, a grand new cathedral was built, using stone from the Isle of Wight. Since the town is in a valley, the encouragement to exploit elevation inherent in a hilltop site did not exist. The building therefore is low, with a squat, square tower. It is, however, very long. Between the burning of Old St Paul's and the construction of Liverpool's Anglican Cathedral, it was the longest in Europe (557 feet). One of the dedicatees of the cathedral was a local monk, Swithun, who, as he lay dying before the building was finished, opted not to be buried inside it but under the grass outside. After he was subsequently made a saint, the clergy ignored his wishes and moved him inside. The result, so legend has it, was incessant rain for forty days. Not far from the cathedral stands Winchester College. This enrolled its first pupils in 1394 and is thought to be the oldest boys' private school in England. It was intended to help boys from low-income families. There are very few of those on its books today. The college has interesting and attractive buildings and grounds and you can take a guided tour of it most days of the year.

Members of the college are known as "Wykehamists"; their motto is "Manners Maketh Man." Among the sporting and related triumphs reported while this book was being written were the appointment of four Wykehamists as national instructors in akido (the most spiritual of the martial arts), and a double triumph over Eton Colllege, in football (1-0) and cricket, when one Tim Lewis scored a fabulous 132 not out.

Most visitors to Winchester are interested in Jane Austen. That was not always the case. The pastry cook who used the house where she had endured her last illness had asked its owners to put up a board recording her stay. He was bothered, he said, by Americans who came in to ask questions without buying anything. But ten years after her death her novels were out of print. He asked for the sign to be taken down because now English people came in to ask who she was. A cathedral verger asked for directions to her grave, asked in return whether "there was anything special about that lady?" As a comic novelist she might have been amused by this, and by the fact that, because her brothers did not want people to think that she had been forced to write novels for money, which they had failed to provide, her memorial in the cathedral did not mention her greatest achievement.

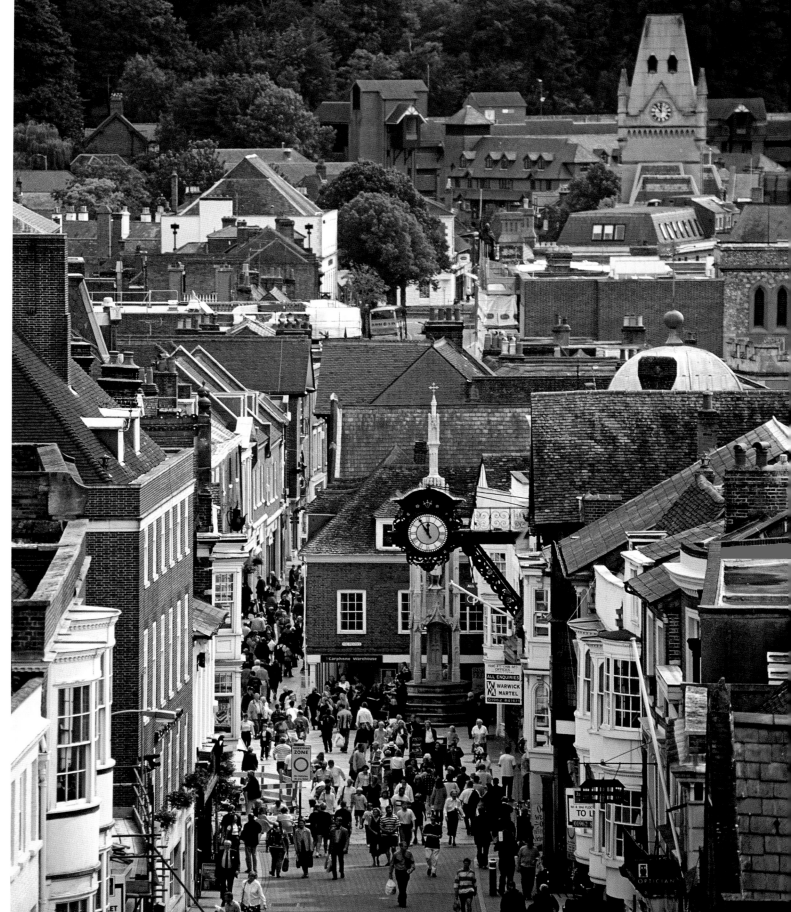

Izaak Walton is also buried in the cathedral. He probably thought of himself as the biographer of several English poets, but he has won lasting fame as author of *The Compleat Angler* (1653). This little book has provoked affection in fishermen all over the world and is seldom out of print. It has also been admired for the self-portrait it almost unwittingly gives of a gentle, contemplative man who found, in casting his bait over the waters, solace from domestic unhappiness and a world turned upside down by civil war, who considered fishermen as a fellowship of more-or-less equals, and thought that we should "study to be quiet."

WINDSOR

SOUTHEAST

THE UPPER CRUST AT HOME AND SCHOOL

WINDSOR CASTLE, BUILT IN 1070 BY WILLIAM THE CONQUEROR, is familiar to television viewers worldwide. Its position on a hill overlooking the river Thames reflects its purpose, to keep guard over the western approaches to London. It is the largest inhabited castle in the world. The queen spends most of her weekends there—she lived there during World War II and prefers it to Buckingham Palace. St George's Hall and Chapel (an outstanding example of perpendicular Gothic architecture) are the home of the ancient and exclusive Order of the Garter. The royal mausoleum, built by Queen Victoria after Prince Albert's death, is at Frogmore, nearby. Across the river is Eton College, the famous private school founded in 1440 by Henry VI, which has educated eighteen British prime ministers. It is not surprising, therefore, that town and castle are synonymous with the British "Establishment"—even more so since, during World War I, George V changed the family's name from "Saxe-Coburg-Gotha" to "Windsor" because of anti-German sentiment. The castle is often used for receptions and dinners for foreign leaders.

Visitors should on no account miss St George's Chapel (which, together with more than one-hundred other rooms, was gutted by fire in 1992 but is now fully restored), the State Apartments—lavishly decorated formal rooms with paintings by Canaletto, Holbein, Leonardo da Vinci, Rembrandt, Rubens and Van Dyck, and a large collection of armor—Queen Mary's Dolls' House (built on a scale of one to twelve, with working elevator, running water, electricity, and a properly stocked wine cellar) and the Drawings Gallery, which shows changing exhibitions of material from the Royal Library, as well as drawings by Michelangelo, Leonardo da Vinci, Holbein, and others.

The town outside the walls has many attractions. Some days you can watch the guards marching up High Street on their way to the ceremonial changing of the guard—which itself can only be seen by going into the castle. The principal building is the Guildhall, venue for many celebrity weddings. The ground floor is an open space, once used as a corn market, with upper floors supported by pillars. Four of these, in the center, in fact support nothing. Apparently the town council thought the building unsafe and asked for additional pillars. Sir Christopher Wren, who had not designed it but was supervising its construction, assured them they were unnecessary. The council persisted. Wren provided four additional pillars but demonstrated that the building was safe by terminating them one inch below the ceiling. Elsewhere there are many quaint Georgian shops, houses, and inns. The Saville and Valley gardens and the gardens at Royal Lodge are worth visiting at almost any time of year.

Across the bridge at Eton College you can visit the Cloisters, Chapel, the oldest classroom, and the Museum. You may catch sight of boys wearing the traditional black trousers, tailcoat, and winged collar. In the early nineteenth century W. E. Gladstone, four times prime minister, wore it; at the end of the twentieth so did Princes William and Harry. Eton's reputation of dealing only with "top people" may throw up amusing confrontations. When William Lang, a trumpeter in the London Symphony Orchestra, was coaching players there, a woman in a shop asked him why he was at the school. "I teach there," he said. She demanded to know *what* he taught. Straight-faced, in his fruity Yorkshire accent, he said, "Elocution."

The royal mausoleum, Frogmore House, stands within the private Home Park of the castle. Various monarchs have enjoyed it as a country residence since the seventeenth century, but the house is especially associated with Queen Victoria. The house and gardens were always a favorite retreat, but after her husband, Prince Albert, was buried there in 1861 the place took on a sacred dimension for her. She was buried with him forty years later. In death the Duke and Duchess of Windsor were permitted to return here after their long exile. Frogmore is not all death, however: Lord Louis Mountbatten (later assassinated by terrorists) was born there. The name, incidentally, means "pool full of frogs."

facing page
The Thames curves placidly through Windsor.

below
Windsor's Guildhall, with its statue of Queen Anne.

far left
Windsor is the oldest and largest inhabited castle in the world.

above
The private apartments at the eastern end of the castle.

left
The guards march to the castle.

To the west of the town is Windsor Great Park (4,800 acres) and at the western edge of the park lies Windsor Forest, in which Shakespeare set the last act of his comedy *The Merry Wives of Windsor* (the original source for Verdi's last opera, *Falstaff*). The play may have been written for performance at Windsor on the occasion in 1597 when a patron of Shakespeare's company was installed as a knight of the Garter. It is interesting that Shakespeare's play, whatever its royal connections, is essentially a bourgeois comedy, which strays frequently into farce as the aristocratic but buffoonlike Falstaff is made to look foolish by two housewives.

C O W E S

YACHTS AND A QUEEN'S SEASIDE HOME

THE ISLE OF WIGHT IS TWENTY-THREE MILES LONG BY THIRTEEN MILES WIDE WITH EXTRAORDINARILY VARIED landscapes, seascapes, and shoreline. The reason for visiting Cowes, therefore, is to see the whole island—unless you go in early August, when you may be swept up in "Cowes Week," the annual regatta, which lasts nine days. Almost 1,000 boats compete in forty different classes of event. Another 200 spectator boats compete for the best view. It happens that the Solent (the western part of the channel between the island and mainland England) is a wonderful place to learn to sail and a wonderful place to display and refine the skills that have been learned. There is a very complex tidal pattern, with an *agger* or double tide, in which there are two briefly separated high waters in each tide. The tides are unusually strong. Harbors and anchorages differ widely in the problems they present. There is continuous busy commercial traffic bound to and from Southampton. The challenges of the sea and the solutions found for them vary from moment to moment. The evenings are a nonstop party: bands and barbecues, cocktails and yacht club balls, with a spectacular pyrotechnical conclusion. Apart from the regatta, there is offshore activity to look at throughout the year.

Yachts moored in Cowes Harbour.

facing page
Queen Victoria's preferred family home, Osborne House.

The other big attraction in Cowes is Osborne House above the Solent, just east of East Cowes. Queen Victoria did not consider either Buckingham Palace or Windsor a suitable family home, and bought the original Osborne House and estate in 1845. The house was too small, however, so Prince Albert designed a new one, which was not finally completed until 1891, long after his death (which desolated Victoria) in 1861. The family had occupied it as soon as the first wing was ready, in 1846. What we see now is a large Italianate three-story mansion with towers at either end, whose interiors reflect the attitudes and territories of Victoria's empire and her role as empress of India. In the Durbar Room, an elaborate banqueting hall, every surface is ornately embellished and strongly colored. Symbols of India abound. Ganesh, the elephant god of good fortune, looks down from a wall and there is a white peacock above the fireplace. The gardens reflect Prince Albert's wide cultural and scientific interests, but also his practicality. His children were taught to grow vegetables and fruit, which they sold to their father at commercial rates for use in the house. Their scaled-down garden tools, branded with their initials, can still be seen. In a Swiss cottage elsewhere on the estate they were taught domestic skills.

The coastline is among the greatest attractions of the Isle of Wight. Just west of Cowes we find coastal woodland, a drowned estuary, and pasture-fringed Thorness Bay. On the south coast a clifftop footpath runs from St Lawrence to the island's western tip. Look out for the "chines": ravines cut through the cliffs by streams, in the past often used by smugglers. At the western end Freshwater Bay has towering cliffs. Nearby are the Needles, three sawtoothed white rocks. Bembridge is the winter resort of thousands of waterfowl. Victoria Country Park, near Yarmouth, has a rocky shoreline with good views across the Solent and, if you get there early enough on the right day in June, an opportunity to assess the contenders in the Round-the-Island Yacht Race.

On the high ground above the Needles is Farringford, now a hotel, once the home (1854-92) of the poet Alfred, Lord Tennyson. He thought the air on the cliffs "worth sixpence a pint." *Crossing the Bar*, a dignified farewell to life that he asked to be placed at the end of all collections of his work, refers to the tide in the mouth of the Solent. "And may there be no moaning of the bar, / When I put out to sea," he writes, "But such a sound as moving seems asleep, / Too full for sound and foam, / When that which drew from out the boundless deep / Turns again home."

36

BARNSTAPLE

SEA, SHIPPING, AND LITERATURE

THE NAME, WHICH PROBABLY INDICATES A POPULAR MEETING PLACE, means "place or pillar of the battle axe." Barnstaple claims to be the oldest borough in England, with a charter dating from 950. Its entry in *The Domesday Book*, a survey of England made in 1085-86 during the reign of William the Conqueror, records that "There are 40 burgesses within the borough and 9 are outside the borough. Among them all they pay 40s… to the King and 20s… to the Bishop of Coutance." Its sheltered mooring on the river Taw allowed it to become a bustling port, at its busiest in the seventeenth century. In the eighteenth century it was known for its pottery and metalware. The arrival of the railways and the silting up of the river killed off most waterborne trade and nowadays it is an agricultural center.

The fishing port at Clovelly.

facing page
Barnstaple's gothic revival Holy Trinity Church, built in 1867.

The town's Heritage Trail will take us to numerous interesting and attractive buildings. The stone-built parish church, with its timber-framed lead spire (warped by a lightning strike in 1810), seventeenth-century wall monuments, decorated organ pipes and case, and stained glass, has stood since 1107. The churchyard is like a miniature cathedral close and contains the freestanding Lady Chapel that was used as a grammar school in the seventeenth century, when John Gay, composer of *The Beggar's Opera*, was a pupil. The Guildhall in High Street is a dignified example of early nineteenth-century British provincial architecture. Butchers Row (1855) consists of ten shops with pilasters of Bath stone, and an overhanging roof with wrought-iron supports. Only two of the shops are now butchers; the others sell local agricultural goods. Pannier Market has operated for a thousand years but its present stylish home, with its high glass-and-timber roof on iron columns, was built in 1855-56. It has been voted one of the top ten food markets in Britain. During the eighteenth century, the Three Tuns Pub was much used by smugglers.

The bridge across the Taw is medieval and notable for its numerous low, narrow arches, and the riverside paths are strikingly attractive. There is a well-liked museum of local history and wildlife. The very popular Annual Fair begins on the Wednesday before September twentieth. Four days of celebration follow a ceremonial opening that survives from ancient times: toasts are drunk in the Guildhall and a huge hand garlanded with flowers, symbolizing the hand of friendship, is displayed. The fair dates from very early in the town's history and was originally a celebration held after the conclusion of the great annual market.

Exmoor, Dartmoor, the lush river valleys, and the North Devon coast offer truly spectacular scenery. Braunton "Great Field" is a relic of medieval methods of cultivation. Braunton Burrows is a wild-dune reserve where marine plants grow in their natural habitat. At Arlington Court there are collections of model ships and horse-drawn vehicles. Bideford, Clovelly and Appledore are charmingly picturesque. From Bideford you can take a ferry trip to Lundy Island, a three-mile-long granite outcrop at the point where the Bristol Channel becomes the Atlantic Ocean. There you may see seals, the island's unique breeds of wild ponies and rabbits and, particularly at migratory times of year, huge flocks of birds. There are some interesting buildings, a population of about eighteen and no motor vehicles.

From Barnstaple you may enjoy exploring some of the Tarka Trail (180 miles), one of the UK's best walks. (On parts of it cycling is also permitted.) This takes you through areas featured in Henry Williamson's classic animal story, *Tarka the Otter*, published in 1927. Rudyard Kipling set his school story *Stalky and Co* near Bideford, where he himself went to school. Clovelly is associated with Charles Kingsley's Elizabethan adventure story *Westward Ho!* (The whole of this area, indeed, has connections with ships that helped defeat the Spanish Armada in 1588.)

B A T H

A SWINEHERD AND A WELSH DANDY

BATH, A UNESCO WORLD HERITAGE SITE, IS SUPERB. More than most, it is a town whose appearance has been governed by its history. Fortunately, that influence has been largely benign. About 860, legend has it, the Celtic Prince Bladud contracted leprosy, went into exile, and became a swineherd. His pigs, coincidentally, came out in a rash, which was cured when they wallowed in pools of hot mud: Bladud followed their

Pulteney Bridge is lined with shops on both sides.

facing page
The Abbey Church towers above the Roman Bath.

example. Once cured, he returned to court, became king, and founded a settlement around the curative pool. Incoming Romans also recognized the spring's therapeutic value and set about turning what they called Aquae Sulis into England's first spa town, building a reservoir and a temple dedicated to Sulis Minerva. (The name combines the Celtic and Roman goddesses of healing: the Romans respected other peoples' deities.) The settlement flourished until the fifth century, when the legions went home. Slow disintegration followed; ruined buildings disappeared under debris. In the tenth century the Saxons built Bath Abbey almost but not quite on top of the Roman remains. Edgar, the first king of all England, was crowned there in 973. The town came to be known as a cloth-making center, as Chaucer mentions in the prologue to *The Canterbury Tales*—

one of the storytellers, the wife of Bath, is a widow who has enjoyed a vigorous sex life with five successive husbands. After the dissolution of the monasteries in the 1530s the abbey was stripped of lead, iron, and glass and left to rot. The citizens of Bath began to restore it some years later.

Bath was revived as a spa town when spas became fashionable during the second half of the seventeenth century. At first it was a disreputable place, notorious for pickpockets, duels, cheating gamblers, and quack doctors. It grew respectable again when the dandified Welshman Richard "Beau" Nash became master of ceremonies. He built a pump room—not the present one, which dates from 1796—that became the social center of the town, characterized by high fashion, order, and discipline. These qualities were given Palladian architectural form by the father and son, both called John Wood, who presided over the growth of Bath in the eighteenth century. John senior designed Queen Square and the Circus; John junior designed Royal Crescent (a majestic semicircle of thirty houses with 114 Ionic columns looking out over Royal Victoria Park, the city's largest green area) and the Assembly Rooms (the interior was destroyed by bombing in 1942 but has been restored). Robert Adam also came, to build the elegant, shop-lined Pulteney Bridge.

It was not until 1727 that Roman remains were discovered in Bath. The Roman bath was only found in 1880, intact and still lined with lead, put in place almost 2,000 years before. The head of Minerva appeared, and a relief of a luxuriously hirsute head, sometimes described as gorgonlike but suggesting to some scholars the sea deity Oceanus. Other museums that make a visit to Bath so pleasantly instructive are twentieth-century foundations. Areas covered include: American life; porcelain, silver, bronze, and eighteenth-century painting; and 300 years of painting in and around Bath. The Museum of Costume in the Assembly Rooms is an especial delight, ranging from a plain linen undershirt (1580s) to the present, via wonders that include an Yves Saint Laurent cocktail dress.

Other authors since Chaucer have taken notice of Bath. Unsurprisingly, references are most frequent in the eighteenth and early nineteenth centuries. Parts of novels by Smollett, Fielding, and Fanny Burney are set in the Assembly and Pump rooms. Dickens, in chapter thirty-six of *The Pickwick Papers*, describes farcical misunderstandings in the Royal Crescent. Jane Austen lived in Bath 1801-1806. She did not want to be there, and passed on her dislike to Anne Elliot in *Persuasion*. But she allows Catherine Morland, in *Northanger Abbey*, a sentiment we may come to share: "Oh! Who can ever be tired of Bath?"

BRADFORD ON-AVON

A JAIL, A TITHE BARN, AND "MILLIE"

THE WORD "AVON" MEANS "RIVER," WHICH MAY EXPLAIN WHY THERE ARE FOUR AVON rivers in the UK. "Bradford" indicates that there was a broad ford here. That is no longer needed because there is the very fine Town Bridge with nine short arches and a domed watch house at the southern end. This was a chapel for the use of pilgrims on their way to Glastonbury and Malmesbury, but was later used as a jail. It has a copper fish as a weathervane and prisoners were said to be "under the fish and over the water." Like other buildings in the town the bridge is built in Cotswold stone, quarried from the hills that extend fifty miles northeast from the area. Further north this stone is honey-colored or golden but here it is pearly white. Its use means that virtually every building in Bradford-on-Avon is attractive. The layout of the town, in a series of terraces on a steep hillside, adds to that attractiveness: the buildings seem to grow out of the hillside. The parish church, Holy Trinity, was built in the twelfth century, and enlarged and refashioned in the fourteenth to sixteenth centuries, when Bradford-on-Avon was a prosperous cloth town. (The Cotswold Hills were at that time grazed by large flocks of sheep.) The two canopied tombs, the wall-painting, and the sculptured female head are all from the fourteenth century. In 1856, across the road, workmen repairing cottages uncovered two reliefs of guardian angels. The vicar managed eventually to confirm that this was the church that had been replaced by Holy Trinity. It was restored during the 1870s. It is very plain outside and in, except for the two hovering angels, and has been described as one of the oldest, smallest (it is less that forty feet long), and most numinous churches in England. In the center of town is the Shambles, a narrow pedestrian lane once a meat market, now a very varied collection of small shops. Most of the houses in the town belonged to weavers during the great days of the cloth trade. You can walk up Conigre Hill (the name means "rabbit warren") to reach the successively higher terraces. The view from the top is worth the effort. At the highest level the eighteenth-century houses at the western end had kitchens made by enlarging caves in the limestone. At the eastern end of the town, the hall is a large seventeenth-century house. Its gardens are open throughout the year. There are Tudor stables, two temples, from the eighteenth and nineteenth centuries, and an octagonal dovecote. In May every year, rafts race along the river from the town to the country park. For some reason, spectators throw eggs at the contestants. In 1995, a grumpy swan attacked every participating raft. Perhaps it was irritated by the waste of eggs.

"Millie" the mill girl greets the Millennium.

facing page
The pilgrim chapel, later a jail, on the nine-arched Town Bridge.

Barton Farm Country Park and the Tithe Barn are at the foot of the hill. Tithe barns existed to store the tenth of the harvest that farmers had to donate to the clergy. This is one of the largest in England, more than 150 feet long, with a steep pitched roof supported by massive curved timbers. As well as the Avon, another waterway also passes through the town—the Kennet and Avon canal, linking London and Bristol. It was closed in 1951. Valiant efforts brought about its restoration and reopening to traffic in 1990. Walk along its towpath in either direction or, if you are an experienced canoeist, hire a canoe.

There is one very popular, modern construction in the town. The Festival of Britain (1951) was intended to raise the nation's spirits as it recovered from the grim 1940s. Bradford turned the site of a demolished building into a festival garden. In 2000 it celebrated the Millennium by redesigning the garden and installing a scupture by John Willatts, a former resident. The subject, a mill girl releasing a bird, symbolizes the woolens industry and the town's hopes for the future. The statue is named after Clotho, Jupiter's daughter who spun the thread of life—but locals call it "Millie."

DORCHESTER

VENGEFUL GODS AND A VENGEFUL JUDGE

DORCHESTER, THE COUNTY SEAT OF DORSET, IS NINE MILES INLAND FROM WEYMOUTH. It stands on the western edge of the region covering several counties that provided the nineteenth-century novelist Thomas Hardy (1840-1928) with settings for his stories. Dorset itself is one of many places still recognizable from Hardy's descriptions, in this case in *The Mayor of Casterbridge* (1886). The manuscript of this novel is displayed in the Dorset County Museum, one of many eighteenth-century houses in Dorchester High Street. At Bere Regis, to the east, the parish church contains memorials to the Turberville family and Hardy used the village as a setting and a version of the family name in *Tess of the D'Urbervilles* (1891). All of Hardy's major novels have tragic endings. People struggle to overcome their fates in a hard, bleak landscape, which they often have to trudge across in dreadful weather. The gods play vengeful games with them—Hardy's plots rely heavily on fateful coincidence. They have lasting qualities just the same, and have proved popular with modern film directors, including Roman Polanski and John Schlesinger. When, in 1895, Hardy's last novel, *Jude the Obscure*, met with what had become the customary complaints about his "pessimism" and "immorality," he abandoned fiction in favor of poetry, which he regarded as superior. The poems he wrote in 1912 in memory of his first wife—"Woman much missed, how you call to me, call to me"—are certainly amongst his greatest works.

Hardy's Cottage, where he was born and from which he walked to school, is at Upper Brockhampton. It has an attractive garden and can be visited. He lived there until 1874, then spent time in London working as an architect and writing, before returning to Dorchester in 1885. There he designed Max Gate, a gloomy house in which he lived until he died. His heart is buried in a family plot in Stinsford churchyard. The rest of his body was interred in Poet's Corner in Westminster Abbey.

The Old Shire Hall still contains the Old Crown Court where in 1834 the six Tolpuddle Martyrs (agricultural laborers who had formed a trade union) were sentenced to seven years' transportation to Botany Bay. They were pardoned in 1836. Six cottages were built in the town as their memorial. Maiden Castle, a hill fort very close to the town, was the site of a battle in 43 when the invading Romans met resistance from the Iron Age inhabitants. Its name could mean either "castle that has never been taken" or "castle so strong that young women could defend it": the past was a politically incorrect time.

Hardy's Cottage, birthplace of the tragic novelist.

facing page
No one knows how old the Cerne Abbas Giant is; his other qualities are not in doubt.

Fortunately for the visitor the landscape around Dorchester is by no means as bleak and unwelcoming as you might conclude from its resident novelist. Maumbury Rings is a stone-age ditch and bank fortification, later an amphitheater. In 1685 Judge Jefferies ordered eighty members of the Monmouth Rebellion to be executed there, after conducting the Dorchester hearing on his "Bloody Assizes" tour in the Antelope Hotel (now a shopping centre). At Cerne Abbas there is a fertility symbol cut into the chalk on a green hillside. This well-endowed, club-wielding figure may represent either Hercules or an Iron Age warrior. Nearby are monastery buildings and a tithe barn rivaling that at Bradford-on-Avon.

At Abbotsbury, a little way along the coast, are another tithe barn, the Sub-Tropical Gardens, the high ridge of pebbles called Chesil Bank (which provides the setting and title of a recent novel by the Booker prize winner Ian McEwan), and a swannery that is worth a visit in the breeding season. Weymouth has been a popular seaside resort since George III first visited it in 1789. A statue commemorates his frequent summer stays. The statue is surrounded by Georgian terraces and hotels. The old town around Custom House Quay is a picture-postcard vision of fishing boats and old seaman's inns. Christopher Wren used limestone from the Isle (a peninsula, in fact) of Portland when building St Paul's Cathedral.

EXETER

CATHEDRAL CITY AND DEMONIC HOUND

EXETER, CATHEDRAL CITY AND COUNTY SEAT OF DEVON, has stood at a crossing point on the river Exe for over 2,000 years. Under the name of Iska it was a center for the Dumnonii, a British tribe. The Romans called it Isca Dumnoniorum and built walls around it, parts of which can still be seen. In Anglo-Saxon times, by then called Execeaster, it was sacked several times by the Danes. In 1068 it rebelled against the Normans but eventually submitted. William built a castle to ensure that they kept their word. Exeter was an important port until c. 1290, when it annoyed the Countess of Devon, who in retaliation built a weir across the river and ruined their trade. It continued, however, to be a prosperous cloth manufacturing center. During the English Civil War it was a Puritan stronghold that was in Royalist hands for eighteen months. Development for some centuries after that was peaceful and prosperous because of the continuing wool trade. The peace was shattered in 1942 when, in retaliation for RAF bombing of Lübeck and Rostock, the Luftwaffe attacked historic British towns. Parts of Exeter's center were destroyed. Nevertheless much of its character survived and damage was rectified during the 1950s.

The sculpture screen on Exeter Cathedral's west front.

facing page
Mol's Coffee House survived the air raid in 1942.

Since Exeter became a university town in 1922, it has been a lively place, day and night. In summer the cathedral green and close are crammed with crowds listening to street musicians. Mol's Coffee House (now a furniture and gift shop) is a very fine Elizabethan black-and-white timber frame building with an impressive front gable and balcony. The remains of the medieval water supply system, which lie under the center of the city, can be explored. The Exeter Guildhall claims to be the oldest municipal building in England still in continuous use. The fifteenth-century structure has a timber-framed roof, made of oak, a massive oak door and eighty carved oak panels of coats of arms of trade guilds, past mayors, and benefactors. A walk along the Exeter Ship Canal, past locks, wetlands, wildlife, and a pub or two, is highly recommended.

The Cathedral Church of St Peter is unusual in that, except for two low Norman towers, which survive (as transepts) from an earlier building, it is unified stylistically, having been built continuously over three generations. The style is, appropriately, called "decorated" and the sculpting of the stonework has to be seen to be believed. On the west front are statues of sixty-six kings, apostles, and saints. The interior is impressively gothic.

The eastern edge of Dartmoor is ten miles west of Exeter. There are car parks from which brief strolls can be taken or you can choose to walk long distances in challenging conditions. On a clear day there are superb views. In winter, the moor is often unforgiving, harsh, and dangerous. Its infamous mists may envelop walkers, robbing them of all sense of direction. Warm clothing, map, and compass skills and a high level of prudence are essential. The dangers and the mists between them have contributed to the characteristic atmosphere of a rich stock of ominous legends, often involving demonic dogs. Arthur Conan Doyle exploited such tales in his Sherlock Holmes story *The Hound of the Baskervilles*.

Exeter is surrounded by places of interest. To the south, on the way to Exmouth (which has some elegant Georgian buildings), is A La Ronde, a sixteen-sided house built by two eccentric sisters in 1796. Killerton House, to the north, holds a collection of eighteenth-to-twentieth-century costumes. Farther north still, beyond Tiverton, is Knightshayes Court, a Victorian Gothic fantasy with spectacular gardens that were designed in the 1960s. (Check opening times before visiting.) Among the many small villages that surround Exeter is Ide, quiet and secluded, with many charming houses. From one of them a carved wooden figure stares at you. Another such village is Kenn, on the edge of the Haldon Hills, from which views of Exeter and Dartmoor may be enjoyed.

HELSTON

"FURRY" DANCE AND LIZARD PENINSULA

THERE IS A STONE IN THE WALL OF THE 500-YEAR-OLD ANGEL HOTEL in Helston once believed to have been dropped there by the Devil when he was confronted by St Michael. This supposed event is what is being celebrated each year on or about May eighth, in what is nowadays Helston's greatest claim to fame, the "furry" dance. In the nineteenth century it was mistakenly called the "floral" dance, but "furry" probably refers to a fair or festival rather than to flowers, although these play their part. The dances and the ceremony of Hal-an-tow, which precedes them, have their origins in pre-Christian fertility rituals. Early in the morning young men go into the woods, returning with garlands and flowers, with which the town and the dancers are draped. The arrival of spring is celebrated with processional dances through the streets all day. Costumes vary considerably from simple fancy dress to the grotesque. Originally there was much sweeping out of houses to symbolize the triumph of light over darkness and cleansing from the dirt and dross of winter, since "Summer is a-come-O and winter is a gone-O."

The Angel Hotel was once the town house of the wealthy Godolphin family.

facing page
Mullion Cove on the Lizard Peninsula offers exciting cliff-top walks.

It was from Lizard Point, c. eleven miles south of Helston, the southernmost point in England, that the Spanish Armada was first sighted in 1588: 138 vessels, with perhaps 7,000 seamen and 17,000 soldiers aboard. The fleet sailed up the English Channel without being seriously troubled by a larger but randomly assembled English force. At Calais their complement of soldiers was supposed to be doubled, but the duke of Parma was not ready when they arrived. The Dutch trapped them in the congested anchorage at Calais Roads; English fireships, sent in next day, caused havoc. Driven out into the channel, they were dispersed by strong southerly winds, which pushed them up the North Sea. Terrible storms met them when they tried to escape around Scotland and Ireland. About two-thirds of them found their way home, but thirty were lost in shipwrecks along inhospitable western coasts. England survived as a maritime nation. The importance of the channel and south coast ports in the defense of England was to a degree reasserted. Helston, an ancient market town, had been one of these until the thirteenth century, when sand and shingle silted up the harbor mouth, in the process creating the largest freshwater lake in Cornwall.

The Lizard Peninsula has many sights and points of interest. Crab, lobster, and mackerel are caught at Porthleven. The beach at Loe Bar is attractive—but do not swim there: currents are very dangerous. Halzephron has cliffs almost 200 feet high. Since a shipwreck centuries ago, Gunwalloe Cove has been supposed to conceal quantities of gold coin. Marconi sent his first trans-Atlantic radio signal from Poldhu Cove in 1901. Goonhilly is the world's largest and oldest communications center, Culdrose the largest helicopter base in Europe. Kynance Cove and cliffs are fierce in winter, serene in summer. Cadgwith is a delightful fishing village, and there is a seal sanctuary on the Helford River at Gweek.

There are delightful walks to be enjoyed on its wooded shores.

While in Cornwall you must eat a Cornish Pasty. This folded circle of pastry, crimped around the curve, encloses meat and root vegetables. Nowadays fillings vary. Formerly, "authentic" contents were as much a matter of dogmatic certainty as Methodism.

Apart from defense and the building and manning of ships, the other local industry in Cornwall and Devon was the mining and processing of tin. Helston was an administrative center of the industry and the name of Coinagehall Street, curving downhill to what used to be the waterfront, with a small stream or "funnel" on either side, reminds us that ingots of tin were brought here for assessment tax payable to the duke of Cornwall. A small slice was taken off at one corner (or "coign") to be tested for quality. Tin mining has taken place for over 2,000 years and possibly for very much longer; the last tin mine in Cornwall closed in 1998. Behind the Guildhall is a folk museum with collections ranging from Bronze Age artifacts to fire engines.

MINEHEAD

GARDENS, WALKS, SHIPS, AND POETS

The Market Cross is one of 200 listed buildings in Dunster.

facing page
Minehead harbor at low tide.

THE NORTH SOMERSET COAST IS MUCH LOVED AS A HOLIDAY DESTINATION. The climate is mild, the coastal scenery dramatic. Inland, Exmoor—home of small, shaggy Exmoor ponies and the largest herd of red deer in England—is a peaceful expanse of heather, bracken, and grass with occasional steep-sided woodland valleys running down to sheltered fishing coves. R. D. Blackmore's *Lorna Doone*, about a family of murderous outlaws, is set there. Dunkery Beacon (51,640 feet high) gives, on a fine day, panoramic views in every direction. Dunster has over 200 buildings listed as being of architectural or historic interest, including a medieval castle and the octagonal Yarn Market built in 1609. To walk through this village is to take a stroll through history. It is also a good place to eat.

Minehead is proud of its parks and gardens (it has won several Britain in Bloom competitions), its Edwardian villas, and the twisting narrow alleyways between thatched cottages in the older part of town. There is always plenty going on worth watching in the pretty harbor. In summer there is a choice of seagoing day trips on either the preserved paddle steamer *Waverly* or the cruise ship *Balmoral*. Ships and the harbor were the town's source of income for several centuries. The fishing fleet caught herring and trade developed with Ireland, Virginia, and the West Indies. In the eighteenth century competition from Bristol and Liverpool and silting up of the harbor brought hard times to Minehead. The next phase in the town's history, however, was already beginning. The poets Wordsworth and Coleridge, who for a time lived nearby, drew the country's attention to the Quantock Hills and Exmoor. Doctors began to advocate sea bathing as a health-giving activity. When the railways reached the town its transformation into a holiday resort was inevitable.

At the western end of the town is North Hill (820 feet), which shelters both the harbor and town below. (The name Minehead has nothing to do with mining: it is derived from either the Welsh or the Celtic word for hill.) You can walk up a steep path known as Church Steps to St Michael's Church, parts of which date from the fourteenth century. There are excellent views of Minehead from its forecourt. Inside there are memorials to the Quirke family, one of whom gave the town a row of almshouses in 1630. Elgin Towers, nearby, is a copy of a Scottish baronial residence. On the open hilltop you will find prehistoric burial mounds, cairns, scattered flints, and traces of medieval farms and fields. There are, of course, views along the coast in both directions.

At 13 Blenheim Road, Minehead, you will find the house where Arthur C. Clarke, author of *2001: A Space Odyssey*, was born in 1917. Much earlier, in 1797 at Nether Stowey, Samuel Taylor Coleridge was interrupted by a person from the delightful village of Porlock, c. six miles west of Minehead, while he was writing down his poem *Kubla Khan*, which had come to him in a drugged dream. When the visitor left, Coleridge found that he had forgotten the rest of the poem—something well over 100 lines. He had a more fortunate experience at Watchet, a little way east of Minehead, having several conversations there with a sailor whose stories, some people believe, inspired him to write his poem *The Rime of the Ancient Mariner*.

Two interesting wild animals breed and live on Exmoor. A hundred and four brood mares were recorded in the *Domesday Book* (1085). They are small and sturdy, with a wide forehead and large eyes, broad-backed and short-legged. Alert, intelligent, and kind, they are ideal for children. Red deer, the largest wild animals in England, have lived on Exmoor since prehistoric times. A few thousand live on the moor, using the woods as a place of safety, eating young shoots of heather, whortleberry, brambles, saplings, grass, acorns, fungi, berries, and ivy—and can be a pest to farmers, raiding fields for corn and root crops. They have eight biting teeth on the lower jaw but none immediately above, biting instead against a hard gum.

50

51

PENZANCE

PIRATES, MOUSEHOLE, AND LAND'S END

WHEN THE LIBRETTIST OF THE MUSICAL THEATRE PARTNERSHIP GILBERT AND SULLIVAN wrote the book and lyrics for *The Pirates of Penzance*, part of the joke was that nobody would associate the quietly respectable Georgian town on the Cornish Riviera with piracy. Smuggling, perhaps. Yet Cornwall, at least in folklore, is associated with the idea of wrecking, the deliberate luring of ships onto rocks so that their cargoes could be salvaged and redistributed. Cornwall was traditionally a rebellious part of the country. It had not been subject to Anglo-Saxon conquest. It resented the centralization of government in London. It regarded itself—warmed as it was and is by the Gulf Stream, with palm trees growing in the Morrab Gardens—as by far the best place in the British Isles for anyone to live and be happy. Its anti-English rebelliousness induced Cornwall, never happy with the established Anglican Church, to embrace Methodism. (John Wesley, Methodism's founder, spoke out against smuggling.) By 1879, when Gilbert wrote his libretto (in a great hurry, in New York), Cornwall was very respectable indeed.

The Sailors' Institute Mission Hall reminds us of past times.

facing page
St Mary the Virgin, the perpendicular gothic parish church, built in the 1830s.

Many Cornish place names begin with the syllable "pen," which means "holy"; the name "Penzance" means "holy headland." The holy well and chapel that attracted this name are no longer there—although the chapel was one of the few buildings in the area spared by Spanish raiders who, in 1595, burned 400 houses. Chapel Street leads from the headland south of the harbor to the town center—and a very strange and interesting street it is. The most remarkable building is the Egyptian House, built by a local geologist in 1836 to house his collection of minerals. The exterior, with its exotic coloring, columns, and statues, to say nothing of its English royal coats of arms, is remarkable. The house where Maria Branwell, mother of the Brontë sisters (the novelists Charlotte, Emily, and Anne), lived as a child is marked with a plaque. The Chapel Street Methodist Church, a capacious, rather imposing building, was built in 1813. There are also the remains of a theater built in 1787 and various restaurants and pubs—including the Admiral Benbow, from the roof of which a pirate gazes seaward.

The great attraction close to Penzance is St Michael's Mount, the island across the bay. It was a center of the Cornish tin trade in pre-Roman times. The archangel St Michael was said to have appeared there in 495. The Normans, struck by the resemblance, asked Benedictine monks from the French Mont-St-Michel to build an abbey there. When he dissolved the monasteries in 1536 Henry VIII incorporated this one in a castle he erected around it as protection against the French. The island and house—as it now is—can be visited, either on foot at low tide, or by ferry. (It is necessary to book ahead in winter.)

In Market Jew Street there is a statue of Sir Humphry Davy, born here in 1778, a remarkable chemist who invented the miners' safety lamp. The Museum has a collection of paintings by the Newlyn School, who flourished just south of Penzance (1880-1900). The gardens and harbor-side walks offer every opportunity to enjoy the warm but airy climate.

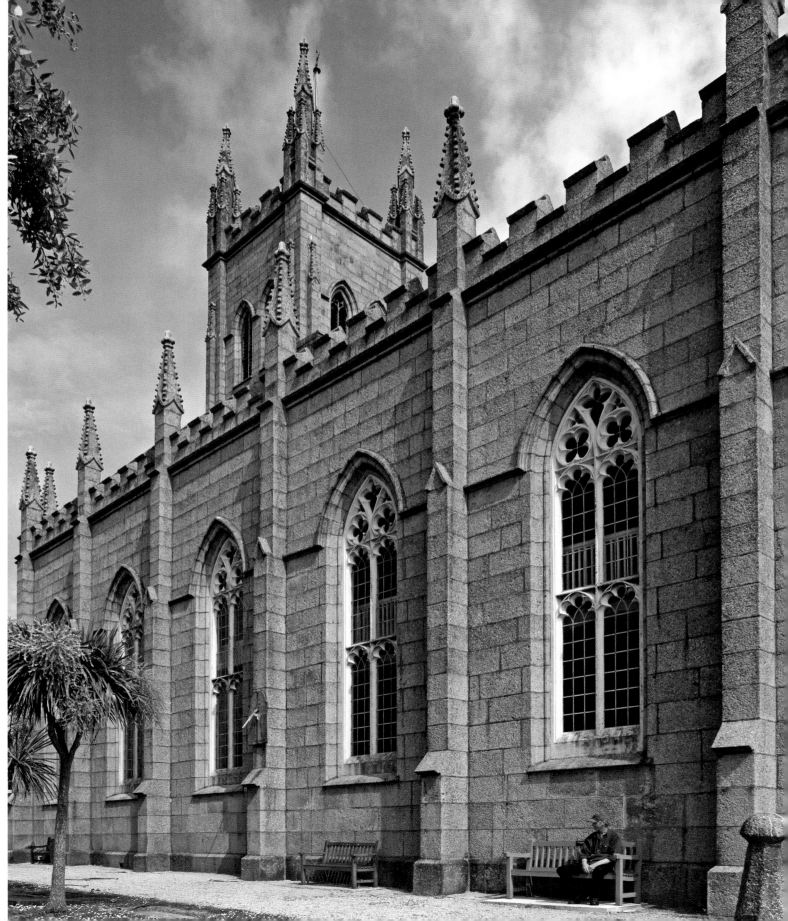

Other reasons for visiting Penzance are scattered around the Land's End peninsula. Inland there are several prehistoric sites. Mousehole (pronounced Mous'l) is a charming small seaside village. The Minack Theater is an open-air performance space high above the sea. Land's End itself is surely as dramatic an image of land and sea as any in the UK, with Atlantic rollers crashing against sixty-foot granite cliffs. Sennen Cove has a pleasant beach. St Ives, northeast of Penzance, has attracted its own art colony, drawn by the quality of the light and the scenic setting. Ben Nicholson, Barbara Hepworth, and Bernard Leach all lived and worked there. The Tate St Ives gallery and many smaller galleries and artists' studios are open to the public.

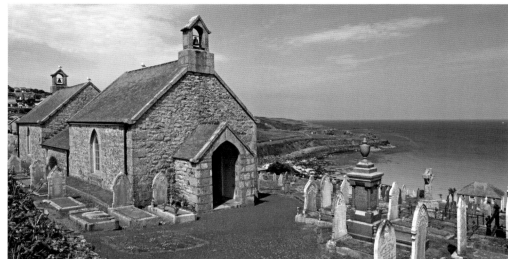

left
The granite cliffs of
Land's End,.

above
The tiny chapel of
St Nicholas on the
headland at St Ives.

About 28 miles off Land's End are the Scilly
Islands, 140 granite islands and granite lumps
whose total area is four and seven-tenths sq.
miles. The largest of the five inhabited islands
is St Mary's. Its capital, Hugh Town (pop. just
over 1,000, one third of the Scillies' total),
straddles a narrow isthmus. Its charming high
street features small shops and stone cottages
whose luxuriant gardens delight the eye with
subtropical blues and reds and an occasional
palm tree. On the hill above ("hugh" means
"hill-spur") stands the eight-pointed Star
Castle. This, built to repel the Spanish
Armada, is now a hotel. Scattered tombs
attest that the islands have been inhabited
since the Bronze Age. Warmed by the Gulf
Stream, they earn much of their income from
flowers and visitors. In centuries past the
islanders exploited the roughness of the
Atlantic by plundering ships that ran, or were
lured, onto the rocks.

left
The Sloop Inn on
the harbor front at St
Ives is one of
Cornwall's oldest
inns.

POOLE

A HARBOR AND A TOUGH LADY

POOLE STANDS ON THE SHORE OF A LARGE (TWENTY-FOUR SQUARE MILES), SHALLOW, almost landlocked harbor, an embarkation point for the D-Day landings in 1944. Like the Solent, it might have been designed for yachtsmen. It has a double high tide, which gives it about fourteen hours of high water every day. It has been a working port since the early Middle Ages. Fishing, piracy, and the timber trade have all flourished

Corfe Castle was deliberately destroyed in the 1640s.

facing page
Visit Poole Quay for traditional fudge, scrumpy cider and expertly cooked fish.

there in the past. Those who pass through nowadays may be oil prospectors, leisure sailors, or passengers catching a ferry to France. Most of Poole's visual interest is focused on the harbor; the old warehouses and new buildings of the waterfront area offer restaurants and bars, and the recently refurbished Waterfront Museum, which reviews 2,000 years of local history—including Poole's century of pottery making. Items made in the 1920s and 1930s are sought by collectors: decorative tiles, stoneware, vases, urns, jugs, bowls, and plates in a huge range of colors, decorations, and finishes. The Lighthouse Arts Center, home to the Bournemouth Symphony Orchestra, is near the Boating Pool.

On the Isle of Purbeck (in fact a peninsula), south of the harbor, stands Corfe Castle. Built by William the Conqueror to garrison the only natural route through Purbeck Hills, it was also an administrative centre where the king would dispense justice in person. By the time of the Spanish Armada it was in private hands; the owner mounted cannon on the walls in case of need. It was fought over twice during the English Civil Wars. Sir John Banks, the owner, was away supporting the Royalist cause elsewhere, so both defensive actions were conducted by Lady Banks. The first time the attackers were beaten off; on the second occasion a treacherous defender let them in. Lady Banks and her garrison were allowed to leave, but the castle itself was reduced by the Parliamentarians to the evocative ruin it is today, rising like broken teeth from the steep limestone hill. There are two small churches dedicated to St Nicholas of Myra close to each other on Purbeck. This is because Nicholas is the patron saint of sailors, and both can be seen from the sea. St Nicholas at Studland is Dorset's most complete Norman Church. On a hilltop not very far away is the Agglestone, a 16 foot high mass of ironstone. The Devil, it seems, fetched it from the Isle of Wight, intending to drop it on either Salisbury Cathedral or Stonehenge, but got tired and dropped it here instead. Swanage is a pleasant seaside resort around a bay where King Alfred defeated a Danish fleet in 877. Rock climbers visit Swanage to test themselves on cliffs west of the town with names such as Dancing Ledges, Blackers Hole and Cattle Troughs.

T.E. Lawrence, the mysterious and controversial "Lawrence of Arabia," bought Clouds Hill Cottage, c. twenty miles west of Poole, in 1925 when he joined the RAF. For the rest of his short life the small brick and tile cottage was a refuge from an existence that his fame (or notoriety) made increasingly difficult. It was here that he worked on revising his classic, if sometimes enigmatic account of his life in Arabia, *The Seven Pillars of Wisdom*. Clouds Hill may be visited in March-October, and contains the simple, austere furnishings he left behind when, in 1935, five days after being discharged from the RAF at the age of 46, he was accidentally killed as he motorcycled homewards.

There is a wealth of nature reserves around Poole Harbour, and an abundance of clean sandy beaches and water sports. If you fancy a fishing trip there are normally good stocks of mackerel. The area's many attractions have had their effect: on Sandbanks, the peninsula north of the entrance to the harbor, once a shanty town: property prices are now very high indeed. Brownsea Island has fine walks and spectacular views; wildlife includes red squirrels, peacocks and deer. There are trails for young smugglers, historians and explorers. In 2007 the scouting movement celebrated the centenary of the experimental Boy Scout camp held on the island by Robert Baden-Powell.

SALISBURY

A CATHEDRAL AND THREE WRITERS

AT THE BEGINNING OF THE THIRTEENTH CENTURY BISHOP POORE OF SALISBURY decided that the town was in the wrong place. According to legend he invited an archer to fire an arrow into the air; where it landed they would build the new city. Be that as it may, we can judge the merits of the two sites for ourselves. The remains of Old Sarum—foundations of a Norman castle and cathedral— are on a hilltop almost two miles north of the present city of Salisbury. There had been a hill fort there since the Iron Age, used by both Romans and Normans. Conflict between military and religious authorities and a shortage of water persuaded the bishop to move elsewhere. The result was a city created on a flat, open site with the largest cathedral close in England, which displays to their maximum effect a number of fine medieval buildings. Salisbury's cathedral, like Exeter's, was built in a relatively short time, thirty-eight years, starting in 1220, in a single style. The tower and its spire, the tallest in England (4,034 feet), were added in 1334. Seen from a distance across riverside meadows (four rivers converge at Salisbury) the building conforms exactly to most people's idea of how a cathedral should look. For many this applies equally in close-up, but some think the

Stonehenge has no rivals for mysterious grandeur.

facing page
Over-decorated or lavishly symbolic? —the west front of Salsibury Cathedral.

west front is over-decorated and dislike the statues, which are Victorian restorations. Fortunately, original statues can be found inside, in the octagonal chapter house, which has sixty scenes from the Old Testament involving c. 200 carved figures. Since 1946 the boys of the Cathedral Choir School have occupied the Bishop's Palace. In 1991 Salisbury made what was to some a startling innovation, by founding the first cathedral girls' choir. This has been a success and operates independently from the boys. In 1998 the girls and the men of the cathedral choir toured America.

Many fine buildings have been preserved in the town outside the close. There are two churches almost as old as the cathedral, two fourteenth-century inns (Haunch of Venison, Rose and Crown), and an ornate fifteenth-century poultry cross, an open-sided building where poultry was sold. The House of John A'Port and the Joiners' Hall are outstanding black-and-white half-timbered structures. Matron's College is a row of almshouses built in the eighteenth century for the use of clerical widows. The museum exhibits remains from Old Sarum and Stonehenge, a Roman mosaic pavement, and a collection of English pottery, china, and glass. There is an interestingly varied display of costumes, including a most elegant 1920s lady.

Outside the town, Stonehenge should not be missed. No one is quite sure what function these concentric rings of standing stones fulfilled but they clearly had something to do with time and the seasons. The stones were erected between 3,000-1,600 BCE, by men who were equally arithmeticians and astronomers. (They were not, despite popular belief, Druids.) Wilton House (c. six and a half miles) has been the home of the earls of Pembroke since Tudor times and its elegance has contributed to such films as *Sense and Sensibility, Pride and Prejudice, Mrs Brown* and *The Madness of King George*. The D-Day invasion of Normandy was planned there. One of the earls was rumored to have smuggled French carpet weavers over in a wine barrel to work in the Wilton carpet factory.

Salisbury has important literary associations. William Golding, the Nobel Prize-winning novelist, who taught in Salisbury until the success of *Lord of the Flies* allowed him to write full-time, wrote, in *The Spire*, about the addition of the spire to the existing building, making out of the historical event a tragedy of human ambition and pride. Anthony Trollope conceived the first of his six "Barchester" novels while wandering about the cathedral close in Salisbury as dusk deepened into night, and it is generally agreed that Thomas Hardy's Melchester is also modeled on Salisbury, the cathedral city nearest to his home in Dorchester, and Tess of the D'Urbervilles is certainly arrested at Stonehenge.

SHERBORNE

AN ABBEY DISSOLVED, A CASTLE BUILT

THE YEARS 1550-1594 HAD A DECISIVE IMPACT ON THE APPEARANCE OF SHERBORNE and explain why the town retains so many unspoiled medieval buildings. Sherborne Abbey had been founded in 705 and its church was the seat of the chief bishopric in Dorset until 1075. The see was then moved to Old Sarum (later Salisbury). The church was rebuilt in the twelfth century and again, after a serious fire, in the fifteenth.

When the monasteries were dissolved there was, as elsewhere, some chance that the buildings would rapidly become ruins. But Sherborne parish bought the church and the other abbey buildings were given to Sherborne College, refounded in 1550 with a new charter from Edward VI. The church is in effect a Norman church wholly transformed, in a mixture of perpendicular and Early English styles. There is fifteenth-century painted glass in the Leweston Chapel and fifteenth-century misericords (projections on the underside of tipped-up choir seats that help the infirm and elderly to stand for long periods during services) in the choir stalls. There are effigies of medieval abbots and an imposing seventeenth-century monument. The fan vaulting in the nave and choir is early, fine, and spectacular.

In 1594 the town acquired a new castle. Elizabeth I had given Sir Walter Raleigh the old one as a residence, but several years of trying convinced him that he could never make it comfortable. He built a new one instead. The state rooms as they are now offer an uninhibited, even exuberant variety of decorative styles: Tudor, Jacobean, Georgian, and Victorian. In them are fine collections of paintings, furniture, and porcelain. In the cellars the visitor can see family artifacts and Raleigh's impressive stone-paved kitchen. The old castle was reduced to a ruin during the Civil War, after having twice been under siege by the Parliamentarians, in 1642 and 1645. When they captured it they knocked down enough of it to ensure that it could not stand against them again. The new castle and the gardens (designed by Lancelot Capability "VL" Brown, who in 1753 also created the lake) are open throughout the summer. There is an abundance of wildlife to be observed. Musical, dramatic, and other events, including a cavalcade and exhibition of vintage cars and motorbikes, are staged there during the summer.

It was Raleigh who introduced to England the habit of smoking tobacco. There is a story that a servant, approaching from behind, saw smoke rising from his master as he sat outside his new castle and threw a pot of ale over him to extinguish the blaze. Sadly, Raleigh's reaction is not recorded.

Where Raleigh failed and Puritans triumphed: Sherbourne Old Castle.

Sherborne is notable for the charm, usefulness and variety of its shops—a violin repairer, a made-to-measure corsetiere, antiques, art galleries and specialist cheese are there, as well as more commonplace retailers. The streets are almost completely unspoiled and in pedestrianized Cheap Street you can look at the buildings from any angle without risk. There are bustling markets on Tuesdays and Thursdays. Annually there is a festival of arts and music centred on the Abbey, a Real Ale Festival hosted by the Rotary Club and, in October, Pack Monday Fair, when street traders take over the town.

Nine miles west of Sherborne is Montacute House, a magnificent H-shaped Elizabethan mansion of local honey-brown Ham stone, with delicate chimneys, parapets, and pinnacles, and curved Flemish gables. Few of the original contents remain, but their place has been taken by a bequest of fine furniture and tapestries—look out for the caparisoned knight in a meadow of spring flowers—and Tudor and Jacobean paintings on loan from the National Portrait Gallery. The gardens follow the original layout while incorporating nineteenth- and twentieth-century features. Nearby is the small, delightful walled garden of Tintinhall House.

facing page
For 500 years St John's Almshouses have in varied ways housed the needy.

TRURO

REBECCA AND THE LOST GARDENS

TRURO IS ALMOST EXACTLY IN THE CENTER OF CORNWALL, making it a natural choice as county seat and cathedral city. It is quite small and not particularly ancient. The Norman castle has now vanished but under its protection Truro became an important river port, market town, and center of the Cornish tin and copper industries. Although it was inland from the sea, this was an advantage at a time when seaborne raiders regularly attacked the coast. There were periods of recession, like the Black Death (starting 1348), which caused a huge exodus from the town, and another in the seventeenth century. In 1695 a visitor described it as "ruinated and disregarded." It had supported the Royalists in the Civil War. When the Parliamentarians captured it, King Charles had to escape via the seaport at Falmouth, ten miles south. During the following 150 years there was intense rivalry between Truro and Falmouth. Falmouth won, taking over most waterborne trade. But owners of tin and copper mines liked to live in Truro and it became a social and shopping center for the county. Truro still has good shops, and two covered markets and an arcade of specialist traders, the Creation Center, supplement more everyday retailers. Do take a stroll through the narrow residential streets—sometimes just a pathway separated from the house fronts by a strip of flower garden.

Truro Cathedral stands among small houses and shops in the old town.

facing page
The ceiling of the main crossing in Truro Cathedral.

In 1876 the Anglican Diocese of Truro was formed and the cathedral begun. The site was cramped and there was no possibility of a surrounding close; nave and spire rise startlingly out of a huddle of shops and houses. Bishop Benson did not want it to resemble any other cathedral; its particular form of imitative Gothic makes it look like something imported from northern France. It has been described as technically impressive and exuberant. The bishop's throne, choir stalls, and font are all worth a look, as is St Mary's aisle, which incorporates part of the original parish church.

Thirty-five miles away on the north coast are the ruins of Tintagel Castle, built by a thirteenth-century earl in the mistaken belief that the clifftop site was the birthplace of King Arthur. This is a dramatic and stirring place nevertheless. South of Tintagel, on Bodmin Moor, you can eat and drink at Jamaica Inn, which inspired Daphne du Maurier's novel about smuggling and romance. Her family home, Ferryside, can still be seen in Fowey (pronounced Foy) on the south coast. Menabilly, the original for Manderley in *Rebecca*, is privately owned. *Rebecca*, *The Birds*, and *Don't Look Now* were unusual takes on the art of the Gothic story, claustrophobic nightmares of psychological exploration afflicting well-behaved people. They, and the films based on them, which du Maurier did not always like, are part of her legacy.

Nature and garden lovers will not want to miss Heligan Gardens and the Eden Project, which are about twenty miles east of Truro. They were respectively restored and created by teams led by Tim Smit. Restoration of the Lost Gardens of Heligan began in 1991. It was the most visited garden in Britain until the Eden Project opened. You enter through rhododendrons to explore a vegetable garden, a valley of subtropical plants, rockery, grotto, wishing well, Italian garden and other curiosities. There is also fascinating wildlife.

The Eden Project opened in 2001. In what was once a disused china clay pit, under huge domes covering almost fourteen square miles, artificial climates have been created and more than 1,000,000 plants from all over the world flourish. The Humid Tropics Biome recreates the natural environment of a tropical forest. The Warm Temperate Biome re-creates a Mediterranean climate: hot, dry summers and cool, wet winters. In a roofless biome we see plant life from Cornwall itself and others from similar climates in Chile, the Himalayas, Asia, and Australia. Exhibitions show how plants provide crops, oils, rope, hemp, and fiber and explain their uses in brewing, fuels, dyestuffs, and natural medicines.

WELLS

TINY CITY, LARGE CATHEDRAL

WELLS, ON THE SOUTHERN EDGE OF SOMERSET'S MENDIP HILLS, describes itself proudly as England's smallest city. It was named after springs in what are now the gardens of the Bishop's Palace, one of the oldest inhabited houses in the country. The first church was built in the eighth century. Athelm, first bishop of Wells, was consecrated about 909, and the church became a cathedral, giving the town city status. After the Norman Conquest (1066) the bishop, John de Vilula, moved his seat to Bath. Wells fell into decline but, after 1136, the clergy (who had become notorious for womanizing, brawling, and thievery) were reformed and the buildings repaired by Robert of Lewes. The present cathedral was begun about 1180, using soft limestone quarried in Doulting, a nearby village. The main structure was consecrated in 1239; the building we see today was completed about a century later. Its most memorable feature is the west front, on which 293 statues represent Jesus in Glory, apostles, saints, bishops, kings, lords, ladies, and characters from scripture and legend.

Inside, the nave is solid but not heavy. The great central tower of the cathedral stands above the point where the nave is crossed by the transepts and to bear its weight, four pointed arches, surmounted by inverted mirror images of themselves, have been built. The effect has been described as theatrical and sensational. Many people will find the Gothic Lady Chapel, with its ingeniously vaulted ceiling and stained-glass windows, more enchantingly beautiful. In the north transept there is an unusual clock: a bearded man in red strikes the hours, and the quarter hours are marked by jousting knights on horseback.

The Bishop's Palace, nearby, has a wide, well-preserved moat that is home to a flock of swans. Their forebears, we are told, were trained to ring a bell hanging from the gatehouse (the bell is still there) when they wanted to be fed. A towered medieval gateway leads from the palace into Wells Market Place. In 1695 the Quaker William Penn, who later founded the American state of Pennsylvania, preached to a large crowd here and was arrested for unlawful assembly. In St Cuthbert Street stands Wells's fifteenth-century parish church, which, during a Protestant rebellion against the Catholic James II, led by James, duke of Monmouth (one of the illegitimate sons of Charles II), housed the men and gunpowder barrels of the Somerset militia. Wells has interesting antiques and clothing shops. In the Market Place, on Saturdays and Wednesdays, you can buy clothes, jewelery, and organic vegetables—even, on the last occasion I was there, large cuddly tigers.

The cathedral choir sings services in this elegant, resonant space.

facing page
The defensively moated gateway to the Bishop's Palace.

Wookey Hole is a cave complex near Wells that—up to 50,000 years ago—provided safe, easy-to-defend homes. Humans and hyenas competed. Both supplied themselves with meat by driving animals off the top of the cliff: bones found at its foot include those of goats, mammoths, rhinoceros, and lions. While the Romans were there, they mined lead and silver. Later on, villagers of Wookey appealed for help against a witch who lurked in the caves. One story is that King Arthur slew her. Another has it that the abbot of Glastonbury appointed an exorciser who, after a spine-tingling encounter, annointed her with holy water and turned her to stone. Today Wookey's spectacular underground scenery is dramatically lit, and guided tours may be taken.

On the northern side of the cathedral stands Wells Cathedral School, one of Britains's five independent specialist music schools. If you have the chance to hear one of their orchestras, bands, or choirs perform, don't miss it. Professional musicians visit the school regularly to coach the players and singers, and an individual's particular tastes and interests are respected. It is a remarkable thing to walk into a school at eight A.M. and hear a wind band rehearsing in the hall while, in other parts of the building, soloists are learning the Brahms Violin Concerto or a Prokofiev piano sonata. Later in the day, you might hear teenage composers introducing and performing their own works.

ALDEBURGH

A TOWN HALF SWALLOWED BY THE SEA

500 YEARS AGO THERE WERE THREE ROADS BETWEEN ALDEBURGH'S half-timbered brick-and-stone Moot Hall and the North Sea. Now there is only one—Aldeburgh's main street. Its varied Georgian houses and older cottages have hardly changed since Victorian times. Beyond that, a wide strip of shingle slopes down to the sea. A lifeboat stands ready for action and fresh fish is sold from small huts. The tide rises and falls by two to ten feet twice every day and what used to be the eastern half of the town has disappeared into it. Above, the sky seems enormous and the light is always changing. Behind a wide sea-wall flows the river Alde, once the town's source of prosperity, providing a flourishing port and shipbuilding center. From it, four ships and many local men were sent to fight the Spanish Armada. *The Golden Hind*, in which, in the 1570s, Francis Drake sailed around the world in two years, ten months, and eighteen days, was built here. At that time the Alde reached the sea just south of the town, but when its mouth was blocked by shingle it had to flow further south into the river Ore, and Aldeburgh ceased to function as a port. Smaller-scale fishing and boatbuilding have continued, however, and the Alde now has its own yacht club. Aldeburgh developed as a seaside resort during the nineteenth century and is often, unsurprisingly, thought of as a conservative town. But in 1908 it elected Britain's first woman mayor, Elizabeth Garrett Anderson, who was also England's first woman doctor.

A fishing boat on the beach at Aldeburgh.

facing page
Aldeburgh's half-timbered Moot Hall was built in c. 1512.

This stretch of England's east coast flatlands has often been a setting for fictional mysteries. Wilkie Collins set part of *No Name* in Aldeburgh. M. R. James told ghost stories about this area and in Dorothy L. Sayers's *The Nine Tailors* murderous church bells pealed in the fens. Malefactors invented by P. D. James stalk the seaside shingle. Arthur Conan Doyle never set a Sherlock Holmes story here, but his friend J. M. Barrie, author of *Peter Pan*, wrote an affectionate parody of one while he was living in Aldeburgh. Perhaps the great original of all these was the early nineteenth-century poet, Aldeburgh-born George Crabbe, with his tale of the misfit and murderer the fisherman Peter Grimes. It was an operatic version of this story that in 1945 gave the composer Benjamin Britten his first big success. Britten loved this area and in 1948, with his partner, the tenor Peter Pears, he inaugurated the Aldeburgh Music Festival. After 1948, most of his music was written for the festival, which is staged in June each year. In 2007, with Britten and Pears dead thirty-one and twenty-one years respectively, it was still drawing enthusiastic audiences to the Suffolk coast.

At first, festival concerts took place in the parish church or the Jubilee Hall, but in 1967 a new principal venue was established, five miles inland, in Snape Maltings, a red-brick Victorian building overlooking the broad, marshy one-time estuary of the Alde. Two years later the building was gutted by fire, but restored in time for the festival in 1970. Guided tours of Britten's last home, the Red House, and the Britten-Pears Library are available in summer. Aldeburgh Church, which arrived at its present form under Henry VIII, contains memorials to George Crabbe (curate there for a time) and Britten. Another local memorial to Britten, Maggie Hambling's sculptured *Scallop Shell*, on the beach, has attracted both rapturous praise and accusations of ugliness and inappropriateness.

Three other churches associated with the festival, all built when the wool trade was most prosperous, are also of more general interest. Blythburgh Church (fifteenth century), damaged by iconoclasts in Cromwell's time, has been compared to a great stranded ship because of its isolated magnificence, but its interior is given a welcoming sense of warmth by the woodwork. Framlingham Church houses many important tombs, a beautiful chancel and a magnificent organ. At Orford we find Norman arcades in the ruined chancel, and fine ornamental stonework. Framlingham and Orford also have interesting castles. Meanwhile, the sea continues, little by little, to eat away the land.

MARKET CROSS PLACE

B U R Y
ST EDMUNDS

WELCOMING INTIMACY

BURY IS NOT GENERALLY A TURBULENT PLACE, but there was a kind of revolt of the townsfolk in 2005 when the Abolish the Town Council Party won a majority on the very town council it proposed to abolish. The town is named after Edmund, king of East Anglia, who, having been defeated in 869 by marauding infidel Danes, refused, as a Christian king, to share power with them. They executed him barbarically. He was reverenced as a martyr and

The Church of St. James became the Cathedral of Edmundsbury in 1914 with the creation of the Diocese of Ipswich and Edmundsbury.

facing page
Near the Cathedral are the ruins of the Abbey Church, a place of pilgrimage since medieval times.

his remains were interred in a monastery at what became a popular place of pilgrimage under the name St Edmundsbury. ("Bury" here means "town.") From 1032, when the monastery church was completed, the monastery became an abbey. The monks planned the town that grew up around it (and which depended upon it) on the grid that survives today. People find the intimate scale very welcoming; the early nineteenth-century radical William Cobbett, thought Bury "the nicest town in the world." Nonetheless, relations between town and monks were not always good: in 1327 there was a "war" between them when abbey buildings were burned and the abbot was held to ransom. Fifty-four years later the town was a major focus of the Peasants' Revolt (mainly about a proposed poll tax); this time the abbot was beheaded and the rebels rioted throughout the abbey. In 1465 the abbey was destroyed by fire; restoration was complete by 1538. Shortly afterward the abbey was dissolved, stripped of valuables, and quarried for building stone. In 1914 a Norman church on the site was designated a cathedral. Within the last few years the tower of this church, never built, was finally completed. Now, as St Edmundsbury Cathedral, it presides over what is left of its much larger predecessor and a large area of varied and delightful gardens.

Bury and its history provides a microcosm of English attitudes toward ancient religious monuments. For much of 2,000 years they might be, simultaneously, places of pilgrimage and resented symbols of oppression. Then, as levels of social and political freedom rose and those of belief and religious observance declined, they started to be loved again and a large cross-section of the population have become supporters of and visitors to these buildings. Few would suggest that anything more than a small minority of the thousands who throng into the cathedrals, abbeys, and parish churches, which are so visible a feature of the British landscape, would be like-

Ickworth House (three miles) is an eccentric neoclassical mansion with a huge rotunda and artworks by Titian and Reynolds. Memorials from the agricultural and industrial pasts are also important. At Blackthorpe Barn there is an expanding arts center in a large sixteenth-century thatched barn. Packenham Watermill is the last working watermill in Suffolk. Lackford Lakes were formed by sand and gravel extraction in the valley of the river Lark, providing a range of aquatic and terrestrial habitats that attract skylarks, lapwing, gray partridge, song thrush, linnet, bullfinch, turtle dove, reed bunting, gadwall, shoveller, pochard, little ringed plover, and water rail. In winter come gadwall, goosanders, and teal. Insects include dragonflies and damselflies.

ly to attend services there, just as few would expect everyone who loves the language of the 1603 English translation of the Bible to think of it as the Word of God. But, however illogical these mixed attitudes may seem, lovers of art, architecture, music, and literature, and those who believe that we have to understand our collective past if we are to make any sense of the present, can only rejoice.

In Bury itself, in the evening, you can buy a drink at The Nutshell. According to the *Guiness Book of Records* this is the smallest pub in Britain. Its floor area is fifteen feet by seven feet six inches. It is probably because it is so small that no food is served. Visitors write enthusiastically about it, although one claimed to be disappointed because there wasn't room to swing his cat. (This is a British joke.) Afterward—or before—see a performance at one of the UK's oldest theaters, the delectable Georgian Theatre Royal. Recently restored, this brilliantly decorated jewel box is one of only three theaters in the UK surviving from the pre-Victorian era. It performs many plays from the eighteenth and early nineteenth centuries.

CAMBRIDGE

CAROLS, INTELLECT, AND PUNTING

ALMOST ANYONE WHO CELEBRATES CHRISTMAS, ALMOST ANYWHERE IN THE WORLD, has probably heard of Cambridge. They will have heard or seen that magical moment of vibrant silence before a boy soprano, sounding simultaneously celestial and of this earth, projects into the tall resonance of King's College Chapel the words "Once, in royal David's city, stood a lowly cattle shed…" He will not have known until seconds before that this time it would be his turn: he has been given no opportunity to be overcome by nerves.

This combination of specialized skill and everyday practicality typifies the place where it is happening. This is where the atom was split and where the structure of DNA was first identified and described. Somebody once joked that the rest of the world was only God's device to ensure that not absolutely everything would happen first at Cambridge. The town and university make an interesting comparison with the other half of the entity known as "Oxbridge" since Thackeray wrote *Pendennis* (1848-50). Oxford is in the humid Thames Valley, sheltered by gentle ranges of hills from every wind that blows. It is synonymous, in fact, with (at least comparative) warmth

The Round Church is the second most visited sight in Cambridge.

facing page
St John's College Chapel has a very distinguished choir.

and relaxed, slippered ease. If, on the other hand, you could see so far, you might gaze eastward from Cambridge and the first visible hump would be the Ural Mountains that separate Russia and Siberia. Similarly, if you gaze north, there's nothing much between you and the North Pole. North and east winds are especially cold in Cambridge, the air unusually clear: no wonder the place is famous for mathematicians and scientists. Its great names over the centuries include Isaac Newton, Bertrand Russell, and Ludwig Wittgenstein, whose statement, "The world is everything that is the case"—simultaneously limpid and opaque—somehow encapsulates the spirit of the place. It was home also to F. R. Leavis—notorious or brilliant according to your point of view—whose relentlessly rigorous assessments of English novelists placed huge emphasis on the moral value of great literature—and the worthlessness of everything else. In recent decades it has become one of the world capitals of information technology. (One of its nicknames is Silicon Fen).

There are many ways of enjoying being outside in Cambridge. Hire a punt and push yourself along the Cam, gazing at the backs of the colleges and watching the movers and shakers of tomorrow doing the same. If you prove to be competent you will have a smooth, elegant trip. If not you may leave your pole behind, stuck in the mud, fall overboard or impede everyone else on the river and be the butt of undergraduate wit. Either way, it is fun and you will remember it for the rest of your life. Look at as many colleges as possible. Stroll along the river to Granchester, listening to and straining to see the skylarks above the meadows. Does the church clock still stand at ten to three, as Rupert Brooke said it did? You will probably catch a glimpse of the outside of the Old Vicarage, source of the title of Brooke's poem, now home to the great bounder and popular novelist Jeffrey Archer.

According to the myth, Oxford is the spiritual home of the gentleman amateur, Cambridge the testing ground of the cool, focused professional. Of their annual sporting contests, Cambridge has won seventy-nine boat races to Oxford's seventy-three, and fifty-seven rugby matches to Oxford's fifty-one.

Music, art, and learning are essential parts of the Cambridge experience. Find out which of the colleges is doing choral evensong and attend. (Getting into the King's Service of Nine Lessons and Carols at Christmas is probably just about as difficult as getting into one of the colleges as a student.) Go to the Fitzwilliam Museum, an elegant building full of elegant art—Venetian masterpieces by Palma Vecchio, Veronese, and Titian, a good selection of Dutch pictures and a fine collection of Rembrandt etchings. Other institutions cover archeology and anthropology and the sciences. Do not miss Kettle's Yard, which would require several pages for an adequate description.

far left
Punting on the Cam is a much-enjoyed, sometimes tricky pastime.

left
The gateway of King's College.

below
Cambridge town center.

Racing fans may like to travel thirteen miles eastward to Newmarket, thought of as the administrative and spiritual home of English racing. (It is home to the occasional scandal as well.) The town lies on open heathland ideal for galloping and the first organized races took place in 1619. The British royal family is to this day famed for its interest in horse racing. King Charles II actually rode in races here. Other royals have been equally enthusiastic, but as spectators, not participants. Many of the thrillers set in the world of racing by Dick Francis, the late Queen Mother's jockey, are set at Newmarket. They have been enjoyed by many readers who have no interest in racing.

COLCHESTER
OYSTERS, CLOCKS, AND CONSTABLE

LIKE MANY TOWNS IN EAST ANGLIA, COLCHESTER WAS A MANUFACTURING and distribution center for the wool trade, which made the region prosperous during the Middle Ages and for some centuries afterward. In Colchester during the twentieth century, wool's place was taken by light engineering, and the eastern and southeastern outskirts of the town are largely occupied by industrial estates. But the central, historical part of Colchester remains pleasantly attractive and interesting. It is a good place, too, from which to visit beautiful spots nearby—a number of villages and a number of sights and places painted by John Constable (1776-1837) one of England's best-loved painters. Colchester's great delicacy, from Roman times onward, has been oysters, and every October an oyster feast marks the start of the season.

People have lived at Colchester for over 3,000 years and it is the oldest recorded town in England. Cunobelin, king of the Catuvellauni, made it his capital c. 10. Forty years later the Romans arrived and made it their first colony, peopling it with ex-soldiers. In 60-61CE Queen Boudicca of the Iceni rebelled against the brutality of Roman rule. Colchester was her first target and she destroyed it. It was resurrected, however, and continued to be an important center of power in the region. The Normans built a large castle keep and this remains, in an excellent state of appearance and repair. It houses a museum, which illustrates life in the town from prehistory to the Civil War, and contains a medieval jail. The castle grounds—proudly described as "an oasis of horticultural splendour"— are extensive, with the river Colne (from which the town may derive part of its name and certainly once derived its standing as a port, along with much of its income) flowing through. Just west of the castle lies the Dutch Quarter, which housed Flemish weavers who arrived in the sixteenth century. On the main street stands the splendid Town Hall, a favorite venue for weddings and civil partnership ceremonies. Equally essential viewing farther along is the Hollytrees Museum in an elegant house from 1719, presenting daily life over 300 years. Just off the main street is Tymperly's Clock Museum, exhibiting another important part of Colchester's commercial history, in a fifteenth-century timber-framed house that belonged to Queen Elizabeth I's physician William Gilberd. All the clocks on display were made in Colchester between 1640 and 1840. Gilberd (also known as Gilbert) was one of the leading scientists of his age. His book *De Magnete* (1600) established the bases of both magnetism and electricity. Galileo regarded him as a leader in the testing of conclusions and beliefs by experiment.

Rooms in Christchurch Mansion in nearby Ipswich represent earlier periods in the town's history.

facing page
St Botolph's Priory, founded in 1103, was England's first Augustinian monastery.

Another favorite venue for weddings and other special events is the Layer Marney Tower, seven miles south of the town. This eight-story Tudor gatehouse was intended as merely part of a very large house, but death intervened. It is a model of Tudor craftsmanship. Visits, unless to public events, have to be arranged privately. At Coggeshall, west of Colchester, is the oldest surviving timber-framed barn in Europe and Paycocke's (c. 1500), a half-timbered house with a remarkable paneled interior. To the east is the Beth Chatto Garden, where an unusual collection of plants has been chosen to suit such unfriendly growing environments as arid, windy slopes, gravel, and bog.

There are frequent trains from Colchester to Ipswich. This latter has largely been rebuilt in modern times but a number of ancient buildings may still be seen. Christchurch Mansion (1548), the town's museum and art gallery, has a collection of Constable's early work when he was painting and drawing in Dedham. If you want to see the settings of some of his most famous works as they are today, go to Dedham, look at the church, which appears in several paintings, then follow the path along the south bank of the River Stour to Flatford Mill, passing on the way Willy Lott's Cottage which appears, much as it is now, in *The Hay Wain*.

LAVENHAM

WOOL ROOM, GUILDHALL, AND CHURCH

THE CHANGES BETWEEN LAVENHAM, AS IT WAS WHEN ITS CATHEDRAL-LIKE parish church was built in the late fifteenth century, and Lavenham today are now neatly encapsulated in the Swan Inn. Part of this, the timber-frame building with the overhanging upper story on the corner of Lady and Water streets, was once the town's wool hall. In 1524 Lavenham was the fourteenth-wealthiest town in England but heavy taxation and disruption of export markets, caused by war on the Continent, sent its fortunes into decline. Most of the timber-framed buildings that make Lavenham today an almost perfectly preserved medieval town, where electric and telephone cables and television aerials are kept strictly out of sight, date from c. 1460-1530. It lives by welcoming visitors and as a home for people who work elsewhere. Hence the change of function at the corner of Lady Street. This key building of the wool trade 600 years ago now blends its ancient oak beams and inglenook fireplaces with luxurious furnishings and fabrics for the comfort of guests. The collection of memorabilia in the Old Bar includes a reminder of recent harsher times—a wall signed by British and American airmen stationed near Lavenham during World War II. Nearby, the remains of USAAF Station 137 are reverting to farmland. These Americans evidently enjoyed their time in Lavenham; they got together to donate an electric blower for the organ in the Church of St Peter and St Paul.

The Swan Inn incorporates the Elizabethan Wool Hall.

facing page
St Peter and St Paul look down from above the door of the church named after them.

To describe Lavenham is necessarily to praise its medieval buildings and street plan, which, ironically, have been preserved by the town's decline. Strolling through the streets you will notice all sorts of details: carved figures on either side of a battered, recessed door, or the oriel windows in the long and varied front of the Guildhall of Corpus Christi. Little Hall, on the town's main square, mirrors, in itself and in its museum, Lavenham over the centuries.

In the countryside roundabout there is much of beauty and interest. At Sudbury is the birthplace museum of Thomas Gainsborough, the eighteenth-century painter of portraits and landscapes. On the way to or from Sudbury you can compare Long Melford's parish church with its Lavenham rival, and enjoy Kentwell Hall (a moated Tudor mansion), its gardens, and rare-breeds farm. Kentwell is a lived-in and loved family home, something it has been for over 500 years. Melford Hall, near the Green at Long Melford, has associations with the children's writer Beatrix Potter. Her original Jemima Puddle-duck toy can be seen there. Notable for its fanciful towers, it was built by a shrewd Tudor lawyer, Sir William Cordell.

There have been four guildhalls in Lavenham at various times. This one became disused as such almost as soon at it was built, c. 1529. The guilds were socioreligious organizations, associated, fatally for them, with late-medieval Catholicism. They were abolished by the Puritan parliament of 1545-47. The building was later used as a prison (the parish lock-up and mortuary is in the back garden), town hall, workhouse, almshouse, and wool store. Upstairs is a museum mainly devoted to the wool trade. (You will learn how many different-colored dyes can be extracted from woad). It also contains a mummified cat, formerly placed in the roof to ward off evil spirits.

The Church of St Peter and St Paul vies with its near neighbour at Long Melford in splendor and general magnificence. Standing on a hilltop, with a square tower 141 feet high, it can be seen for miles around. Its bells, by the same token, can be heard from afar, particularly the deep tone of the great tenor bell made by Miles Graye in 625. The wood carving in the interior is intricate and beautiful, although it has been stained an inappropriately dark color, probably at the same time as the stained glass in the otherwise lovely Lady Chapel was replaced. Assessments of the glass vary from "unfortunate" to "hideous, most truly awful."

NORWICH

WALKING, BOATING, AND LOOKING

IN 1700, WOOL AND AGRICULTURE HAD MADE NORWICH THE SECOND-RICHEST CITY after London. The Industrial Revolution changed that forever. But although it may no longer be the commercial force it once was, Norwich is a delightful town. It is a wonderful place to explore on foot—or, if you want to go further afield, by river bus. You might like to start with the 160 or so stalls laid out under the multicolored striped

St Ethelbert's Gate was built as penance by townsfolk who had attacked monks.

facing page
The Church of St Peter Mancroft dominates Norwich Marketplace.

awnings of its open-air market (Mon.-Sat., 9-5). Founded in 1075, it is still one of the largest—and most enjoyable—in England. You might not need to buy fresh fish, meat, cheese, fruit, or vegetables, but may find something to take home as a souvenir among the hats, shoes, and books on sale. On one side of the market, making a corner with the twentieth-century City Hall, is the Guildhall, instantly identifiable by its fine checkered flint front. Built in 1407-13 soon after Norwich was granted a charter allowing it a mayor and two sheriffs, it was used for civic and judicial functions for 500 years. Then it became the city's tourist information center. It has a good café.

Two blocks away from the market, inside a deep, steep-sided moat, is the square castle. Despite standing well above the city, this foursquare, almost cubic structure in pale stone looks squat and (even given the elaborate yet relentlessly symmetrical fluting and relief work on its identical facades) grim. (However, Colman's Mustard used it on their labels.) The Normans built the Castle 900 years ago as a royal palace. Then, from the thirteenth century until 1894 it was a jail. Since then it has housed the city's museum collections. Amongst the paintings there are notable eighteenth- and twentieth-century English collections but probably most interest attaches to the intermediate local group known as the Norwich School, in particular John Crome and John Sell Cotman. Crome (1768-1821) was influenced by Dutch landscape painters but depended equally on direct observation of nature in his oil paintings of heathland, woods, and tranquil rivers. Cotman (1782-1842) was a watercolorist. Some of his finest works were done, early in his career, in Wales and Yorkshire. He spent his middle years in Norwich before being appointed professor of drawing at King's College, London, a job that relieved him of the burdens of inadequate income. In addition to archaeological displays, there are fine collections of silverware (the sort used in civic offices to impress visitors) and ceramic teapots of every size and shape, illustrating the ways in which the pottery industry kept in touch over 250 years with every shift in fashion and taste.

Not far from the castle are Elm Hill and Tombland, the two oldest streets, which have surviving medieval buildings pleasingly scattered amongst small modern shops. Tombland, a short walk from the Cathedral Close, was in 1271 the scene of a pitched battle between citizens and monks that lasted several days. Early on, the cathedral was badly damaged: by fire, the collapse of the tower, and by reformers of various sorts. Despite all the necessary remodeling and rebuilding, it retains the appearance of a great Anglo-Norman abbey church. We cannot fail to be struck by the length and height of the nave and the lierne vaulting and decorative central bosses in the ceiling. In one of these bosses is a charming carving of the Last Supper, reduced to seven diners.

Bridewell and Strangers' Hall museums are old buildings featuring, respectively, industrial and commercial life, and domestic life. The river Wensum is a lovely and important feature of Norwich. There is a riverside walk that will lead you past fascinating buildings and bridges and the occasional pub. (The rule in Norwich is keep on looking at everything as you move about: there is always another detail to enjoy.) You can also use the river bus to take a tour of the Norfolk Broads, medieval peat diggings that gave the area 124 miles of shallow lakes and waterways when water levels rose in the thirteenth century. Wildlife is abundant and includes Britain's largest butterfly, the swallowtail, and many, many birds.

Norwich offers a wide range of architectural eras and styles. Most of these are historical in that they date from more than a hundred years ago. But there are exceptions. Three miles west of the city, on the campus of the University of East Anglia, is the Sainsbury Center for Visual Arts (opened 1978). Its most remarkable feature is its lack of internal walls from which artworks can be hung or against which they may be arranged. Displays have to be freestanding. This allows visitors to view exhibits in constantly changing visual, stylistic and historical perspectives. In a way this is true of Norwich at large. Every period from the Middle Ages onward can be viewed in relation to other periods, either simultaneously or by moving a few yards. Looking at the town in this way we begin to feel the history of England coming—if not exactly alive, at least into visual focus. This is very much a city to walk through, looking at everything with alert, eager eyes.

left
Norwich Guildhall is the largest medieval city hall in England.

above
The Wild Man pub and neighboring shops are typical of the Norwich town center.

below
Royal Arcade houses small, elegant, specialized boutiques.

SOUTHWOLD
POST-COLONIAL RETIREMENT

SOUTHWOLD SAILORS' READING ROOM WAS BUILT IN 1864 as a memorial to a local man who had a brief but colorful naval career. The intention was to keep sailors out of pubs and give them something worthwhile to read. It must have enjoyed some popularity, for the Website is full of affectionate reminiscences, either from men who actually used it or their fond families. In those days the waterfront at Southwold was crammed with fishing boats and their crews were familiar figures. There are still boats to be seen but of a different sort and with smaller crews in pursuit, mainly, of leisure. The town is an interesting, sometimes puzzling place. It has many features of the standard picture postcard seaside town. There is a pier, a row of (rather expensive) beach house, the beach itself, the odd boat. There are remnants of historic shoreline defenses. From Gun Hill Green a row of cannon points over the bay where the last major naval battle in British waters was fought—English v. Dutch in 1672. It was an inconclusive affair, although the English were badly mauled by superior Dutch numbers and Lord Sandwich was killed.

Several accidents of history have kept Southwold able to feel exclusive. One was the closure of the railway line to London in 1929. Another was the "Greens," frequent areas of well-kept lawn, planted as firebreaks after a disaster in 1659, which have helped restrain indiscriminate building. Finally, there was an influx of colonial-service families from India. One such family, in the 1920s, was that of George Orwell (author of *Animal Farm* and *Nineteen Eighty-Four*), who found the social atmosphere of the town oppressive—but then he did tend to imagine that creditors or enemies were lurking unseen but seeing behind the net curtains. The loss of the railway meant that Southwold could never become "East-End-on-Sea." Instead, as the historian Simon Schama remarks, it was "Little Raj-by-the-sea": quiet, relaxed, above all "select." The lighthouse stands along a street of houses.

Southwold's former importance is indicated by the hugeness and solidity of the fifteenth-century St Edmund King and Martyr Church (see under BURY ST EDMUNDS). The interior has many notable features. Axe-wielding Iconoclasts damaged the font in the seventeenth century; its cover has been reproduced from existing plans, but the stonework remains as they left it. Similarly, the remains of the magnificently carved rood screen are partially defaced. A model of a famous local lifeboat hangs below angels painted on the ceiling beams. Jack o' the Clock, a helmeted figure in chain mail with metal knee spikes, holds a sword and an axe; when services are about to begin he strikes a bell.

facing page
A rented beach house combines immediate access to the sea with a degree of privacy.

below
The Church of St Edmund King and Martyr is a treasure trove of ecclesiastical crafts.

Inland from Southwold is Blythburgh, with its huge church (see under ALDEBURGH). Dunwich, the most famous of the eroded towns, is a few miles farther south. Once the seat of the kings of Anglia, and also of bishops, it was the largest port in Suffolk. But ever since the great storm of 1326 it has been under attack by the sea. The last of its twelve churches crashed into the sea in 1919. Dunwich Heath is an important nature reserve, with nightjars, a rare butterfly, and the also rare Dunwich rose. At the adjoining Minismere Reserve you can use observation blinds to watch a variety of birds.

With its quiet roads and relative lack of challenging hills, the Suffolk coast is an excellent place for excursions on a bicycle. It is, however, an area where beauty tends to be tinged with melancholy. Certainly Covehithe offers beauty and melancholy in equal parts. At its height the population was 300; now, coastal erosion having taken its toll, only a few cottages remain. Its remarkable feature is the ruins of a large church, built by a wealthy benefactor. In 1672 stones from the ruin were used to build a tiny replacement church within the ruined nave.

SWAFFHAM

LEGEND AND CIVIC PRIDE

A LEGEND ASSOCIATED WITH THE LOCALITY TELLS US SOMETHING ABOUT SWAFFHAM'S sense of its own identity. (The essence of the story, however, can be found in folktales from elsewhere in Britain, central Europe, and *The Arabian Nights*.) A peddler from Swaffham dreamed that if he went to London Bridge he would be told something greatly to his advantage. He walked there with his dog. Someone who thought him

a fool told him that he himself had dreamed that he would find money under a tree in a peddler's garden in Swaffham—but he was not so credulous as to waste time and money doing that. The peddler went home, dug in his garden and found a large sum of money in a pot. Later, someone interpreted some writing on the pot, and he dug again, finding an equal sum of money. He was generous and successful with these windfalls and became a wealthy man. The story has become attached to Swaffham and its parish church of St Peter and St Paul because a Mr Chapman (which means merchant, or up-market peddler) was a generous benefactor, financing the building of the north aisle of the church. In the church itself we may see medieval carvings on clergy stalls associated with merchant/peddler Chapman that show a peddler with his dog and a merchant and his wife in their shop. It is easy to suppose that Swaffham's merchant class interpreted the story as epitomizing their preparedness to seek their fortune in the place where they lived and their benevolent generosity to fellow citizens once they had succeeded. The carved and painted wooden sign near the marketplace, announcing the town to visitors, shows a man and his dog on a journey.

The domed Market Cross, with Ceres, Goddess of crops and fertility.

facing page
The magnificent fifteenth-century hammer-beam roof in St Peter and St Paul Church.

Be all that as it may, Swaffham today announces in its layout and buildings that it is a place where men made money (from wool and agriculture) and spent it beautifying their town. They sold their wares in the wedge-shaped marketplace, in the shadow of Ceres, goddess of plenty. This stands atop the impressive pillared and domed Market Cross built by Horace Walpole, son of England's first prime minister and author of the Gothic horror story *The Castle of Otranto*. (Nowadays there is a market there every Saturday.) They worshiped under the hammer-beamed ceiling with its guardian angels, in the Church of St Peter and St Paul, and gave their daughters in marriage there to suitable young men (that is, the sons of other men like themselves) selected during balls at the Assembly Rooms. They exchanged their corn at the imposing brick Corn Exchange decorated with carved medallions of sheaves of wheat.

At Castle Acre, three miles north of Swaffham, there is an impressive mound and enclosed land Norman castle (the village, on a grid laid down by the Normans, stands within the outer bailey) and the resplendently decorated, three-door Norman front of a Cluniac priory. Five miles southwest is Oxburgh Hall and Gardens. This has a fortified gatehouse eighty-four feet high, the gardens are colorful, and you can see some examples of the Oxburgh Hangings, worked by Mary, queen of Scots and her companion Bess of Hardwicke, while she waited for her cousin Queen Elizabeth to decide her fate. Much of the decoration is Tudor, but some rooms were later romantically embellished in accordance with High Victorian Catholic taste.

A journey of about eighty-five miles will take you to and from the residence used by the present Queen Elizabeth at Christmas, Sandringham House. This may be visited between April and October (but is closed for one week in July: check before setting out). There is a great deal to see, including gardens and country park, exhibits to do with hunting, shooting, and horse racing, and a display of royal cars spanning nearly a century. Among these is the first motorcar owned by a member of the British monarchy, a 1900 Daimler Phaeton, and the splendid 1939 Merryweather fire engine used by the estate's own fire brigade. King's Lynn, an attractive port with buildings that reflect its colorful maritime history, is six miles northwest of Swaffham.

BURFORD

CROMWELL AND NELL GWYN

THE NAME INDICATES A RIVER FORD BENEATH A HILL FORT AND IN ANGLO-SAXON times that is what it was. The very attractive main street runs down the hill to the river Windrush, crossed now by a narrow three-arched bridge rather than a ford. When the wool trade flourished under the Tudors, the Tolsey, an open ground floor with a hall above, was built halfway up the hill; market stalls operated downstairs while above them wool merchants debated their business.

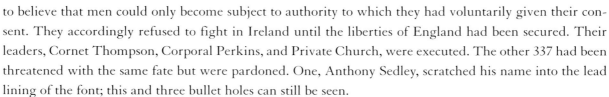

The Church of St John the Baptist at the bottom of the hill has had an occasionally tempestuous history. In 1530 a wealthy cloth merchant was charged with possessing a Bible in English. Since he was young, the authorities did not punish him in the usual manner: branding on both cheeks. In 1628 Lady Tanfield, widow of the unpopular lord of the manor, was refused permission to build a memorial tomb in the church. She sent her builders in regardless. Later, she joined her husband in the colorful, marble-columned installation that survives. During the Civil War, Oliver Cromwell used the church as a prison for 340 mutinous soldiers. These men had been influenced by Levellers to believe that men could only become subject to authority to which they had voluntarily given their consent. They accordingly refused to fight in Ireland until the liberties of England had been secured. Their leaders, Cornet Thompson, Corporal Perkins, and Private Church, were executed. The other 337 had been threatened with the same fate but were pardoned. One, Anthony Sedley, scratched his name into the lead lining of the font; this and three bullet holes can still be seen.

Burford offers fine furniture as well as attractive houses.

facing page
The Cotswold Arms is a traditional "no nonsense" pub.

At Swinbrook, just east of Burford and also on the Windrush, the Church of St Mary has an unusual wall in its chancel. On two sets of shelves like three-tiered bunks, lie two sets of effigies of three seventeenth-century knights. One set lies in full armor, with swords, propping up their heads on one hand. The second set is more relaxed: no helmets, no swords, torso propped on one elbow, rather oddly wearing wigs. The three were members of the Fettiplace family, who arrived in c. 1490 and built a large mansion, which has now disappeared. In the graveyard a Cotswold-stone slab marks the grave of Nancy Mitford, who grew up nearby and described the experience in affectionately comic terms in her first novel, *The Pursuit of Love*. She and her sisters hated their house and called it "Swinebrook" and plotted to escape. It was so cold that they hid in the linen cupboard to get warm. Their parents did not believe in education for girls and their father is portrayed as hating "smartly dressed women, socialists, and foreigners." Unfair, no doubt, but funny.

In the Georgian era Burford acquired many of the elegant houses that we see today. During the great coaching age of the eighteenth and early nineteenth centuries Burford was an important stop on the route from London to the West of England and Wales and many of the larger buildings in the town were inns, providing travellers on long journeys with a comfortable overnight stay. It is easy to guess which buildings were once coaching inns: coach-sized archways lead from the street into what were once inn yards. A few are still hotels or pubs. Like most Cotswold towns, Burford is built largely from local stone; in the gentle sunlight of morning and evening it is golden and magical.

After the restoration of the monarchy in 1660, the George Inn at Burford must have been an envied focus of local attention and gossip, for it was visited on a number of occasions by two very great, somewhat scandalous celebrities: Charles II and his mistress, the comic actress and former orange seller, Nell Gwyn. Charles's marriage to Catherine of Braganza was childless; Nell Gwyn, like numerous other women, bore him a son, or possibly two. No doubt the "merry monarch" gave the George's attentive host the instruction which, on his death-bed, he gave the duchess of Portsmouth (his other favorite mistress): "Do not let poor Nelly starve."

CHELTENHAM

A PUMP ROOM AND A ROLLING STONE

CHELTENHAM AND GLOUCESTER ARE IN THE SAME COUNTY, only twelve miles apart but are very different towns. Cheltenham's character is influenced by its position on the western edge of the Cotswold Hills and its warm, humid climate. Like Southwold it was favored as a retirement place by people returning from India. It mounts annual, internationally celebrated festivals—of music, literature, and horse racing. Having been an unremarkable market town, it became a fashionable spa after mineral springs were discovered in 1715. It was noticed, legend has it, that pigeons drinking the water were unusually plump and glossy. In c. 1780 the first pump room was opened. Visitor numbers were much boosted after 1788 when George III made his first of many appearances and again in 1816 when the duke of Wellington, recently victorious at Waterloo, took the waters.

Much of the Regency and neoclassical architecture that characterizes the central part of the town was built during this period or soon after, most notably the Pittville Pump Room (1825-30). This cost over 40,000 British pounds, a huge sum at the time. When the culture of taking the waters declined, it fell on hard times. By the 1940s, when it housed British and American Army personnel, it was in the grip of dry rot. Public subscriptions and funding bodies rescued it, and now, fully restored, it is in use most days of the year for public or private events, including conferences, concerts, and weddings. Its attractive gardens feature an artificial boating lake.

Cheltenham has an unusually spacious center around the Promenade. On the western side of this wide street stands the town's finest Regency terrace, now the municipal offices. The central pedestrian rectangle of the Promenade has elm and chestnut trees, flower beds, lawns, and park benches. There is a fountain, a statue commemorating the Antarctic explorer Edward Wilson, born in the town, and a whimsical sculpture of a cow and a rabbit sitting affectionately together on a bench. At the southern end you will find the Imperial Gardens, overlooked by another of the town's magnificent Regency buildings, the Queen's Hotel. On the southern side of the gardens stands, more modestly, Cheltenham Town Hall, home to a wide variety of cultural events. The recently restored Montpelier Gardens (host to an annual cheese festival) has a splendid bandstand. Nearby, the ironwork of Cheltenham's earliest Regency terrace, Royal Crescent, is worthy of study. Originally planned as two blocks with a roadway between, it was eventually built as a single block of eighteen houses.

Cheltenham's Regency Municipal Offices.

facing page
Regency elegance and luxuriant greenery at Pittville.

If there are plenty of floral spaces within the town, there are many more outside it. The Cotswolds are a haven for a wide variety of flowers that are elsewhere becoming rare. Scarlet poppies stipple the cornfields. Snowdrops carpet the woods in spring. Bluebell woods are a familiar sight, and the purple spires of foxgloves push through ferns in the Forest of Dean. More formally, gardens at Sudely Castle, Stanway House, and Snowshill Manor will repay a visit.

Gustav Holst, composer of *The Planets*, Ralph Richardson, theater and film actor, and Brian Jones of the Rolling Stones were born in Cheltenham. There is a small museum at Holst's birthplace and a bust of Jones in Beechwood Shopping Center. But when developers planned to name a new street "Brian Jones Close" there was vociferous, successful opposition. Another cultural fuss occurred in 1968, when *If...*, about rebellion in a boys' private school, was filmed at Cheltenham College. Some townsfolk, however, appeared as extras in the climactic scene, when rebels fill the school chapel with smoke during a speech by a visiting major general, then open fire from the rooftops as the crowd pours into the quadrangle.

CHIPPING CAMPDEN

SHIN-KICKING AND ENGLISHNESS

THE UK MAY HAVE TO WAIT UNTIL 2112 TO STAGE THE OLYMPIC GAMES a second time, but "Dover's Olimpick Games" have been staged every summer since 1963 on Dover's Hill, Chipping Campden. The event began, with the permission of James I, in 1612. It was banned by the Puritans and again by a prim vicar in 1851. The modern event is more restrained than the old but some of the original sports remain.

Shin-kicking, for instance, in which contestants hold their opponent by the shoulder and try to kick his legs out from under him. The Championship of the Hill tests a range of skills, including a sack race in which the sack is tied around the neck. Contests begin when a cannon is fired. The evening ends with fireworks, a torchlight procession into the center of the town, and dancing in the square. Next day, during the event known as Scuttlebrook Wake, the May Queen is crowned, followed by a fancy-dress parade and maypole and morris dancing.

This town is devoted to the maintenance of local traditions. The Campden Trust was set up in 1929 to keep alive the skills of stone carving and repair, which are necessary to maintain the Cotswold stone buildings. Perhaps this is why Chipping Campden is always described in such terms as "the quintessence of Englishness," "the most picturesque town in Britain," "the jewel of the Cotswolds," or "a unified picture of golden-colored and lichen-patched stone." No one could say that these claims are exaggerated.

We start, however, with ruins. Sir Baptist Hicks (c. 1551–1629), First Viscount Campden, who accumulated wealth by lending money to the extravagant James I, was always ready to spend it in his hometown. He built Campden Manor in 1613; Royalist soldiers burnt it down after the Parliamentarians won the Civil War. Opposite, unharmed, is a row of almshouses, also built by Hicks. Chipping Campden High Street is one of the treasures of the UK. In the center of this, Hicks built the Market Hall (1627). Standing within it you can look either way along the main street and see a view virtually unchanged for centuries. A little bit away is the "great, golden, Perpendicular" church of St James's. A church has stood here since before 1180, but, starting in 1260, a 250-year transformation produced more-or-less the building we see today: among other things, a reconstructed nave c. 1290, monumental brasses, ornate tombs, and macabre swathed figures in grave clothes. A window over the chancel arch that reminds us of the Last Judgment lights the nave.

Tidily trimmed thatched roofs are a feature of this town.

facing page
The Market Hall, built in 1627, is one of the treasures of the Cotswolds.

Strolling through Chipping Campden High Street we may notice one of the town's strangest features—its passion for sundials. There are seven in this street alone and evidence that there were others. (Some scratches in the church stonework serve the same purpose.) Grevel House (c. 1380, perhaps the oldest house in the street) has one—but, oddly, it dates only from 1815. There are many thatched houses in the town and the shaping of the thatch around upstairs windows sometimes resembles particularly bushy eyebrows. It cannot be a matter for surprise that Pier Paolo Pasolini used the town as a setting for his film *The Canterbury Tales*.

Broadway, sometimes described as 'the show village of England', is three miles away. Tudor, Jacobean, and Georgian building in Cotswold stone the color of the most golden honey you can imagine, gaze contentedly at each other across the broad village street. Unfortunately, their view is in summer, sometimes obscured by visiting tourist coaches. Other "must visit" places are the gardens at Kiftsgate Court and Hidcote Manor. Also close at hand is Burnt Norton, unfortunately not generally open to the public unless they are guests at a wedding. Those interested in twentieth-century poetry will recognize the name as the title of the first of the *Four Quartets* by T. S. Eliot, who was a frequent visitor there.

CHIPPING NORTON

BLISSFUL TWEEDS, HORSE-DRAWN BEER

CHIPPING NORTON, AFFECTIONATELY REFERRED TO AS "CHIPPY" by locals, is the highest town in Oxfordshire. "Chipping" means "market" and for some centuries Chipping Norton market was the commercial hub of the Evenlode Valley. Its importance increased when the wool trade made the Cotswolds the richest part of England. As with many other towns in the area, the attractive buildings we see today reflect the town's prosperous past. It continued, however, to be a wool town longer than most, for the Bliss Mill went on making tweed until 1980. William Bliss was the town's great benefactor, having brought in the newest technology of the Industrial Revolution in the early nineteenth century. The large mill that still stands today was built in 1876, to a rather curious design. A large square building with turreted corners and a round domed tower on one side, it would look like a country house were it not for the enormous chimney, as high again as the tower itself, protruding from the dome. It has now been converted into luxury apartment and leisure facilities. Another survivor of the wool trade is the annual "Mop Fair." This began in the thirteenth century when King John granted a charter for a wool fair. Over time this became an informal kind of employment exchange, at which prospective employers and employees became acquainted.

The Church of St Mary has a tall, well-lit nave.

facing page
Bliss Mill, now luxury apartments, manufactured tweed until 1980.

Among other interesting buildings in the town, St Mary's Church has an elegant square tower and a tall nave, lit by large, high windows, the whole set in a delightfully green churchyard. Its priest was hanged from the tower in 1549 for resisting the imposition of the English Book of Common Prayer. In the marketplace we find a very grand, pillared town hall. The fine row of eight almshouses was founded and funded by Henry Cornish. Ten of his twelve children died in childhood, which was possibly a factor contributing to his generosity, along with his strong belief in giving aid to the deserving poor. Unusually for a town of this size, there is an active and enterprising theater, with a program including plays, films, music, and dance. It has perfect acoustics, occupying as it does a building erected in 1888, by a firm specializing in music halls, as a Salvation Army citadel. There cannot be many theaters displaying an inscription like this one: "These stones were laid by 100 of those who through great persecution boldly and conscientiously served their God." A blue plaque commemorates the Reverend Edward Stone (1702-68) who discovered the active ingredient in aspirin while living in the town.

A short walk will take you to the enigmatic circle of standing stones, solitary king stone and dolmen (burial chamber), known collectively as the Rollright Stones, via the village of Salford. Broughton Castle ("the most beautiful in all England" according to one writer), with its lake, woods, and gardens, is twelve miles away on the road to Banbury. You may well remember seeing parts of it in *Shakespeare in Love*, *The Madness of King George*, or *Joseph Andrews*. Broughton's owner, Lord Saye, thought that *Joseph Andrews* sounded like "good clean fun" and was slightly disconcerted to see topless nuns on his front lawn. Hook Norton Brewery is a few miles from "Chippy" and you may see its horsedrawn dray and bowler-hatted driver delivering barrels of beer to the town's pubs.

At Rousham (twelve miles) we find gardens on the banks of the river Cherwell, designed by William Kent in the eighteenth century. Kent made use of the natural elements and contours of the landscape to produce an elegant and engaging ensemble of cascades, ponds, temples, and a seven-arched portico. There is a touching memorial to "Ringwood: an otter-hound of extraordinary sagacity." But, be aware that children are not admitted. Great Tew, a secluded village of houses with box hedges with a sixteenth-century pub is worth a visit. The house where Winston Churchill was born, Blenheim Palace, is twelve miles away at Woodstock. If you visit the palace, allow plenty of time. (See under WOODSTOCK).

CIRENCESTER

SPARROWS ON FIRE, ROMANS AS TEXANS

facing page
The church porch once doubled as the Town Hall.

below
Wool paid for some wonderful churches, as St John the Baptist demonstrates.

CIRENCESTER (ONCE PRONOUNCED "SISSITTER" BY LOCALS) IS TODAY A SMALL country town, but for two periods in its history it was of national importance. In Roman times only London was larger than this 250-acre fortress at a crossroads where three major roads met: Akeman Street, Ermine Way, and Fosse Way. During the Middle Ages it had the largest wool market in England. After the Industrial Revolution and the decline of the cloth trade, it became an agricultural center: the Royal Agricultural College was founded there in 1845. Because of a story told by a thirteenth-century abbot it was sometimes called "sparrow city." When the Saxons were besieging it, the abbot insisted, the resident Britons kept them at bay for six years. An observant Saxon noticed that sparrows that nested in the thatched roofs of the city flew into the surrounding fields. He trapped a number of them, tied burning straw to them and set them free. They flew back to their nests and set fire to the city.

The Church of St John the Baptist is the largest and most splendid of the Cotswold "wool" churches—indeed, you may be surprised to learn that it is not a cathedral. Its skyline is extremely detailed. The nave and aisles bristle with decorative parapets and pinnacles, as does the tower. Inside we are at once impressed by the great height of the nave. The details are equally impressive: splendid memorials, spectacular and varied stained glass, Bristol brass candlesticks. The fan vaulting in St Katherine's Chapel is delightful. The painted and gilded pulpit, one of very few remaining pre-Reformation pulpits in Gloucestershire, is of the style known, for obvious reasons, as "wine-glass." The three-story porch with its elaborate decorative stone framework served for a time as the town hall. The church stands on the edge of what were once the grounds of Cirencester Abbey, now a public park. Of the abbey, only a small arched Norman gatehouse remains.

Along Market Place from the church is the Fleece Hotel. Its smartly maintained black-and-white timber-framed facade leads into an interior that has been unaggressively modernized. The Corinium Museum will give you an idea of what life has been like here from Roman times on. Its exhibits include mosaics and other artifacts, reconstructed sites, and paintings. You may, if you, choose, dress up as a Roman soldier, complete with sword. Just west of the town is the Roman Amphitheater: a circle of mounds surrounding a flat central area where performances would have taken place. If you are in Cirencester on a Monday or a Friday, be sure to take time to watch the market traders doing the work they have done for more than 2,000 years.

About six miles north of Cirencester is Chedworth Roman Villa, said to be the best place in the country for exploring and understanding a large Roman country house. According to its owners, the National Trust, it "strongly suggests the Roman equivalent of a Texan ranch." Its walls now stand only a foot or two high, but the many fine mosaics were preserved by silt until uncovered and saved in 1864. The dining-room floor has a red, white, and blue pattern, with Bacchic satyrs capering drunkenly. Two other particularly exquisite floors identify two bathing areas: one much resembling a sauna, the other a Turkish bath. The surroundings, a wooded Cotswold valley, are glorious.

The headwaters of the Thames rise, four miles from Cirencester, at a spot marked by a statue of Old Father Thames. This trickle grows into the longest English river and the second-longest in the UK after the Severn. It flows, gathering breadth and volume from tributaries in the hills from which it has carved out its valley, through Gloucestershire, Wiltshire, Oxfordshire, Berkshire, and London. It passes through great towns and cities—Oxford, Reading, Maidenhead, Windsor, and London before spilling into the North Sea. Queen Elizabeth II was greatly amused by a trip up it she shared with Sir Winston Churchill: "One saw this dirty commercial river as one came up and he was describing it as the silver thread which runs through the history of Britain." It is, of course, both those things.

GLOUCESTER

A DAMP DOCTOR AND A PUZZLED TAILOR

ACCORDING TO THE NURSERY RHYME DESIGNED TO TEACH CHILDREN HOW to pronounce the town's name, "Doctor Foster went to Gloucester / In a shower of rain. / He stepped in a puddle / Right up to his middle / And never went there again." The rhyme was first recorded in 1844 but may refer to a visit by Edward I (1239-1307), whose horse got stuck in mud. We may hope for a drier, cleaner fate. Although Gloucester is

Gloucester still has an active port, although its warehouses now have other uses.

facing page
Gloucester Cathedral's magnificent nave, facing eastwards through the screen and organ loft.

many miles from the open sea, it is a port, linked by canal to Sharpness Docks on the estuary of the Severn, a river that, confusingly, also flows through Gloucester itself. In the Middle Ages the port was an essential link with the outside world for the Cotswold wool producers and after wool's importance declined it dealt with timber, corn, metals, wines, and spirits. Nowadays local light industry keeps it busy and it is also used as the departure point for cruises on the canal and the Severn and as dry-docking for maintenance and restoration of vessels. Interesting ships are frequently seen there. For that reason and for itself, the area is often used as a film location. It has also become more generally useful: the warehouses have been converted into apartments, the National Waterways Museum, an antiques center, shops, and restaurants.

The city had great military significance in Roman times and later, because of its proximity to Wales and because it was the most convenient fording place on the Severn. There was a royal castle next to where the cathedral now stands and monarchs were frequently in residence there. The abbey was founded in 861 and the present cathedral was begun in 1089. It was in many ways an innovative building. The local stone masons developed two new techniques of vaulting: "fan" in the magnificent cloisters, and "lierne," in the south transept and choir. The vast east window is a memorial to Gloucester knights killed at Crécy (1346) and Calais (1347). Earlier, in 1327, the rather unsatisfactory King Edward II was murdered at Berkeley Castle (which may be visited), nine miles southwest of the city. He is buried in the cathedral, which became a popular place of pilgrimage for some time afterward. When the monasteries were dissolved, the church survived as the seat of the newly constituted diocese of Gloucester, for which, as we feast our eyes and hearts, we may be grateful. It is good to go back after dark to see the exterior of the cathedral floodlit. The recently cleaned and restored tower is a majestic and captivating sight. The building is a musical center as well: in rotation with Hereford and Worcester, Gloucester hosts the Three Choirs Festival every third year.

The House of the Tailor of Gloucester, which the children's author Beatrix Potter used as the setting for a story, is in College Court . The Union Inn pub in Westgate Street was once the shop of the real Tailor of Gloucester, John Pritchard. In 1897 Beatrix Potter's cousin told her that the Mayor of Gloucester had ordered a new suit, which Pritchard left unfinished overnight; when he returned next day it was, mysteriously, finished except for one buttonhole. (There was a reasonable explanation: his assistants, too drunk to go home, had sheltered in the shop and worked on the suit until they ran out of thread.) Pritchard put a sign in his window: "Come to Pritchard's, where the waistcoats are made at night by the fairies."

Sir Peter Scott (1909-89), son of Antarctic explorer Robert Falcon Scott, was an artist, ornithologist, broadcaster, and sportsman (Olympic dinghy sailor, ice skater, British Open Gliding Champion, and skipper of a yacht in the America's Cup in 1964). In 1946, after wartime naval service, he founded Slimbridge Wildfowl Trust, the birthplace of modern conservation. Eleven miles southwest of Gloucester, 120 acres of wetlands beside the river Severn provide a winter home for huge flocks of geese, ducks, and swans. Slimbridge is also the only place on earth where you can see all six species of flamingoes. Scott's broadcasts, art works, and ornithological expeditions to Iceland, Australasia, and the Pacific all furthered the cause.

TEWKESBURY

AN ENGLISH SURVIVOR

THE RIVER AVON, FLOWING SOUTH FROM STRATFORD, joins the river Severn at this market town in Gloucestershire. From the point of view of those who love it as it is today, with many of its medieval, Tudor, and Georgian buildings surviving intact, and the huge tower of the abbey church standing guard over all, Tewkesbury has had three major pieces of good fortune during its almost two millennia of recorded history. The first was the purchase by the townsfolk of the abbey church from Henry VIII when he dissolved the abbey itself. (They paid him 453 pounds.) Second was the town's nonparticipation in the Industrial Revolution. The third was not an event (or nonevent) but a situation. Squeezed by the two rivers and the associated flood plain, it is virtually the same size and shape as it was in medieval times.

Architecturally, Tewkesbury Abbey is in some ways a sister of Gloucester Cathedral but there are also many differences. The most obvious is the west front, which is unique. The effect is of elongated Romanesque, with six curved arches, linked and recessed. These frame a large window (pointed rather than curved) above a low, further recessed door. The whole looks outward onto a secluded small lawn, with three low, flat tombs, irregularly arranged. (The porched entrance on the north side is the one normally used.) The east end has small semicircular chapels on each side. This is a very large building, as the enormous round pillars and sturdily crisscrossed vaulting of the interior indicate. The tower, although it is so well in scale that it does not look excessively large, is fourty-six feet square and 150 feet high. That the religious history of this small town is more complicated than the presence of this powerful symbol of established doctrine might suggest is demonstrated by the Old Baptist Chapel and Burial Ground (1655), in a small court virtually across the road. This dissenters' meeting house may be the oldest in southern England. It is now used for exhibitions and may be visited free. Whether you see abbey or chapel first, the contrast between the small, plain chapel and the large, magnificent abbey is startling. The buildings, of course, symbolize the theological and liturgical differences between the Established Church (not nearly as far from Catholicism as dissenters would have wished) and the Protestant sect. Further contrast is provided by the tolerantly relaxed feeling of the Bell Hotel (formerly the Bell Inn), a very large black-and-white timber-framed building nearby. In 2007, Tewksbury was one of the areas worst hit by the torrential rain and resulting floods that turned parts of England into huge pools of destructive water. It is cold comfort to say that this sort of thing has happened before—but it has, and, as before, tremendous community efforts are being devoted to repairing the damage. It will still be worth coming here.

Mention of all the fascinating historical buildings in Tewkesbury would demand more space than is available: this is quite simply a town to walk through with your eyes wide open. Printed guides to the Heritage Trail, which will take you on foot around all the sights, are available. Do explore also the narrow alleys of shops. The John Moore Countryside Museum commemorates a local writer, a pioneer of conservation, who recorded his delight in the locality in several books, which are usually available on sale. Don't neglect the rivers. (You can take a boating tour, or hire a boat and explore for yourself.) This town looks very good from the water. If you feel like it take in Twyning's riverside pub, 6 miles north on the River Avon.

The Battle of Tewkesbury was fought in 1471, after grueling forced marches, by Yorkists and Lancastrians, opposing factions in the Wars of the Roses (1455-85—see under LANCASTER). The Yorkists wanted to prevent the Lancastrians from reaching Wales. Shakespeare gives the Lancastrian Queen Margaret a rousing speech before the battle, which ends: "Why, courage then—what cannot be avoided / 'Twere childish weakness to lament or fear," referring to the fact that her side is outnumbered; the battle marked the near extinction of their cause—but trouble continued until Richard III was killed at Bosworth in 1485, when the Tudors took over. You may visit the battlefield at Tewkesbury; the battle is reenacted during the Medieval Festival in July.

facing page
Characteristic buildings in Church Street.

below
The twelfth-century tower of Tewkesbury Abbey dominates the small town.

BUXTON

SPA WATERS, OPERA, AND CAVERNS

THE EARLS AND, LATER, DUKES OF DEVONSHIRE HAVE LIVED AT CHATSWORTH HOUSE, in the Peak District in Derbyshire, since the sixteenth century. During that time they have been assiduous art collectors and developers and landscapers of their estates. Chatsworth, originally Elizabethan, was transformed between 1686 and 1707 into the Baroque mansion we see today. In the late eighteenth century the fifth duke turned his attention to the spa and market town of Buxton, thirteen miles west of the house, and developed it as Bath and Cheltenham were being developed to attract the fashionable classes. Protégés of the architects and landscapers who had developed Chatsworth were set to work and today's remarkable town, high in the Pennine Hills (the highest of its size in England), is—with sundry harmonious additions—the result. (The mineral water is now commercially bottled, but a revolt by the townsfolk prevented an attempt to close the public fountain called St Anne's Well, where local people can bottle their own and visitors can sample a glass.)

The Concert Hall in Pavilion Gardens.

facing page
Buxton's Edwardian Opera House.

The dukes commissioned a crescent reminiscent of Royal Crescent in Bath, other elegant public buildings, and the gardens, which include a giant conservatory, the Winter Gardens. In 1871 a glass-and-iron Pavilion, later to incorporate a concert hall, was built and the gardens were renamed accordingly as the Pavilion Gardens. It has been said that they "would bring distinction to any capital city." The trees, the lawns, the iron bridges over the river Wye, the views of hilltops and moorlands outside the town, and the stylish houses and shops within it make up a treasurable townscape. A further gem was added in 1903 when the Brixton Opera House opened. The architect, Frank Matcham, was responsible for exquisite theaters in every quarter of the United Kingdom, from Brighton to Aberdeen, to Belfast, Yarmouth, Cardiff, London, and Portsmouth, with dozens more in between.

Buxton had become widely known for its annual festival devoted to the comic operettas of Gilbert and Sullivan and eventually it began to seem that the town cried out to be the venue for an annual celebration of the arts more generally. The Festival of Opera, Music, and Literature was inaugurated in 1979, offering a crowded program of events every July over approximately a fortnight. Its specialty is the staging of little-known operas, but there are events suitable to every taste in the broad mainstream of the arts. The only problem is obtaining tickets, so do not wait until you get there before booking.

Chatsworth House itself, with garden, farmyard, adventure playground, gift shops, and restaurant is open every day from March until just before Christmas and provides a complete day out with something for everyone to enjoy, from famous works of art, young animals, and the spectacular fountains in the garden to the finest shopping, food, and drink and many miles of free walks. Haddon Hall, near Bakewell, is an amazingly complete medieval manor house, with battlements, stone entrance with gargoyles, chapel, and a banqueting hall with minstrels' gallery—unchanged for 600 years. There are fine gardens. On the way you might like to stop in Bakewell to sample its traditional sweet pudding: jam topped with a mixture of ground almonds, sugar, eggs, and butter.

Buxton is on the edge of the more hospitable southern part of the Peak District. Short excursions can be made in the immediate neighborhood. Poole's Cavern, in Buxton Country Park on the edge of the town, is a spectacular series of limestone chambers. Guided tours leave every half an hour, and the chambers' names include, intriguingly: Great Dome, Flitch of Bacon, Poached Egg, Frozen Waterfall, and the Sculpture Chamber. Elsewhere in the country park, Solomon's Temple, twenty-minutes' walk from the cavern, is a tower built as a folly, from which you have panoramic views of the High Peak District, with its plateaus intersected by steep-sided valleys and crags, and of Buxton itself.

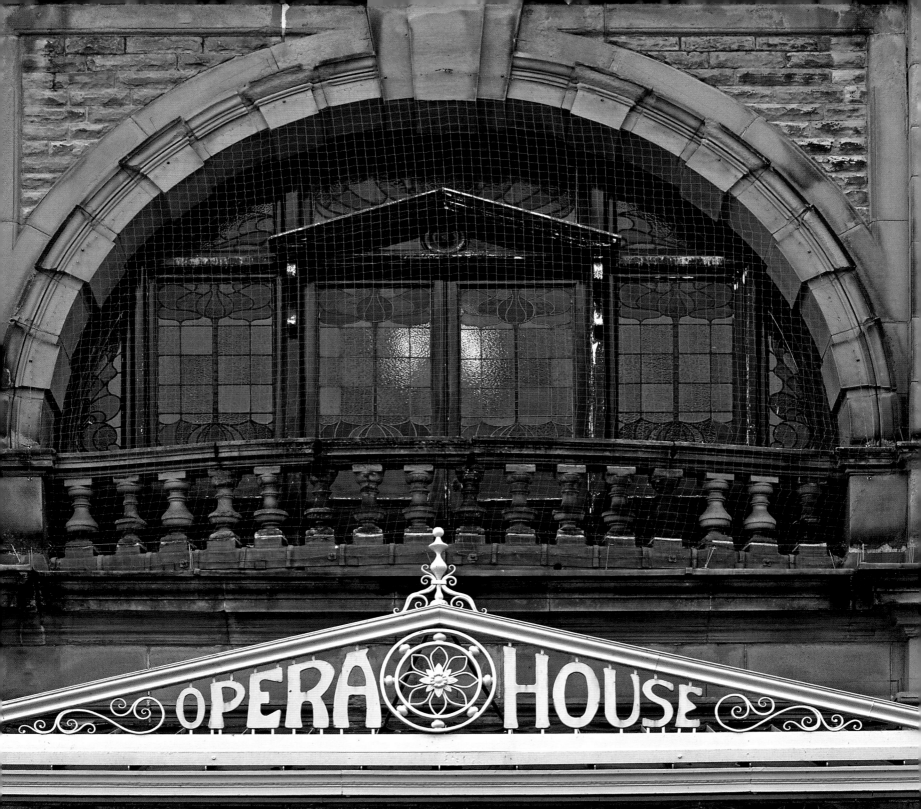

LINCOLN

A CATHEDRAL, A POET, AND A PIE SHOP

LINCOLN STANDS ON A SOLITARY HILL COMMANDING THE SURROUNDING FENS. When the Normans came in 1066 it was one of the most important cities in England and William the Conqueror set out to establish a strong presence there. Pausing only to drive the Saxons living at the top of the hill down to the plains below, he built a new castle and cathedral where their homes had been. In c.1141 the cathedral was rebuilt, with the magnificent Norman doors we see today. In 1185 the building, except the west front, was reduced to a heap of rubble by either an earthquake or catastrophic subsidence. The political situation demanded that a replacement be provided immediately. A new, longer building was begun beyond the rubble at the east end, extending westward as the rubble was cleared. When they arrived within a few meters of the west front it became clear that the axis of the new structure was slightly askew. It was too late to do anything but turn a little to the right. The resulting bend in the nave can be seen inside the church but is more easily observed from the top of the central tower, to which suitably fit people can be taken on a guided tour. The cathedral and its three towers can be seen from many miles away across the fens. The houses and other buildings around it seem only to tug at its skirts. Walking up the bluntly-named Steep Street from the town center makes any visit feel like a pilgrimage.

The Exchequer Gate separates the Cathedral Close from the rest of the city.

facing page
The towers of Lincoln Cathedral by night.

Just south of the cathedral are the remains of the Bishop's Palace. On the northern side stands G.F. Watts's statue of the Victorian Poet Laureate, Alfred Lord Tennyson (1809-1892) walking with his dog Lufra. Tennyson was born and grew up at Somersby, twenty miles east of Lincoln, where his father was the very moody rector. Lincoln Library houses the Tennyson Research Center, the most significant Tennyson archive in the world. The family's social and business papers will provide a researcher or lover of Tennyson's poetry with many fascinating insights. It is advisable to arrange appointments in advance. Elsewhere in the town there is a working windmill, not far from the Museum of Lincolnshire Life. The exhibits there illustrate domestic, community, and commercial life. The row of traditional shops is particularly interesting, and there are extensive exhibitions of crafts, transport, agriculture (especially agricultural machinery), and industrial heritage. There is also an authentic World War I tank. You will find other vivid representations of local life in works by significant nineteenth-century Lincolnshire-born artists exhibited in the Usher Art Gallery, downhill from the cathedral.

No visit to Lincoln is complete without the nearest thing to mountaineering you will find in the Fens—a walk up and down Steep Street. Near the top, just as your legs are about to give out, you will find a fascinating second-hand bookshop. If you are going to be there at lunch or dinnertime, book a table at Brown's Pie Shop. Its pies are excellent and generous, as are the many other dishes it serves. At the foot of the hill is another well-known restaurant, in the twelfth-century Jew's House. Medieval Lincoln had numerous Jewish residents, because the Normans encouraged them to settle in provincial towns in order to stimulate the growth of trade.

For many years Lincoln seemed a remote and quiet place—not on a main road, not on the way to anywhere else. At the foot of the hill, Brayford Pool, now one of its attractive features, was surrounded by derelict, rat-infested wasteland. After 1990, a use was found for it. There was a feeling that Lincoln should have a university of its own: money was raised and strings were pulled; in 1996 the queen opened the new university campus. Many people welcome as appropriate the contrast between the gleaming high-tech buildings at Brayford Pool and the historic architecture of the rest of the city. The influx of students has revivified more than Brayford Pool. Lincoln remains a quiet, very friendly place but now it buzzes gently.

above
The nave, choir
screen and organ of
Lincoln Cathedral.

right
Remains of the
medieval Bishop's
Palace.

left
Bishop Fleming's
tomb shows him
robed and as a
sheeted corpse:
the earliest such in
England.

As you might expect, Lincoln Cathedral has played an important part in the intellectual life of the city for many centuries. This tradition is continued by the Lincoln School of Theology and Ministry Studies, organized in partnership the University of Lincoln, and other interested educational bodies, which between them provide school's academic staff. Both the Church of England and the Methodist Church recognized it as a training school for their clergy. The cathedral also has an excellent library, almost lost during the Civil War but rescued by the dean after the Restoration in 1660. Sir Christopher Wren was commissioned to design an elegant new building, completed in 1676.

MATLOCK

SPAS, CAVERNS, AND CRAGS

MATLOCK IS ANOTHER TOWN THAT FLOURISHED DURING THE NINETEENTH CENTURY because of the belief that spa waters were good for people's health. Most of these spas were established in beautiful areas surrounded by attractive, often dramatic countryside; Matlock is no exception. The town is situated on the river Derwent, on the southeastern edge of the Peak District. It falls fairly clearly into three parts. Matlock Bridge was the site of the original settlement, an agricultural hamlet. On the hillside above the bridge is Matlock Bank. A spring of tepid water was discovered there in 1690, and over the following decades hotels were built to promote its use in hydrotherapy. This form of alternative medicine had been commended from the time of Hippocrates (460-370 BCE) onward and in the eighteenth and nineteenth centuries gained further impetus from its association with fashion for holidaying in spa towns. John Smedley (1803-1874), a teetotaler manufacturer of woolen underclothing in the Derwent Valley Mills (now a UNESCO World Heritage Site), enters the story. Driven by strong convictions and an eye to the main chance, he built a large treatment center (since 1955 home to the Derbyshire County Council). After the railway arrived in 1849, Matlock flourished as a spa and medical center for a century. Visitors traveled up the hill from the railway station by tram, and until the lines were taken up Matlock boasted one of the steepest tramways in England. (A spa also sprang up in the third segment of the town, Matlock Bath, one mile south.) Smedley built himself a large house, Riber Castle, the ruins of which dominate the town from the summit of a hill. A century after the railways started bringing health-seekers to Matlock, however, the war and postwar austerity left it looking rather drab. And the National Health Service, inaugurated in 1948, had little time for hydrotherapy. Nevertheless, Matlock today is drab no longer. It is a solid, Victorian place, with neat stone houses distributed in rows up the hill. The Matlock Bath, by contrast, offers a more frivolous version: whitewashed cottages instead of stone houses on its hillside—and a few too many souvenir shops along the river. In between Matlock Bank and Matlock Bath stands another dominating eminence, the 750-foot Heights of Abraham, so called because of its resemblance to cliffs scaled by General Wolfe before he lost his life driving the French out of Canada in 1759. For visitors the climb is easier: there is a cable car from which you will enjoy magnificent views of Matlock Bath and the Derwent Valley. (Queen Victoria went up on a donkey.) Guided tours of Rutland Cavern and Great Masson Cavern, both part natural and part lead mines, are included in the price of admission.

Matlock Bath Hydro (1883) is now an aquarium.

facing page
Matlock has a wide range of small shops.

On the opposite bank of the Derwent stands another lofty crag, High Tor. There is a public park on the summit—but be warned: the cliffs are not fenced. Leaflets are available outlining other walks in the area, including the Matlock Town Trail and the Matlock Bath Walk. On Saturday and Sunday evenings during September and October there are spectacular illuminations at Matlock Bath, with the addition, on three Saturdays, of a fireworks display. Also in Matlock Bath you may visit the Peak District Mining Museum and a working mine.

Places within easy reach by car include Haddon Hall and Chatsworth House (see under BUXTON). At Eyam, in 1665, a bale of infected cloth from plague-stricken London brought the deadly disease into the town. Led by their rector, the people of the village put themselves into quarantine to protect other hamlets nearby. For 13 months no one was allowed in and no one left: 250 of the population of c. 300 died. Whole families died and were buried together. Eyam is now a large and pleasant village with many architectural gems. Well Dressing, Sheep Roast, and the Plague Commemorative Service held in the cave that served as the church during their period in isolation are popular annual events.

OXFORD

PRIME MINISTERS AND DREAMING SPIRES

IN OXFORD IN 1860, DURING A DEBATE ON CHARLES DARWIN'S *Origin of Species* (1859), the bishop of Oxford asked the biologist Thomas Huxley whether it was through his grandfather or grandmother that he claimed his descent from a monkey. Huxley replied that he would not be ashamed to have a monkey for a grandfather but he would be ashamed to have any connection with a man who used his "restless and versatile intellect" and "aimless rhetoric" to obscure the truth. The anecdote illustrates Oxford's dual character: forward-thinking but innately conservative. One of its graduates, Matthew Arnold, poet and inspector of schools, in two unforgettable phrases stamped an image of town and university on the minds of the educated world. Oxford was, he wrote, a "sweet city, with her dreaming spires," "unravaged by the fierce intellectual life of our century… home of lost causes…" Arnold, who was a nostalgic romantic, may not have been entirely accurate about Oxford even as it was in the mid-nineteenth century. Today, the university's Begbroke Science Park advertises itself as an environment where "world-class scientists work alongside industrialists, decision-makers and entrepreneurs to translate cutting-edge research into commercial opportunities." This is the oldest university in the English-speaking world, it boasts many famous alumni. The UK has had almost sixty prime ministers since the title became generally used in the eighteenth century and twenty-seven of them have been Oxford graduates. Twenty-three overseas heads of state were educated there. The playwright Bernard Shaw would have thought such statistics meaningless. Declining an invitation to speak there, he declared majestically that "The business of Oxford is to create a few scholars and a great many gentlemen."

Oxford stands where Anglo-Saxon farmers drove their cattle from one water-meadow to another across a shallow part of the river Thames—hence Ox-ford. The name "Thames" reminds us of another of Oxford's lost causes. A misapprehension about the origins of the name *Tamesis* gave rise to the Oxford custom of referring to the river as the Isis. Leaving the name aside, there can be few more delightful things than walking into the town along the riverside path on a misty morning when the rowing crews are out. Those who glide past may include veterans of the annual Oxford and Cambridge Boat Race, potential Olympic medallists—or simply people who, in the words of Kenneth Grahame (who did not go to the university but was at school in Oxford) like "messing about in boats." As well as the river, there are many green spaces in or near Oxford to wander in.

A Coat of Arms above the Brasenose College gateway.

facing page
The Radcliffe Camera is now the main reading room of the Bodleian Library.

Oxford is not only a university city. In the suburb of Cowley, associated with car manufacture since 1912, the revived Mini is still produced by BMW. That said, however, most visitors will want to see the river, the colleges, and the museums. Most colleges can be visited during the afternoons. At Christ Church you will see many locations used in the Harry Potter films. At Magdalen College, on May 1 at six A.M., the college choir sings from the top of the tower to welcome the summer. At Lincoln College you can visit the rooms once occupied by John Wesley, founder of Methodism. The chapel of New College (new in 1379!) has El Greco's painting of St James. Other colleges are equally worthy of your attention.

Take a tour of the Bodleian Library, founded in 1320, one of the world's great libraries. Next door is the Radcliffe Camera, a circular room now the Bodleian's main reading room. The Divinity School has one of the finest Gothic interiors in Oxford, with spectacular vaulting and bosses representing biblical scenes. The Ashmolean and Oxford museums are both of great interest. My favorites, however, are the University and Pitt Rivers museums, conveniently housed in one building. The first has a collection of dinosaur remains (another lost cause!) and a stuffed dodo. A statue of Queen Victoria's husband, Prince Albert, gazes proudly at them. Pitt Rivers is an ethnographical collection of totems and masks and other such items along with some fascinating musical instruments.

Of the many novels set in Oxford, *Zuleika Dobson* by Max Beerbohm is one of the most amusing. Zuleika, a beautiful young adventuress, entices, then rejects, innumerable undergradute suitors, driving them to suicide. *Zuleika Dobson* apart, Oxford has many other literary associations. At the Eagle and Child you can drink in the room where J.R.R. Tolkien read parts of *The Lord of the Rings* to the Inklings, a group including C. S. Lewis, author of the Narnia stories and books about Christianity. Among novels wholly or partly set in Oxford are Evelyn Waugh's *Brideshead Revisited*, Colin Dexter's Inspector Morse novels, Edmund Crispin's *The Moving Toyshop*, Dorothy L. Sayers's *Gaudy Night*, Hardy's *Jude the Obscure*, and Philip Pullman's *His Dark Materials*. Lewis Carroll, author of *Alice in Wonderland*, taught mathematics at Oxford and the Alice books play with mathematical, philosophical, and linguistic paradoxes.

left
Official university religious services take place in the Church of St Mary the Virgin.

above
The Museum of Oxford exhibits range from a mammoth's tooth to a Morris car engine.

below
The principal meetings and public ceremonies of the university take place in the Sheldonian Theater.

STAMFORD

CLOTH–OF–GOLD, BULLS, AND A DYNASTY

STAMFORD IS A SMALL TOWN THAT NEVERTHELESS CONTAINS, IN ST MARTIN'S CHURCHYARD, the grave of the largest ever Englishman. Daniel Lambert weighed 742 pounds when he died at Stamford Races in 1809. A waxwork of him can be seen in the town's museum. A less gross, but still substantial, claim to fame is that Stamford's famously durable cloth was used to make the several hundred luxurious tents and pavilions

The spectacular west front of Burghley House.

facing page
Around 1900 the Protestants of Stamford were perturbed by High Church practices in St Mary's Church.

for the "Field of the Cloth of Gold" diplomatic encounter between Henry VIII and Francis I of France in 1520. The meeting failed to keep the peace between France and England but its setting was a great success. Stamford dates back to Anglo-Saxon times. Under the Danes it was capital of the Fens. This extensive (2,450 square miles) area of marsh was drained in the seventeenth century and its rich black soil produces an abundance of cereals, vegetables, and bulbs. But, since most parts of the Fens are below sea level, the sea defenses have to be rigorously maintained against the ever-present threat of flooding. After the cloth trade declined, Stamford earned its living as a staging post on the Great North Road from London to York. The advantage of this turn of historical events is that, as at Lavenham, the medieval layout of the center (winding streets and cobbled alleys) remains, as do five of the ten medieval churches. (Like Oxford, Stamford is a town of "dreaming spires.") There are also many fine seventeenth- and eighteenth-century houses. (Look out for the chinoiserie porch on Barn Hill.) Unsurprisingly, Stamford was chosen as the main setting for the film *Pride and Prejudice* starring Keira Knightley, Matthew Macfadyen, and Dame Judi Dench. If all this strikes us as excessively genteel, we might note that until 1835, during the annual Bull Run, a bull was goaded into rampaging through the streets, creating mayhem. The banning of this event was the earliest success of the campaign for the prevention of cruelty to animals.

One of the great political country houses of England, Burghley House, lies on the southern edge of the town. This took William Cecil, first Lord Burghley, more than thirty years to build. During that time, and for four decades all told, he was Elizabeth I's secretary of state and spymaster. In his later years he was a

Burghley House is a huge architectural fantasy with a spectacular roofline. Cupolas with pinnacles abound; pinnacles without cupolas stand along the parapet of the west front; chimney pots are disguised as classical pillars; the central clock tower is an obelisk. In the Great Hall there is a Queen Anne cistern made from 187 pounds of silver, used as a wine cooler, said to be the largest in the world. As if in warning of the dangers attendant on having so much wine available, there is, just through a door, the Hell Staircase, the ceiling of which shows Hell as a cat's mouth crammed with sinners. Somewhat illogically, perhaps, this leads upward to the Heaven Room, where gods and goddesses tumble playfully from the ceiling and walls.

rather conservative but very efficient administrator of a system that was beginning to show its age. His descendants have had a similar influence over the fortunes of Stamford, protecting their own position by resisting change in the town. One of them arranged matters so that the main East Coast railway line went through Peterborough, nine miles eastward, rather than through Stamford.

In 1845 the arrival of
the railways in
Peterborough—
previously a small
market town—led to
industrial expansion
and population
growth that left
Stamford far behind,
in some respects to
its advantage.
Peterborough's
population is now
156,000 and it
remains an
important center of
industry and
railways. The twelfth-
century cathedral
suffered much
damage in 1643
from Cromwell's
iconoclastic troops,
who smashed
everything they
could reach and
even managed to
weaken the
structure. Some
parts were lost
forever but much
has been restored—
and the painted
wooden ceiling was
too far above their
heads for them to
destroy.
Peterborough is a
link in the Eastern
Counties chain of
cathedrals, which
includes Durham,
York, Lincoln,
Peterborough,
Norwich, Ely,
Southwark, and
Canterbury. The
splendor of the
buildings and the
scenery near them
makes for an
enjoyable tour.

STOKE ON-TRENT

POTTERY, POTTERY, AND MORE POTTERY

THE STORY OF STOKE-ON-TRENT IS THE STORY OF POTTERY, and three of the great names of the industry—Minton, Spode, and Wedgwood—flourished here. It has to be understood that Stoke-on-Trent is not, as politically constituted today, a small town, since it consists of an amalgamation of six towns, known collectively as "the Potteries," but administratively as Stoke-on-Trent. Each of the six, however, has to some extent retained its individuality. Nor is Stoke, in the picture-postcard sense, strictly a beautiful town; or, rather, it has many beauties but they are mainly to be found in museum displays. Some of these include original buildings such as kilns, as well as carts and other equipment used in pottery manufacture. Anyone who enjoys the beauty of the products will surely find fascination, even a kind of grandeur (if also some uneasiness) in imagining the process.

Pottery was made in this area 3,500 years ago. The City Museum in Hanley has examples of cremation urns from this period. There were pottery kilns operating in both Roman and medieval times. But pottery was no more important here than anywhere else until the seventeenth century. At that point it was realized that the vast supplies of marl clay, coal, and water (along with deposits of iron, copper, and lead to provide the oxides used in glazing), made it ideal for the development of potteries devoted to production of fine goods on an industrial scale. Nowadays the local marl clay, only ever of average quality, has been replaced by a blend of china clay, ball clay, flint, and ground stone from other places. For English bone china, burnt, powdered animal bone is added to the mixture, giving the finished product great strength.

The Gladstone Pottery Museum preserves a complete Victorian pottery that produced ordinary, everyday tableware, tiles, and sanitary items. It has five giant "bottle" kilns ("bottle" refers to their shape). You will see the terrible, unhealthy conditions in which men, women, and children worked there. Every surface was thick with clay dust and the lead and silica clay used in the process brought disease with them. Lead poisoning affected people's blood, stomach, kidneys, nervous system, and brain. Silicosis attacked their lungs. Crude death rates and deaths from lung disease were well above the national average. Few workers in such places lived past forty, until health and safety legislation began to take effect in the early twentieth century. As you leave the museum you will see a tile, from the nose cone of the NASA Shuttle spacecraft of 1981, which is able to withstand temperatures on reentry of 1,357°. The singer Robbie Williams spent his childhood in Stoke, where his mother owned a pub. According to her, he loves the place and its people.

A pottery plaque for a pottery museum.

facing page
A hundred years ago hundreds of these bottle ovens dominated Stoke's skyline.

The Etruria Industrial Museum marks the place where Wedgwood began work. It may be visited, but the 1903 boiler is only "in steam" seven times a year. There is general agreement that Wedgwood was the most important individual figure in the story of pottery at Stoke and that he was immensely skillful as both potter and entrepreneur. There is a memorial tablet to him in the Church of St Peter ad Vincula, and a bronze statue of him faces the railway station. However, the range of work that has been done in Stoke, as the museums indicate, is ample testimony to another truth, that there were others who were also imaginative, inventive, and forward-looking.

The Potteries Museum and Art Gallery traces the story of pottery in the area and houses possibly the world's largest collection of locally produced ceramics alongside an art collection that demonstrates links between potters and their colleagues in the other arts. There is also a World War II Spitfire, brainchild of local aircraft designer Reginald Mitchell. In 1934, convalescing from cancer, Mitchell visited Germany, where he realized that Britain would be open to attack if it did not possess a potent defensive fighter plane. A driven man, he threw himself into developing the Spitfire. The result revolutionized fighter-plane design—but he did not live to see it in action. He would have been distressed by problems that hampered its production in the years after his death in 1937. The aircraft was technologically advanced, and industrial capacity limited—problems solved just in time.

STRATFORD
UPON–AVON

PLAYWRIGHT, PUNDITS, PROPERTIES

WE KNOW MORE ABOUT, SAY, QUEEN ELIZABETH I, THAN WE DO ABOUT SHAKESPEARE, but there is no need to exaggerate our degree of ignorance, as is often done by people eager to prove (for reasons that are almost invariably tainted with intellectual snobbery) that he did not write the plays that bear his name. Because no lists of pupils remain, such self-opinionated pundits argue, we cannot say he was educated at the King's New School, a grammar school that would have given him the classical drilling that lies behind the plays. More pertinently, however, it would have been extremely odd had he not been a pupil there. He was born in 1564 in a house on Henley Street and baptized in the Holy Trinity parish church, by the river Avon, where he lies buried. His life's work as a playwright was mainly done in London but he grew up and married in Stratford (where his wife, Anne Hathaway, their eldest daughter, Susanna, and their twins, Hamnet and Judith, remained, in a cottage belonging to Anne's family). He bought property there as soon as he could afford to and returned to live in style and comfort for the last few years of his life. His plays contain not only complex rhetoric but also similes of transparent simplicity, derived obviously from the life of the country around Stratford.

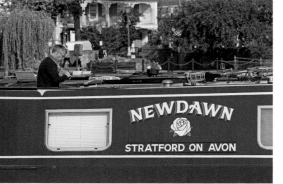

River boats crowd the canal basin opposite the Royal Shakespeare Theatre.

facing page
The Stars and Stripes graces Harvard House, home of the mother of the founder of Harvard University.

Visits to Stratford should obviously include Holy Trinity, the birthplace, the grammar school, and Anne Hathaway's cottage. Three other properties in Stratford have direct or likely associations with Shakespeare. Nash's House in Chapel Lane belonged to the husband of Shakespeare's granddaughter Elizabeth. It opens onto the garden of New Place, the house Shakespeare bought in 1597 and lived in, whenever he could get away from London, until his death in 1616. His daughter Susanna and her husband, Dr John Hall, probably lived in Hall's Croft, in Old Town Street, before she inherited New Place from her father. After seeing the house, furniture, paintings, and an exhibition illustrating obscure medical practices of the time, it is pleasant to take afternoon tea in the garden. Outside the town, a house thought to have been Shakespeare's mother's home before her marriage, Mary Arden's House at Wilmcote, was declared in 2000 to have been misidentified. The identification and the name have been transferred to the farm next door. Since, however, the first house remained a working farm until 1930 and its outbuildings have survived, along with many meticulously preserved features of a prosperous Tudor farm, it is well worth a visit on its own account.

Shakespeare was first formally celebrated at Stratford when actor-manager David Garrick organized a three-day Jubilee in 1769. In 1864 came celebrations of his tercentenary. After 1879, summer festivals of the plays were given in the first Shakespeare Memorial Theater. That was destroyed by fire in 1926 and replaced by the Royal Shakespeare Theater, a 1,300-seat building that served from 1932 to 2007. In 1961 Peter Hall formed the Royal Shakespeare Company (RSC), which performed all year round in Stratford and in London. Under a series of directors the company has done much excellent work, surviving occasional crises, financial and otherwise. Visitors can see their productions of plays by Shakespeare, his contemporaries, and later playwrights.

The Royal Shakespeare Theater's Main House is at the time of writing beginning to be transformed to bring it more into line with a modern audience's expectations. Productions continue to be staged at the Swan (a thrust stage surrounded by stalls and galleries on three sides). When work on the main house has been completed, it is hoped that there will once again be three theatres showing RSC productions: the main house, the Swan, and a smaller theater, staging mainly modern or experimental work. The RSC Collection and Gallery exhibits paintings, photographs, and other objects associated with Shakespeare's plays and productions of them, particularly at Stratford.

Shakespeare gazes over Bancroft Gardens and the river Avon.

Katherine Rogers, mother of John Harvard, who founded Harvard University, lived at Harvard House in the main street. Harvard himself was born in London. He studied at Cambridge, became a clergyman and went to America. In 1638 he died, leaving books and money to the recently established college, which was named in his honor. Harvard House was restored in 1910 through the efforts of the popular novelist, author of *The Sorrows of Satan*, Marie Corelli. Ms Corelli lived at Mason Croft in Church Street and kept her own gondola on the Avon, complete with Venetian gondolier. Her novels, writes Jonathan Keates, are "sensation-seeking, ever so faintly naughty, and full of half-baked metaphysics."

left
This substantial "cottage" belonged to the family of Anne Hathaway, who married Shakespeare in 1582.

below
Many of the half-timbered buildings in Stratford are genuine; some are not.

WARWICK

ROMANCE, A KINGMAKER, AND REVENGE

WARWICK CASTLE LOOKS COMPLETE AND WELL KEPT only because of nineteenth-century restoration. It is a romantic site nevertheless. It puts you in mind of wicked King John, Robin Hood, ladies in distress, bandits awaiting unwary travelers on roads through forests, forelock-tugging peasants, and violently grasping lords of the manor—in short, the whole technicolored fantasy of English history that Hollywood so enjoyed

during the 1930s, '40s, and '50s. Errol Flynn, jaw clenched, cannot be far away and, surely, the lovely Janet Leigh must be watching from behind the bars of that high window, waiting for Tony Curtis to come ambling over the hill on his white horse. Perhaps Danny Kaye will appear as the court jester. For all its appearance of romantic unreality, however, this castle was the family home of the earls of Warwick until 1978. The best-known member of the family is Richard Neville, who exercised great power and influence during the first phase of the Wars of the Roses, deposing Henry VI and putting Edward IV in his place, then reversing the procedure. This gained him his nickname "Warwick the Kingmaker." Edward, however, took revenge in 1471, by defeating and killing Warwick at the Battle of Barnet.

Imagine yourself as a member of a house party at the castle in 1898.

facing page
From this walkway and these towers bowmen picked off attackers during the Wars of the Roses.

William the Conqueror built Warwick Castle on its cliff overlooking the Avon in 1068. It has three tall towers (one twelve-sided, one square with rounded turrets at the corners, one cloverlike) and other shorter ones. Bowmen moved along walkways on its curtain walls, finding the best point for picking off whatever attackers were trying to get in. It has a chapel, great hall, and state rooms, and a suite of rooms set up to show you what a house party for the Prince of Wales was like in 1898. It has a conservatory, peacock garden, and Victorian rose garden. And in this setting you can come and let your hair down at kingmaker's feasts and highwayman's suppers. Or you can simply gaze at the world's largest *trebuchet*—a huge wooden machine designed to sling boulders at the castle wall—and give thanks that you will never be there when one lands.

Elsewhere in Warwick, the museum in the seventeenth-century Market Hall houses giant fossils, live

Other places close by are worth visiting. Kenilworth Castle is an impressively large assemblage of ruined but not unrecognizable fortifications and palatial apartments, visited, liked, and exploited by such monarchs as John, Henry V, Henry VIII, and Elizabeth I. Right next door to Warwick, Leamington Spa, like other spas, became fashionable in the nineteenth century, especially after a visit in 1838 by Queen Victoria, who added the prefix "Royal," to its name. Many buildings from that period of reflected glory remain and there are some attractive shops.

bees and the Sheldon tapestry map. The Lord Leycester Hospital is a group of fourteenth- and fifteenth-century timber-framed buildings near the Norman town gate, used for several centuries as a home for returned soldiers, with a chapel, great hall, galleried courtyard, and guildhall. The restored Master's Garden re-creates the original Elizabethan garden design.

Finally, if you have no other plans to visit the theatrical center on the river Avon, Stratford (see under STRATFORD-UPON-AVON) is only seven miles away. Many buildings there are worth seeing even if you are not interested in Shakespeare. In the countryside nearby are Charlcote Park (which Elizabeth I visited in 1572, somewhat before the time when Shakespeare is said to have been in danger of arrest for poaching deer in the park, forcing him to flee to London; there is no evidence to confirm this story. Indeed, there were probably no deer for him to poach.) Nearby is the charming crossroads market town of Henley-in-Arden, with its timber-framed houses and church set in a spacious churchyard.

WOODSTOCK

BATTLE, PALACE, DYNASTY

JOHN CHURCHILL, DUKE OF MARLBOROUGH (1650-1722), was the most successful general and the leading European statesman of his age. In 1704, during the War of the Spanish Succession, in which the French tried to unite a large part of mainland Europe under their overall domination, Marlborough led British and Dutch armies to a very significant victory over a larger French army at Blindhelm ("Blenheim" to the English), by the Danube in Bavaria. Anne, queen of England, a chronic invalid (after seventeen pregnancies who can blame her?) and a shrewd politician, rewarded him and boosted her own image by making him Duke of Marlborough and giving him an estate and palace at Woodstock. (Later, after disagreements about the scale of the building, royal subsidy was withdrawn and Marlborough had to complete Blenheim Palace at his own expense.)

above and facing page
Distant and close-up views of the grandly ceremonial frontage of Blenheim Palace, birthplace of Winston Churchill.

Despite the disagreements, this baroque masterpiece (a World Heritage Site since 1987) stands as designed by two of the leading architects of the eighteenth century, Sir John Vanburgh (soldier, dramatist, and architect) and Nicolas Hawksmoor. (They had earlier drawn the plans of another very grand private house, Castle Howard—see under YORK). The park and gardens as we now see them are principally the work of later generations; "Capability" Brown relandscaped the park in 1764-74. Marlborough's descendants continued to be important in English political life: Winston Spencer Churchill ("the saviour of his country" according to the historian A.J.P. Taylor) was born in Blenheim Palace in 1874 and was buried in the churchyard at Bladon, nearby, in 1965. Three staterooms, entrance, saloon, green writing room, and red and green drawing rooms occupy the central front. Wings and courtyards on either side accommodate the Long Library, the chapel, a clock tower, and the more domestic areas. All the principal rooms can be visited and there are several areas devoted to exhibitions on aspects of the palace, the life of Winston Churchill, and other subjects. The sumptuous formal gardens (which include, amongst many other things, the magnificent Water Terraces) are reminiscent of chateaus in France and Italy. A stroll through the park will show you how an awkward stretch of marshland may be transformed into a thing of beauty. Interest for all the family will be found in the Pleasure Gardens (reached by a miniature train): adventure playground, maze, model of a Woodstock street, putting greens, giant chess and checkers sets and a butterfly house. When you visit, allow all or most of a day to get your money's worth. I hope you like it more than Marlborough's duchess, who said, "I mortally hate all gardens and architecture."

Woodstock is a very agreeable small town, once famed for glove-making, now a center for antique shops, and artworks. The "Town Gate" is one of the entrances to the Palace. The Oxfordshire County Museum is at Fletchers House in Park Street. Flat and compact, Woodstock prides itself on its friendliness and safety. It proved less than safe for Rosamund, mistress of Henry II. Legend, at least, has it that she died there, poisoned by Eleanor, Henry's jealous Queen. Sir Walter Scott's novel *Woodstock* vividly describes events in the locality in 1651, when, following defeat in the Battle of Worcester, the future King Charles II hid for a time in what was then a royal lodge and park.

Oxford is seven miles away (see under OXFORD) and will repay, at the very least, a day or two's attention. Rousham House and gardens (see under CHIPPING NORTON) are 7 miles north. The sprawling village of North Leigh, 7 miles southwest, boasts a late Saxon church with a chantry chapel dating from c. 1439, a Roman villa and a windmill. Further on, near Witney, is Cogges Manor, which houses a museum of rural life in Oxfordshire in Victorian times. There you can meet traditional breeds of farm animals (and help feed them) and ask the housemaids and farmhands how there lives differ from your own. Witney itself makes blankets, and the Wool Hall is one of numerous buildings worth looking at.

WORCESTER

MIDLANDS

MUSIC, CRICKET, AND A CATHOLIC COMPOSER

IN 1930, ONE OF WORCESTER'S FAMOUS SONS (and one of England's greatest composers), Sir Edward Elgar, had long been in retirement. His wife, Alice, had died in 1930. About then, too, he substantially lost faith in two other elements in his life that had sustained him through the years before the success of the *Enigma Variations* (1899) made him famous: his Roman Catholic faith and his belief in the moral greatness of the British. The *Cello Concerto* (1919) had been his last major work and its elegiac note seemed to sum up his situation. Awash, as he saw it, in a sea of vulgarity and mindless imperialism, he despaired. The only thing that made him even think of composing was his friendship for the playwright George Bernard Shaw. (Significantly, Alice Elgar had not liked the rationalistic, witty Shaw: she thought his views were "poison.") Elgar had some sketches for a third symphony, but although he thrashed away at them on the piano from time to time, he had in effect decided that sketches were what they would remain. (They did until Anthony Payne's completed version of the work was performed in 1998). But from London a man called Whitely kept inviting him to write a test piece for the National Brass Band Championships at the Crystal Palace. When the fee he offered rose to 150 pounds, Elgar gave way. He was not poor but he was not rich either, and he had developed a taste for betting on horses. He produced his *Severn Suite*, a hymn of love for Worcester, the city where, because he was the son of a Catholic tradesman (owner of a music shop) he had grown up as an outsider, cut off from polite society by religion and class. The suite's four movements celebrated the sights and imagined sights of old Worcester: the castle, a tournament beneath its walls, the cathedral and the commandery—this last a medieval hospital whose uses over the centuries included being a Royalist headquarters in the Civil War. It has recently been restored and is now a building you must not miss. The main hall is magnificent, and all of the many other rooms provide fascinating insights into the life and architecture of the many different eras during which the building has been in existence. The gardens repay at least a quick look.

Elgar's story tells us a huge amount about his home city—and about the West of England generally. It was musical (Worcester shares the Three Choirs Festival with its neighbors, Gloucester and Hereford). It had a long history, with buildings or remnants of buildings to match. It had remained Royalist, Anglican, provincial, politically conservative, and socially stratified. Tradesmen, including music teachers came to the back door, never the front. Elgar chafed against some of these things: as a nationally recognized composer he thought that he was an exceptional case. But, at another level of his personality, he also shared most of them.

If Elgar is one part of the identity of the city, the cathedral (which as an institution deplored his Catholicism) is another. Attend a match at the cricket grounds across the Severn on a fine day. What do you see and hear? Green grass, white flannels, the healthy thwack of willow bat on leather ball, the river flowing peacefully by. Beyond, the square-towered thirteenth- to fourteenth-century cathedral, with its Victorian Gothic choir and lawns sloping down to meet their reflections in the placid water. Ducks and swans serenely floating. What picture could better sum up the Englishness felt by those who distrusted Elgar as an outsider? He, of course, loved it too.

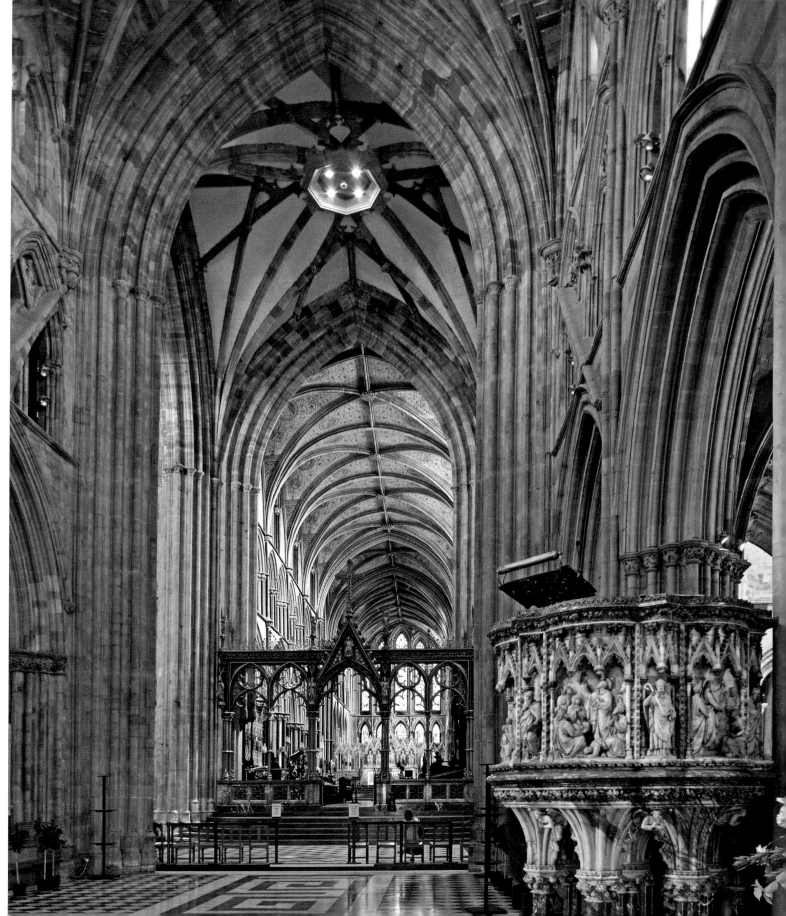

Alice Elgar, older than her husband and several rungs higher on the social ladder, was his entry card to Worcester society. The marriage, its termination by her death, and the fact that it did not altogether prevent him falling platonically in love with a succession of younger women, is a further clue to the emotional power that welled up through his personal repressions and sense of propriety when he composed his great symphonic works, but otherwise induced him to cultivate the manner of a natty middle-class gentleman. But under the smart clothes he was a vulnerable and emotional man. World War I distressed him terribly. But what upset him most was not the slaughter in the trenches but the sufferings of wholly innocent creatures: "Pity," he exclaimed, "the poor horses!"

CHESTER

CITY WALLS AND AN EMINENT VICTORIAN

CHESTER, LIKE THE CASTLE TOWNS ACROSS THE BORDER IN WALES, was, by the laws put in place by Edward I, an English city. No Welsh were allowed to live within the walls or be there between sunset and dawn. This reflects the central fact about the town's history. It was a frontier garrison town from Roman times onward, its function being to keep the Welsh out. The Roman defenses eventually became the city walls, which, much rebuilt, are still there. A stroll along them is an agreeable early evening treat. Set in a loop of the river Dee, Chester was also the nearest English port to Ireland, and its trade with Scotland, Wales, and Europe made it rich during medieval times.

Chester's shopping arcades, the Rows, were medieval in origin, but the present buildings date only from the Victorian Era. Shops on the first floor have recently been restored again. Sadly, they now house the same chain stores as have taken over virtually every town center in the UK. In their thirteenth- and fourteenth-century origins and until perhaps thirty years ago, they were small, quirky, and useful. However, again like many other towns, Chester has begun to resist destructive modernization. Plans to build over the Roman amphitheater have been abandoned; what remains is being carefully excavated. Unfortunately, all that remains of Chester's Castle, a Norman stone structure overlooking the river Dee, is fragments of the twelfth-century inner wall, the flag tower, and the original inner gateway, the Agricola Tower.

Chester Cathedral, formerly an abbey, is also medieval in origin. It is built, however, in soft red local sandstone, which crumbles. Restoration, therefore, is more-or-less continuous, and this has made the building architecturally confusing. From some angles it is extremely impressive, from others less so. One remarkable feature is the polygonal apse, with its very tall "candle-snuffer" polygonal roof. The Victorian restorer who put it there claimed to have evidence for its accuracy, and this is now thought to be possible, although there are doubts about the extreme height of the roof. Inside, although the building is not particularly long, there is an impression of length, fostered by its height and narrowness. The choir stalls are greatly admired as are the screen and decoration above and behind the stalls. One of the carved misericords under the tip-up seats (designed to enable elderly monks to stand for long periods), shows a wife beating her husband.

The Anglo-Saxon ruins of St John's house a ghostly monk.

facing page
The Eastgate Clock on the city walls.

Outside the walls, in the bend of the river, is the Roodee, which since 1540 has served as the town's racecourse, said to be the oldest still in use in England. Race meetings, but also polo and concerts are staged there. Other places of interest can be found not far away. South of Wrexham, twelve miles away, is Erddig, an eighteenth-century mansion where you can find out how a well-managed and apparently happy estate was run. The photographs of the staff in the servants' hall are charming and illuminating. Nearby is Erddig Farm World where you will learn how farms work in the present day, and there is plenty for children to enjoy.

The village of Hawarden, six miles west, is associated with the great nineteenth-century prime minister W.E. Gladstone, who is buried in the church there. The family still lives in the castle around the corner; limited walking in the attached park is possible. Next to the church is the St Deiniol's Gladstone Memorial Library. You can see a collection of photographs, documents, and statuary outlining his life, and at appropriate times, most days, have tea or coffee and a cake, or lunch. Or, if you want to do some research in humanities or divinity, you can become a resident for a day, a week, or a year and enjoy the luxury of distraction-free work in a splendid library.

HEREFORD

THE RIVER WYE AND PILES OF BOOKS

HEREFORD IS THE WESTERNMOST POINT OF THE TRIANGLE OF CATHEDRAL cities that promote the Three Choirs Festival (see also GLOUCESTER and WORCESTER). It is essentially a market town where local farm produce, including the cattle that bear its name, is sold. Opposite the covered market is the Old House (1621) a three-storied black-and-white building and a very startling thing to find in a modern shopping precinct. It is now a museum showing domestic life in the early seventeenth century. There are many other interesting museums, exhibiting, to give a few examples, a Roman mosaic, watercolors by local artists, and cider making.

A good place to get an overall view of the cathedral is Bishop's Meadow, on the banks of the river Wye, from where its burly tower is seen to best advantage. Closer up and particularly in the interior it is clear that the building is in places a jumble of restorations and alterations, some of which have proved controversial. Batsford and Fry, writing in 1934, described Sir Giles Gilbert Scott's Victorian choir screen as "tortured... a melancholy commentary on the transience of even the most eminent taste." Someone at the cathedral clearly agreed, because the screen was removed in 1966 and sent to a museum in Coventry. Pevsner, fifty years after Batsford and Fry, regretted this "great loss to Hereford," praising the screen as "a High Victorian monument of the first order." Some of the other alterations, not very well managed, followed the collapse of the west front and part of the nave in 1786. No one, it seems, much likes the early twentieth-century replacement of the front itself.

There are some fascinating items on view in other parts of the building. There is the *Mappa Mundi*, drawn by a clergyman in 1290. It shows the world as a circle centered on Jerusalem, with the Garden of Eden nearby. At the edges blood-curdling monsters are shown awaiting anyone who ventures too far. In the library, the volumes are chained to the shelves. They can be read on the hinged lectern on one of the lower shelves, but not removed.

Eastward from Hereford the town of Ledbury is attractive and relaxed. It claims, justifiably, to be one of the finest black-and-white towns in the country. Elsewhere, walkers can explore the Wye Valley Walk, upstream and downstream. The stretch between Hereford and Ross-on-Wye (sixteen miles) is gentle countryside. Beyond Ross the ground becomes rocky and the terrain more dramatic: a meandering gorge passes the Forest of Dean and Symonds Yat; briefly it reenters Wales and passes Monmouth, a town certainly worth inspection; after Monmouth it forms the Welsh border and passes by Tintern Abbey.

facing page
The Cathedral bathed in sunlight.

below
The ornate Town Hall was built in 1904.

Hereford was founded in the seventh century as a garrison whose purpose was to keep the Welsh out of England. In the eighth century it became the capital of the Kingdom of West Mercia under King Offa, who built the defensive earthwork known as Offa's Dyke along the whole length of the Welsh border, from the mouth of the Dee in the north to the mouth of the Severn in the south. In the seventeenth century Hereford had a difficult civil war. It was held by the Royalists much of the time and was therefore constantly subject to raids by the Parliamentarians, and even suffered a siege by the Scots. Nowadays the Special Air Service Regiment, a prestigious, highly trained group, whose motto is "Who Dares, Wins," is based there.

If you are a book-lover take an outing to Hay-on-Wye. This small Welsh town lists thirty-eight bookshops on its official Website. Most sell second-hand books, and some specialize in particular areas of literature or subject matter; others are splendid lucky dips. If your house is already bursting at the seams with books, you had better not go to Hay; the problem will only get worse. Every May there is a literary festival there, which (in the words of its own publicity), offers "a gathering in the staggering beauty of the Brecon Beacons National Park" of writers, comedians, and musicians that have the capacity to change our lives, to share new visions of the world, and to do that incredibly sexy thing—to renew our sense of wonder.

L U D L O W

FOOD AND A LAND OF LOST CONTENT

THE TOWN AND THE COUNTY OF SHROPSHIRE HAVE THEIR OWN POET laureate in A. E. Housman (1859-1936) who, however, was born in Worcestershire and lived most of his life in London and Cambridge, in both of which universities he was a professor of Latin. Nonetheless, he made of a (partly imaginary) Shropshire his "land of lost content" and wrote about it obsessively. Many of his poems reflect also his homosexuality and his distress at the numbers of young men slaughtered during the 1914-18 war.

"The lads in their hundreds to Ludlow come in for the fair, / There's men from the barn and the forge and the mill and the fold, / The lads for the girls and the lads for the liquor are there, / And there with the rest are the lads that will never be old."

facing page
Castle, Church
tower, charming
houses, gentle hills;
few towns can rival
this.

below
The Feathers Hotel
has been called
"that prodigy of
timber framed
houses."

Housman's ashes were scattered in the churchyard of St Laurence's Church and there is a memorial to him on the north wall. St Laurence is a grand and lofty structure with beautifully carved choir stalls and a splendid perpendicular chancel. Its 130-foot tower supports a peal of eight bells that is important in the development of change ringing in England. In 2003 the pugnacious restaurant critic Jonathan Meades praised Ludlow as "the exception that proves the rule of provincial Britain's gastronomic backwardness." That reputation has continued, although Shaun Hill, the restaurateur who first hit the headlines, has lately moved elsewhere. There are still seven restaurants in or near Ludlow listed in the Michelin guide to Great Britain. Why should this be? Some attribute it to Hill's dynamic presence. Others believe that the annual food festival, which has attracted as many as 12,000 visitors over three days, has created and, so to speak, nourished the phenomenon. There is perhaps a cause more basic than either of these. Ludlow is at the center of one of the greatest food-producing areas in the UK, and the town has a tremendous array of specialist shops selling locally produced fare. There are six independent butchers, all of whom produce their own sausages. There is additionally a farmer's market. Nor is this gastronomic plenty used only by prestigious gourmet restaurants. Ludlow claims that it has an eating place for every taste and budget and that in any of them you are almost certainly going to eat better than you would in their equivalents elsewhere. I can think of few more appealing prospects than being allowed to test that claim, at leisure over a suitably lengthy period of time.

Whenever you arrive in Ludlow you are likely to have an immediate impression of a place that is lively and active without being frenetic, a place where people feel it a pleasure rather than a tiresome social duty to be free with their time in community activities, church groups, and the like. It is certainly a pleasant and sociable place to browse in bookshops—and in whatever other sort of shops appeal to you.

Splendid as it is, St Laurence's Church does not outshine the rest of the town. More than 500 buildings in Ludlow are listed for their architectural merit. The church backs onto the Bull Ring, a street with many ornate structures, including The Bull and Feathers inns. The latter is an amazing Jacobean three-story black-and-white building whose upper stories jut progressively further over the pavement below. The museum has an important geological section as a tribute to Sir Roderick Murchison, a Victorian geologist who established a classification and dating of fossils in the different layers of graywacke rock underlying the red sandstone of Ludlow and adjoining areas. The museum has a collection of 20,000 fossils, including some of the oldest known to man.

Like other towns in these parts, Ludlow began as a garrison against the Welsh. During the Middle Ages it was the seat of the Lord President of the Council of the Marches (the areas along the Welsh border). Its castle, now a very substantial ruin, was well positioned on a hill near the confluence of the rivers Teme and Corve and built with stone quarried on the site. It drew water from a deep well sunk through the hill to the level of the river Teme. In 1689 it was abandoned, having been considerably damaged during the Civil War. Nowadays, well kept up, it provides a backdrop that in itself contributes markedly to the impact and atmosphere of the many enjoyable theatrical, musical, events and exhibitions that are presented there.

SHREWSBURY

WAR, PEACE, AND WRITERS

IN ITS TIME, SHREWSBURY HAS BEEN POLITICALLY IMPORTANT TO SEVERAL PEOPLES: Welsh, Anglo-Saxons, Normans, rebels, and royalists. Why? It's near what is now the Welsh border and is flanked on three sides by a loop of the river Severn some two miles across. With the fourth, unenclosed, side protected by a red sandstone castle built in 1083, it was, during the turbulent centuries before England and Wales reached an accommodation with each other—or, as some Welsh would express it, before England became dominant (and arrogant with it)—, a fortress border town that both sides very much wanted to control. (The bridges crossing the river on either side are known as "the Welsh bridge" and "the English bridge.")

Names are also a point of contention. "Shrewsbury" is, according to educated opinion, pronounced "Shrowsbury." The existing spelling is, apparently, the result of a mistake by some orthographer long ago. Similarly, when the county of which it is the seat was, in 1974, renamed "Salop"—a conveniently shorter name derived from Anglo-Saxon—its good folk rebelled. (The word's similarity to the French word for "slut" was particularly irritating to the area's MEP.) The name reverted to "Shropshire" in 1980. Despite all these wrangles, Shrewsbury is virtually a synonym for English comfort and contentment, remaining essentially a rural market town. Possibly as a result of that calm it has preserved much of its medieval and Tudor historic center (more than 600 listed buildings), along with the pleasing, slow-paced West Country accent found, with variations, everywhere from Devon to Chester. The surface was ruffled, perhaps, when Robert Clive (1725-1774), one of the creators of British India and MP for Shrewsbury from 1761, reformed the Indian civil service, drew heavy criticism and, weakened by ill health, killed himself (in London).

Shrewsbury has many literary connections. A. E. Housman (see under LUDLOW) wrote of it, "High the vanes of Shrewsbury gleam, Islanded in Severn Stream." Wilfred Owen, the poet who wrote *Anthem for Doomed Youth* and was killed in the trenches one week before the 1918 armistice, spent formative years there. George Farquhar set his comedy *The Recruiting Officer* in a town very like Shrewsbury as did Ellis Peters in her medieval crime stories featuring the monk-detective Brother Cadfael.

Shrewsbury Center is an area to wander around, looking and marvelling. With 600-plus buildings to choose from it would be invidious to direct you in any particular direction. Outside the town, walk on the moors at Long Mynd, and through the wooded glories of Wenlock Edge.

The Square offers indoor and outdoor entertainment.

facing page
St Chad's has a circular nave and Industrial Revolution pillars and banisters.

The calm, peace, and gentleness of Shrewsbury today is embodied in Quarry Park and within that in the Dingle, an area sometimes called "Shrewsbury's Enchanted Garden." In 1647, a woman was burned at the stake there after poisoning her husband. The Dingle itself was created between 1875 and 1879. During World War II, it was used for farming. In 1946 Percy Thrower, who gained fame as the host of the immensely popular BBC radio program *Gardner's World*, was appointed the park superintendent and transformed it to what it is today, making it a perfect place to relax and contemplate. It is full of color during the summer and the shaded benches are perfect for hot, sunny days.

Shrewsbury School, like Sherborne School, was founded in the 1550s by Edward VI. It has produced an odd crop of old boys, such as Sir Philip Sidney, the Elizabethan poet who died in battle, Edward German, composer of the operetta *Merrie England*, and Michael Heseltine, dyslexic conservative politician, famed for brandishing the mace of the House of Commons during a particularly fierce debate. The one who had most effect on the world is Charles Darwin, writer of *On the Origin of Species*, a foundation text of evolution. In 1961 a group of 1950s pupils—Ingrams, Rushton, Booker, and Foot—founded *Private Eye*, the satirical magazine. It continues to make Britain laugh at the follies of its public figures to this day.

BEVERLEY

GEORGIAN, GOTHIC, LOCAL PRIDE

IN PARTS OF BEVERLEY YOU MIGHT ALMOST EXPECT A LADY—dressed as Jane Austen would have dressed—to step daintily from one of the pillared front doors. Making her graceful, dignified way to the pinnacled west front of the Gothic Minster for morning service, she would greet friends and acquaintances with a ready smile and a few decorous—if occasionally barbed—pleasantries. Its an appealing thought. The road markings, of course—the assertive double yellow lines, the triangles at intersections (and, possibly, aircraft rumbling overhead)—give the game away: Beverley is a Georgian small town that has somehow survived into the age of cars, the aircraft, and the Internet. The Minster has survived much longer than the houses, the present building having been rebuilt after a fire in 1188. The earliest part of it that remains today is the decorated nave. It avoided the worst ravages of the Reformation, partly because of the conservative attitudes prevalent in the diocese of York, partly because it was administered by secular canons, not monks.

The Minster was a thorn in the flesh as far as the administration of justice was concerned. Like Durham it was a chartered sanctuary, which is to say that even serious criminals could take refuge there for thirty days and, by swearing an oath of obedience to the lord of the locality, avoid punishment. This was overruled in 1487 for a case of high treason—in this case rebellion against the king. Despite the degree of security it enjoyed, by 1713 it needed thorough restoration to save it from ruination. A cathedral in all but name, the building will repay lengthy contemplation. This is especially true of the choir stalls and the misericords on their undersides.

One medieval gate, North Bar, remains; these gates were so constructed that goods being taken to market could be stopped and examined and a toll imposed. Be sure also to see St Mary's Church, the other Gothic church in Beverley, for its groups of sculpted figures and for the rabbit walking on its hind legs with a satchel over its shoulder, said to be the inspiration for the white rabbit in Lewis Carroll's *Alice in Wonderland*. As you may recall, Carroll's rabbit is perpetually anxious about being late and is given to "looking anxiously about… as if it had lost something" and muttering "The Duchess! The Duchess! Oh my dear paws! Oh my fur and whiskers! She'll get me executed as sure as ferrets are ferrets!" The stone original looks rather content with things as they are, which in Beverley seems entirely reasonable.

County Hall is the administrative headquarters for the East Riding.

facing page
Saints, bishops, warriors, and kings surround the west door of Beverley Minster.

A click on What's On in Beverley's Website suggests that everything that's "on" in Beverley occurs at the town's racecourse. The course is west of the town in Beverley Westwood, a large area of pasture land. It promises "a stunning location" and "a range of modern facilities catering for everything from exquisite fine dining and corporate entertainment to picnics with the family" plus, of course "the exhilaration of watching competitive racing and the excitement of cheering your chosen horse past the winning post." We should all be so lucky. The course specializes in "themed days" of racing; most of the themes are teasingly vague: Family Fun Day, Journal Ladies Day, Revved Up Raceday, Totesport Bullet Day, and Bank Holiday Bonanza. Perhaps you have to be there to get the point.

Yorkshire as a county has a proud sense of its own identity. Indeed, Yorkshiremen sometimes give the impression that they come from an independent country rather than a mere county. In 1974, parts of Yorkshire, including Beverley, were transferred to a new county called "Humberside." Great discontent resulted and "Humberside" was abolished in 1996. The rest of England, especially the great rival county across the Pennines, Lancashire, sometimes has strong views about Yorkshiremen. A letter published in the *Guardian* in 2004, apropos the argument over whether or not Robin Hood was actually from Yorkshire, summed up these views. "As Robin Hood wore bright green clothes, had a band of merry, not gruff, men and gave his money away, there is no way he could have hailed from Yorkshire." Judge for yourself.

HARROGATE

A MYSTERY, GARDENS, AND AN ABBEY

THE ONLY UNSOLVED MYSTERY CONNECTED WITH AGATHA CHRISTIE played itself out in Harrogate. In 1926 the thirty-six-year-old creator of Hercule Poirot and Miss Marple disappeared from her home in southern England after discovering that her husband, Colonel Archie Christie, was having an affair with a younger woman. There was a furor; Archie was briefly suspected of murder. When she was found in a Harrogate hotel, it was reported that she was suffering from amnesia. Nonetheless, she was registered there under the surname of Archie's mistress. In 1930 she married, happily, the archaeologist Max Mallowan.

By the time of Mrs Christie's enigmatic sojourn Harrogate was evolving into its present self, but during the three decades before 1914 there were almost ninety medicinal springs there, making it a convenient recuperative stopover for aristocrats leaving the rigors of the London season for grouse shooting in Scotland. As is usual in spa towns, however fashionable, some disobliging travelers complained about the smell. Celia Fiennes was an English diarist who, motivated by intense curiosity, undertook journeys through England in 1685-1703. Her remarkable journal of those travels was lost for more than 140 years and was rediscovered only in 1885 and republished in 1888 as *Through England on a Side Saddle*. Among her observations of Harrogate was the following: "The Sulphur or Stinking Spaw [sic] not improperly termed, for the Smell being so strong and offensive that I could not force my horse near the Well." The springs are not used now, although a Turkish bath may still be enjoyed in a setting that has been described as "a visual feast of tiled Victoriana." What remains is a superlatively elegant town, with delightful public gardens—it calls itself "England's floral town." As well as agricultural and flower shows, it hosts conferences, trade fairs, and a music festival. It is an excellent base from which to explore the Dales (see under MASHAM) and the North Yorkshire Moors (see under HELMSLEY).

Harrogate's buildings are wonderfully various. You can move from the mix of square and knobbly pillars at the entrance to the Royal Baths past rows of small, friendly shops looking onto lawns and pathways, to the octagonal elegance of the pumphouse, to the vine-garlanded brick pillars of the Valley Gardens Sun Pavilion… And, having gazed at all these, you will have hardly begun. And if the formal arrangements of urban architecture and gardens pall briefly, you can refresh yourself with a stroll or a picnic in The Stray, 200 acres of jealously preserved open common land that wraps around the southern end of the "old town."

The northerly latitude of the Harlow Carr Garden and its challenging growing conditions (exposed site, temperature range of –11C to +30C, annual mean temperature of +7C with frosts sometimes continuing into early June) help us understand what can be grown in the north. Rainfall often exceeding thirty-nine inches per year means that drainage is a constant consideration. ("Carr" means "land reclaimed from bog.") The fifty-eight acres at 550 feet above sea level are in a shallow valley divided by Harlow Beck—hence the spectacular Streamside Garden. The soil varies between silver sand and alluvial silt and very heavy clays that can, if not improved, become baked hard in summer and sticky and waterlogged in winter. Extreme acidity is another characteristic. Anyone seriously interested in gardening should visit this place.

facing page
The Royal Baths are a Moorish survival from Harrogate's heyday as a spa town.

below
The first Betty's Café (1919) seen from Montpelier Gardens.

The very substantial ruins of Fountains Abbey, a UNESCO World Heritage Site, stand eleven miles northwest of Harrogate. First Benedictine, then Cistercian, it became the wealthiest religious house in Britain. With the dissolution of the monasteries in the 1530s it fell into ruin. In the 1720s, the MP for nearby Ripon began developing the area, creating an elaborate ensemble of ponds, lake, canal, and water garden, set among meadows and woods, the whole dotted with classical temples, banqueting house, and Anne Boleyn's Seat. The abbey has no roofs left and many walls are now only a foot or two high, but enough remains to show the shape and magnificence of the building. The tower stands virtually complete, as does the vaulted dormitory undercroft where fleeces were stored. Close by is Fountains Mill, a fine survivor.

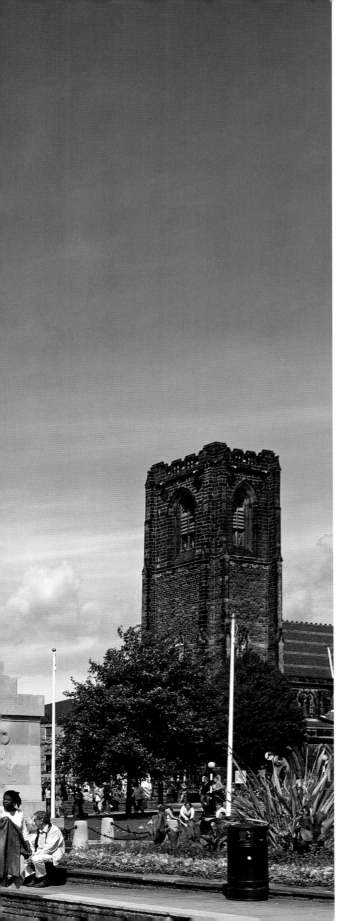

Ripley Castle is a fortified manor house.

The present occupant of Harewood House, the seventh earl of Harewood, has had a distinguished career as an opera administrator.

The Cenotaph, a memorial to war dead, is a popular meeting place.

Harrogate is within easy reach of many other places described in this book. The Yorkshire Dales are on its western doorstep. Ripon is ten miles north. York is fifteen miles east. On the way to or from it you will pass through Knaresborough, one of Britain's oldest towns, mentioned in the Domesday Book as having six ploughlands and eleven outlying estates. There are fine eighteenth-century houses and, nearby, Mother Shipton's Cave, which has been a tourist attraction since 1630. It was presented as the birthplace of a local prophetess. Objects such as umbrellas and soft toys have been hung there and have become limestone replicas of themselves. Ripley Castle, where Oliver Cromwell once stayed, is a bus ride away.

HAWORTH

MOORS, A PARSON, AND A MAIN STREET

IT WAS IN HAWORTH PARSONAGE THAT POSSIBLY THE WORLD'S MOST FAMOUS literary family threesome, the Brontë sisters, grew up, and imagined, first of all, their poetic fantasy about an alternative world called Gondal, then their novels. Two other sisters died very young. Charlotte, the oldest survivor, lived longest (but only until her fortieth year), traveled furthest, and wrote four novels. *Jane Eyre*, possibly the most accessible of the sisters' fictions, is her best known. Anne, the youngest and shortest lived, wrote two novels. Their scapegrace brother, Branwell, dissolved his short life in opium, drink, and irresponsible behavior. A family portrait shows the three sisters with a space between them from which Branwell has apparently been painted out. Emily survived one year less than Branwell and wrote one novel, *Wuthering Heights*. It remains, after more than 150 years, wild and strange, despite literary and other developments that have intervened since it was published in 1847. On the moors near Haworth are two houses that may have contributed to the novel. The first, Top Withins, is derelict. In any case it was its location, not its structure, that made Emily press it into service as Wuthering Heights itself. Penden Hall, nearby, may have provided the model for Thrushcross Grange.

A visit to this area is not for the faint-hearted, nor for those who prize comfort above all other things. Even today—even when the sun is shining and the air is still—there is a feeling of wildness; the moors, which neither loom nor plunge into depths, make you sense instinctively that you are not welcome. It may indeed be this antisocial aspect of her native landscape that appealed to Emily. Charlotte wrote of it that "The scenery of these hills is not grand, it is not romantic; it is scarcely striking. Long low moors, dark little heaths, shut in valleys… it is only higher up deep in amongst the ridges of the moors that Imagination can find rest for the sole of her foot; and even if she finds it there she must be a solitude loving raven, no gentle dove." And she wrote of Emily's attitude to the place that "She found in the bleak solitude many and dear delights; and not the least and best loved was liberty." Emily herself wrote in *Wuthering Heights* of "'wuthering' being a significant provincial adjective, descriptive of the atmospheric tumult to which its station is exposed in stormy weather… one may guess the power of the north wind blowing over the edge, by the excessive slant of a few stunted firs at the end of the house…"

Even the railway station is picturesque.

facing page
The main street is now prettier than it was when Branwell Brontë roistered here.

Patrick Brontë, the parson, was the son of Northern Irish peasants who had got himself into Cambridge entirely by his own efforts. He was an eccentric, conscientious, benevolent man. His relationship with Emily was particularly close. He seems to have felt that she, not Branwell, should have been his son. He taught her to shoot with pistols. (He practiced himself, at a regular time each day, leaning out of a parsonage window and using the church spire as a target.) He educated his daughters and allowed them almost unrestricted access to his own library, that of the Mechanics Institute in Keighly and perhaps that at Ponden Hall. He did not encourage them to make friends among people of their own age. Instead they developed "a bone-deep indifference to the rest of the world," which secured their "extraordinary artistic autonomy."

The church (the family tomb is under a pillar) and the parsonage (now the Brontë Museum) are, of course, essential stops for visitors. If you have it in you, go also onto the moors and seek out Top Withens, to see whether your imagination can find "rest for the sole of its foot." Do explore Haworth's steep, cobbled main street. Here, between B&Bs and self-catering cottages, are small shops, none of which can be much like those that were there when Patrick Brontë was parson of the parish but which are in their own present day terms pleasant and interesting. Away from Haworth, near Skipton (c. five miles) you will find the ruins of Bolton Priory and one of the most beautiful areas of Wharfdale (see under MASHAM), including the "Strid," a spectacular gorge.

140

HELMSLEY

ABBEY, MOORS, AND LAURENCE STERNE

HELMSLEY IS A VERY PRETTY MARKET TOWN WITH A VERY SMALL POPULATION. Nowadays it may be thought of as a peaceful backwater. In the seventeenth century life was more hectic. Then it was a weaving town and the loom operators were famous for "their thirsts, their songs, and their leather breeches." The local fair was a carnival of fisticuffs and intoxication. Today Helmsley is a magnet for those who love walking. The castle in the

The pretty Tudor Rose Restaurant in this pretty town.

facing page
In 1644 the Parliamentarians reduced Helmsley's defences to this broken stump.

town was virtually impregnable, although with typical stubbornness the Parliamentarians managed to capture it after a three-month siege in 1644. Helmsley is centrally situated amongst a host of attractions, many of which are within walking distance. There is a plentiful supply of great country houses. At Nunnington Hall we find a seventeenth-century manor house that combines Elizabethan and Stuart styles, among others. It has alluring surroundings, a finely panelled Oak Hall and a collection of twenty-two miniature furnished rooms. Duncombe Park, having been a family home for nearly three centuries, a hospital, and a girls' school was bought in 1985 by Lord Feversham, restored, and opened to the public in 1990. Castle Howard, as seen in the TV version of Evelyn Waugh's *Brideshead Revisited*, is outside walking distance but is worth whatever it takes to get there—a vast pile, designed by Vanburgh (who died on the job) and Hawksmoor, who also collaborated on Blenheim Palace (see under WOODSTOCK).

A signpost within the town indicates the footpath to Rievaulx Abbey (six miles) founded in 1132 by monks of the Cistercian order sent by Bernard of Clairvaux. (He almost immediately had occasion to be concerned about the impetuosity of a newly elected abbot there, William of Fitzherbert, and the violence of his supporters.) This is an easy crosscountry walk through the edge of the North York Moors, the last part of it alongside the river Dale. Set in a steep wooded valley, the ruins are both dramatic and extensive. Above the abbey is the Rievaulx Terrace, a landscaped promenade that may have been designed by Vanburgh. The remains of another Cistercian abbey, including the green-and-yellow glazed tiled floor, can be seen at Byland, some way southwest of Rievaulx. About eight miles west of Helmsley is Sutton Bank, whose one-in-four gradient is thought something of a trial by motorists. The compensation is panoramic views and a walk around a white horse cut into one of the slopes. Unlike numerous other such decorations of the landscape this one dates only from the nineteenth century.

The North York Moors National Park wraps round Helmsley on the western and northern sides. These scenic hills, which extend as far as the cliffs on the North Sea coast, are much beloved of walkers and there are many trails to follow. If you don't feel up to walking you can always ride on the North Yorkshire Moors Railway between Pickering and Grosmont. If you do you will see the railway station at Goathland, which features in the Harry Potter films as the station nearest to Hogworts School. There are, of course, many charming villages in the area. One of the most delightful, Hutton Le Hole, is only 7 miles from Helmsley. It has a large village green, often grazed by sheep, surrounded by limestone cottages with red pantiled roofs. The excellent Ryedale Folk Museum illustrates the life of a Romano-British agricultural community.

At Coxwold (seven miles) is Shandy Hall. The novelist Laurence Sterne was vicar at Coxwold from1760 to 1768 and this, now a museum, was his vicarage. He named it after his most famous character, the narrator of *The Life and Opinions of Tristram Shandy*, which he wrote (at high speed) while living here. Although the book contradicts virtually every expectation we might have of a novel, many critics regard it as one of the high points of English fiction. It is, in the words of fellow novelist Malcolm Bradbury, a "dark, mortal comedy that uses the play of the mind as a survival mechanism." Its influence can be detected in Joyce, Beckett, Nabokov, and Borges, as well as in such comedy series as *The Goon Show*, *Monty Python*, and *Fawlty Towers*. Sterne's contemporary Dr Johnson said that *Tristram Shandy* "did not last." He was wrong.

KINGSTON UPON HULL
PERCEPTIONS AND RENEWALS

THIS ENTRY MAY SEEM INAPPROPRIATE TO THIS BOOK. As recently as 2003 the East Riding Local Strategic Partnership discussed the matter of perceptions of Hull amongst people who had never been there and agreed that in most cases these were either negative or nonexistent. Recent restoration of the Docklands and of a number of important buildings has been completed, to the point that there is now certainly a small town within Hull that is worthy of inclusion in this book. What follows is intended as recognition of the attractiveness of the Old Town of Hull and its historical importance.

The Docklands were always the heart of the town and Hull (as it is most often known) has been an important port since medieval times. Daniel Defoe utilized that fact and several other important characteristics of the town in his most famous novel, *Robinson Crusoe*. Crusoe's father is described as "a foreigner of Bremen, who settled first at Hull. He got a good estate by merchandise, and leaving off his trade, lived afterward at York…" This was published in 1719. He returned to Hull in his nonfictional account of *A Tour through the Whole Island of Great Britain*: "I believe there is more business done in Hull than in any town of its bigness in Europe." Eventually Hull would be for a time the third-busiest port in Britain. Naturally, it attracted the attention of German bombers during World War II. Later on, in common with the rest of Britain's fishing industry, Hull's fishing fleet went into decline, but otherwise it recovered and continues to be a busy ferry and freighter port.

But as well as being busy with trade Hull's dockland is now a pleasant place to stroll, sit, and admire views, as are the pedestrianised streets, many of them winding alleyways, in the city center. Hull is justifiably proud of its Museum Quarter: a grouping of museums, a number of them free, exploring aspects of the life of Hull and the East Riding of Yorkshire. One is the house in which William Wilberforce, the anti-slavery campaigner, lived. (Finishing in 2007 the house has undergone a multi-million-pound refurbishment.) Another is an actual lightship. The Streetlife Transport Museum is the busiest and noisiest. All are fascinating, not least the huge aquarium in a spectacular landmark building, the Deep. They say that you can dine there, at the Two Rivers Restaurant, "with the sharks." We must conclude that things have changed since the poet Philip Larkin, never a man to pull his punches when he was feeling aggrieved, wrote to a friend that Hull was "a terrible dump."

facing page
The shopping center and Maritime Museum at Princess Dock.

below
The City Hall and Queen Victoria Memorial in downtown Hull.

Two very famous English poets had connections with Hull. Andrew Marvel was its MP for almost twenty years after 1659; he made his mark in the House of Commons by brawling with Thomas Clifford, an extremist with Catholic sympathies. Some of his best-loved poems, including *The Garden*, reflect his own love of Yorkshire. He writes that the experience of sitting in a favorite garden annihilates "…all that's made / To a green thought in a green shade." Philip Larkin, the master of the negative perception, as quoted elsewhere, was the university librarian in Hull for most of his working life. His dislike of the town is unsurprising, since he appeared to dislike most things, places, and people. His poems express this, but without themselves inducing negative feelings in the reader. They are so exact in their identification of what bores or frightens him that they seldom fail to give pleasure.

Holderness, a rich agricultural low plain, formed principally by erosion farther up the coast, lies east of Hull. It only attached itself to the mainland in the 1830s. Its straight flat roads and fields of oats and barley remind us of Holland. The area curves out into the sea for c. twenty miles. Its tip, Spurn Head, is a reserve for seals and migrating birds. At the very end the curve turns into a hooklike spit. On its inner side are the UK's only permanently manned lifeboat station and the base for pilots who guide ships into port. Both are there because of the dangerous and treacherous underwater sandbanks; equally, both will be moving soon because the spit, formed by eroded material, is being eroded in its turn.

MASHAM

BEER, BUTTER, CHEESE, AND DALES

MASHAM (PRONOUNCED AS IF IT HAD NO "H") IS PRETTILY ENDOWED WITH GREENERY, water, a druid's temple, charming streets and buildings. What are its other attractions? Walkers and beer lovers will have different answers. Masham has been since 1827 the site of Theakston's brewery. It has been claimed that there are more flavors in the Theakston's beers brewed in Masham than in an entire wine-growing region of France. This claim would take extensive and expensive research to substantiate. Visitors with strong heads and long purses may wish to do at least some groundwork. Theakston's offers a year-round range of classic ales and a program of seasonal ales brewed every other month. The classic range includes one celebrated item marked by its eccentric spelling—the "Old Peculier." This is deep, dark ruby in color, fruity, mellow, and warming on the nose, full-bodied and malty in taste. Brewed from the "traditional fuggle hop" it is notably strong. The seasonal ales include "Grouse Beater" and "Cooper's Butt."

The beer garden of this pub has spectacular views over the River Ure and Wensleydale.

The other brewery in Masham, The Black Sheep, resulted from a takeover of Theakston's by a larger firm. One of the family, faced with unappealing choices such as working for someone else or leaving Masham, opened the new, traditional brewery in 1992. Its beers now sell in pubs all over the Yorkshire Dales. Both Theakston's and Black Sheep breweries have visitors' centers.

The Dales National Park is a series of steep-sided valleys intersecting the Pennine Hills, which run north and south from Derbyshire to the Scottish border. This is a farming landscape but also provides recreation and delight for walkers. There are three major dales and several smaller ones. There is also an underworld of caverns, potholes, and passages, with rivers and waterfalls. Masham is well placed as a base for exploring the area, by car and on foot. The largest of the dales is Wensleydale, famous for its cheese and as the setting for James Herriott's books about veterinarians, known under the collective title *All Creatures Great and Small*. At Hawes (twenty-four miles), the highest market town in England, there are large sheep and cattle markets in the summer. Also at Hawes the Dales Countryside Museum illustrates the eighteenth- and nineteenth-century butter and cheese making techniques and equipment that made Wensleydale celebrated. Just north is Hardraw Force, England's tallest single-drop waterfall. You can walk behind the waterfall without getting wet. At the Aysgarth Falls, on the way back to Masham (nineteen miles), the river Ure hurls itself downward across a series of limestone platforms.

Swaledale is the most northerly of the dales. A good place to start exploring it is Richmond (nineteen miles). The ruined Norman castle above the town was built in the eleventh century to protect the valley of the river Swale. Richmond is now the regimental headquarters of the Green Howards, whose museum—in a converted medieval church in the marketplace—may be visited. Just off the marketplace is a Georgian theater about thirty years older than the one in Bury St Edmunds. The winding alleys in Richmond are attractive. Swaledale made its money from wool, and sheep still flock on its higher slopes whatever the weather. On the Green at Reeth, upriver from Richmond, is the Swaledale Folk Museum, which interests itself in lead mining, wool, and brass bands.

facing page
Visiting ringers are invited to try the bells of St Mary's, Masham.

146

Wharfdale, the southernmost of the large dales, has some lovely villages, such as Burnsall and Buckden. Around the village of Bolton Abbey and the ruins of Bolton Priory are twenty-eight miles of walks, some suitable for disabled people and children. Further up into the Pennines, from Malham you can take a more demanding walk that can last over four hours, depending on the time available. (At the end of it you can catch a bus back to Malham.) At its most extensive, this will take in Malham Tarn and Nature Reserve, spectacular cliff and gorge scenery, Malham Cove, and the gorge at Gordale Scar (subject of an immense painting by James Ward) and a naturally formed limestone pavement at Malham Lings.

RIPON

A HORN, A WEST FRONT, AND A CRYPT

IN RIPON MARKET SQUARE JUST BEFORE NINE EACH EVENING A DIFFERENT SMALL CROWD—say six or seven visitors—gathers. At nine exactly a man wearing a brown jacket with scarlet collar and cuffs and a piratical black hat appears, carrying a substantial length of horn from some very large animal. He plays a fanfare, exchanges a word or two with his audience, then goes off for a mug of ale. He is the Wakeman. This was a medieval office. The horn call signaled that he was now on duty and would watch wakefully through the night, ensuring the safety of the citizenry. If he failed to perform this duty adequately he would have to compensate anyone who had paid the yearly toll of two pence per household. There is a building in the square called the Wakeman's House, but of course he no longer lives there. The horn, along with the town's original charter, is supposed to have been given by Alfred the Great in 886. Be that as it may, the evening ritual gives you the feel of Ripon. It has a long history. It is a cathedral city, with a taste for ceremonial ways of doing things. And it is quite a small town. Not so small as Wells, but not much bigger.

Ripon's cathedral, however, is smaller. It has only been a cathedral since 1836, although for some of the previous 1,200 years the church on this site was a kind of sub-cathedral within the northern part of the enormous diocese of York. Nikolaus Pevsner thinks Ripon's Early English west front one of the noblest in England. Other writers dislike the nineteenth-century "purification" in which decorative tracery and mullions were removed, making it cold, featureless, or barren. It may be a pity that the spires have gone from the tops of the three towers. I am with Pevsner regarding the west front.

Within the cathedral there is a mixture of styles, thought by most writers to be uncomfortable. The great point of interest is the crypt, which is one of the earliest surviving pieces of Christian building in England. This may have been built by St Wilfrid, first abbot of the then abbey, in c. 670. Sadly, however, it has been filled up with display cases in which the cathedral's treasures can be put permanently and safely on show.

Around a corner on the northern side of the cathedral is the Prison and Police Museum, a sobering reminder of what a "House of Correction" was like in past ages. Fountains Abbey (see under HARROGATE) is 2 miles away.

The east front of Ripon Cathedral.

facing page
Ripon's Market Square, described by Daniel Defoe as the "most beautiful square that is to be seen in England".

One of two grand houses within easy reach of Ripon is Norton Conyers (three miles), a mid-fourteenth-century house with later additions, which has been the home of the Graham family since 1624. Its main rooms contain fine seventeenth- and eighteenth-century furniture; a table in the hall dates from the Middle Ages. Charlotte Brontë was a visitor in 1839 and heard the legend of a madwoman who had in the previous century been confined in the attics. When she wrote *Jane Eyre* eight years later the madwoman became the original of the mad Mrs Rochester, while Norton Conyers provided details for Mr Rochester's house, Thornfield Hall. The discovery in the house in November 2004 of a secret staircase, as clearly described in *Jane Eyre*, aroused worldwide interest. There are about two acres of gardens.

Newby Hall, the family home of Mr and Mrs Richard Compton, is an exceptional example of eighteenth century interior decoration. Built in the 1690s in the style of Sir Christopher Wren, it was enlarged and adapted by John Carr and subsequently, Robert Adam. The contents of the house, collected by a Compton ancestor on the Grand Tour, include the Gobelin's tapestries, classical statuary, and Chippendale furniture. There is also an unusual collection of chamber pots. Outside are twenty-five acres of glorious gardens, including the national collection ofdogwoods. Newby's famed double herbaceous borders form the main axis, off which are numerous formal, compartmented gardens: a rose garden, water garden, autumn garden, and tropical garden.

left
Fountains Abbey is now a magnificent ruin.

above
The Choir and East Window of Ripon Cathedral.

below
The Water Garden at Studley.

From Ripon it is easily possible to visit Harrogate and to investigate at least the eastern edge of the Yorkshire Dales. Nidderdale is the nearest and can be explored starting from the self-styled "Capital of Nidderdale," Pately Bridge, an attractive, colorfully floral market town. It also has the Nidderdale Museum, which traces the history and activities of the area during the past two centuries. Pately Bridge is an ideal center for walking, mountain biking, riding, fishing, pot-holing, and rock climbing. At the head of the dale is How Stean Gorge, a spectacular cleft in the limestone through which the stream tumbles. At Brimham Rocks there are what look like piles of large, irregular, stone discs and, a little west of the dale proper, in Stump Cross Caverns, you will find, underground, equally strange formations coupled with amazing colors.

SCARBOROUGH

HEALTH, FOOD, AND PIRATES

PEOPLE HAVE TAKEN REFUGE ON THIS HEADLAND—which rises c. 330 feet out of the sea and is approachable only along a narrow rock spur—for about 4,000 years. Until the restoration of the Stuart monarchy in 1600 it had, unsurprisingly, a somewhat martial history. The remains of a Roman signal station may be seen on the headland, alongside the gate, a chunk of the keep and other traces of a Norman castle (1158). The castle survived many sieges over almost 500 years, but in 1645 it was, like so many others in Royalist areas, captured—the defenders having been reduced to boiling their boots for food—then largely knocked down by Parliamentary forces. By then, in 1626, Scarborough's mineral water springs had been proclaimed to have medicinal qualities, curing more or less everything, including hypochondria. (They had been promoted since 1620 by a Mrs Elizabeth Farrow, who, so it is said, had decided that anything that tasted so disgusting must in some way be good for you.) Since then (the taste of the waters apart) much of Scarborough's work and local pride has been devoted to giving visitors a good time, especially after a doctor announced that sea bathing from the town's two beaches was especially healthy.

In 1779, during the American War of Independence, the American John Paul Jones captured a British two-decker (which had previously put the guns of his own ship out of action) off Scarborough, causing the British ambassador in Washington much irritation. A less well-documented tale of enterprise at sea tells us that Robin Hood went out with some fishermen from Scarborough, boarded a French vessel that attacked them, and seized a bag of gold, which he distributed amongst his shipmates.

Numerous literary luminaries have been associated with Scarborough. Anne Brontë, the quietest yet in some ways the most independent of the Brontë sisters (see under HAWORTH) died in Scarborough, a place she had been taken to during summer holidays by one of the families who employed her as a governess. Her first novel, *Agnes Grey*, is set there. Sacheverel and Edith Sitwell, along with Susan Hill, author of *The Woman in Black* (a dramatized version of which was first performed in Scarborough and has been running in London's Fortune Theatre since 1989) were all born here. So were the actor Charles Laughton, who played Henry VIII and Rembrandt in famous films and directed Robert Mitchum in *The Night of the Hunter*; Frederick Leighton, painter of historic genre canvases for the chastely cultivated Victorian collector; and the scientific pioneer George Cayley whose important discoveries in aerodynamics during the first half of the nineteenth century, were not taken seriously—but whose work was eventually recognized and put to use long after he died.

Scarborough attained unexpected international celebrity among gourmets when Giorgio Alessio, who opened his restaurant, La Lanterna ("an English temple of Italian cuisine" and "Yorkshire with an Italian accent") in the town over thirty years ago, published *White Truffle Yorkshire Pudding*, which, he wrote, was intended to show the Italian and Piemontese way of cooking, with Scarborough in the middle, "because I live here and can buy wonderful prime local products, which are sometimes taken for granted." The book has sold well in Italy and America and all over the world. The playwright Alan Ayckbourn discovered La Lanterna on his way home from a show and swore an oath to keep the place open even if it meant eating there every night. "What devotion!" he wrote in self mockery, "What sacrifice!"

facing page
The steeply jumbled buildings on the headland at Scarborough.

below
St Mary's originally had two towers at its west front.

From 1972 until 2008 Alan Ayckbourn was the artistic director of what is now the Stephen Joseph Theatre Company in Scarborough. A prolific dramatist, he produced his seventieth full length play in 2007. Most of the seventy are comedies of manners, exposing the eccentricities and follies of the English middle classes. Some border on tragedy. Most were originally performed in Scarborough; many have also run in London. He frequently experiments with dramatic form. An ingenious device he has used three times is a trilogy whose three parts tell the same general story from three different points of view. One of his more unlikely fans is the avant-garde French film director Alain Resnais, who has filmed three of Ayckbourn's plays.

WHITBY

DRACULA AND CAPTAIN COOK

IT WAS IN A BOOK BORROWED FROM THE WHITBY PUBLIC LIBRARY that Bram Stoker first saw the name he would eventually attach to the eponymous Transylvanian vampire in his best-known horror novel *Dracula* (1897). He set a large part of his story in Whitby, and has Mina Murray, one of the people whose diaries and letters form the narrative, describe the town in enthusiastic terms. "This is a lovely place. The little river, the Esk, runs through a deep valley, which broadens out as it comes near the harbour. A great viaduct runs across, with high piers, through which the view seems somehow further away than it really is… The houses of the old town… are all red-roofed, and seem piled up one over the other anyhow… Right over the town is the ruin of Whitby Abbey, which was sacked by the Danes…" Dracula arrives in the town having swum ashore after a shipwreck, in the guise of a wolf, and scampers up the 199 steps to a churchyard very like that of St Mary's, Whitby. Shocking and distressing events follow. Another, more respectable resident, Captain James Cook was a naval apprentice in Whitby and it was from here that he set sail in the *Endeavour* in 1768 on the voyage to the South Seas, where he observed the transit of Venus, mapped New Zealand, and took formal possession of part of Australia.

Much earlier, Whitby had played an important role in the establishment of the Christian Church in England and in the determination of its loyalties within Christianity at large. The Irish monks who had sent missions to England and Scotland and established monasteries, were at odds with the Roman mission to Canterbury over, among other things, the dating of Easter. At the Synod of Whitby (664) the Celts reluctantly accepted the desirability of being in agreement with southern English Christians and with Rome. Later in the same century, Caedmon, a cowherd at the monastery in the town, had a dream in which he was commanded to sing. He sang a hymn telling the story of Creation. Next day he told the abbess, who told him another Bible story and asked him to sing about that. He became a monk and spent the rest of his life composing English poetry on religious subjects. It is now thought that some of the works attributed to him were by later writers, but, as the earliest vernacular poet in English whose work survives, he was an important and influential figure in the development of Christian devotion in England. Another cleric and poet, Lewis Carroll, is said to have conceived part of *Through the Looking Glass* (1872) while walking on the beach west of Whitby. The Walrus and the Carpenter, engaged in a similar stroll, "…wept like anything to see / Such quantities of sand: / 'If only this were cleared away,'/ They said, 'it would be grand!'"

Whitby waterfront, with a replica of Captain Cook's ship the Endeavour.

facing page
The ruined hilltop abbey where Caedmon wrote his poems.

Whitby Harbor is the estuary of the river Esk and divides the town in two, with the Old Town on the left or western bank. Berthed vessels are close to everything the town has to offer. Like the town the harbor is a mix of old and new. The jetties are piled high with colorful framed fishing nets. Traditional fishing cobles, modern trawlers, leisure craft, and cargo vessels are all moored there. The house where James Cook lived as an apprentice, now the Captain Cook Memorial Museum, housing watercolors done on Cook's voyages, and period furniture, is on the harborside. All the requirements of a busy small port are available: repair workshops, coal bunkers, ice, a fish market, chandlers, and cargo handling.

High above the harbor are the ruins of the abbey, with, in the graveyard, a cross erected in memory of Caedmon in 1898. Nearby is St Mary's Church. Originally Norman, the building has later additions: twisted wood columns, box pews, and Victorian ear trumpets. Whitby is close to the North York Moors National Park (see under HELMSLEY) with its wonderful scenery and wildlife. You may choose to go on a guided tour of the Dracula Trail. The guide will do his best to frighten you. Otherwise you can walk the trail in daylight—then, perhaps read chapters six through eleven of the book, just before bedtime. Whitby Museum and Pannet Art Gallery have collections of art, photography, maps, and jet jewelry, traditionally made here.

Y O R K

ROMANS, MYSTERIES, AND "BRIDESHEAD"

THE ROMANS ARRIVED HERE DURING THE FIRST CENTURY. It was then called "Eborakon," a name indicating the presence of yew trees. They made it their military headquarters in north Britain and Latinized its name as "Eboracum." The emperor Hadrian conducted his campaigns and built his wall seventy-five miles further north of the city to keep the Scots out. A bishop of York attended the Council of Arles in 314. (Bishops and archbishops of York have retained the Roman name, signing themselves "Ebor." The present incumbent, since 2005, is a Ugandan, Dr John Sentamu.) The Romans withdrew in 407 and the Saxons who followed called York "Eoforwick." They hung on until 867, when the Danes took charge and called it "Jorvik." Two more centuries elapsed before, in 1066, shortly before being himself killed by the Normans at Hastings, King Harold killed his near namesake, Harald of Norway, at Stamford Bridge; the Danes left. "Jorvik" became York again and, with a population of 8,000, was the second-largest city in Britain.

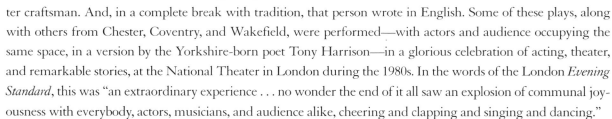

Clifford's Tower, site of a massacre of Jews in 1190.

facing page
The crowded, dynamic skyline of central York.

At some time between 1300 and 1500, the York Mystery Plays were written and performed. (The word "mystery" here means "trade secret" and the plays were written for and performed by members of trade guilds.) Who wrote them? We don't know. But whoever it was was a master craftsman. And, in a complete break with tradition, that person wrote in English. Some of these plays, along with others from Chester, Coventry, and Wakefield, were performed—with actors and audience occupying the same space, in a version by the Yorkshire-born poet Tony Harrison—in a glorious celebration of acting, theater, and remarkable stories, at the National Theater in London during the 1980s. In the words of the London *Evening Standard*, this was "an extraordinary experience . . . no wonder the end of it all saw an explosion of communal joyousness with everybody, actors, musicians, and audience alike, cheering and clapping and singing and dancing."

York's history is unusually well preserved in its present-day fabric. The city walls are virtually complete; the Shambles is a half-timbered medieval street; there are complete Georgian terraces. The Jorvik Viking Center reconstructs York's streets as they would have been in 975. The collections at the National Railway Museum include more than a hundred locomotives and nearly 200 other items of rolling stock. Permanent displays include "Palaces on Wheels": royal saloons, bedrooms, dining rooms, and day saloons dating back to the nineteenth century. Other items include the *Mallard*, the world's fastest steam locomotive, a replica of the first railway engine, Robert Stephenson's *Rocket* and, bizarrely, a lock of Stephenson's hair.

The discussion of the Cathedral Church of St Peter (York Minster) in Nikolaus Pevsner's *The Cathedrals of England* occupies fifty pages. The Minster is the largest Gothic Church north of the Alps and has the largest collection of stained glass in the UK. The ideal way to explore it is to begin by walking around the city walls, which will give the best views of it from outside and a clear indication of its size and shape. Then move in closer and walk around the outside. The west front is "of an elaboration hardly paralleled English Gothic." Then go inside. The word "stunning" is badly overused by writers who like something, but much of the interior of York Minster is definitely a candidate for that description.

Only the keep of York Castle remains as, in effect, a memorial to one of the worst acts of violence in English history. In 1190, Richard "the Lion Heart" succeeded to the throne, before leaving to join the ridiculous Third Crusade, which captured Constantinople rather than Jerusalem. Leading Jews had attempted to attend his coronation, causing great offence to those Englishmen who hated them and envied their financial status. Violence erupted all over East Anglia and moved north to York. Jewish houses were torched; their occupants took refuge in this tower. Screaming mobs gathered outside; an Augustinian monk gave them his blessing. 150 Jews committed suicide. 52 of York's Christian citizens were punished.

Castle Howard, featured in the television version of Evelyn Waugh's *Brideshead Revisited*, is six miles northeast of York (you can take a bus). This is another case of a grand design by Sir John Vanburgh put into execution by Nicholas Hawksmoor. The Howard family has lived there since 1712. The house itself and its furnishings and decoration are sumptuous and delightful. Allow enough time to do them all justice. (There are almost 200 listed buildings and monuments on the 1,000-acre estate.) Perhaps Castle Howard is a little too magnificent to stand in for Brideshead—but since Evelyn Waugh was consciously writing a panegyric for a way of life he thought, partly mistakenly, had gone for ever and, as he later admitted, "piled it on rather, with passionate sincerity," an element of adoring exaggeration is inherent in the book and therefore appropriate also in the adaptation.

above
Monkbar, York's tallest medieval gate.

right
Duncombe Place, St Wilfrid's Catholic Church and York Minster.

far right
A magnificent house and garden: Castle Howard.

BAMBURGH

A CASTLE, A RESCUE, AND A HOLY PLACE

THE NORTH SEA COAST NEAR BAMBURGH IS PICTURESQUE AND IDYLLIC. The beaches stretch for miles. In Bamburgh itself, standing spectacularly some 260 feet above the sea, is a red sandstone castle, once the seat of the kingdom of Northumbria. This rocky eminence has been occupied since the prehistoric period. At the end of the Middle Ages the castle fell into obscurity until it was bought in 1894 by an arms dealer named, appro-

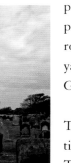

In St Aidan's Churchyard is a memorial to Grace Darling which is visible out to sea.

facing page
Bamburgh's restored Norman castle.

priately enough, Armstrong. His family still lives there. There are collections of china, porcelain, furniture, paintings, arms, and armor. The public is able to visit the museum room, grand king's hall, cross hall, the armory, and the Victorian scullery. In the church-yard of the magnificent Norman church by the village green is the grave of local heroine Grace Darling.

A mile or so off the coast the Farne Islands just about keep their heads above water. There are between fifteen and twenty-eight of these low islets, depending on the state of the tide. Boat trips to the islands can be taken from Seahouse, a little way south of Bamburgh. They are a sea-bird sanctuary and there is a colony of gray seals. In 1999, 182 species of birds were recorded. Twenty-two of them breed there; the rest are migratory. In 2005 there were 55,674 pairs of puffin, 23,458 pairs of guillemot, and so on down to five nests of pied wagtail.

You may also take a cruise to Lindisfarne, on Holy Island a few miles north. Or, at low tide you can walk across or take a taxi. The ruins of a Benedictine priory are there but the island is now principally occu-pied by another restored castle. It was restored by Sir Edwin Lutyens, architect of New Delhi, and the walled garden was designed by the celebrated Gertrude Jekyll, with whom he often collaborated. The island is known as the "cradle of Christianity." It was from here that St Aidan and St Cuthbert spread the Christian message in the seventh century. The illustrated *Lindisfarne Gospels* is now in the British Library. This legacy of an artist monk in the early eighth century is a precious testament to the tenacity of Christ-ian belief during one of the most turbulent periods of British history. Medieval manuscripts were usually the work of a number of people: some wrote the text; others added pictures and decoration. This book, however, is the work of one remarkably gifted man who, so a note added later tells us, was Eadfrith, bishop of Lindis-farne 698-721. It is one of the earliest survivals of the Gospel texts in any form of English. The monks were forced to flee the island by repeated Viking raids in 875 and took the Gospels with them, saving the book from almost certain destruction.

On September 7, 1838 nobody except the few inhabitants of the Farne Islands had heard of Grace Darling, the lighthouse keeper's twenty-two year-old daughter. Days later her name was known over much of the world. In a terrible storm the steamer *Forfarshire* ran aground on an island more than a mile from the lighthouse. Grace and her father rowed through mountainous seas at great risk to themselves and rescued the survivors. Grace was feted internationally. Sadly, she died young in 1842. A museum to commemorate her life was established in Bamburgh in 1938, across the green from the Norman church. The museum houses the rescue boat, Grace's dresses, letters, and family belongings and much commemorative ware.

160

The Laidley Worm of Spindleston-Heugh is a ballad first published in 1778. It supposedly dated from 1272, but it is a reasonable suspicion that the Reverend Robert Lambert, who "discovered" it, actually wrote it himself, drawing on a considerable knowledge of local folklore. It tells a wicked-stepmother story, set in Bamburgh Castle. A new queen, jealous of her stepdaughter's beauty, turns her into a loathsome worm with venomous breath. The only person who can help her is her brother who, naturally, is far away. When he returns he gives the worm "kisses three." She becomes a beautiful woman once more—but the queen is turned into a toad and lurks under rocks spitting venom at beautiful young women.

BERWICK
UPON–TWEED
FRONTIER RIVER TOWN, FOUR BRIDGES

BERWICK-UPON-TWEED, THE NORTHERNMOST TOWN IN ENGLAND, is on the northern side of the river Tweed, which until almost that point marks the border between England and Scotland. From the twelfth to the fifteenth century the two countries contested possession of Berwick and its castle (which had been built by the English king, Edward I, c. 1300). Control changed hands thirteen times during that turbulent period. King Henry VI ceded the town to the Scots in 1461 in return for their help during the Wars of the Roses, but in 1482 Edward IV took it back again. The Scots made no further claim. From 1551 to 1746 it was regarded as a neutral town. After the Act of Union (1707) the matter became relatively unimportant. An anomaly remains: Berwick is a town in England, while Berwickshire is a district in the Scottish Borders.

Little is left of Edward's castle. A curtain wall runs down the hill from the railway station to the river; the station's down platform is on the site of the castle's great hall. The Elizabethan town walls, however, remain—high and wide, one and a half miles long, they circle the town. They are faced with carefully cut stone and there are five very large arrowhead bastions. But when they were built (1558-69) the days of defensive walls were over: these walls have never been attacked. Berwick has therefore inherited a spacious promenade. It has also inherited three bridges: two marvels of different kinds, one apparently misconceived. Nearest the sea is the Old Bridge, built on the orders of King James I of England (King James VI of Scotland) when he crossed a rickety wooden one on his way south to inherit the English crown in 1603. Its red stone and gentle, low arches make it supremely elegant. Furthest inland is Robert Stephenson's railway viaduct, built more than two centuries later. Its twenty-eight tall arches carry railway tracks 126 feet above the water. In between is an unloved concrete bridge from 1928, carrying the main road north. It seems, however, to have been built in the wrong place and causes frequent traffic jams.

Holy Trinity Church, unusually, was built during Oliver Cromwell's Parliamentarian Commonwealth. It combines Gothic and Renaissance features. Lacking spire or tower, its exterior looks unexpectedly unecclesiastical; its interior has Tuscan columns and Venetian windows. The nearby Barracks (1717-21, built, like much else in Berwick, with stone from the castle) is confident and well-proportioned. It houses the King's Own Scottish Borderers' Regimental Museum, an art gallery, and By Beat of Drum, illustrating the history of British infantrymen. The town hall and much of the domestic architecture in the town also repay inspection.

Five miles west of Berwick, on the banks of the river Tweed, is Paxton House, one of the finest Palladian country houses in Britain. It also has a superb, well-documented collection of Chippendale furniture, and richly styled rosewood suites supplied in 1813-14 by William Trotter for the new library and picture gallery—some of the finest Regency period Scottish furniture in existence. The picture gallery is a magnificent and spectacular space, which exhibits over seventy paintings from the National Galleries of Scotland, focusing on British art from 1760 to 1840, the heyday of Paxton House itself. There are masterpieces by Raeburn, Wilkie, and Lawrence amongst many of local interest such as Sam Bough's *Berwick upon Tweed* and the Reverend John Thomson's *Fast Castle*.

Close to Paxton House is a surprisingly little-known structure. The Union Suspension Bridge (1820) is the oldest surviving carriage suspension bridge in Britain still open to vehicular traffic. Until completion of Thomas Telford's Menai Bridge linking Anglesey to the Welsh mainland (1826), the Union Bridge was also the UK's only suspension bridge designed to carry vehicles. It was built by Captain (later Sir) Samuel Brown R.N. (1776-1852), a chain manufacturer, and John Rennie (1761-1821), a consultant engineer. The delicate-looking bridge apart, this is a beautiful and peaceful spot: curving river, trees, fields, grazing sheep, a solitary house. Here, as A.J. Youngman observes, we find ancient peace blending with pioneering accomplishment.

facing page
The Old Bridge over the River Tweed.

below
St Andrew's is one of only eight Church of Scotland congregations in England.

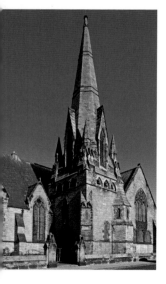

D U R H A M

NORMANS, FARMERS, MINERS, QUAKERS

AT DURHAM A HIGH ROCKY HILL, ROUGHLY OBLONG IN SHAPE, is surrounded on three sides by a tight loop of the river Wear. On this "island" as it was once called (the bridges at the landward end are only c. 300 yards apart), stands an ensemble of buildings—cathedral, castle, and monastery—within a townscape that, Pevsner's *Cathedrals of England* suggests, "is almost to the same degree the visual foil to the monuments that it must have been two and five hundred years ago." Together, they make "one of the great experiences of Europe" for the eyes and minds of those who appreciate and understand architecture. The city was built here in 995, when the see of Lindisfarne was transferred to Durham to escape Danish attacks (see under BAMBURGH). The city would be the last resting place of the venerable St Cuthbert, who was soon joined by the venerable Bede, the first English historian. The central ensemble was rather unusual—but so was the politicoreligious situation in Durham. Durham was a County Palatine, which meant that the earl had royal privileges within his own county. Durham had its own parliament, sending no representatives to London. (This changed only in 1678.) The men of the county did military service for the earl, not the king. Furthermore, the earl was, like a German prince of the Church, also the bishop. And the religious community at Durham had always consisted of monks under a bishop. Thus, in Durham it was natural to place cathedral, castle, and monastery alongside each other.

The Castle is one of Durham's central ensemble of medieval buildings.

facing page
The Pulpit and Choir in Durham Cathedral.

As at York, it is best to see the cathedral from various viewpoints around the city before going into it. (Pevsner lists a number of possibilities.) I will mention only some interesting oddities inside. The chevrons and lozenges decorating pillars in the nave are uncommon further south but are found here and in Scotland in Norman buildings. The pillars and arches in the Galilee Chapel seem strikingly reminiscent of the Cordoba Mosque, although Pevsner finds their origins elsewhere. But there is agreement that the chapel is in deliberate contrast with the rest of the building. Whereas the cathedral is an expression of Norman strength, the chapel is an exercise in delicacy and lightness. But, of all of the sights inside and ouside, in the city, it is the magnificent, elevated townscape, as seen from a suitably all-encompassing vantage point, that leaves the greatest impression. One visiting American spoke for many of us, when Nathaniel Hawthorne visited Durham once and came upon a sudden vista of the cathedral: "I paused upon the bridge, and admired and wondered at the beauty and glory of this scene . . . it was grand, venerable, and sweet, all at once; I never saw so lovely and magnificent a scene, nor, being content with this, do I care to see a better."

At Beamish Open Air Museum (c. twelve miles), the selling point is that if you step onto one of their trams you will be transported into the past. You need not assume, however, that what is offered is an exercise in soft-focus nostalgia. What is there is 300 acres of countryside and establishments from the nineteenth and early twentieth centuries functioning much as they would have done when they were part of the everyday world. At Pockerly Manor, we see an 1820s house, lit by candlelight, from which a farmer—not an aristocrat—ran the farm with the aid of his family and employees. Elsewhere are a near-the-surface coal mine and the associated miners' village, a 1913 railway station, and numerous other period exhibits.

Barnard Castle (twenty-four miles) is a characterful town with old shopfronts, a cobbled market, and a ruined castle. Nearby is a museum, purpose-built in the style of a French chateau by a rich man and his imaginatively extravagant wife. The art collection offers a comprehensive survey of European painting from the fifteenth to the nineteenth centuries, which is particularly strong on Italy and Spain. Clocks, porcelain, furniture, musical instruments, toys, and tapestries are also there in profusion. Middleton-in-Teesdale, an eighteenth-century lead-mining village, is eight miles away. Nowadays it is an attractive market town on the Pennine Way, with a rich network of public footpaths through magnificent scenery.

AMBLESIDE

LAKES, FELLS, AND WRITERS

AMBLESIDE, A MAINLY VICTORIAN MARKET TOWN AT THE NORTHERN END of Lake Windermere, is a good base from which to explore the Lake District. It suits people with literary interests who don't want too much strenuous walking. It also has good shops selling outdoor clothing, crafts, and specialist foods. If you were to read that featureless modern buildings have damaged Ambleside's picturesque beauty you might assume that this was a recent opinion. In fact the complainant was the poet Wordsworth, writing in 1810. Nevertheless he concluded that the town retained "a store of picturesque materials." Wordsworth's assessment stands today. Seen from a slight distance with the church spire rising above autumnal trees, Ambleside gladdens the spirits. (It is probably best to come here in spring or autumn when the colors are striking and the visitors are fewer.)

In a quirky way, too, it has a variety of attractions, some unexpected. (And, it must be said, some of Wordsworth's "modern" buildings are now themselves "picturesque," as happens often with age.) The market garden has a miniature replica of London's Crystal Palace. On a tiny bridge over Stock Beck, there is a small two-story house, built, alleged-

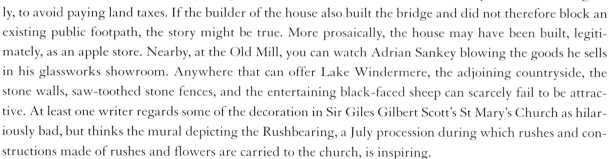

above and facing page
Characteristic Lake District buildings in Ambleside.

ly, to avoid paying land taxes. If the builder of the house also built the bridge and did not therefore block an existing public footpath, the story might be true. More prosaically, the house may have been built, legitimately, as an apple store. Nearby, at the Old Mill, you can watch Adrian Sankey blowing the goods he sells in his glassworks showroom. Anywhere that can offer Lake Windermere, the adjoining countryside, the stone walls, saw-toothed stone fences, and the entertaining black-faced sheep can scarcely fail to be attractive. At least one writer regards some of the decoration in Sir Giles Gilbert Scott's St Mary's Church as hilariously bad, but thinks the mural depicting the Rushbearing, a July procession during which rushes and constructions made of rushes and flowers are carried to the church, is inspiring.

Northwest of Ambleside are two delectable small lakes, Rydal Water and Grasmere. Avoid the main road and use the minor one, or walk—one possible route is described on the town's Website as "soft"—ideal for those "recuperating from heart attacks, violent hangovers, or loss of a leg." Another local walk, along Tarn Path, takes us from Rydal Mount, overlooking Rydal Water, where Worsdworth spent his last thirty-seven affluent years as distributor of stamps, to Dove Cottage, in Grasmere, where he spent the previous seven years, in far more restricted conditions and writing better poetry.

A walk to Troutbeck and back makes a pleasant and virtuous day's outing. From Ambleside there is a gentle ascent, becoming stiffer to Wansfell Pike, giving panoramic views over Windermere and the fells. Thereafter you descend by grassy moorland to Nanny Lane and Troutbeck. Three members of the Arts and Crafts Movement— Burne-Jones, William Morris, and Madox-Brown—made Jesus Church's east window. Townend, the home of the Browne family, yeomen farmers, for over four centuries until 1950, is a wonderful example of Lakeland domestic architecture—and the village is full of strong local building. Return along Robin Lane to High Skeighyll, then alongside Jenkyn's Crag, with its lovely view of Windermere, and down to Ambleside.

Numerous writers other than Wordsworth have lived in or near Ambleside: Mrs Hemans, ("The boy stood on the burning deck / Whence all but he had fled…"); Harriet Martineau, writer on politics, economics, and travel; Beatrix Potter at Near Sawrey, west of Lake Windermere (the background for six of her tales). Matthew Arnold, poet and critic, spent his last years there. The Armitt Collection, in a single room above the library, a remarkable treasure chest of books and papers relating to the area, was established with the support of those already mentioned, John Ruskin and others. The German Dadaist poet and painter Kurt Schwitters took refuge from the Nazis here in 1942.

CARLISLE

A BORDER AND A WALL

CARLISLE CASTLE IS A LARGE WALLED ENCLOSURE FRONTED BY WELL-KEPT LAWNS. The enclosure is five-sided but the keep and gateway are, vertically and horizontally, defiantly square. This is a no-nonsense, "Don't imagine you can come in here" structure, a medieval fortress that has watched over its city for nine centuries. You can explore fascinating ancient chambers, stairways, and dungeons and find the legendary "licking stones" where parched Jacobite prisoners found enough moisture to keep themselves alive until they were executed on Gallows Hill.

Nearby stands what is left of Carlisle Cathedral. As Batsford and Fry remark, "only its head and shoulders survive." There is perhaps a kind of poetic justice in this. In the twelfth century, it seems, Hadrian's Wall was used as a quarry from which to build this nave; during the seventeenth, three-quarters of it was knocked down, probably by Parliamentarians to build additional defensive walls. Parts of two bays remain and the west front is "a patch." We have, however, the transept and choir, a Norman structure transformed during the fourteenth century. The choir stalls are a forest of Gothic pinnacles; the glorious East Window has four lights on either side forming pointed panels, with the central ninth light expanding like a bud about to open.

This figure decorates the ends of beams supporting the Guildhall Museum.

facing page
The starry vault of England's smallest cathedral.

Carlisle and the Scots have obviously not always been friends. Today, however, the city is the main shopping, commercial, and industrial center for the northern half of Cumbria and parts of southern Scotland. Because of its strategic position, Carlisle became in the nineteenth century an important railway city, with seven companies sharing use of the platforms and extensive goods yards of Carlisle Citadel Station. The station was built in a Tudor Gothic style to harmonize with the crenellated round towers of the Citadel, the southern entrance to the city. The station is a splendidly over-the-top building in several senses. It is the northern terminus of the rather special, extremely picturesque Settle to Carlisle Railway. This runs seventy miles through the Eden Valley and the Pennines. Seventeen ravines are spanned by viaducts and there are fourteen tunnels. You may be able to take a train drawn by a steam locomotive.

The emperor Hadrian built 173 miles of wall across the north of England in the second century to keep Picts and other Caledonians out of Roman Britain. Some of it runs through the northern suburbs of Carlisle, which was established as a Roman settlement to help administer and maintain it. It had sixteen fortresses, and a fortified gateway every mile. Much of it no longer stands but the parts that remain are well looked after and the countryside makes a wonderful backdrop. It is possible to walk the whole way along paths beside the wall or on its original line. Or, of course, you can pay a short visit for a morning or an afternoon. The wall was declared a UNESCO World Heritage Site in 1987.

In Tullie House, a seventeenth-century private house set in gardens behind an imposing modern entrance, you can travel in time through Carlisle's Roman period, grind corn with the Celts, endure the Civil War, and be terrified by marauding family gangs who made many a Border wife a widow. The wildlife dome takes you through a day in eight minutes. You can also see many Pre-Raphaelite paintings and drawings.

Rose Castle, the palace of the bishops of Carlisle, is six miles south. It is not usually open to the public but a nearby public footpath allows enough of a view for you to ponder the ways in which a three-towered fortress made up of remnants from different ages has been transformed into a Victorian country house. Lanercost Priory, founded about 1166, is ten miles northeast. At the dissolution, some of it was converted into Dacre Hall. The rest fell into disrepair but c. 1740 it was decided to restore the nave for use as a parish church. Later, stained-glass windows by Sir Edward Burne-Jones were added. The remaining ruins are well kept and the setting very attractive. Birdoswald Roman fort is nearby.

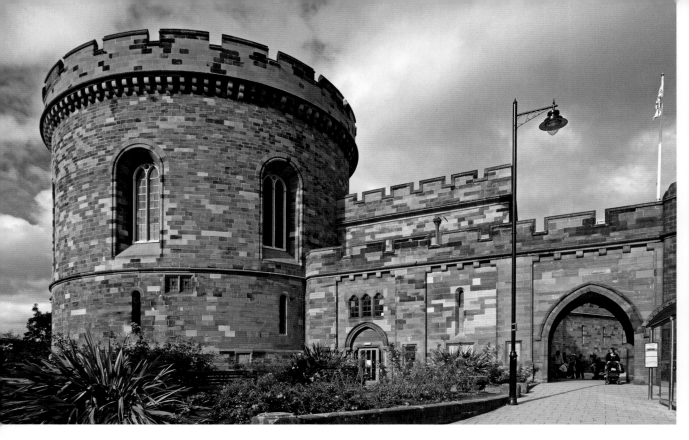

The Carlisle poet Robert Anderson (1770-1833), wrote poems in the Cumberland dialect evoking scenes from ordinary local life, such as a young woman waiting (after her parents have gone to sleep) for her lover to arrive. He also dealt with sports: horse racing, wrestling, quoits, football, running, jumping, throwing, and hunting of otters, badgers, and hares. He published his *Poetical Works* with autobiography in 1820. His grave is in the churchyard of Carlisle Cathedral and there is a marble monument to him inside the building. Because the Cumberland dialect is confined to relatively few people he is virtually unknown outside his native county despite efforts to bring his work before a wider public. Four lines from *The Impatient Lassie* will give you the flavor: "Now, key for seeghs and suggar words,/ Wi' kisses nit a few —/O but this warl's a paradise,/When lovers they pruive true!"

far above
The Citadel is the southern entrance to Carlisle.

above
Carlisle Castle, with its outer gatehouse (c. 1167), known as De Ireby's Tower.

right
The remains of Hadrian's Wall curve across the undulating spaces of northern England.

KENDAL

FELLS, LAKES, AND CHURCHES

IN 1793 A TRAVELER DESCRIBED KENDAL AS A "REMARKABLY NEAT and well-built marketing and manufacturing town… in a pleasant and healthy situation." Another visitor, 200 years later, thinks it must be among the best of places to live, instancing houses with gardens close to the center, good coffee, great bookshops, a lively arts center (The Brewery) and, perhaps above all, striking views in every direction. A Flemish weaver, John Renne, settled here in 1331 and its early prosperity came from the wool trade; the town's motto translates as "cloth is my bread." It was, indeed, bread-and-butter-quality, workaday stuff, fit only for the "three misbegotten knaves in Kendal green" whom Shakespeare's Falstaff alleged had mugged him.

The Stricklandgate
Shopping Centre.

facing page
Kendal's Victorian
Town Hall and
Assembly Rooms.

Kendal marked the end of easygoing travel on the way north. If indeed it is the "southern gateway to the Lake District" it opens onto difficult terrain. However, 350 packhorses weekly brought the wares of clothmakers in the surrounding fells to be sold there. High volume counterbalanced low margins. Like the wool churches of East Anglia and the Cotswolds, Kendal's parish church is impressively large. Two aisles on either side of the nave and thirty-two columns break up the 140-by-103-foot interior. As in the Galilee Chapel in Durham Cathedral (although stylistically very different), the changing perspectives are reminiscent of Córdoba. Restoration during the nineteenth century stripped color from both interior and exterior walls, which had been exuberantly decorated for the previous 200 years. A pity, perhaps. A hat used to hang behind the door, said to belong to a cavalier who burst into Sunday morning service with violent intentions toward a Parliamentarian magistrate. Sir Walter Scott made use of the incident in his narrative poem *Rokeby* (1813), though this can hardly be why the hat disappeared some sixty years later.

Abbot Hall (1759), next door, is one of several museums that are counted, at least locally, among England's best. The ground floor houses furniture, and pictures by Turner and George Romney. Romney was emotionally highly wrought (he had enjoyed, if that is the word, an obsessive relationship with the woman who became Lady Emma Hamilton, Admiral Nelson's mistress), and, as pictures shown here suggest, had

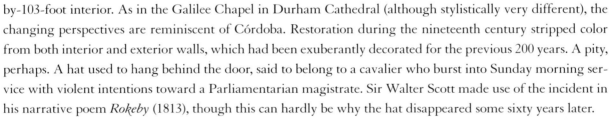

Kendal Mint Cake, made by three small factories in the town, is a bar of concentrated sugar and peppermint, offering climbers and walkers an easily absorbed energy booster. (New York's customs authorities once banned it, on the grounds that products labeled "cake" should have flour in them. A whole shipment was dumped in the Atlantic.) The mixture, as was accidentally discovered, turns cloudy when stirred long enough. Once set, it is cut into bars. Thereafter it will not melt, nor be affected in any other way by adverse conditions. Polar explorers use it— and it reached a high point, so to speak, when Hillary and Tenzing carried it to the summit of Everest in 1953.

tired of the blandness of the society portraits he painted in London. He was something of a loner as far as the art world was concerned, preferring to socialize with literary people. His plans to paint large literary and historical works seldom advanced beyond sepia drawings—although he did contribute to John Boydell's nine-volume illustrated Shakespeare. The pictures we see in Kendal are there because, ill and depressed, he lived in Kendal (where he had learned portrait painting as a young man) from 1799 until his death in 1802. Across the courtyard in the old stable block is the rewarding Museum of Lakeland Life.

Alfred Wainwright (1907-91), who tirelessly charted the fells in seven celebrated books reproduced from his own meticulously lettered and drawn manuscripts, lived in Kendal, where he became borough treasurer in 1949. His alcoholic father blighted his childhood in Blackburn, Lancashire. His life was transformed in one respect when he discovered the Lake District—but domestically this made little difference. His first marriage was unhappy—he hardly spoke to his wife—and he was not a good father. His biographer, Hunter Davies, is of the opinion that had he been happy he would have walked less and written nothing. Stories about how he avoided or refused contact with his admirers are legion.

KESWICK

INSPIRATIONAL SCENERY, HEAVY RAIN

KESWICK IS AT THE NORTHERN END OF DERWENT WATER. The heights of Skiddaw and Blencathra loom above it. A visiting organist and composer from Newcastle, Mr Arnison, described Derwent Water and Skiddaw as "Beauty lying in the lap of Horror!" The poets and brothers-in-law Coleridge and Southey lived with their families in Greta Hall nearby. Coleridge was initially thrilled, writing to a friend (clearly a man with whom he shared some of his pleasures, "I would that I could wrap up the view from my house in a pill of opium and send it to you!" Later he wished that "it had but a more genial climate!" Other writers inspired by the place include Ruskin (whose earliest memory was the view "through the hollows in the mossy roots, over the crag into the dark lake"), Beatrix Potter (see "Owl Island" in *The Tale of Squirrel Nutkin*), Keats ("rich and magnificent... sublime and graceful") and, of course, Wordsworth ("The woods, and distant Skiddaw's lofty height, / Were bronzed with deepest radiance"). It was Derwent Water that prompted a local vicar, Canon Rawnsley, to found the National Trust in 1895. The essayist Hazlitt was less high-minded. When a local lass to whom he made improper, public, and peremptory advances rejected his suggestions, he lifted her skirts and smacked her bottom. Keswick's outraged citizenry ran him out of town. Coleridge, his host, was much embarrassed.

The Moot Hall was once a prison.

facing page
Skiddaw looms over Keswick and Derwent Water.

In the nineteenth century a German company mined metallic ores. Managers and skilled workers brought over from Germany attracted local disapproval, partly because they drank a great deal, partly because they built a bath house and used it frequently. There was also a flourishing pencil industry, which continues, much reduced, to this day. Formerly, smuggling of graphite from Borrowdale to the pencil factories also prospered. There is the Pencil Museum, where you can see "escapers' pencils," supplied to RAF pilots flying over Germany, with tiny compasses and maps hidden under the eraser: a poetically just response, perhaps, to the habits of German mine managers. Keswick is now, unfortunately, dependent upon visitors, notably earnest Evangelical Christians attending conventions and conferences. Accommodating the crowds has, in various ways (notably the large car park) made it less beautiful than it was. But the visitors (earnest evangelicals apart) have not come for the town so much as its surroundings. Let us give thanks that the astonishingly changing light and the views remain, undiminished in scope and splendor. And, just to mention a tiny detail, the low humped bridges over local streams (themselves gushing merrily) are a delight. As for the weather, one optimistic writer on the lakes suggests that although "it does rain quite often... it doesn't do so for long."

You can hire various sorts of boat to explore Derwent Water, and may land on most of the islands. St Herbert's Island is recommended for picnics. A circular building of which some stones remain may have been the cell Herbert built for himself; the stones are sometimes used in barbecue pits. St Herbert was a friend of St Cuthbert, monk and bishop of Lindisfarne, who may have visited the island. Cuthbert prophesied that he and Herbert would die on the same day, which they duly did, on March 20, 687. Derwent Island has been known by other names, including that of Pocklington, a banker who decorated it with a villa, a fort, and a circle of monoliths. Wordsworth derided them as "puerilities."

Borrowdale, the valley whence came the "lead" for the pencils, is at the southern end of Derwent Water. At its highest point is Sty Head Tarn, the wettest place in England (average annual rainfall 172 inches). The wettest *inhabited* place, Seathwaite, is lower down. Over the exceedingly steep Honister Pass at Gatesgarth, take in the view over Buttermere, and of the great ridge of High Stile and Red Pike. Further on is Crummock Water, with the bulk of Brackenthwaite Fell and Grasmoor towering above it. Much smaller Loweswater lies amid farms and woodland. As the National Trust, which owns all three, and much else hereabouts, observes, "In only eight miles harsh wilderness has become pastoral beauty."

LANCASTER

FOUR DYNASTIES

LANCASTER CASTLE STANDS ON A MOUND ABOVE THE RIVER LUNE. Its low, square, crenelated towers and air of stubborn determination remind us that the three kings between 1399 and 1461 (Henrys IV-VI) were Lancastrians; and that the so-called Wars of the Roses, which followed, used to be understood as a dynastic contest between Lancastrians (red rose) and Yorkists (white rose). In its final years it certainly was that, but its earlier phases—plots, rebellions, and battles—were a chaotic argument about the nature and sources of royal power. When Henry VII seized the throne in 1485 he determined to reinforce his claim by presenting himself as a Lancastrian who had united warring parties by marrying Elizabeth of York. There was some truth in this, of course, but the presentation had more to do with neat, happy endings than with historical reality. Henry's tidied-up views lie behind the history plays of William Shakespeare—but he was too much of a reporter to suggest that the early phases of the conflict were other than arbitrary and opportunist.

The Lancastrians were descended from one of the most contradictory characters in English history, John of Gaunt, duke of Lancaster. John's life, as Norman F. Cantor argues, embodies the politics of his age. He was not able to be a shining, romantic great leader, like Alexander the Great; he was constrained by circumstances and by the need to attract and keep the support of others. "He was a hero, but a flawed and unfortunate one. He was more the representative of his world than its saviour." He aroused hostility in many different quarters. Shakespeare captures the complex problems of the period (while presenting Gaunt as far less self-interested than he actually was) in the celebrated deathbed speech in *Richard II*, in which Gaunt combines eloquent patriotism with disquiet and foreboding: "This royal throne of kings, this sceptred isle…This other Eden, demi-paradise…this earth, this realm, this England" is "now bound in with shame / With inky blots and rotten parchment bonds. / That England that was wont to conquer others / Hath made a shameful conquest of itself."

The castle in Lancaster is commonly called "John of Gaunt's Castle." It has dominated Lancaster for 1,000 years and is one of the best-preserved in the country. In 1612 ten women from the Forest of Pendle, accused of witchcraft, a number of murders, and an attempt to blow up the castle, were tried here. The charges and confessions are still argued about. The Grand Jury Room is improbably beautifully furnished and paneled by Gillows. Don't miss the remarkable choir stalls in St Mary's Church, and visit the market to see, if not taste, Lancashire's traditional working-class diet— chip butty (sandwich) with tomato or brown sauce, and pig's trotters.

facing page
A statue of John of Gaunt on the castle gateway.

below
The Storey Institute (1891) houses an art gallery.

In *HMS Pinafore* (1878) the captain's daughter, Josephine, contemplating marriage with an ordinary seaman, sings about things she will have to sacrifice, including "Rich Oriental rugs, luxurious sofa pillows / And everything that isn't old, from Gillows." Gillows began trading in Lancaster c. 1730, taking advantage of the slave trade, in that ships returning to Lancaster from the West Indies brought supplies of mahogany from Jamaica, Cuba, and Honduras. In c. 1800 Gillow's invented the extending table. Later it specialized in outfitting luxury yachts and liners. It merged with Warings of Liverpool in 1903 and disappeared inside a take-over after 1945. Its Lancaster showroom is now a nightclub.

James Williamson
and his son
produced linoleum
and oilcloth in vast
quantities for export
all over the world,
dominating the
market for almost a
century. His son,
James Williamson
the Younger, later
Lord Ashton, ran the
company single-
handed until 1930
and spent much of
his very large wealth
on buildings in
Lancaster, including
the huge town hall
and, high on a hill,
with views of the
town, Morecambe
Bay, and the
Lakeland hills, the
Ashton Memorial,
built in honor of his
late wife. The
stonework of this
domed baroque folly
may appear pale
yellow, pure white,
or deep orange at
different times of
day. It is used as a
concert hall.

The seaside resort of Morecambe, three miles northwest of Lancaster, has a five-mile promenade along the beach at the southern end of the broad sweep of Morecambe Bay. There you may take the sea air while enjoying splendid views of the mountains of the Lake District. The bay itself is treacherous. The vast flat sands visible at low tide hide areas of quicksand that can trap you like setting concrete, while the tides sweep in faster than most people can run. There have been many fatal accidents to walkers and cockle pickers, most recently in 2004 when twenty-one Chinese, employed by an exploitative entrepreneur, were drowned.

The local comedian who took his stage name from the town, Eric Morecambe, is commemorated by a statue on the waterfront, which captures his posture in the jig that he and his straight man, Ernie Wise, danced as they made their exit singing the song "Bring Me Sunshine."

above
An extravagant memorial to Lady Ashton.

below
Lancaster City Museum occupies the former town hall.

right
The Benedictine Priory, now the Parish Church of St Mary.

PENRITH

RUSTLERS AND INCENDIARY SCOTS

IN ST ANDREW'S CHURCHYARD, PENRITH, THERE IS AN ENSEMBLE OF LARGE STONES. These, naturally, have for hundreds of years stimulated those with a taste for sensational legend. Two groups of stippled hogback Saxon graves lie head to toe outside the north door of the church. A tall vertical spike stands at each end. A giant's bones and swords were said to have been dug up here in the sixteenth century and the four graves are supposed be the doubtless calcified remains of wild boars he killed in the forest. The likely truth is that the graves are graves and the spikes are the damaged remains of Saxon crosses. The crosses, presumably added after conversion, were small in proportion to the height. The lower part of the spike would probably have been decorated with pagan imagery. Another example, better preserved, is at Gosforth, across Cumbria near the Irish Sea. The remarkable color scheme inside the church moves from stained glass and painting around the altar up attractive slender pillars, past the gallery to an elegant ceiling.

The church's square battlemented tower has walls three feet thick, suggesting that it doubled as a bell tower and small fortress capable of resisting short sieges; Penrith's position on the road from Scotland made it, from Roman times onward, a frontier town. The lanes that separate its central markets—with, nowadays, their remarkably varied pubs—form what used to be the outskirts and were deliberately made narrow and crooked to help keep out raiders calling on market day to capture livestock. Considerable parts of the walls of Penrith Castle, now a roofless large square, remain. Begun in 1399 it was improved and enlarged over the next seventy years, becoming a royal fortress for Richard, duke of Gloucester, later the wicked Richard III portrayed so unsympathetically by Shakespeare. Near a delightful stone bridge over the river Eamont, enough of the walls, internal as well as external, of the Norman-built Brougham Castle, remain for us to see how it worked. Despite its presence, however, the Scots sent a large army in 1345, which burned Penrith and carried away great numbers of prisoners.

Across the road from the church is the Tudor Coffee Room, once the Dame Anne Birkett School. William and Dorothy Wordsworth had grandparents in Penrith, dour folk whose company William did not much enjoy. He and his sister were probably quite pleased to get out to the nursery school during 1766 and 1777. The two oldest streets, Burrowgate and Sandgate, date from the thirteenth century. The Penrith Museum and Tourist Information Center are housed in the former Robinson's School, an Elizabethan building that was altered in 1670 and used as a school until the early 1970's. The recently refurbished museum covers the history, geology, and archaeology of the Penrith area.

Penrith Beacon, high above the town on top of Beacon Hill, was built in 1719, on a spot where beacons have been lit to signal war or emergency since the time of Henry VIII. It gives magnificent panoramic views. That of Ullswater is especially fine. This is sometimes called "the Queen of the Lakes"; Wordsworth thought it had "the happiest combination of beauty and grandeur" of any of them. It was on its shores that he "wandered lonely as a cloud / That floats on high or vales and hills, / When all at once I saw a crowd, /A host, of golden daffodils..." Victorian steamers ply the lake in summer: their predecessors used to fire cannons, provoking seven-fold echoes from the fells above.

Patterdale, at the
southern end of
Ullswater, may be
named after St
Patrick, who may
have visited the
area. Visitors to St
Patrick's Church are
reminded that
"Helvellyn [a 3,116-
foot peak nearby]
praises God, but
please do not bring
it into church on
your boots."
Surrounded as it is
by mountains and
water—Grisedale
Tarn, Angle Tarn,
Brothers Water—
Patterdale is a
popular starting
point for walkers. St
Patrick's is a small
Victorian building
containing well-
known tapestries by
Ann Macbeth.
Sheepdog trials,
sheep shearing, and
hound trailing are
some of the country
activities you can
watch hereabouts.
Patterdale and its
surroundings
inspired John
McCabe's
composition
Cloudcatcher Fells
(1985).

A Y R

BRIDGES, WRITERS, AND A STAIRCASE

BRIDGES ARE IMPORTANT IN AYR. THE RIVER AYR WAS FIRST SPANNED within the town 800 years ago. That old bridge, as rebuilt in stone in 1470, is still used by pedestrians. There have been two more recent ones, the first built in 1788. Scotland's national poet, Robert Burns, wrote an amusing dialogue between the two bridges in which the old bridge tells the newcomer that "I'll be a brig when ye're a shapeless cairn," and indeed the new bridge was washed away in flooding in the 1870s. A second new bridge was built in 1878. Ayr has grown out of a settlement serving a castle built in 1197 at a time when it was still virtually a border town. Its street plan largely survives from that era. It has had a racecourse since 1770 and during the nineteenth century the long beach to the south helped it become a popular a seaside resort. Ayr was for centuries the distribution center for the west coast of Scotland, importing goods in bulk from America, England, and Spain and shipping them on. Eventually, however, Glasgow overtook it. The town's first castle was demolished by Cromwell's forces in 1654 and replaced by a huge citadel. Much of its outer wall remains. Apart from that and the bridges, important buildings include the Town Hall, with its remarkable spire, the Wallace Tower (1833), and Loudoun Hall, Scotland's oldest merchant's house (1513).

During the 1760s a bank was founded in Ayr that issued "accommodation bills"—loans for companies in urgent need of risk capital and little to offer as security. It was very popular but its spectacular crash in 1773 damaged confidence. However, in true Scottish fashion it did eventually pay all its bills—and in the long term helped transfer wealth from consumption by the upper classes into development. The use of capital in this way was analyzed by Adam Smith in *The Wealth of Nations* in 1776.

Robert Burns (1759-1796), a different kind of Scotsman, was born in Alloway, now a suburb of Ayr. The cottage is still there, with some of the original furniture and, next door, a display of manuscripts. In *Tam O' Shanter*, he describes Tam getting drunk in Ayr on market day, then meeting a coven of witches on his ride home, where his "sulky, sullen dame" is "nursing her wrath to keep it warm." The story is based on events in the life of an Alloway farmer. The Tam O' Shanter pub is in Ayr High Street. It was for a time a Burns museum but is now a pub once more. If you are in Ayr on January 25 you can expect enthusiastic celebrations of Burns's birthday with everyone roaring out probably the best-known of his song lyrics: "Should ould acquaintance be forgot / And never brought to mind?" it asks. The answer is "We'll tak a cup o' kindness yet, / For auld lang syne" (old time's sake). Burns espoused individual liberty and had a sure ear for Scottish speech.

Ayr Pavilion and the Steven Memorial Fountain on the sea front.

facing page
The second "new bridge", built in 1879.

Another writer, George Douglas Brown (1869-1902), went to school at Ayr Academy in the 1880s. He was greatly encouraged by one of his teachers, but his life and work were shaped by his hatred of his father, an overbearing farmer. He was illegitimate, and the relationship was never affectionate. It is reflected also in his use of pen names. He cut off most of his links with Ayrshire after his mother's death in 1895. His best novel, still in print, is *The House with the Green Shutters* (1901). It tells the story of John Gourlay, clearly a version of his father, and describes life in a claustrophobic small town (not modeled on Ayr).

Culzean (pronounced Cullain) Castle will make you gasp and widen your eyes as will its clifftop outlook to the Isles of Arran. A medieval tower house when this was a border area, it was remodeled after 1777 by the architect Robert Adam (1728-1792), "a typically hard-headed Scot, canny and remorselessly ambitious, yet with a tender, romantic side…" His master stroke here is the oval staircase, which looks as if everything were built around it. But it came last, using a limited space to unify separate blocks. Other features include: walled garden, swan pond, deer park, fountain court, bird watching, wildlife, beaches, old estate buildings, and caves. One floor (now partly available as hotel accommodations) was given to General Eisenhower in tribute to his work in World War II.

LINLITHGOW

GREAT HALL, PANORAMAS, A REFORMER

LINLITHGOW LIES IN A QUIET RURAL AREA, SEPARATED BY ROUNDED HILLS from the industrial tumult of central Scotland. As a commuter town it offers quick journeys to Scotland's two major cities, Edinburgh and Glasgow, and to Stirling (see under STIRLING). It is also a convenient place from which to explore the Scottish Borders by road (or even, for some areas, by bus).

Linlithgow itself has frequently had a role in Scottish history. There was a royal palace here in the twelfth century. The present palace, a surprisingly complete, pigeon-inhabited shell, is above the town and is especially princely looking when floodlit. The roof is missing but many of the rooms are very well preserved. The ninety-four-foot Great Hall is particularly impressive. The numerous rooms, passages, and stairways may disorient you, but a glance through a window into the central courtyard will reorient you. The floor consists of stone slabs. Mary, Queen of Scots, executed by Elizabeth I in 1587, was born here in 1542. Two centuries later, during the rebellion of Bonnie Prince Charlie, English forces were apparently responsible for the loss of the roof when they tried to warm their quarters by burning bedding straw. The fantastical fountain in the courtyard, built in 1537, was restored to active life in 2005. The castle is said to be haunted by the ghost of a woman. The custodian in 1973 claimed that he and his wife and some visitors had seen the shape of a woman near the main entrance. Clad in a blue gown, she walked purposefully toward the nearby church, disappearing before reaching it. Her appearances normally occur in April (sometimes in September), always in the mornings at about nine o'clock. Some people have heard a rustle of clothing at that time. The church, St Michael's, has suffered at the hands of Puritan reformer John Knox, Parliamentary soldiers, and, according to some, of those who replaced the long-collapsed stone crown on the tower with a wood and aluminium "crown of thorns" in 1964.

Below the castle is the attractive Lough (try to see a sunset or a sunrise there), with swans that are said to have left when Cromwell's Parliamentarians arrived, returning only at the restoration of the monarchy. The park alongside the loch is sometimes occupied by flocks of swan, geese, and ducks.

Boat trips can be taken from the Linlithgow Canal Center (you can also walk along the canal), and the story of the area is told in Annet House in the main street. Linlithgow Tours will arrange guided tours including the canal and other nearby attractions according to your requirements as to duration and strenuousness. If you want a good meal you might try Champany's, an inn just two miles from the center of town across the M9. You can stay there as well, and you have a choice of dining in the Main Restaurant ("surely the best steak house in Britain," writes Richenda Miers, "but more than that,") or the cheaper but also excellent Chop and Ale House.

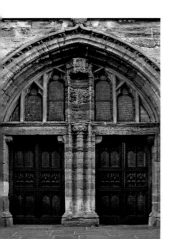

The doors of St Michael's Church.

facing page
Linlithgow Castle and St Michael's Church seen across the lough.

There is delightful country south of Linlithgow. Stroll first through pinewoods up Cockleroy Hill. (The name may indicate royal infidelities, or something more innocent.) From the summit you will see thirty-six signposted landmarks. The most remote is Goat Fell, more than sixty miles away on the Island of Arran. Carry on to Cairnpapple Hill (c. two miles), where you will see coast to coast, from Goat Fell to Bass Rock, at the mouth of the Firth of Forth. Then go down to Torpichden Preceptory. This, a rare remnant of an obscure corner of Scottish history, is the tower and transepts of a church of the Knights Hospitaller of the Order of St John of Jerusalem—whose only other establishment in Britain was in

UNESCO's World Heritage Site, New Lanark, is c. twenty-two miles south of Linlithgow. Its cotton mills, driven by the waters of the river Clyde, attracted wide attention when Robert Owen, manager and part-owner (1800-25), abolished child labor and corporal punishment and provided workers and their families with decent homes, schools and evening classes, free health care, and affordable food. The mills and housing are preserved in this, Scotland's most important memorial to the Industrial Revolution. After visiting mill and museum, take a walk through the Clyde Gorge to the Falls of Clyde, which have been painted by J.M.W. Turner, Jacon More, Alexander Nasmyth, and James Ward, among many others.

MELROSE

ASCETICS, RUGBY, AND LOYAL HORSES

A REFORMIST, PURITAN TENDENCY WAS AN EARLY CHARACTERISTIC of the Church in Scotland, not least at Melrose. King David I (son of the learned St Margaret) and other monarchs felt that monasticism was a way of life that ought to be testing. The orders of monks invited into Scotland were chosen only after thorough appraisal of their readiness to be tested, their piety and their asceticism. This was especially so in the case of the Cistercians who arrived from Rievaulx and founded Melrose Abbey in 1136. The order arose when a group of monks left the monastery at Molesmes, which had become very wealthy, to found a new house at Citeaux, where they would observe very strictly the *Rule* of St Benedict, rejecting any unsanctioned practice, such as the wearing of comfortable, warm garments and the use of bedclothes. At Melrose, what was left of the abbey after Henry VIII, during the course of his attempt to take over the crown of Scotland, had had his way with it, still stands. Thomas Pennant described its rose-pink glory in 1771: "The south side and the east window are elegant past description; the windows lofty, the tracery light, yet strong. The church had been in the form of a cross, and of considerable dimensions; the pillars clustered: their capitals enriched with most beautiful foliage of vine leaves and grapes. A window at the north end of the transept represents the crown of thorns. The rich work of the outside is done with uncommon delicacy and cunning. The spires or pinnacles that grace the roof; the brackets and niches, that, till 1649 [that is, when Cromwell's soldiers found them] were adorned with statues, are matchless performances." Apparently the gargoyle on the south wall of a pig playing the bagpipes did not offend Cromwellian religious sensibilities.

Melrose has two other claims to international fame. One is Sir Walter Scott. The other is the invention, in 1883, of seven-a-side rugby, by Ned Haigh, a local butcher. (The date when the fifteen-a-side game came into being is disputed, but the evidence seems to point to about 1841.) Rugby is (or was) a passion in southern Scotland, marked by moral earnestness, competitive vigor, and conservative attitudes. Unsurprisingly, the invention of "sevens" was the result of a financial problem. (The price of admission had been doubled from threepence to sixpence and attendance had diminished.) The "Melrose Sevens" tournament is held each year in April. When I visited it, we were held up for five or six minutes by what a policeman apologized for as an "awful traffic jam." The small-scale, short game allows the rounds and finals of a tournament to be fitted into one ground over a weekend. Now that rugby is a professional game and increasingly popular, international tournaments take place around the world every year.

The Bank of Scotland and Rhymer's Fare on Market Square.

facing page
What Cromwell's soldiers spared of Melrose's Cistercian Abbey.

Sir Walter Scott (1771-1832) was a lawyer, novelist, and poet. From 1826, facing debts of 130,000 pounds, he labored for six years to repay them, a process ending only with his death and the sale of his copyrights. His early novels, dealing with the history of Scotland since 1745, and some of his poems, are admired. Later work, produced under dreadful pressure, is uneven. His house, Abbotsford, near Melrose, stands for everything that was important to him: the beauty of the Scottish Borders, his collection of antiquities, his library, and, perhaps fatally, his idea of himself as a landed gentleman. It is more medieval fantasy than architectural gem, but it helps us understand and like its owner.

Scott's View is on the other side of Melrose from Abbotsford, on a road passing above the river Tweed, with a view toward the Eildon Hills. This range of three small hills was said to have been one hill split into three by a demon working for a Scottish wizard during the twelfth century. The story is even more than usually obviously untrue: the Romans knew the hills as "trimontium" (three mountains). Scott stopped to look at the view whenever he passed that way. When his funeral cortege reached the spot, so it is said, the horses pulling the hearse to Dryburgh Abbey left the road unbidden and paused a few minutes there. I hope that this story is true.

Melrose is an excellent base for exploring the Scottish Borders by car. This is a landscape of rolling hills, rippling rivers, and vast reservoirs; of threatening skies, sudden downpours, and lingering patches of snow; of strange stone towers in the middle of nowhere, ruined abbeys, stately houses, and stone cottages; of head-butting sheep, dog trials, and striving rugby players; of tales of "old, unhappy, far off things, and battles long ago," like those Wordsworth heard (elsewhere in Scotland) from a solitary Highland lass singing in a field; and of many beautiful small towns. At Ettrick there is a memorial to yet another great Scottish writer, James Hogg, farmer, poet, novelist, and friend of Sir Walter Scott, with whom he shared a passion for traditional Borders ballads. Hogg's *Confessions of a Justified Sinner* ranks with Robert Burns's *Holy Willie's Prayer* as an examination of Scottish Calvinism.

left
Abbotsford,
Sir Walter Scott's
manorial home on
the river Tweed.

far above
The stand-up
reading desk in the
library at
Abbotsford.

above
A reception room at
Abbotsford.

PERTH

LOWLANDS MEET HIGHLANDS

IN THE OPENING CHAPTER OF *THE FAIR MAID OF PERTH*, Scott writes of a traveler who "beheld, stretching beneath him, the valley of the Tay, traversed by its ample and lordly stream; the town of Perth, with its two large meadows, or 'inches,' its steeples, and its towers; the hills of Moncrieff and Kinnoul faintly rising into picturesque rocks, partly clothed with woods; the rich margin of the river studded with elegant mansions; and the distant view of the huge Grampian mountains, the northern screen of this exquisite landscape." The traveler leaving the motorway today will see much the same view. The "inches" are attractive, spacious riverside parks, with good Georgian terraced houses across the road. Sadly, too many interesting old buildings have been replaced by very dull modern ones, but that process was halted and once again, with its pedestrianized shopping streets and inventive floral displays, Perth can sensibly be referred to as a fair city.

Perth and Stirling were long thought of as gateways to the Highlands, Perth partly because it is at the point nearest the sea where the Tay can easily be bridged. When the great divide between tamed and wild Scotland moved from the Firth of Forth to the edge of the highlands, Perth became a border town. It was subjected to seven sieges at various times. Some were mounted by the English but none of the powers that held sway in England, from the Romans on, were interested in establishing rule over the Highlands; rather they wanted to protect themselves against raids by cattle stealers and the like. Their difficulties with the Scots arose largely from the racial and social diffuseness of the peoples living in Scotland. A mixture of British, Welsh, and Anglo-Saxons inhabited the area north of Hadrian's Wall. The Picts were established in the middle and the highlands were occupied by Gaelic-speaking Scots—who had come there from Ireland. The Picts and Scots united in 843, but the mixed grouping in the south did not join them until 1018. When the Normans arrived they regarded Scotland as part of their territory without doing much about it. In 1296, however, Edward I invaded Scotland and removed the Stone of Destiny (on which Scottish monarchs were crowned) to Westminster Abbey. (It was returned to Edinburgh Castle in 1996—although it will be taken to London for future coronations.) William Wallace began a long war of independence. For about 350 years before 1452, Perth was Scotland's capital. Later there were two further moments when events there were of national importance. In St John's Church in 1559 John Knox preached what became his standard iconoclastic sermon urging Christians to purge their churches of idolatry. The congregation obliged by wreaking havoc there and at Scone Abbey nearby. In 1618 Perth was the setting for James I's attempt to make the Church of Scotland more like the Church of England. He achieved little change, created much ill will—and never visited Scotland again.

facing page
St Matthew's Church and the Sheriff Court, on the banks of the river Tay.

below
Scone Castle, which has Perth's racecourse on its grounds.

Lower City Mills is a Georgian oatmeal mill (Scottish oats and the porridge made from them are famous worldwide). Balhousie Castle is the headquarters of the Black Watch, and houses their regimental museum. Perth's art gallery and museum, among the oldest in Scotland, concentrate on local history and the whisky industry. The Branklyn Garden attracts gardeners and botanists from all over the world to see its rhododendrons, alpines, herbaceous and peat-garden plants—and the striking blue Himalayan poppy.

Outside the town, the line between highlands and lowlands can be examined from the summit of Kinnoul Hill, where you will find spectacular views to the Cairngorm Mountains in the north, the Loch Earn hills in the west, and the Ochil and Lomond hills in the south. Scone Palace, a restoration of the replacement for the abbey and palace destroyed by John Knox's followers, can be visited. The town's racecourse has a splendid setting on the palace grounds. Half an hour at the Perth Market bull sales will give you a glimpse of wonderfully characterful bucolic faces. Further afield, many of the more popular areas in the southern highlands can be reached quite easily.

ST ANDREWS

GOLF, PURGES, AND A BUNKER

ONE EXCELLENT REASON FOR GOING TO ST ANDREWS IS TO BE A STUDENT. Scotland's oldest university was founded at St Andrews early in the fifteenth century. Its standing amongst British universities is good; its smallness and relative remoteness are not necessarily disadvantages. The second-in-line to the throne, Prince William, studied there.

The other reason for going to St Andrews is, of course, to play golf. The game's origins are lost in the mists of time. Its name has been thought to come from a Dutch word for club, but, as *The Oxford Dictionary of English Etymology* stiffly observes, "there are difficulties of form and use in the way of that commonly given derivation." We know that golf was popular in Scotland in 1457, because in that year a royal decree forbade it—on the grounds that it interfered with archery practice, and therefore with the defense of the realm. But in 1502 a peace treaty made it possible for everyone, including all subsequent Stuart monarchs, to play. The Royal and Ancient Golf Club of St Andrews was not the first such body, there having been an earlier one in Edinburgh, but it holds a preeminent position, having administered golf's rules and other matters since 1897 until recently, when these responsibilities were devolved to a group of companies. The club has a worldwide membership of 2,400.

The Old Course at St Andrews (there are ten in all, suited to every range of skill and experience) was named best in the world outside the USA in a poll in *Golf Digest* in 2005. A great test for golfers, it is a public course and welcomes any golfer with a handicap of twenty-four or under (thirty-six for ladies). Some of its more idiosyncratic features are Swilcan Burn, a stream that meanders in front of the first green, and its celebrated (if that is the word) bunkers: Four Stroke (once in it, you lose at least one stroke); Hell (the largest); Beardies, Kitchen, Grave, and Sutherland. The last commemorates a member in 1869 who was outraged when an existing bunker was filled in. He made such a fuss that two cousins re-created it in dead of night and left a note with his name on it. The final hazard is a road running behind a green. In 984 this determined the result of the Open Championship. The Old Course used to have a hard, fiery quality that posed enormous challenges to players' skills; an automatic watering system mitigated the problems to some extent.

On one side of the golf courses, where the river Eden meets tidal mudflats, we may see, according to season, gray plover, oystercatcher, knot, dunlin, pink-footed geese, black-tailed godwit, shelduck, and eider.

St Andrews has three main streets and numerous narrow cobbled alleyways, all of which lead to the ruins of St Andrews Cathedral, once the largest in Scotland. If you can climb 158 steps, St Rule's Tower gives splendid views of town and sea. In the same year, 1559, as John Knox urged the parishioners of Perth to "purge idolatry," he exhorted those of St Andrews to "cleanse the temple." This they did. Having cleansed it they left it to decay. Knox saw himself as the spiritual heir of "the preacher of Protestantism," George Wishart, who was burnt at the stake in 1546 in St Andrews—and may or may not have participated in a plot by Fifeshire lairds to slay the pro-French Catholic bishop, Cardinal Beaton. Legend has it that Beaton (the father of several illegitimate children) watched Wishart burn. The plotters got to him soon afterward and pickled his corpse in brine.

Despite its name and proximity to St Andrews (seven miles), Scotland's Secret Bunker has nothing to do with golf. Hidden beneath what appears to be a farmhouse but is actually a guard post, it consists of nearly 24,000 square feet of secret accommodations on two levels. The one-hundred-foot-deep hole has a shock-absorbing foundation of gravel and an outer shell of ten feet of solid concrete reinforced every two inches with inch-thick tungsten rods lined with brick. It was intended as the headquarters of government in the event of nuclear war. Nowadays, should you wish, you can go there to buy an inscribed T-shirt or mug, attend a rock concert, eat, or be married—or to reflect on the waste and expense of the Cold War.

We have seen (under CANTERBURY) that the English comic novelist P. G. Wodehouse was an enthusiastic golfer. He refers to St Andrews frequently in his stories. Think of Archibald, who tries obsessively to improve but spends much time on (or rather off) the fairway at his New York club retrieving lost balls. "His inability to do a hole in single figures did not handicap him at Cape Pleasant as it might have done at St. Andrews." Then there is the legalistically minded Oldest Member who, overseeing a round between rivals in love, will not allow any infringement of the rules, however unikely the circumstances. He ends the resulting acrimonious discussion by baring his head and saying that he obeys "the rules which were drawn up by the Committee of the Royal and Ancient at St Andrews . . . I have always respected them and will not deviate on this occasion from the policy of a lifetime."

below
Some colleges were rebuilt in neo-Jacobean style in the 1820s.

right
The Younger Hall of the university's Music Center.

far right
The view across St Andrew's Bay from St Andrews Castle.

STIRLING

STRATEGY, VIOLENCE, BEAUTY

LIKE PERTH, STIRLING IS A GATEWAY TOWN—OR, TO BORROW THE WORDS of Alexander Smith, "Stirling, like a huge brooch, clasps Highlands and Lowlands together." People have lived in its environs for almost 6,000 years, during the Middle Stone Age, the Bronze Age, and the Iron Age, from which traces of forts remain. The Romans were in the neighborhood in the first century CE, but there is no evidence that they tried to fortify the remarkable rock that has dictated the nature of Stirling's subsequent history. We might not expect to find the remains of a volcano in central Scotland but that is what Stirling is built on, a great lump of solidified black lava left behind when a volcano eroded away. The rock is crowned by Stirling Castle, which looks out over the flat surrounding plain. King Arthur is supposed to have captured an original wooden castle from the Saxons. Most of the replacement we see today is from the fifteenth and sixteenth centuries. It remains the finest example of Renaissance architecture in Scotland; French masons did much of the work. In 1488 an abbot who was also an alchemist and a charlatan attempted to fly from the castle walls. He reached the foot of the cliff more rapidly than he expected and did not survive.

The hilltop gateway into Stirling Castle.

facing page
The Municipal Buildings were influenced by Baroque style.

Whether or not King Arthur had anything to do with it, the castle did not lack drama in its first few centuries when it was often used as a royal residence. It commanded the road north into the Highlands and northeast Scotland, and the fords over the river Forth, which gave it a unique strategic importance. In 1314, during Scotland's fight for independence, Edward II decided to relieve the besieged English garrison at Stirling. He was defeated by his own incompetence and the skillful and cunning generalship of Robert the Bruce, at Bannockburn, a little south of the town. When he tried to take refuge in the castle, the governor told him that the castle had to be surrendered to the Scots. (The Bannockburn Heritage Center and the National Wallace Monument are both worth a visit.) In 1452 the castle was the scene of a bizarre incident. King James II, suspecting the eighth earl of Douglas of treason, summoned him there, stabbed him to death, and threw his body out of a window into the garden. In 1543, nine-month-old Princess Mary was crowned Queen of Scots in the Chapel Royal, a ceremony that set her on the road to execution. At the end of 1745, Bonnie Prince Charlie, the young pretender, who wanted to restore the Stuart monarchy, wasted more than a month, which could have been better spent elsewhere, in an unsuccessful attempt to capture Stirling Castle. When Stirling University was created in 1967 it was the first completely new university establishment in Scotland since Edinburgh in 1583. It has a high reputation and a pleasant campus.

The Argyll and Sutherland Highlanders have their Headquarters and Regimental Museum in Stirling Castle. The paved square at the centre of the building is called the Lion's Den. One guidebook states firmly that both James III and IV actually kept lions. Others have reservations. Another suggestion, that plays were occasionally performed there, seems far more practicable and likely. A macabre object, the Beheading Stone, can be seen in an iron cage on Gowan Hill. It was an important instrument of policy for James I (1394-1437). When, after twenty years in exile, he was finally able to establish himself as king, he executed his principal rival, the Duke of Albany, and three other members of the family.

Next to the castle stands the Church of the Holy Rude (cross). Although the reforming Calvinists of Scotland rejected not only ornaments in churches, but often the churches themselves, Holy Rude escaped destruction, while losing its ornamentation. Its beauties attract enthusiastic commendation from visitors worldwide. Stirling Old Town, on the sides of the hill below the castle, has a number of interesting buildings. Argyll's Lodging, the seventeenth-century townhouse of the dukes of Argyll, is the most complete surviving example of its period in Scotland. French influence is strong, particularly in the conical roofs of the rounded turrets at each corner. Look also at the facade of Mar's Wark, nearby.

INVERNESS

A ROUT, A CANAL, AND "NESSIE"

INVERNESS IS OFTEN DESCRIBED AS "THE CAPITAL OF THE HIGHLANDS" and it is an ideal center from which to explore that dramatic, romantic, and majestic area. Until the Jacobite Rebellion in the eighteenth century, relatively few outsiders visited an area generally regarded as wild, or even barbarous. But rebellion provoked the construction of roads, and roads inevitably brought visitors when peace was restored. The half-hour rout at Culloden Moor (1746) five miles from Inverness, the last battle on British soil, effectively ended the rebellion—but repercussions and reprisals continued long afterward. The successful English general— "Butcher" Cumberland or "Stinking Billy," the rest of whose military career was inglorious, abundantly earned his nicknames during the months following the battle as he destroyed the Jacobite social base. The rebellion had largely been supported by Highland clans, which were regarded as debt-ridden petty despotisms by Lowlanders and Englishmen. Lowlanders kept their distance from the more punitive aspects of the actions of the English government but did not necessarily disapprove of its aims. The breakup of the clan system and mass migration across the Atlantic and elsewhere followed. There has been a program of restoration at Culloden so that it is now more evocative of the battle than it has been for many decades.

Inverness has a history in which fact and fable interact, as in, for example, Shakespeare's play *Macbeth*, which simplifies the story of Macbeth's murderous progress toward the Scottish throne and shortens his reign. But it is possible that the first Castle of Inverness was in fact destroyed in revenge for the death of King Duncan at Macbeth's hands. There have been several castles on the site since. There is some difference of opinion about the present one, a Victorian edifice thought by some to dominate the town, by others to resemble a toy fort—an effect possibly enhanced by its pink brickwork and the white curtains hanging in its tall windows. St Andrew's Cathedral (1866-74) is another pink building, with twin towers, an octagonal chapter house, and an elaborate interior. The most attractive things in Inverness all have to do with the succession of bodies of water to which it is attached: Loch Ness, the river Ness, the Caledonian Canal (see below), and the Moray Firth. A walk in either direction along the river will bring much pleasure. Ness Island is a public park consisting of islands linked by bridges.

Cawdor Castle, where you can see some elegant and atmospheric interiors and delightful gardens, was not built until considerably after the deaths of Macbeth and Duncan. It was not, however, Shakespeare who introduced it into the story but one of his sources. In a fit of noble candor, the fifth earl Cawdor remarked, "I wish the Bard had never written his damned play!"

Thomas Telford's spectacular Caledonian Canal is one of the notable waterways of the world, offering grandly dramatic scenery and abundant wildlife. The Northwest Highlands cram the horizon on one side, the Grampian Mountains on the other. The Great Glen—through which the Caledonian Canal runs from southwest to northeast, linking the Atlantic with the North Sea—is the region's natural line of communication. Stretching sixty miles from Fort William to Inverness, with twenty-two man-made miles linking Loch Lochy, Loch Oich, Loch Ness, and Loch Dochfour, the canal is important in the Highlands' economy. Cabin cruisers can be hired and passenger cruises run in summer.

facing page
The Gothic St Stephen's Church and the Free Church seen across the suspension footbridge.

below
A monument to Queen's Own Cameron Highlanders who died in Egypt in the 1880s.

Loch Ness is twenty-four miles long and considerably over a mile wide. With a maximum depth of c. 800 feet, it is the second-deepest freshwater loch in the UK, behind Loch Morar. It is very cold. Its steep wooded banks create a wind tunnel and surprisingly rough water at times. The ruins of Castle Urquhart are impressive but if you visit in summer try to get there early before coach parties determined to spot the Loch Ness monster appear. The glens that open off westward are worth exploring, particularly Glen Urquhart, which leads into Glen Affric and, further south, Glen Moriston. Fort Augustus, tiny, busy, has a clansmen center and a Caledonian Canal heritage center. Its former Benedictine monastery is now a block of luxury flats.

The Loch Ness monster (popularly referred to as "Nessie") is first mentioned in the biography of St Columba (521-597) written by St Adamnan almost a century after the subject's death. Dating and Columba's showy miracles when confronting the monster inspire skepticism. Modern photographs and films of Nessie have been exposed as fakes. In 2003, when Lloyd Scott spent twelve days walking along the bottom of the loch in a diving suit to raise money for children with leukemia, he reported no sightings. Sonar surveys have added nothing. Arguments in favor of Nessie depend on the supposed depth of concealing mud in the loch, or on a possibility that the monster arrives periodically by tunnel from some other, unspecified, body of water. We may be sure that no one earning a living from tourists in the area wants to hear proof that Nessie does not exist.

left
Urquhart Castle
above Loch Ness.

above
Inverness Town
House was the
venue for the only
British Cabinet
meeting outside
London, in 1921.

below
Inverness Castle now
houses the Sheriff
Court.

201

LERWICK

FIRE FESTIVAL, ELEMENTAL SCENERY

THE SHETLAND ISLANDS AND THEIR CAPITAL, LERWICK, are closer to the Arctic Circle than to most of England, and closer to Norway than to much of Scotland. Unsurprisingly, although Shetland was for a time part of the Norse jarldom (earldom) of Orkney, until it fell apart in 1065, it was governed by Norway after 1195. But in 1469 when King Christian was short of money for a daughter's dowry, he mortgaged Orkney and Shetland to Scotland. Since then, Shetland has been part of Scotland—but only up to a point. When they speak of "the mainland" Shetlanders mean their own largest island, not Scotland. The legacy of Norwegian rule can be heard in the place names and dialect. The name Lerwick, for example, comes from the Old Norse for "muddy bay." One of the more extrovert examples of inherited Norseness is, however, to some extent an invented ceremonial that has existed in its present form for only just over a century. On the last Tuesday of January every year, the largest fire festival in Europe, "Up Helly Aa," lightens up the depths of the near-Arctic winter night. After a blazing torchlight procession of up to a thousand male "guizers" through the packed streets of Lerwick, a full-size replica Viking longship is ceremonially burned. (The head "guizer" is dressed as a hero from the Norse sagas, the rest in whatever fancy dress they choose: the event is sometimes referred to as "transvestite Tuesday.") The "guizers" and onlookers then repair to local halls for a night of revelry, dancing, and partying. The next day is—necessarily perhaps—a public holiday. The event has never been cancelled for bad weather, a proud boast given that gales and hurricanes, rain and snowstorms are commonplace at that time of year.

The Shetland Hotel in "da toon."

facing page
A "guizer" and his Viking warriors in the "Up Helly Aa" procession.

Lerwick is a lively and picturesque port. Originally it earned its living from fishing, but lairds from Scotland took over the trade and ran it to their own advantage. After the war (when Shetlanders helped the Norwegian resistance in many courageous ways, principally by ferrying fugitives from Nazi vengeance across to the Shetlands), the economy revived with the discovery of oil under the North Sea. This was well handled by the Shetland Council and part of the boom was used to improve roads, housing, and other infrastructures.

Lerwick is known as "da toon." Commercial Street, Shetland's principal forum for business and gossip, is "da street." Narrow, winding, a little away from the sea, it moderates the worst weather. Up the hill is the splendid Victorian Town Hall, built by public subscription. If nothing else is happening, go in and look around, particularly at the stained-glass windows celebrating Shetland's history. Climb the tower, the town's highest point. Most of Lerwick's nightlife takes place in people's houses, but there are signs that restaurants now take proper advantage of superb local products. Fish, and lamb fed on heather and seaweed, can be superb. Local fiddle playing provides virtuosic fun.

But the oil boom is now over. Shetland must look to tourism for continued prosperity. Lerwick harbor is still fairly busy with ferries, fishing boats, oilrig supply, seismic survey vessels, and ships from the various navies active in these latitudes present in profusion. In summer local and visiting pleasure craft are added to the mix. But questions about possible future directions for this fragile economy are being asked with increasing urgency.

Scalloway, on an attractive bay c. five miles west, was the capital until 200 years ago. It was the headquarters of the Shetland Bus, the organization that helped Norwegian resistance fighters escape the Nazis. Mainland is by far the biggest of about a hundred Shetland Islands: many of the others can be visited by boat. The Shetland landscape is unlike any other part of the UK. The light seems supernaturally clear to visitors and the sights it illuminates are elemental: sea, islands, cliffs, beaches, roaming Shetland ponies, apparently wild, but all actually owned by someone, birds and prehistoric remains. Shetland's sheep include one breed that, for historical reasons, cannot eat grass but lives off seaweed.

O B A N

SHELTERED HARBOR, EXPOSED ISLANDS

OBAN WRAPS ITSELF COMFORTABLY AROUND ITS BAY AND HARBOR, overlooked by the silhouette of MacCaig's Folly, an imitation, never completed, of the Roman Colosseum. (MacCaig was a local philanthropist who began the building simply to provide employment. He planned to fill its niches with statues of himself and his family but when he died the project was abandoned.) Although it is a seaside town on the west coast, Oban is some way from the open Atlantic. The island of Kerrera lies across the width of the harbor, sheltering it from westerly winds; ferries entering the harbor from either north or south have to hug the coast. Beyond Kerrera, the island of Mull provides further protection. Many other islands, some small, some rather large, are scattered north and south. Oban came into being as a fishing village in the late eighteenth century and achieved its present Victorian solidity through the nineteenth century's enthusiasm for seaside resorts—and, of course, the arrival of the railway.

It is usually worthwhile to spend some time simply looking at the boats moored around the harbor in Oban—watch, too, for seals scavenging in the bay. If you are interested in whisky, sign up for a guided tour of the Oban Distillery. Part of your admission can be redeemed against the price of a bottle—and it also includes a dram at the end of the tour. The War and Peace Exhibition is full of interest of an unusual kind, telling the story of Oban in wartime, when it was a flying-boat base, a mustering point for Atlantic convoys and a training center for the D-Day landings. There is also more general material about old Oban, the ferries, the fishing and maritime industries, the railway, and local sport. Enthusiastic local volunteers staff the exhibition and admission is free.

A leisurely stroll along the coast road at the northern end of Oban will take you to the ruin of Dunollie Castle, once the seat of the MacDougalls, the lords of Lorne, who owned a third of Scotland. There's a small steep hill to climb, but the view overlooking the northern entrance of Oban harbor is delightful. Further north, on a different road, stands what is left of Dunstaffnage Castle, square with round towers at the corners, which has played an important role in Scottish history. This was the site of the capital of Dalriada, the original Kingdom of the Scots between the fifth century and 843. The Stone of Destiny (see under PERTH) was brought here from Ireland via Iona. Glencoe, site of a notorious massacre in 1692 is about thirty-five miles north of Oban. Following the Jacobite rebellion of 1689-90, the Campbells, on behalf of the government, tricked the Jacobite Macdonalds into giving them hospitality, then murdered forty of their hosts. Many who escaped died in winter storms. King William, who had not authorized the slaughter, did not punish its perpetrators.

Ferries link Oban with Kerrera, Mull (see under TOBERMORY), Colonsay, Lismore, Coll, Tiree, Barra, and South Uist. Truly, it is "The Gateway to the Hebrides." All of these islands offer pleasant walks. Kerrera is a good place to escape to when summer crowds in Oban become stifling. Colonsay offers heather, some woodland, plant and bird life, wild goats and rabbits, a fine quasitropical garden and some glorious beaches. Lismore, which does not rise much above sea level, offers gentle walking and cycling. Coll and Tiree resemble the Outer Hebrides rather than the Inner. Both are exposed to strong winds from the Atlantic—but also enjoy some of the longest hours of sunshine available in Scotland.

facing page
McCaig's Folly, modeled on the Colisseum stands illuminated above Oban.

below
The asymmetrical frontage and truncated pinnacles of the Caledonian overlook Oban's waterfront.

It takes almost five hours to reach Barra by ferry, so it would be wise to arrange to stay at least overnight. Try to be there when there is a *ceilhid* (pronounced kayley). This is party with Scottish traditional dancing and whisky—and you will be made welcome as either spectator or participant. You will notice that those watching are concentrating single-mindedly on the dancers' feet. Look out for *ceilhids* throughout the Highlands, also for Highland Games and Sheepdog Trials—and throughout Scotland for a game of shinty, an alarming version of hockey, with few restrictions on how and where you may hit the ball. It has used formalized rules since 1893 and is played by women and children as well as men.

PITLOCHRY
MOUNTAINS, WALKS, ISOLATION

YOU MIGHT BE WELL ADVISED TO AVOID PITLOCHRY'S MAIN STREET as far as possible; the succession of tartan memento emporiums may lower your spirits. Other aspects of the town and its surroundings are a different matter. The Victorian architecture, friendly inns, pubs and restaurants, and museums provide much to look at and explore at leisure. During the summer season at the Pitlochry Festival Theater a wide range of plays, musicals and other events is presented in rotation so that, for example, by taking in two matinées you could see seven different shows in five days. There are some exciting independent shops. Outside the town, Highland Perthshire has a wealth of lochs, rivers, woodland, and dramatic mountain backdrops. Many guided walks and tours are available. In early summer you may watch salmon swimming up the spectacular ladder built into the hydroelectric power station—a succession of thirty-four chambers allowing them to bypass the station on their way back to the spawning grounds where they themselves hatched.

You should not miss the opportunity of having a look at the Cairngorms. But do bear in mind that the weather in the area can change without warning, and that between September and May near-Arctic blizzards may sweep in at almost any time. There have been many fatalities in the past. (There has been less snow in the last decade than used to fall, but the possibility remains.) Ensure that you have very adequate, warm, and appropriate clothing—and tell someone where you intend to go. If you drive up the A9 to Kingussie, then take the B9152 and follow signs to Cairn Gorm, the Reindeer Center, and the Coir Cas car park, whence a funicular railway will take you to the Ptarmigan restaurant, 340 feet short of the summit (4,084 feet). In order to protect a mountain that has suffered from overpopularity and being easy to climb—on one side, not on the other—only skiers are allowed to go outside and on to the summit, but, assuming the weather is suitable, you will have excellent views. There are about thirty ski runs in this area, spread over two valleys. Few of them are "black runs" demanding advanced technique, but the changeable weather and strong winds can make them fairly demanding all the same. These mountains are characteristically rounded and surrounded by high plateaus. Everything is cut by *corries* (more or less rounded, near-vertical shady hollows, which protect alpine plants) and steep-sided glens. This landscape supports a sub-Arctic ecosystem that is unique in the British Isles.

If you are interested in animals you may, on the way back to Pitlochry, like to walk among reindeer at the Cairgorm Reindeer Center, walk through the Rothiemurchus estate, with its Highland cattle, or drive through the Kincraig Highland Wildlife Park, where you will see bison, wolves, and wild boar, all once common in the Highlands. At Rothiemurchus you can walk, go fishing, shoot clay pigeons, and see the everyday life of a working Highland estate.

The Dunfallandy Stone near Pitlochry is a large eighth-century Pictish slab of red sandstone carved with symbolic signs and Biblical figures. At Dunkeld there are small houses rebuilt after a battle in the eighteenth century and a ruined cathedral, the choir of which is still used as a church. Beatrix Potter set her Peter Rabbit stories here. Blair Castle gives insights into the changing lives of Highland aristocrats during 700 years. Killiekrankie Walk is an easy ten-mile walk through a river gorge and around Loch Faskally. Catch a bus to Killiecrankie Visitors' Center for a free guided tour. You may feel skeptical at the spot where a soldier "leapt the river" to escape Jacobites in 1689.

facing page
Some roads are steep, but the views offer a reward.

below
Round Towers with conical tops like witches hats are characteristic of Pitlochry.

206

For a memorably scenic outing travel west past Loch Tummel and Loch Rannoch to Rannoch Station, where the road ends. There you will discover what it is to be isolated. Only trains disturb the quiet of Rannoch Moor, an uninhabited and uninhabitable wilderness. David Balfour, on the run with Alan Breck in Robert Louis Stevenson's *Kidnapped*, describes it thus: "The mist rose and died away, and showed us that country lying waste as the sea…Much of it was red with heather; much of the rest broken up with bogs and…peaty pools…" Between the two lochs you will pass Schiehallion, the "fairy hill." At the eastern end of Loch Tummel you can enjoy the "Queen's View" down the loch to that "fairy hill."

STORNOWAY

SEA, AIR, AND SABBATH

STORNOWAY HAS A FINE NATURAL HARBOR IN AN INLET ON THE SOUTHERN SIDE of the hooklike Eye peninsula on the east coast of the island of Lewis and Harris. (Lewis and Harris are not separate islands—but the mountains between them have often made them behave as if they were. They have retained separate identities.) Lewis is the largest island in Outer Hebrides (Western Isles) and Stornoway (pop. 8,000) the largest town. It is the administrative center and its name is familiar to those who follow British weather forecasts. It is linked to the mainland by ferry and air.

Stornoway was a historic burgh in the sixteenth century and a fishing port in the eighteenth century. After 1918, the islanders' fierce, reactionary independence in daily life and religion (see opposite) seems—they might not agree—to have worked to their disadvantage. Lord Leverhulme bought the island and spent something approaching a million pounds trying to eradicate poverty and modernize its life. The islanders preferred running their own crofts to being organized by the philanthropic lord. When he was forced to withdraw, there was severe unemployment, with consequential poverty; 1,000 men migrated to America. It follows, therefore, that Lewis is in the fullest sense of the word an otherworldly place. But that otherworldliness, together with its remoteness and its refusal to be pushed into doing anything that goes against its conscience or customs, is what gives the island its particular character and, in a sense, its beauty. Lewis is perhaps a place for the seeker after curiousness rather than the aesthete. Its checkered history has made Stornoway a town of mixed effects, and until recently some of them were fairly grim. But in 2005 a regeneration plan was launched. Many parts of the town now look, in a restrained way, fresh and bright. Buildings originally designed simply to keep out the weather have been given carefully considered refurbishment. Some adventurous restaurants have opened. Undeniably, the level of activity in the port has shrunk. Once, barrels of pickled herring crowded the docksides and the deep, sheltered water was alive with more than a thousand coastal steamers. Today most of the catch is taken direct to the mainland. However, a reduced fleet of fishing boats still anchors at Cromwell Street Quay. The interior of Lewis Castle is not open; but the well-kept gardens are worth visiting as are the Western Isles Museum, the Lanntair Gallery, and the Lewis Loom Center, where you can learn about the Harris Tweed industry, which exists in both parts of the island. Harris Tweed is a loosely woven material made from woolen yarns dyed in different colors and is favored for skirts, jackets, scarves, and suits by the country gentry of the UK. It has nothing to do with the river Tweed, the original term being in fact "tweel."

The delightful gardens of Lewis Castle are open to the public.

facing page
The Old Town Hall, seen here from the harbour, was built in 1905.

When touring Lewis it is wise to collect a leaflet giving place names in both English and Gaelic, since road signs are not always helpful. You can take a circular coach tour. Public buses—which double as school buses at the appropriate times—will take you to particular areas. In the southwest you will see mountains, in the southeast many, many lochs. The center is undulating moorland. Outside Stornoway most of the population is strung out along the northwest coast, which also features many of the most popular sights, including the Butt of Lewis and Arnol's Black House Museum. There is much fertile croft land, many fine beaches, and the air is very fresh and unpolluted. This is a place to unwind.

One thing that Lewis and Harris have very much in common is Sabbath Day observance. This is because the influence of the minority Calvinist group called the "Wee Frees," which broke away from the newly unified Church in 1900, remains strong. In consequence, most things that happen as a matter of course on weekdays do not happen on Sunday. Many transport links to and within the island cease to operate. Shops, gas stations, cafés, pubs, and attractions are closed. Either be very sure of how you will cope with this, or avoid being there between Saturday afternoon and Monday morning. Filmgoers who have seen Lars von Trier's film *Breaking the Waves* will have some idea of the rather intense atmosphere.

TOBERMORY

GAMES, MENDELSSOHN, AND PEACE

IF YOU WERE A CHILD IN THE UK IN THE 1970S AND WATCHED TELEVISION, you probably thought that Tobermory was an elderly, furry creature with a long nose wearing a bowler hat and a leather vest, living with his family in a burrow on Wimbledon Common, recycling things dropped by humans. You might, however, have realized that some of the family had chosen their own names by sticking a pin at random into an atlas and have deduced that Tobermory was the name of a place. And what a place it is! Arriving by ferry from Oban, sailing the length of the Sound of Mull, you see the town itself only at the last moment, as the ferry turns into Tobermory Bay. Ahead of you is a pinkish-brown stone church with a pinnacled spire beyond a stone-embanked waterfront. To your right, boats are moored at stone jetties. Beyond is a row of smart buildings, some with pink, yellow, or blue fronts. Behind them, a thickly wooded hillside, with houses peeping through the trees below what appears to be a flat hilltop.

The waterfront is a kaleidoscope of colored buildings.

facing page
On higher ground larger and grander buildings enjoy panoramic views.

If you have come over for the Highland Games, that is where you will be bound. Highland Games are held all over Scotland from late May to mid-September. Events you may expect to see include: tossing the caber (pron. cabber) a large tree-trunk or equivalent object); tugs of war; wrestling; field events and foot and cycle races that use a handicapping system (which gives weaker competitors more of a chance) to make the competition (fierce but friendly) closer and more exciting. Interspersed will be Highland dancing, solo piping, and pipe bands, all clad in the proper kilts, short-sleeved shirts, and knee-length woolen stockings. Adults and children have their own separate events. If the weather is good you will enjoy the views as well as the sport. If rain and mist come down you will sit on your waterproof under your umbrella, reflecting that the solo pipers, especially if playing a lament, sound especially evocative in these conditions. There are two sorts of bagpipes in use in Scotland. "Warm-wind" pipes are blown with the mouth and, associated with the Highlands, are used in outdoor events. "Cold-wind" pipes, blown by a bellows operated by the player's elbow, are associated with the Lowlands, have a sweeter tone, and are used indoors.

Whether you return to Oban on the ferry or are staying on you will have the chance to enjoy a *ceilhid* (see under OBAN) either as watcher or participant. Later you might see a production, local or visiting, at the Mull Theater. Theater (and games) apart, possibly the most dramatic event to startle Tobermory occurred in 1588. A Spanish galleon, on the run after the debacle of the Armada, exploded and sank in the bay. It was rumored to have thirty million gold ducats on board. None of this fortune has ever been recovered.

Roads on Mull mainly follow its indented coastline. If you pause to absorb every stunning view progress will be slow, but who cares? Torosay Castle is a very pleasing country house, with a tearoom, craft shop, gardens, and farm. Duart Castle stands on a headland nearby. It was the home of Fitzroy Maclean, diplomat and traveler, whose book *Eastern Approaches* describes the time when he was sent by Winston Churchill to deal with Marshall Tito and his Communist guerillas in what was then Yugoslavia. The castle has featured in several movies, including the classic Powell and Pressburger romantic comedy *I Know Where I'm Going* (1945), about a young woman who plans to marry for money but is ambushed by love.

Two islands west of Mull are interesting in quite different ways. Staffa (seven miles) is difficult to visit since you can only land from small boats in calm weather. It was made famous by a description of it by the naturalist Sir Joseph Banks, published in 1772. Its cliffs are made up of hexagonal or pentagonal basalt columns. Mendelssohn visited the island in 1829; his overture *Fingal's Cave* evokes the varying moods of the sea in this out-of-the-way spot. On Iona, near Mull's southwest tip, is a restored Benedictine abbey you can visit for a day, or stay longer (in fairly spartan accommodations) sharing the life of the abbey: meals, worship, chores, and social events. Even by the standards of the Scottish islands, this is a very peaceful place.

ABERGAVENNY

LOCAL HERITAGE, WORLD HERITAGE

THE MARKET TOWN OF ABERGAVENNY LIES IN THE VALLEY of the river Usk surrounded on three sides by the southern end of the Black Mountains. The river crossing and lines of communication and supply in the Usk Valley caused defense works to be built here between 4,000 BCE and the twelfth century. Like most Welsh towns before the ages of iron and coal, Abergavenny began as a Norman borough. It suffered from being simultaneously a Welsh town and an English frontier post. Among many towns smitten by the Black Death, Abergavenny was peculiarly unlucky to suffer additionally the full destructive force of Owain Glyndwr's Welsh patriotism in 1404. It recovered with the establisment during the sixteenth and seventeenth centuries of tanning and weaving. Abergavenny flannel became a recognized brand. Prosperity continued when Abergavenny became a spa town during the eighteenth century. Milk from its goats was considered good for tuberculosis; the goats' hair was made into fashionable wigs. In the mid-eighteenth century, John Wesley, preaching Methodism to the frequently enthusiastic Welsh, found that his congregation here was the best-dressed in Wales. When the spa, like others elsewhere, became unfashionable, the coming of the railways, and development of iron and coal industries nearby, kept it going economically.

St Mary's Church was once a Benedictine priory.

facing page
Abergavenny is a gateway to the Black Mountains.

All this has left behind a town in which the typical features line up: castle, market, large church (originally part of a monastery dissolved by Henry VIII). But, underlying these, its original importance, as a southern gateway into Wales, remains. It's "southern" that is important. From quite early in Welsh history, the southeast corner of the country, an area of 1,500 square miles at most, bounded by the English Border, the river Severn, the Bristol Channel, and the Black Mountains, was its most populous and prosperous part. This was the segment the English wanted to get hold of; farther north all they wanted was to keep the wild and hairy natives, as they saw them, at bay. When things calmed down in later centuries, or, as the Welsh would have it, when English hegemony became a stranglehold, the rugged scenery, the remote seacoasts, the art, crafts, and costumes of north and west Wales began to interest the English as tourists. Later still, however, the English have come to be seen in parts of Wales as robbers, not visitors. Should Welsh reservoirs send water to English cities? Should Welsh houses become the weekend cottages of English middle managers?

North of Abergavenny, the Black Mountains have preserved almost unimaginable aspects of traditional Welsh life—not least because some areas were untouched by the Reformation. From the mountain road between Abergavenny and Hay-on-Wye (see under HEREFORD), visit the remains of Llanthony Abbey and Capel-y-ffin, where Father Ignatius, a notable Welsh eccentric who collected misfits, attempted in 1869 to establish an Anglican Benedictine order. When, eventually, he failed, the place passed to Eric Gill (1882-1940), whose heady mixture of Roman Catholic medievalism, art, and forbidden sex also proved unstable. Bizarrely, there is also a Welsh Baptist chapel on the site.

Visitors will not encounter hostility in Abergavenny. It is a comfortable town. But where it is and what it is arise from conflicts never entirely resolved.

The Brecon Beacons are west of Abergavenny, immediately north of the Rhondda Valley, former center of coal mining. Here, as neighbors, beacons and valleys exemplify the essence and the contradictions of South Wales: coal mining and countryside, overcrowding and solitude. The UK's élite regiment, the SAS, begins its training on the beacons, testing applicants by inviting them to carry thirty-two pound Bergens (backpacks) over fifteen miles of rough terrain, a test known for some reason as "The Fan Dance." Fortunately, ordinary visitors may simply enjoy the high level ridge walk known as the Brecon Horseshoe, or other walks and activities. West of the Beacons is the wild area known (in the singular) as Black Mountain.

Blaenafon, five miles from Abergavenny, was declared a UNESCO World Heritage Site in 2000. Here you may follow the rise and fall of a Welsh mining and industrial area. Other places worth a visit at greater, but not daunting, distances are: Caerleon, a well-preserved amphitheater, part of the base of the Roman Second Augustan Legion in the second century; Monmouth, with reminders of Henry V and buildings from the eighteenth and nineteenth centuries; and the remains of Tintern Abbey, in a field on the banks of the river Wye. Wordsworth, a man who preferred solitude to almost anyone else's company, celebrated his return after "five summers, with the length / Of five long winters…" to "…these steep and lofty cliffs, / That on a wild, secluded scene impress / Thoughts of more deep seclusion…" If seclusion is not often available at Tintern Abbey nowadays, he is partly to blame.

ABERYSTWYTH

THE ATHENS OF CARDIGAN BAY

ABERYSTWYTH SITS IN THE CURVE OF CARDIGAN BAY, with Constitution Hill at its northern end and the harbor (now, perhaps inevitably, a marina) at the other, looking out at the Irish Sea. (A funicular railway will take you up Constitution Hill to the camera obscura on its summit.) The town has been described at various times as "a very dirty, black, smoky place," "the unofficial capital of Welsh-speaking Wales," "the Biarritz of Wales," and "the Athens of Cardigan Bay." The first characterization, penned by Daniel Defoe in the 1720s, has long been irrelevant; the others remain apt. The Welsh Language Society was founded here (as recently, surprisingly, as 1963) and the town houses both its own university and the National Library of Wales. The library, won after stiff competition with Cardiff, is a treasure house of Welsh culture. The splendid, much-loved neo-Gothic old university building was originally intended as a hotel; the hotel's gable mosaic of Archimedes receiving emblems of science and industry seems to have found its proper home with the change of use. This, the first college of the federal University of Wales, is especially notable for having the world's first Department of International Politics, and a well-regarded Department of Theater, Film, and Television Studies, responsible, so David Barnes suggests, for having "an entire generation of Welsh youth transfer its ambitions from the pulpit to the TV studio." It was also one of the first universities in Britain to award degrees to female students. Near the old university building stand the remains of a castle built by Edward I after his campaign in Wales in 1277. When built it was among the greatest in Wales: an innovative structure in which walls-within-walls allowed guards to defend the stronghold from several heights without firing upon their own men. Now, having gradually lost its strategic significance and been neglected, it is merely the remnants of towers and foundations. As elsewhere, Oliver Cromwell finished the job of ruination after the English Civil War.

The beach in and south of the town provides a very pleasant walk on a fine day, as does the Edwardian Promenade in Aberystwyth itself. There is a wishing well there where for five pence you may whisper your deepest hopes. My two granddaughters did this one balmy summer evening. Later we discovered that the younger had wished to get her money back, the older that everyone in the world would be happy that night. Fortunately that night did not turn out as did the night of January 14, 1938, when ninety-mile-per-hour winds lashed the town, reaching a climax at about five A.M. Next day the town had to start adapting to the sight of water lapping a crumbling low cliff where the promenade had been. Half of the pier had also gone. The Ceredigon Museum will tell you the full story.

A ruined castle guards the southern approaches to the town.

facing page
At the northern end the Cliff Railway takes you to the view.

Take the Vale of Rheidol (narrow-gauge) Railway to Devil's Bridge. From the center of this quiet village, a walk (there is a small charge) will take you to the point where the river Mynach drops 300 feet to meet the river Rheidol. There are three bridges over the river, built one above the other. The lowest was built by the devil himself to allow a local woman to rescue her cow from the other side of the gorge. Part of the bargain was that he would take the soul of the first creature to cross the bridge. Being a woman of wit and resource she sent her puppy across first—which is why the devil has the soul of a dog.

Dafydd ap Gwilym (c. 1320-80), one of Wales's greatest poets, lived in Aberystwyth most of his life. He visited towns and houses of the gentry throughout Wales, entertaining his hosts with his poetry. He was clearly a trained bard, influenced by native poets who wrote in praise of princely patrons and by wandering scholars from Provence. He was, however, notably racier and jollier than most other Welsh poets, as is shown by his most often quoted poem *The Girls of Llnabadarn* (Llanbadarn is now a suburb of Aberystwyth), complaining that they invariably rejected his advances. But, whatever his success rate with the women at home, he had a widespread reputation as a successful philanderer.

BEAUMARIS

CASTLES IN WALES

The Norman Conquest (1066) scarcely affected northwestern Wales at first. Hereditarily chieftains, technically vassals of the Anglo-Norman kings, ruled their domains much as they pleased. Two centuries later, however, Edward I thought the situation required resolution in his favor. He achieved this in the late thirteenth century, establishing Beaumaris on Anglesey Island, across the Menai Straits from mainland Wales. The Norman French name (meaning "beautiful marsh") was a clear indication that this was an outpost of royal power. Its purpose was to prevent food (Anglesey was the main grain-growing area in Wales) or other aid being sent from Anglesey to rebels on the Welsh mainland.

Generally, Edward's campaigns against the Welsh were successful, although the need for them arose partly from his highhanded enforcement of what he took to be his rights as feudal lord. The chain of castles he left behind him is a triumph of architecture and propaganda, announcing solidly and magnificently where power lay and how effectively the wishes of the powerful could be enforced, a point reinforced by the rule, which applied for a long time, that only English people could live in Beaumaris town. Edward won his triumphs over the Welsh by meticulous and efficient mustering of men and resources rather than brilliance as a general. Of the castles he built—throughout Wales but more especially in the west and north—Beaumaris is the eighth, last, and most elegant. It took over thirty-five years to build—and even then was not completed. At one time more than 3,500 people were working on it. It cost about fifteen hundred pounds. All the castles together cost eighty thousand pounds: many millions in today's terms. No wonder Edward's son faced a financial crisis.

Beaumaris is a concentric castle, like that at Aberystwyth, with a moat (which drained the marsh) and two sets of walls. On the inner edge of the moat is the first, lower wall. It has round towers (which give fewer blind spots than square ones) at the corners and at intervals in between. The narrow outer ward—in effect no-man's-land, and a trap for anyone caught there—led to the second wall, much higher and with much larger round towers, from which deadly showers of arrows could be easily and accurately directed. The inner ward, an assembly area for the defenders, was lined with a hall, granary, kitchens, and stables.

One of the incomplete towers at Beaumaris.

facing page
A moat with ducks; a castle with two walls.

The Welsh have described Anglesey differently at different times. One name may mean "Island on the End." When it was covered by trees it was called "The Dark Island," and it has also been known as "The Mother of Wales" because of its fertility. It has always resisted invasions, by the Romans and later by the Normans. In 78, however, Agricola conquered it by enterprising and unexpected means. He had no fleet. He therefore used his best men, who had been trained to swim with their arms and horses alongside them. Their sudden appearance, mounted and armed, on the Anglesea shore of the Menai Strait made the defenders, Tacitus tells us, "lose their heads. What could embarrass or defeat a foe who attacked like that?"

The castle was considered impregnable, but this was never much put to the test. It seems never to have been seriously attacked, although Owain Glyndwr may have held it briefly during 1403-1404. It was surrendered to the Parliamentarians in 1648. On this occasion they did not proceed to its destruction. Beaumaris remains one of the best-preserved concentric castles in the UK.

Before the Romans swam across to Anglesey it was a druidic stronghold. It is the largest island in the UK, but the European Community refuses to subsidise it as such, ruling that the bridges across the Menai Strait have integrated it with the mainland. In fact, neither Telford's elegant road bridge (1818-26) nor Stephenson's railway bridge (1850) was built to unify Anglesey and Wales, but to further England's political and commercial purposes in Ireland, which can be reached by sea from Holyhead. And, despite Agricola's feat, tides, currents, and shifting sandbars make the strait notoriously difficult for shipping. In form and spirit Anglesey is an island, whatever the European Community may say.

CAERNARFON

POLICY IN STONE, LINGUISTIC RESISTANCE

THERE IS A STRONG CASE FOR SUGGESTING THAT CAERNARFON CASTLE, different in form and scale from other castles built in Wales by Edward I, is a conscious (and successful) attempt by him to state in stone his political attitudes and ambitions in Wales. The castle incorporates part of an earlier one built by the earl of Chester 200 years earlier, precisely because Edward thought of himself as reasserting an existing right. The locality's Christian and Roman associations were emphasized: the castle has polygonal towers and bands of colored masonry built into the gray stone walls, both in deliberate imitation of fortifications Edward had seen in Constantinople. During rebuilding, a body believed to be that of Emperor Constantine's father (local legend had it that Constantine had been born in the neighborhood), was reburied in the church that was also being built. The king's tower was decorated with imperial eagles. And, the clincher, Edward arranged for his heir to be born there and be called Prince of Wales, thus establishing that he and his successors were rightful rulers of Wales. The accommodations within the castle for royalty in residence are palatial. Furthermore, like the other castles in north Wales, it did its primary job; most were from time to time besieged, but very few rebels ever got inside one. To state as one Welsh writer does, that "It is all show… inside there is nothing of substance, an unintended but effective architectural metaphor for a bully's bluster" seems perverse and inadequate. "Some bully! Some bluster!" as Winston Churchill might have said. But the writer also concedes that the castle is "an extraordinarily impressive piece of architecture, rightly… on the UNESCO World Heritage list." Caernarfon was the linchpin of Edward's scheme for governing north Wales. Commanding the southern end of the Menai Straits, it ensured the quickest possible sea communications and provisioning for the castles strung along the north and west coasts, from Conwy to Aberystwyth—and, of course, could be reached by ships from Chester, just across the English border. On land, the Welsh were efficient at intercepting and pillaging supply trains; but the English, at that stage, did rule the waves.

Have a look at what remains of the town walls, and the church, which was at one time incorporated into them. Palace Street, which used to offer a choice of fourteen inns and taverns, retains a number of buildings from the seventeenth and eighteenth centuries and a more recent—and splendid—Market Hall. During Caernarfon's heyday as a port, Northgate Street was known as "Four-and-Six Street"—referring to the shillings and pence required to secure a sailor a room, a bottle of gin, and a woman for the night.

The Seiont Estuary is home to many fishing boats and pleasure craft.

facing page
The bands of colored masonry in the castle walls were copied from Constantinople.

Although Edward I's castles worked for some purposes, they failed in others. The idea that the English crown might gain legitimacy in Wales through resident princes of Wales, sank without trace. No Prince of Wales has ever shown any inclination to live there. The latest two were formally invested with the title at Caernarfon, then went back to England. Rather more importantly, perhaps, Caernarfonshire has remained stubbornly unconquered. Admittedly the proportion of its population who conducted ordinary life in Welsh fell between 1901 and 1991 from 89 percent to 61.5 percent—but of those percentages a proportion avoids using English altogether. Some nationalists regard even bilingual road signs as a craven compromise.

Caernarfon Air World has pleasure flights over the castles of northwest Wales and the mountains of Snowdonia. Those who want to climb Mount Snowdon (3,559 feet) the easy way use the mountain railway. There are several walkable paths to the summit. The least interesting simply follows the railway track. The most interesting, the Horseshoe Path, demands a considerable degree of experience and the ability to negotiate two sharp, rocky ridges, possibly in strong winds. Don't try to be brave, take advice about your route, take proper clothing, and be ready for changes in the weather. Don't wander into the mountains by yourself. Do tell someone concerned for your wellbeing where you intend to go and what time you expect to return.

If you find time to visit the National Slate Museum at Llanberis you will walk into an industry that once roofed Wales and whose output can be seen on rooftops in many parts of the UK. The museum is housed in restored Victorian workshops under Elidir Mountain, near the vast Dinorwig quarry. There are four quarrymen's houses, rescued from demolition in Blaenau Ffestiniog and reassembled to recapture significant periods in the history of the slate industry. One is furnished in the manner of the 1860s, another reflects the Penrhyn Strike of 1901, and a third the time of the quarry's closure in 1969. You can also visit the Chief Engineer's House, refurnished to reflect life in 1911. An additional attraction is that the National Museum stands in a dramatically beautiful landscape on the shores of Llyn Padarn, at the terminus of the Llanberis Lake Railway, which runs along the shore.

above
This pub, originally a customs house, is reputedly haunted.

right
Caernarfon Castle is the largest in Wales.

CARDIGAN

CHAPELS, SEALS, AND BUTTERFLIES

THE NAME "CARDIGAN" IS, AS SO OFTEN IN WALES, the result of a botched English attempt to pronounce a Welsh original. In this case that original is "Ceredigion" ("land of Ceredig"). The town therefore has no connection with either the seventh earl of Cardigan (who led the charge of the Light Brigade) or the woolen button-up jackets named after him. The actual town has character enough without need of such associations. Imagine a port within the estuary of a river, built largely in the eighteenth and nineteenth centuries, with Georgian and Victorian buildings and winding streets to match. Imagine a collection of fine Welsh chapels—whatever you think of what went on inside them, these buildings have a dignity and human interest—homely, classical, or perhaps merely respectable—as great in its way as that of most churches and cathedrals. (Their pews, sadly, suggest that the Welsh have a sturdy disregard for creature comforts.) Imagine the lively Mwldan Theater presenting its varied shows and musical events in what was once an abattoir. (I wonder if they have ever done *Sweeny Todd* there.) Then, having done your imagining, go to Cardigan to find out how far imagination falls short of reality.

After a long period of agitation, the medieval castle (1093) has at last come out of private ownership and is being restored. It has an important role in history of a competitive but not warlike kind: in 1171 it was host to the first nationally organized *eisteddfod*. Many other older buildings have also been refurbished, often with excellent effect. But Cardigan is not without problems for those who live there. Some young people see it as a place they have to escape if they wish to pursue any kind of ambition. They also say, apropos leisure activities, that "there is nothing to do," ignoring, presumably, well-intentioned mention of Sea Scouts and other such possibilities, let alone the sturdy suggestion that you can only be bored if you are yourself boring. One option less open to the discontented nowadays is that of emigration to North America. In the eighteenth and nineteenth centuries the Port of Cardigan was an important center of this activity, taking people to New Brunswick in Canada or to New York and other US ports. The forebears of the American architect Frank Lloyd Wright, from Llandysul, twenty miles upriver, were among those who took the latter course. Cardigan clearly realizes that one way of promoting prosperity is to welcome visitors. The list of annual events and festivals staged here is impressive. It includes an Outdoor Festival (sailing, surfing, climbing, kayaking, walking, canoeing, mountain biking); an annual regatta; agricultural show; coracle racing; and a food and river festival celebrating locally produced food.

facing page
Estimates of the age of this bridge vary from 400 to 800 years.

below
The Guild Hall embodies the prosperity and pride of nineteenth-century Cardigan.

Cardigan Bay is home to one of only two resident groups of bottlenose dolphins in the UK. There are thought to be about 120 of them. They grow to be about twelve feet long and can weigh something in the region of 800 pounds. They live for more than forty years and produce only one calf in three years. You can see them almost anywhere from the coast of Cardigan Bay. At Cardigan Island Farm Park (on the mainland; the island is a bird sanctuary) they are joined by a colony of Atlantic gray seals, which bask on exposed rocks at low tide, especially during warm weather. They seem to enjoy floating in the sea, staring at the strange creatures watching them from the clifftops.

The northern end of the Pembrokeshire Coastal Path is at St Dogmaels, across the river from Cardigan. The other end is 186 miles away. St Dogmaels has a ruined abbey and a parish church with inscriptions in Latin and Ogham, an alphabet used long ago for writing Irish and Pictish. The popular beach (which, however, never seems crowded) at Poppit Sands marks the beginning of the path proper. At Cemaes Head the path goes close to the edge of the 400-foot cliffs. Be wary! Walkers in this area remark upon butterflies, bluebells, gorse and profuse wildflowers, the geological formations and the distance you can see through the clean air. They also mention that the walk at this point is "taxing."

C O N W Y

WALLS AND WATERFALLS

Among Conwy's many attractive and charming features are its perfectly preserved, virtually complete medieval town walls. A walk along any of those considerable sections that have been fully restored will tell you a great deal about what life in a medieval town was like. They are 4,200 feet long and thirty feet high, with twenty-one round towers and three double-towered gates. They were built to keep Welshmen out; only on specific market days could the Welsh come into town. The only gap in them is at the point where local traffic enters the town. This is right by the castle, another of Edward I's legacies. Its eight towers—from which you can enjoy spectacular views of the town, coastline, and countryside—and connecting walls are all intact. (Be sure to see the Chapel Royal, in Chapel Tower.) Unlike Edward's other Welsh castles, all of which are concentric in design, this is essentially a rectangle—albeit with one rather angular side. It is built on a rocky outcrop below which the River Gyffin flows into the River Conwy, providing a moat.

Two-hundred buildings of architectural interest are listed in Conwy. St Mary's Church, which has a fifteenth-century rood screen, is in the center of a block, surrounded by lawns. It was still being built for the monks of Aberconway Abbey when Edward sent them elsewhere so that Aberconway, as it was then known, could become an English garrison town. The

Inside its medieval walls Conwy has many fine buildings.

facing page
At night especially, Conwy Castle looks like the stuff of legend.

abbey was being built under patronage of Llewelyn the Great, perhaps medieval Wales's most successful leader. A statue of him surmounts a pillar in nearby Lancaster Square. He's a splendid-looking chap: gold crown, orange moustache, scarlet cloak over his chain mail, and a scarlet-and-gold shield displaying four lions. There's a sixteenth-century nobleman's house called Plas Mawr ("the Great Mansion"—modest-looking outside but very grand inside) and a wealthy merchant's equivalent, Aberconwy House. This has a stone ground floor with timbering above; the rooms are decorated so as to illustrate different periods in its history. For a contrast with these large houses, go through the gates to the Quayside to see the smallest house in the UK. This is ten feet high and consists of two rooms one above the other, both nine feet by five feet. The last inhabitant, a century and a half ago, is said to have been six feet six inches tall. Conwy is also the Teapot Capital of North Wales: at Teapot World you may compare 1,000 of these useful domestic objects.

If at any time when exploring the town you wonder what has happened to all the through traffic, it is actually passing under your feet, in the UK's first immersed tube tunnel. Thomas Telford's suspension bridge (1826), designed to blend with the castle standing above it, was (after a struggle) preserved for the use of pedestrians, rather than demolished, when it was replaced in 1958.

The river Conwy flows through spectacular scenery from southern Snowdonia. Most spectacular is the series of waterfalls near Betws-y-Coed. Also nearby are Thomas Telford's Waterloo Bridge, and Ty Hyll (the Ugly House) built, legend has it, between sunset and sunrise, with walls, roof, and smoking chimney, allowing the builders to claim its freehold according to the law at the time. About five miles upriver from Conwy is Bodnant. There, above the river, with views across Snowdonia, you are offered Italianate terraces and formal lawns, rhododendrons, magnolias, camellias, a fifty-five-yard tunnel of golden laburnums, a wooded valley, stream, and a wild garden.

Conwy is within convenient reach of many other pleasant towns and beauty spots. Llandudno (see under LLANDUDNO) is a short distance north. Further afield, Bangor, with its cathedral and university, may be regarded as the cultural capital of north Wales. It is Welsh-speaking and strongly nationalist. The small villages dotted about the mountains are full of picturesque buildings and the best way of spending a day out of the town is probably to take local advice as to which of many possible walks are best adapted to your degree of fitness, experience, and interests. You will find many to choose from. Remember always that weather conditions can change quickly, so be prepared.

KNIGHTON

CALLING ALL WALKERS

KNIGHTON'S (ENGLISH) NAME REFERS TO THE KNIGHTS who kept peace in the border country. Its Welsh name is "Tref y Clawdd," "town on the dyke," referring to the fact that the town, uniquely, straddles Offa's Dyke, the defensive earthwork built along the Welsh border by King Offa (ruled 757-796). Knighton is in fact a Saxon settlement overrun by the Welsh—which is why we find here a Welsh border town with an English name. In Offa's time, Welshmen who crossed over to England had to be escorted during their visit and seen back onto Welsh soil before nightfall. There was a famous victory nearby when, in 1402, during the course of his rebellion against Henry IV, Owain Glyndwr, abandoning his usual guerilla tactics, confronted a large English force in a pass south of Knighton, routing them and capturing their leader. Shakespeare noted reports of atrocities: "…upon whose dead corpse(s) there was such misuse, / Such beastly shameless transformation, / By those Welshwomen done as may not be / Without much shame retold or spoken of." Nowadays Knighton is not a hotbed of Welsh nationalism; Welsh has not been spoken there for centuries. Its people shop in Ludlow, catch a train in Shropshire, and go to church in the diocese of Hereford. But, although Knightonians may be neither passionately Welsh nor English, they (and visitors) are passionate about their town: "the most lovely place in the world"; "one of the most beautiful towns in Mid Wales"; "the countryside is breathtaking": these are typical comments.

Knighton is built on a hillside. At the top there used to be a castle. The castle mound remains, giving a good view up and down the valley of the river Teme. At the bottom of the hill, St Edward's Church, surrounded by grass and trees, stands on a promontory above the river. Its square medieval tower remains (with an added pyramidal pergola for the eight bells). The Victorian interior is characteristic but fairly restrained. No medieval fittings survived the rebuilding, which was finished in 1877. From the church the main street leads upward to the market square, which has a charming Victorian clock tower: Big Ben in miniature in interestingly patterned gray stone, highlighted with light brown. Above the square is the Narrows, a Tudor street of small shops. In Broad Street stands the Old House, a medieval structure in which a framework of curved timbers supports the roof, which has a hole in it rather than a chimney. In the same street, the George and Dragon is a listed seventeenth-century coaching inn.

In 2001 Knighton acquired the UK's only Spaceguard Center, an independent observatory, impressively well-equipped. Opened in 2001 by Jay Tate, a former British Army officer, Spaceguard monitors the possible threats to our planet posed by "near-earth objects."

Some of the best-preserved sections of Offa's Dyke are in or near Knighton. Since 1971, following a campaign by a Knighton schoolteacher, the eighty miles that survive can be walked; the path attracts thousands of walkers every year. Frank Noble began his crusade in the 1960s by founding the Offa's Dyke Association. Then he persuaded farmers' wives along the dyke to open up spare bedrooms to walkers; now there are hundreds of places to stay along the route, including four-star hotels, guest houses, and farms. Walkers come from all over the world but the majority of overseas visitors are Dutch. Knighton is very aware that its economy now depends upon hikers and the trains that bring them.

facing page
In Knighton the countryside is always just around the corner.

below
St Edward's Church, with its interesting tower, is at the foot of the hill.

The River Teme Walk stays close to the secluded river for much of its ninety-three miles but in places takes to the hills. The Teme flows rapidly in its upper reaches but becomes placid as it passes, falling almost 900 feet, through Knighton, Ludlow, and Tenbury Wells to the Severn. Water level has been variable in recent years, partly because of extraction by farmers. In 2007 the problem went into reverse and the path had to be closed because of flooding. Nevertheless, in normal circumstances, A. E. Housman's celebratory words still apply: "In valleys of springs of rivers, / By Ony and Teme and Clun, / The country for easy livers, / The quietest under the sun..." In spring, damson, apple, and hawthorn blossom make the path especially inspiring.

LLANDRINDOD WELLS
A VICTORIAN REVIVAL

LLANDRINDOD MEANS "CHURCH OF THE TRINITY"; "Wells" was added during the nineteenth century, by the railway company, anxious to drum up trade. Thus Llandrindod became a spa town. (The spa waters had been known since Roman times. The mid-nineteenth-century pump room was closed and demolished in 1971 but reopened in 1983 as part of a deliberate revival of Llandrindod's Victorian heritage. (The railway station was "revictorianized" in 1990). Every year on August 18-26 a Victorian festival is staged, with around 200 programed events and 150 impromptu street performances. Horse and carriage, penny-farthing bicycles, buttered muffins, a Punch and Judy puppet show, and a palmist enliven the streets. Street organs and bandstand concerts fill the air with music. A Victorian fairground appears. Other annual events are less tied to the Victorian theme. In September comes the Heart of Wales Walking Festival: eleven guided walks (all-day or half-day walks, with a theme such as churches, natural history, or geology, and shorter walks within the town). Terrain covered varies from gently rolling countryside to moderately rugged hills, with narrow valleys, ancient hill forts, riverside paths, traces of Roman occupation, and other items of historical interest to add variety. At the beginning of May there is the Drama Festival Week, while the Royal Welsh Show, the largest agricultural show in the UK, comes in July to Llanelwedd, six miles south of the town. Among its delights and novelties are wood-chopping contests, dogs shepherding geese, and displays of riding and firing by the Royal Household Artillery.

Until the mid-eighteenth century there was no town where Llandrindod now stands—only a few scattered farming communities, the Llanerch Inn, and two thirteenth-century churches. Both churches are still used. One overlooks the town and the lake from a hill just south of town, the other is in a beauty spot that, although only just over a mile away, seems remote, known locally as Shaky Bridge. In 1749 an entrepreneur built a hotel between the town church and the lake. There were rooms for several hundred visitors, who could enjoy billiards, racing balls, and assemblies, and employ the services of milliners, hatters, and hairdressers. The first attempt to exploit the waters was badly handled, developing an unseemly reputation. The growth of the town remained slow, despite the railway, until 1880, when the Radnor County Council made the town its headquarters. Numbers of residents and visitors (up to 80,000 a year) continued to rise until the war of 1914-18 broke out. Thereafter Llandrindod was in decline. But now visitors are increasing greatly and the town, with its red brick villas and public buildings, has been given a thorough visual makeover. It looks and feels good.

Originally the Carnegie Library, Amgueddfa houses entrancing small collections.

facing page
Farm building nestling among trees and hedged fields near Llandridndod Wells, with open mountain landscape beyond.

East of Llandrindod is Radnor Forest, not a forest in the modern sense, but in the medieval sense of "an unenclosed area used for hunting": this was once a royal hunting ground. It is a land of hill farming, great heather clad moorlands and steep, narrow valleys. You will find plantations of upland spruce on its higher ground, and larch, douglas fir, and broadleafs in the more sheltered valleys. This is excellent walking country and while exploring it you may see any of the following: foxes, badgers, rabbits, hares, and roe deer on the ground; buzzards, goshawks, and hen harriers in the air.

St Stephen's at Old Radnor is the area's most celebrated church. Next to it is the site known as Old Radnor Castle. There is debate about the age and the purpose of this D-shape ditch—and no evidence of stone fortification. Apropos the church, it is likely that the Normans misunderstood the name of the Welsh Saint Ystyffan for that of the first Christian martyr; there is no other authentic dedication to Stephen in Wales. The church is built in gray stone with a slate roof and has a castellated square tower. Inside, its rood screen, in the fifteenth-century Gloucestershire style, and the round stone font with four squat feet (carved from a dolerite boulder dropped here by a glacier) are the most remarkable features.

LLANDUDNO

LOVELY FOR THE CHILDREN

LLANDUDNO STRADDLES A PENINSULA IN NORTH WALES. It has a large but also elegant crescent moon of beach, with hills at either end, backed by Victorian three-storied buildings. Donkeys take small, rapturous children for rides over the sands. There is a delightful pier. Some writers would have us believe that the place is in a time warp. More small children, again rapturous, cheer and laugh as they watch—good heavens!— Punch and Judy engaging in bruising domestic violence for entertainment. Doting parents or grandparents look on. Have they no idea how damaging and sexist this sort of show is? The adults look, in fact, as if they were remembering times they spent here during their own childhoods, enjoying the same delights all over again, including the feeling of discovering that this is what it is to be on holiday and that holidays are magic. Perhaps this is why people come to Llandudno: to get away from the riven, multicultural jungle they leave behind in Birmingham, London, or Cardiff. Here they can revisit an earlier time when things seemed less complicated: a time when *The Dam Busters* was the exciting new film, when Gracie Fields was modern music, and when *Peyton Place*, that dreadful movie, which they somehow saw (by accident, of course), signaled, all too accurately, imminent moral collapse.

Llandudno's location—on a side road leading only to itself—is symptomatic. If you come here you step out of the mainstream. In another way its location is profoundly contradictory. This is a very un-Welsh place. It might just as well be on the coast of Yorkshire, on the far side of this crowded and kaleidoscopic island. Or even on the south coast, somewhere between Brighton and Eastbourne. Two questions therefore arise: How did it come to be here? What is it for? Llandudno was created—invented, one might almost say—when a member of the Mostyn family in Conwy sold off this part of the family estate. Two Welsh architects, working in Liverpool, were commissioned and the resort was built in ten years. Its uniformity of architectural style has been preserved; that is part, if not all, of its charm. I have only ever been to Llandudno in late September, so cannot speak for it at the height of summer. But my suspicion is that even then, at the time of year when other British seaside resorts are rowdy and even, toward midnight, somewhat disgusting, Llandudno keeps its dignity. In September it is almost bewilderingly free of the litter and general dross that in most seaside towns make a generally tolerant but still sensitive person wonder whether the fears of moral and social degradation were not, after all, justified.

Llandudno's two headlands are Great Orme's Head and Little Orme's Head. For those of an indolent dispostion, Great Orme offers a choice of tramway or cable car to ride to the top.

Graceful Victorian buildings provide a backdrop for the curving beach.

facing page
The pier was built in 1878, is 1,234 feet long and reaches a graciously domed conclusion.

The geology, wildlife, archaeology, and landscape of the Great Orme are such that much of it is preserved as a Special Area of Conservation, Site of Special Scientific Interest, and Heritage Coast. Visiting naturalists delight in the butterflies, spiders, and birds. These arrive naturally but the area also maintains a flock of more than 150 Kashmiri goats. From the Bronze Age until the nineteenth century, copper was mined here. Excavated mine workings can be visited, along with a Neolithic burial chamber from c. 3,000 BCE. The attractive Church of St Tudno commemorates an early Welsh saint, who founded a church here in the sixth century, which was replaced in the thirteenth century.

Some guide books state that Llandudno is where Lewis Carroll told his young friend Alice Liddell the stories of the White Rabbit and the Mad Hatter, which he later wrote down and published as *Alice in Wonderland* (1863). Factually minded spoilsports point out that there is no evidence that Carroll was ever in Llandudno. (Alice and her family certainly were, at the holiday home on West Shore that they built and kept for eleven years.) The Alice in Wonderland Center in Trinity Square is aware of this lack of evidence and concentrates on Alice herself and the "Alice" books. The second of these, *Through the Looking Glass*, was written in 1868 after a chance encounter between Carroll and another Alice, a distant cousin called Alice Raikes.

LLANGOLLEN
"GENTLE ARE ITS SONGS"

LLANGOLLEN IS QUINTESSENTIAL NORTH WALES: a pretty town on a river in the bottom of a deep valley. The river is the Dee (meaning "divine"). This flows out of Lake Bala, twenty miles southwest of Llangollen on the fringe of Snowdonia; forms, after passing through it, part of the Welsh border; executes a U-turn around the English city of Chester; goes briefly home to Wales; then enters the Irish Sea. The sands, mudflats, and quicksands exposed at its mouth at low tide are notoriously treacherous.

The bridge over the Dee at Llangollen is one of the traditional Seven Wonders of Wales listed in an anonymous rhyme written, apparently, by an English tourist: "Pistyll Rhaeadr and Wrexham steeple, / Snowdon's mountain without its people, / Overton yew trees, St Winefride wells, Llangollen bridge and Gresford bells." John Trevor, later Bishop of St Asaph, built the bridge in the fourteenth century. Probably the first stone bridge over the Dee, it is a most elegant structure.

For much of the year life in Langollen is quiet, even introspective, but for a week each July the town is transformed by cosmopolitan hubbub. This is the time of the International Eisteddfod, when Llangollen is packed with dancers, singers, musicians, and merrymakers from many different nations, clad in national costumes. Founded in 1947, this was an attempt to heal the scars left by World War II: an international folk festival, along the lines of the Welsh National Eisteddfod but open to competitors from places as diverse as Ukraine, Morocco, and Patagonia. One of the early competitors was the tenor Luciano Pavarotti, still then a member of a Modena choir; he returned to give a goodwill concert in 1995. The motto of the gathering is touchingly simple: "Blessed is the world that sings, / Gentle are its songs."

Just outside Llangollen, on the steep road north to Horseshoe Pass, are the ruins of Valle Crucis Abbey, founded by Cistercians in 1201. In the fifteenth century many Welsh poets wrote of its delights. Shortly before its final dissolution, Abbot Robert Salbri is recorded as having been removed from Valle Crucis on charges of minting his own money and of being a highway robber. He was imprisoned in the Tower of London. Another, earlier abbot met Owain Glyndwr, the Welsh patriot, walking in the hills one morning. "You have risen early, Master Abbot," said the guerilla leader. "Nay, sire," replied the Abbot. "It is you who have risen early—a hundred years before your time." On a high, grassy hill northeast of the town stand the ruins of Castell Dinas Bran, a thirteenth-century castle built within the ramparts of an Iron Age hill fort. Severely damaged during Edward I's wars of conquest, it was never repaired.

The "Ladies of Langollen" entertained visiting writers in this enlarged cottage.

facing page
The Cistercians chose a typically remote site for Valle Crucis Abbey.

Most visitors want to see Plas Newydd ("new hall"), home during the early nineteenth century of the "Ladies of Llangollen." Eleanor Butler and Sarah Ponsonby came from Ireland to live in a cottage, which they enlarged and redecorated in the Gothic style. They dressed in men's clothes and lived in "friendship, celibacy, and the knitting of blue stockings," with a maid, their dog Flirt, and their cat Mrs Tatters. Among their visitors were Wordsworth (who wrote them a sonnet, concluding: "Sisters in love, a love allowed to climb, / Even on this earth, above the reach of time!"—but upset them by referring to their "low-roofed cot"); and Sir Walter Scott, who noted their resemblance to "respectable superannuated clergymen."

Do find time to take a trip on the Llangollen canal. You will experience a wonder of Wales equal to any of the listed seven. During the Industrial Revolution, when canals were being built to transport raw materials and manufactured goods all over the British Isles, William Telford faced the problem of taking the Shropshire Union Canal across the narrow, steep-sided Dee valley. His answer was the justly famous Pontcysyllte Aqueduct, the longest and highest in Britain. Completed in 1805, 121 feet high and 1,007 feet long, it carries the canal in a cast-iron trough supported by eighteen piers. To sail across it looking down at the Dee river valley beneath you is truly an exhilarating experience.

ST DAVID'S

PAGANS, MONKS, AND PILGRIMS

facing page
Locally quarried stone increases our feeling that the cathedral is entirely at home in its setting.

below
Remains of the Bishop's Palace

ST DAVID'S IS A PARADOXICAL PLACE. IT IS A VILLAGE that is called a city because it has a cathedral. That cathedral is by far the biggest building in the village—indeed it is the largest church in Wales—yet as you approach and drive into the village, it cannot be seen. Only when you've gone looking do you find the wooded, bowl-shape hollow where it stands. Why does this splendid large building, with its equally splendid Bishop's Palace and Bishop's Great Hall (both now consisting only of beautiful sets of walls) shrink so coyly away from notice? Why, come to that, is there a cathedral city out on the end of a peninsula that itself has the sense of being on the other side of nowhere? And why, unlike Chichester's equivalent center for the proclamation of Christianity, does it hide from observers at sea as well as those on land?

Around 550 David established a monastery here. (We know very little about him with any certainty; the earliest biography, written five centuries later, was essentially a propagandist work asserting the claims of the Welsh Church to independence from Canterbury.) When he and the monks arrived, so the story goes, they found a bevy of naked young women sporting in this "Valley of Roses," as it was known, drafted in by resident pagans to cure them of chastity and other such follies. We are to understand that they remained steadfast against temptation. David became, in due course, the patron saint of Wales. The cathedral was built in the twelfth century, the Bishop's Palace a century later. Like the monastery, they were built in the valley in order that Viking raiders sailing past should not be drawn to plunder them. The settlement nearby had suffered at least one damaging raid.

It cannot be denied that the cathedral sits very comfortably in its setting. Its beauties are many, both inside and out. The floor plan is cruciform. There is much exquisite carving; the misericords are frequently humorous as well. Two ceilings in the cathedral are particularly remarkable. That of the nave is somewhat lower than the actual roof, in golden Irish oak. The arches, bosses, and coffering, in slightly darker timber, are elaborately carved and there is some colored inlay. The square tower lantern ceiling is fan vaulted with a colorful cruciform arrangement of panels. The rood screen dividing nave from choir is equally delightful. Bishop Vaughan's chapel has a fan-vaulted Tudor roof. (The tomb of Edmund Tudor, father of Henry VII, first of the Tudor kings, is elaborately decorated with brass figures and heraldic emblems, and occupies a place of honor at the high altar. There is some attractive stained glass, some of it no more than sixty years old. In a shrine on the south side of the nave there is a statue of St David preaching. A dove, representing the Holy Spirit, perches on his shoulder, recalling that such an incident was reported as having occurred while he was addressing a conference of bishops. Finally, don't miss the Celtic grave marker embedded in the wall.

Because St David's is a recognized place of pilgrimage (two visits to St David's were reckoned the equal of one visit to Rome) it is well provided with a variety of places to stay, tearooms, restaurants, bookshops, and gift shops. A number of painters, sculptors, photographers, and artists of other kinds live and work in or near St David's. A look around the galleries here is always interesting and tempting. So are locally made chocolates. There are a number of music festivals based in the cathedral and it is also a venue used by festivals based in other towns.

A sixty-nine-mile circular tour can be made from St David's. Black sand at Abreiddy Beach is followed by Porthgain's mixture of seaside and industrial remains. (Book a table at the Shed Bistro.) On via Tregwyny Woollen Mill and the Iron-Age fort at Strumble Head, to Lower Fishguard, once a fishing village, now a boating harbor. Turning inland we pass through the Gwaun Valley, where otters and native woodlands survive, and the Llysyfran Country Park. (You can stop at both for enjoyable walks.) We return to the Sea at Slova, which has a boating harbor, working woolen mill, and a butterfly farm—then on to St David's. From there, on another day, we can walk in either direction along the Pembrokeshire Coast Path.

left
Pentre Ifan Cromlech burial ground is one of many druidical and Celtic sites in Pembrokeshire.

below
Near Pentre Ifan we find the thatched Iron Age roundhouses of Castell Henlyss.

left
The peninsula at Fishguard gives a taste of the Pembrokeshire Coastal Path.

Fishguard and Haverford West are both sixteen miles from St David's. Fishguard Lower Town was used as the setting for the film version of what Dylan Thomas's friend, Glyn Jones, calls "his preposterous and utterly convincing 'play for radio' *Under Milk Wood*." In 1997 seven women of Fishguard completed an "Invasion Tapestry" commemorating the appearance in Cardigan Bay 200 years earlier of a comically mismanaged French invading party. According to one account the ship was scared off by a single blank cannon shot; another has it that a force landed but its American commander decided that military operations would "tend only to bloodshed." Yet another tale has a force of local women in red cloaks marching fiercely upon the intruders, rendering them panicstricken. Haverford West has an attractive Town Hall, a number of handsome town houses, a Norman castle that houses a museum, and a number of good churches.

TENBY

"LITTLE ENGLAND BEYOND WALES"

ON NEW YEAR'S DAY CHILDREN IN TENBY SHOWER SPECTATORS with drops of water shaken from holly or twigs dipped in water. One writer remarks appropriately dryly that the spectators "donate money as thanks for their good fortune." The tradition may be related to winter fertility rites. Tenby was the birthplace of Robert Recorde (c. 1510-1558), the mathematician who invented the equals sign. Tenby and Pembrokeshire gave the artist Augustus John (1879-1961) more that just a birthplace: swimming here once, he injured his head, an accident that seems to have turned him from the cautious, rather timid man and artist he had previously been into a roaring extrovert with a large sexual appetite.

Tenby may strike visitors as more English than Welsh, and it is in fact part of "little England beyond Wales." This lies to the south of a cultural frontier called "the Landsker," between the Welsh-speaking and English-speaking parts of Pembrokeshire or, more generally, between Welsh-speaking middle and north Wales, and the southwestern fringe of people of Viking, Norman, and Flemish descent who in times past spoke a distinctive dialect of English. Historically the word "Landsker" has wandered in and out of official and general use. Nowadays various businesses and agencies use it as a trade name. The Normans built a chain of castles along the Landsker to keep wilder folk at bay; some have vanished, others survive to various degrees. Tenby was an important port until the end of the sixteenth century. Its economy revived in the eighteenth and nineteenth centuries, particularly after the railway started to bring an annual influx of fashionable holidaymakers. It has to a considerable extent resisted overcommercialization; the thirteenth-century town walls largely survive, Georgian houses overlook the harbor and beaches, and the narrow streets and passages of the medieval clifftop town have been preserved. Early frescoes can be seen on the interior walls of the Tudor Merchant's House and there is a partly medieval restaurant next door.

The rebuilding in the fifteenth century of St Mary's Church, complete with a very tall steeple, is testimony to the prosperity of the town at that time. Its interior is pleasingly light and airy and there is much to delight the eye, including a barrel roof with carved bosses and stained glass by John Eamer Kempe (1834-1907), the Tractarian architect and glass painter. Prevented by a speech impediment from becoming a clergyman, he expressed his fervent belief by beautifying church interiors. His use of green, ruby, and blue glass, with areas of silver stain, is refreshing and reflects his preference for fifteenth-century treatment of stained glass. On the subject of color we may note the existence of the Tenby daffodil, a rare wild plant, found only in Pembrokeshire, more erect and of deeper color than usual. These may still be found in graveyards.

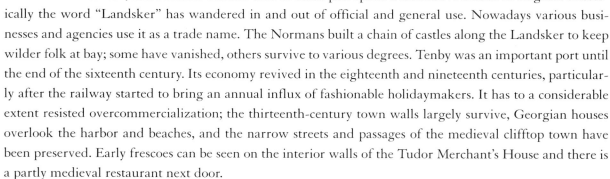

Castle Beach is one of Tenby's three very different beaches.

facing page
The decorative ironwork and porches of these cottages illustrate Tenby's English character.

Gerald of Wales (c. 1146-1223) was born in Manorbier, near Tenby, and described it as "the pleasantest spot in Wales." The castle we see today in an idyllic setting overlooking the sea is thirteenth-century, not the one in which Gerald was born. Holidaymakers can rent the house inside its walls. Gerald, said to be tall, with bushy eyebrows and vast energy, wanted to become bishop of St David's and was twice elected as such but rejected by Canterbury, which feared he might declare the Welsh Church independent. He devoted himself instead to writing four keenly observant, if sometimes tendentious and exaggerated, topographical books, two each about Wales and Ireland.

If you are in Tenby for several days in summer you may feel the need for a few hours of peace and quiet. A ferry trip to Caldey Island will answer that need. There was a monastery there in the fifth century. During the twentieth century the island was tenanted first by Anglican Benedictines, who later transferred their loyalty to Roman Catholicism and, since 1928, by Trappist Cistercians from Chimay in Belgium. Caldey is Norse for "cold," but the island's microclimate allows the monks to grow vegetables, herbs, and flowers and produce widely famed perfumes, chocolate, and shortbread. You may join a guided tour or explore in your own time, perhaps incorporating a picnic. There is an expansive, uncrowded beach at Priory Bay.

ARMAGH

CITY OF SAINTS AND SCHOLARS

Like Wells and St Andrews, Armagh is a small town, which is called a city because it has a cathedral. Two cathedrals, in fact: one Protestant, one Catholic. Both buildings are called "St Patrick's Cathedral." Both archbishops have the title "Archbishop of Armagh and Primate of all Ireland." A wit once spoke of "Armagh, where two cathedrals sit on opposing hills, like the horns of a dilemma." It is a dilemma that troubled Northern Ireland greatly during the twentieth century.

St Patrick's Protestant Catholic Cathedral is a sober building.

facing page
St Patrick's Catholic Cathedral is an exuberant exercise in neo-Gothic decoration.

There was a settlement here c. 370 BCE, founded by Queen Macha of the Red Locks, from whom its name derives. St Patrick arrived in the fifth century CE, converted the king and was given the means to found an archbishopric. (Armagh therefore predates Canterbury as a Christian center.) Patrick also set about making the town a seat of learning. As a medieval poet put it, "I found in Armagh, the splendid, / Meekness, wisdom, and prudence blended." We know a good deal about this period from *The Book of Armagh*, the very beautiful work of a monastic scribe, which contains a life of St Patrick, the text of the Gospels and other material. It is now at Trinity College Dublin. The religious fracturing of Ireland began with the Norman Conquest; the Normans wanted a church based on parishes and dioceses rather than on monasteries. They also ruled that no Irishman could ever become archbishop. The Reformation made little headway at first, but the Act of Supremacy imposed by Henry VIII in 1537, the establishment of the Church of Ireland in 1560 (by the Irish parliament in Dublin), and increasing immigration from England and Scotland were all factors in the growth of Protestantism, particularly in the political centers. Although Armagh remained the primatial city it suffered a decline from its great days, not least through being burned to the ground by Norse raiders. In 989 it had been described as "the most melancholy spot in the kingdom"; and it continued to suffer destructive attacks in the centuries following.

Everything changed in the late eighteenth century. Archbishop Robinson took one look at the dismal town to which he had been appointed and decided to spend much of his enormous wealth on improving his see. In succession he built an episcopal palace, public library, royal school, public infirmary, jail, and barracks.

Apart from St Patrick, two other archbishops of Armagh have attracted particular attention. The Protestant James Ussher, archbishop after 1625, was a good and careful scholar. Sadly for his reputation he is best known today for his painstaking chronology of Biblical history, which established that the world was created in 4,004 BCE. The Catholic Oliver Plunkett, archbishop after 1669, fell a victim to the panic created by Titus Oates, who spread stories of a popish plot to murder King Charles II and replace him with his Catholic brother, James. Plunkett was arrested, taken to London, tried, and executed for treason in 1681.

He lit and paved the streets, planted trees, and built terraces of three-storied houses. He also restored the cathedral, less successfully—much that was good in the old one disappeared. (The Roman Catholic cathedral has a handsome Gothic exterior and a garishly decorated, Italianate interior.) Good buildings were added later to the Archbishop's benefactions: a courthouse, market house, and the Bank of Ireland.

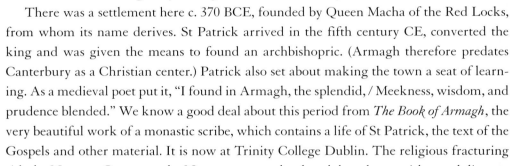

Ireland's largest lake, Lough Neagh, is about fifteen miles from Armagh. In the winter it is visited by thousands of waterfowl and it supports vast numbers of eels. There are many rural beauty spots in south Armagh, among the mountains, bogs, nature parks, and cultural activity centers. In particular, Slieve Gullion Forest Park should not be missed. Among great houses worth visiting are Gosford Castle, the UK's first Norman Revival house, built in 1820 and Castle Leslie, an extravagant baronial mansion with an extensive collection of Italian paintings and objets d'art, with an equestrian center attached. Its publicity tells us, accurately, that its "links with reality are tenuous indeed."

DERRY

"THE TOWN I LOVED SO WELL"

THE RIVER FOYLE WINDS MAJESTICALLY THROUGH THE MODERN CITY and port of Derry. Above its left bank stands the last walled city built in Ireland: the only one whose walls still stand complete. In most towns in the UK, history is comfortably in the past. This is not so in Derry, an epicenter of the "Troubles," which ravaged Northern Ireland after 1969. Perhaps these will have come to an end with the reestablishment of power-sharing in Northern Ireland in 2007—but at the time of writing, Derry still awaits publication of the Saville Report on the thirteen deaths resulting from the "Bloody Sunday" civil-rights protest march in 1972. (Lord Saville began hearing evidence in 1998.)

St Columba founded an abbey in an oak grove (*Daire*) at Derry in c. 546. Early in the seventeenth century the English captured the town and an association of trade guilds was formed in London for the purpose of planting an English colony there. Its name was changed to Londonderry—still used officially in England, but seldom in Ireland. The town walls—almost a mile long, twenty-five feet high and twenty-eight feet thick—were built (1614-19) to protect the colonists. Catholics lived outside the walls, in the Bogside. In 1789 Derry resisted a 105-day siege by the forces of the Catholic James II. When the governor suggested surrender he was expelled and apprentice boys locked the gates behind him. (The incident is ceremonially reenacted annually.) Following the power-sharing agreement in 2007 there is hope that "the bright, brand new day," wished for by local songwriter Phil Coulter in *The Town I Loved So Well*, has at last arrived.

The walls are a popular attraction and you may take a guided tour of them. On the side nearest the river are seven cannons given by Elizabeth I and the London guilds. A plaque commemorates Captain Michael Browning, who captained the ship *Mountjoy*, which broke the Catholic blockade and ended the siege in 1599. Within these walls, St Columba's Cathedral (Protestant, 1628–33) has been described as "Planter's Gothic" and contains objects and monuments from the seventeenth century, as well as Victorian and modern additions. The Apprentice Boys' Memorial Hall (1877) honors the thirteen boys who locked the gates in 1789. It houses a social club and a museum and may be visited by arrangement. Outside the walls the Courthouse (1817), Georgian houses, St Columba's Church (Catholic, 1873, on the site of the original abbey), and the Guildhall (1912) are all of interest.

Also, of course, there is the Bogside, the Catholic area where the Bloody Sunday shootings took place. This is scarcely beautiful but the sign YOU ARE NOW ENTERING FREE DERRY, a Bloody Sunday wall painting, and a memorial to the hunger strikers in the Maze Prison all provide a stark reminder of the violence that ruled there for thirty years. .

Derry has a wide range of museums: Tower (complete history of Derry); Harbor (maritime connections); Riverwatch (river and loughs); Workhouse (Famine, Battle of the Atlantic); Amelia Earhart, (the American aviatrix). Prehen House, home of the colorful Knox family and one of the Northwest's most historic buildings, stands next to the famous woods, commanding panoramic views of Derry, the river Foyle, and the hills beyond. Shirt making on an industrial scale began in Derry over 150 years ago; the Glenaden Shirt Museum was opened—in a former shirt factory—in 2004, by a group of local women with among them several hundred years' experience of making shirts.

facing page
The Guildhall in Shipquay Street, Derry—or Londonderry, according to where your loyalties lie.

below
The Diamond War memorial is one of Derry's prominent landmarks.

The town is never the whole story in Ireland: look outside it. You can fish in season for salmon and sea trout in the river Foyle. Birds flock in great numbers on Lough Foyle, including, in early winter, brent geese and whooper swans. Eastward (about forty miles; there is a bus) stands one of Ireland's most famous sights, the Giant's Causeway, a coastal formation of basalt columns. This was once believed to be one end of a road made by Fingal, a mythical giant, to his cave on Staffa, in the Inner Hebrides, where there is a similar formation. Going west, you may like to hire a car and cross the border into Donegal, which combines spectacular coastal scenery with lush vegetation and attractive villages.

Differences of religious opinion have had tragic effects in Derry in the past. But as well as tragedy there has been comedy. Among the many demons that Northern Ireland Protestants abhor is alcohol. The notable playwright, IRA man, and drinker, Brendan Behan, once found himself in need of a bottle of wine in Derry on a Sunday. (All anecdotes coming from Behan himself are, it has to be said, untrustworthy.) The only possible source was a pharmacy run by a teetotaller who refused to serve him. She was won round when told he was a Calathumpian, a sect of which she had never heard—unsurprisingly, since he had invented it on the spur of the moment. Calalthumpians, he explained, ate the stalks of cabbages but not the leaves and, following New Testament practice, drank only wine with their meals. She decided that she should not "interfere with any man's covenant with God," and gave him a bottle.

below
Nearby, the ruins of Dunluce Castle perch above the undermining sea.

above
These low columns mark one end of a supposed gigantic bridge to the Scottish island of Staffa.

right
Derry's wildest pubs and clubs can be found—or avoided!—in Waterloo Street.

ENNISKILLEN

A BOMB, BEAUTY, AND A SOVIET SPY

THE WORLD AT LARGE FIRST HEARD OF ENNISKILLEN on November 8, 1987. People had gathered at the Cenotaph for the annual Remembrance Day Service, to pay respect to the dead of two world wars. That morning eleven of them joined the number of those killed in pursuance of a perceived better world. The IRA had planted a bomb in a nearby hall. Later, when the organization realized how hugely it had lost the sympathy even of those who accepted its case for a united Ireland, it apologized.

The problem, as always in Ireland, had to do with history. Ireland had never been subjected to Roman rule. It was thinly populated and not notably attuned to the idea of living in towns. Although Christianity arrived earlier there than it did in England, it was confined largely to monasteries or towns like Armagh, which had grown up around them. Ireland was governed, insofar as it was governed at all, by a rabble of clans, which were usually at war with each other. Its desirable agricultural land attracted the attention of its aggressive neighbors across the Irish Sea. In the twelfth century Henry II invaded it and established English rule in a fairly limited area, known as "the pale," around Dublin. (To be, in the traditional English phrase, "beyond the pale" was to be lawless and ignorant.) Fortified by their mission to civilize and by the lure of an apparently defenseless target, the English, under Elizabeth I, James I, and Oliver Cromwell, established what they called "plantations," which in effect meant rewarding English people for services rendered by giving them a large estate in Ireland. Thus it was that the area around Enniskillen ceased to be ruled by the Clan Maguire and became the domain of one William Cole. The locals cannot have been entirely dismayed, since less than a century later they were staunchly Protestant and, with Derry, supported William of Orange in resisting the Catholic James II. Nonetheless, the "plantations" shaped the pattern of Irish history for 400 years—and led with horrible, seemingly inevitable directness to the bombing in 1987.

Is Enniskillen a beautiful town? It has every natural advantage. It is largely surrounded by the river Erne, which southeast and northwest of the town broadens into the upper and lower loughs of Erne. Lake isles, so beloved of W. B. Yeats, are plentiful. So are picture book Irish villages (on either side of the border between Northern Ireland and Eire, not far away). Enniskillen Castle presents an array of nineteenth century barracks buildings surrounding the medieval castle keep; to the south, with its distinctive turrets is the seventeenth-century Watergate, which guarded the ford across the river.

Castle Coole,
a magnificent
neo-classical house
completed in 1798.

facing page
The 600-year-old
castle and St
Michael's Roman
Catholic Church.

Devenish Island in lower Lough Erne is reached by boat from the town. There you will find the remains of a monastery, a round tower with sculptured heads on its cornice, and St Mary's Abbey. At Florence Court on the edge of the wild Cuilcagh Mountains, the first Lord Mount Florence was able to use inherited wealth to build himself a very grand house indeed. The chief pleasure of its interior is the plasterwork, variously described as "exquisite" and "riotous," done by a Dublin *stuccadore*. A few miles away, Castle Coole was built by the noble lord's brother-in-law, in a deliberate attempt to outdo Florence Court. He ran out of funds before it was finished but his son was able to complete the work after his death.

Portora Royal School has educated and exported some diverse "old boys." Brian Goold-Verschoyle, for example, became a Soviet spy, lost favor with Stalin, and died in the Gulag. The hymn writer Henry Francis Lyte, who saw "change and decay... all around" and anticipated the moment when "Heaven's morning breaks and earth's vain shadows flee," was there in the late eighteenth century. Oscar Wilde, who wrote *The Importance of Being Earnest*, one of the greatest of all stage comedies, followed in the mid-nineteenth century. Samuel Beckett, who wrote *Waiting for Godot*, which is to existentialism what *Earnest* is to comedy, was there in the early 1900s. Coincidentally, all three writers died in France.

ADDRESSES

The National Trust
(England, Wales, Northern Ireland)
PO Box 39
Warrington WA5 7WD
phone +44 (0) 870 458 4000
fax +44 (0) 870 609 0345
enquiries@thenationaltrust.org.uk
minicomb +44 (0) 870 240 3207

The National Trust for Scotland
Wemyss House, 28 Charlotte Square
Edinburgh, Scotland EH2 4ET
phone +44 (0) 844 493 2100
fax +44 (0) 131 243 9301
information@nts.org.uk

English Heritage
Customer Services Department
PO Box 569
Swindon SN2 2YP
phone +44 (0) 870 333 1181
fax +44 (0) 1793 414926
customers@english-heritage.org.uk

abergavenny (wales)

Abergavenny Tourist Information Centre
Swan Meadow, Cross Street
Abergavennny, Monmouthshire NP7 5HH
phone +44 (0) 1873 857588
abergavenny.tic@monmouthshire.gov.uk

Abergavenny Hotel and Y Fenni Restaurant
21 Monmouth Road
Abergavenny, Monmouthshire NP7 5HF
phone +44 (0) 1873 855324
fax +44 (0) 1873 852193

The Angel Hotel
15 Cross Street
Abergavenny, Monmouthshire NP7 5EN UK
phone +44 (0) 1873 857121
fax +44 (0) 1873 858059
mail@angelhotelabergavenny.com

Llanwenarth Hotel and Riverside Restaurant
Brecon Road
Abergavenny (3 m), Monmouthshire NP81EP
phone +44 (0) 1873 810550
fax +44 (0) 1873 811880
info@llanwenarthhotel.com

Park Guest House
36 Hereford Rd,
Abergavenny, Monmouthshire NP75RA
phone +44 (0) 1873 853715
info@parkguesthouse.co.uk

The Hardwick Restaurant
Abergavenny, Monmouthshire NP79AA
phone +44 (0) 1873 854220

The Malthouse Italian Restaurant
Lion Street
Abergavenny, Monmouthshire NP75PB
phone +44 (0) 1873 859960

Abergavenny Museum
The Castle, Castle Street
Abergavenny, Monmouthshire
phone +44 (0) 1873 854282
www.abergavennymuseum.co.uk

Skenfrith Castle
Skenfrith
nr Abergavenny, Monmouthshire NP7 8UH
phone +44 (0) 1874 625515
skenfrithcastle@nationaltrust.org.uk

Big Pit: National Mining Museum
Blaenafon, Gwent NP4 9XP
phone +44 (0) 1495 790311
www.nmgw.ac.uk/bigpit

Roman Legionary Museum, Caerleon
High Street
Caerleon, Newport, Gwent NP18 1AE
phone +44 (0) 1633 423134
www.nmgw.ac.uk/rlm/rlmhome.html

Cyfarthfa Castle and Art Gallery
Brecon Road
Merthyr Tydfil, Mid Glamorgan CF47 8RE
phone +44 (0) 1685 723112

The Kymin
Monmouth, Monmouthshire NP25 3SE
phone +44 (0) 1600 719241
kymin@nationaltrust.org.uk

aberystwyth (wales)

Aberystwyth Tourist Information Centre
Terrace Road
Aberystwyth, Ceredigon SY23 2AG
phone +44 (0) 1970 612125
fax +44 (0) 1970 612125
aberystwythtic@ceredigion.gov.uk

Harry's Restaurant Hotel
40-46 North Parade
Aberystwyth, Ceredigon SY23 2NF
phone +44 (0) 1970 612647
fax +44 (0) 1970 627068

Richmond Hotel
The Promenade, 44/45 Marine Terrace
Aberystwyth, Ceredigon SY23 2BX
phone +44 (0) 1970 612201
fax +44 (0) 1970 626706
reservations@richmondhotel.uk.com

Bodalwyn Guest House
Queen's Avenue
Aberystwyth, Ceredigon SY23 2EG
phone +44 (0) 1970 612578
fax +44 (0) 1970 639261

Savannah Guest House
27 Queens Road
Aberystwyth, Ceredigon SY23 2HN
phone +44 (0) 1970 615131

Gannets Bistro
St James Square
Aberystwyth, Ceredigon SY23 1DL
phone +44 (0) 1970 617164

Le Vignoble
31 Eastgate
Aberystwyth, Ceredigon SY23 2AR
phone +44 (0) 1970 630800

Little Italy
51 North Parade
Aberystwyth, Ceredigon SY23 2JN
phone +44 (0) 1970 625707

National Library of Wales
The University of Wales
Buarth Mawr
Aberystwyth, Ceredigon SY23 3BU
phone +44 (0) 1970 632800
www.llgc.org.uk

Aberystwyth School of Art Collection
The University of Wales
Buarth Mawr
Aberystwyth, Ceredigon SY23 1NE
phone +44 (0) 1970 622460

Ceramics Gallery
School of Art, University of Wales
Buarth Mawr
Aberystwyth, Ceredigon SY23 1NE
phone +44 (0) 1970 622460

aldeburgh (east anglia)

Aldeburgh Tourist Information Centre
152 High Street
Aldeburgh, Suffolk IP15 5AQ
phone/fax +44 (0) 1728 453 637
atic@suffolkcoastal.gov.uk
http://www.suffolkcoastal.gov.uk/

The Brudenell
The Parade
Aldeburgh, Suffolk
phone +44 (0) 1728 452 071
info@brudenellhotel.co.uk
www.brudenellhotel.co.uk

The Wentworth Hotel
Wentworth Road
Aldeburgh, Suffolk IP15 5BD
phone +44 (0) 1728 452312
fax +44 (0) 1728 454343
stay@wentworth-aldeburgh.com

The Lighthouse
77 High Street
Aldeburgh, Suffolk
phone/fax +44 (0) 1728 453 377
sarafox@diron.co.uk
www.lighthouserestaurant.co.uk

152
152 High Street
Aldeburgh, Suffolk IP15 5AX
phone +44 (0) 1728 454 594
info@152aldeburgh.co.uk

Regatta
171/173 High Street,
Aldeburgh, Suffolk IP15 5AN
phone +44 (0) 1728 452 011
fax +44 (0) 1728 453 324.
regatta.restaurant@aldeburgh.sagehost.co

Snape Maltings
nr Aldeburgh, Suffolk IP17 1SR
phone +44 (0) 1728 688303
info@snapemaltings.co.uk

Orford Ness National Nature Reserve
Quay Office
Orford Quay
Orford, Woodbridge, Suffolk IP12 2NU
phone +44 (0) 1728 648024
orfordness@nationaltrust.org.uk

Sutton Hoo
Sutton Hoo
Woodbridge, Suffolk IP12 3DJ
phone +44 (0) 1394 389 700
www.nationaltrust.org.uk

ambleside (lake district & northwest)

Ambleside Tourist Information Centre
Central Buildings, Market Cross
Ambleside, Cumbria LA22 9BS
phone +44 (0) 15394 32582 /31576
tic@thehubofambleside.com

The Ambleside Salutation Hotel
Lake Road
Ambleside, Cumbria LA22 9BX
phone +44 (0) 15394 32244
fax +44 (0) 15394 34157
enquiries@hotelambleside.uk.com

Rothay Manor Hotel and Restaurant
Rothay Bridge
Ambleside, Cumbria LA22 OEH UK
phone +44 (0) 15394 33605
fax +44 (0) 15394 33607
hotel@rothaymanor.co.uk

Brathay Lodge
Rothay Road
Ambleside, Cumbria LA22 0EE
phone +44 (0) 15394 32000
info@brathay-lodge.com

Elder Grove
Lake Road
Ambleside, Cumbria LA22 0DB
phone +44 (0) 15394 32504
fax +44 (0) 15394 32251
info@eldergrove.co.uk

The Log House Restaurant and Bar
Lake Road
Ambleside, Cumbria LA22 0DN
phone: +44 (0) 15394 31077
nicola@loghouse.co.uk

Lucy's on a Plate
Church Street
Ambleside, Cumbria LA22 0BU
phone +44 (0) 15394 31191
info@lucysofambleside.co.uk

Armitt Museum and Library
Rydal Road
Ambleside, Cumbria LA22 9BL
phone +44 (0) 15394 31212
info@armitt.com

Stagshire Garden
Ambleside, Cumbria LA22 0HE
phone +44 (0) 15394 46027
stagshaw@nationaltrust.org.uk

Beatrix Potter Gallery
Main Street
Hawkshead, Cumbria LA22 0NS
phone +44 (0) 15394 36355
beatrixpottergallery@nationaltrust.org.uk

Coniston andTarn Hows
Boon Crag
Coniston, Cumbria LA21 8AQ
phone + (0) 15394 41197
Coniston@nationaltrust.org.uk

Blackwell
Bowness-on-Windermere, Cumbria LA23 3JR
phone +44 (0) 15394 46139
www.blackwell.org.uk

Brantwood
Coniston, Cumbria LA21 8AD
phone +44 (0) 15394 41396
www.brantwood.org.uk/

Dove Cottage
and the Wordsworth Museum
Town End
Grasmere, Cumbria LA22 9SH
phone +44 (0) 15394 35544
www.wordsworth.org.uk

Fell Foot Park
Newby Bridge
Ulverston, Cumbria LA12 8NN

Gondola
Pier Cottage
Coniston, Cumbria LA21 8AJ
phone +44 (0) 15394 41288
gondola@nationaltrust.org.uk

Ruskin Museum
Yewdale Road
Coniston, Cumbria LA21 8DU
phone +44 (0) 1539 441164
www.ruskinmuseum.com

Grassmere and Great Langdale
High Close, Loughrigg
Ambleside, Cumbria LA22 9HH
phone +44 (0) 15394 37663
grasmere@nationaltrust.org.uk

Hill Top
with **Hawkshead and Claife**
Hill Top
nr Sawrey
Ambleside, Cumbria LA22 0LF
phone +44 (0) 115394 36269

Townend
Troutbeck
Windermere, Cumbria LA23 1LB
phone +44 (0) 15394 32628
townend@nationaltrust.org.uk

Windermere and Troutbeck
(including Bridge House)
St Catherine's
Patterdale Road
Windermere, Cumbria LA23 1NH
phone +44 (0) 15394 46027
windermere@nationaltrust.org.uk@nationaltru
st.org.uk

armagh (northern ireland)

Armagh Tourist Information Centre
40 English Street
Armagh, Northern Ireland BT61 7BA
phone +44 (0) 28 3752 1800
fax +44 (0) 28 3752 8329
info@visitarmagh.com
www.visitarmagh.com

Armagh City Hotel
2 Friary Road
Armagh, Northern Ireland BT60 4FR
phone +44 (0) 28 3751 8888

fax +44 (0) 28 3751 2777
info@armaghcityhotel.com

Charlemont Arms Hotel
57-65 English Street
Armagh, Northern Ireland
phone +44 (0) 28 3752 2028
fax +44 (0) 28 3752 6979
info@charlemontarmshotel.com

Fairylands Country House
25 Navan Fort Road
Armagh, Northern Ireland BT60 4PM
phone +44 (0) 28 3751 0315
info@fairylands.net

Hillview Lodge
33 Newtownhamilton Road,
Armagh, Northern Ireland BT60 2PL
phone +44 (0) 28 3752 20
info@hillviewlodge.com

The Stage Bar and Bistro
The Market Place Theatre, Market St, Keady,
Armagh, Northern Ireland BT60 3RP
phone +44 (0) 28 3752 1828
fax +44 (0) 28 3752 1822
info@thestagearmagh.com

Stonebridge Restaurant
74 Legacorry Road
Richhill (Armagh ca 6 m)
County Armagh, Northern Ireland BT61 9LF
phone +44 (0) 28 3887 0024
fax +44 (0) 28 3887 9673
info@stonebridgerestaurant.co.uk

Zio
7 Market Street
Armagh, Northern Ireland BT61 7BW
phone +44 (0) 28 3752 2299

The Market Place
Armagh Theatre and Arts Centre
Market Street
Armagh, County Armagh,
Northern Ireland BT61 7BW
phone +44 (0) 28 3752 1821
admin@themarketplacearmagh.com

Ardress House
64 Ardress Road
Annaghmore
Portadown
County Armagh, Northern Ireland BT62 1SQ
phone +44 (0) 28 8778 4753
ardress@nationaltrust.org.uk

The Argory
144 Derrycaw Road
Moy
Dungannon
County Armagh, Northern Ireland BT71 6NA
phone +44 (0) 28 8778 4753
argory@nationaltrust.orguk

Derrymore House
Bessbrook
Newry
County Armagh, Northern Ireland BT35 7EF
phone+44 (0) 28 8778 4753
derrymore@nationaltrust.org.uk

ayr (scottish lowlands)

Ayr Tourist Information Centre
22 Sandgate,
Ayr, Scotland KA7 1BW
phone +44 (0) 1292 288 688
fax +44 (0) 1292 288 686
http://www.ayrshire-arran.com

The Abbotsford Hotel
and Bells Wynd Restaurant
14 Corsehill Road
Ayr, Scotland KA7 2ST
phone +44 (0) 1292 261506
fax +44 (0) 1292 261606
info@abbotsfordhotel.co.uk

Western House Hotel
and Jockey Club Restaurant
Ayr Racecourse, 2-6 Whitletts Road
Ayr, Scotland KA8 0JE
phone +44 (0) 870 8505666
faz +44 (0) 870 5665667
info@ayr-racecourse.co.uk

Belmont Guest House
15 Park Circus
Ayr, Scotland KA7 2DJ
phone +44 (0) 1292 265588
fax +44 (0) 1292 29030
belmontguesthouse@btinternet.com

Coila Guest House
10 Holmston Road
Ayr, Scotland KA7 3BB
phone +44 (0) 1292 262642
info@coila.co.uk

Langley Bank Guest House
39 Carrick Road
Ayr, Scotland KA7 2RD
phone +44 (0) 1292 264246
fax +44 (0) 1292 282628
langleybank@ukonline.co.uk

Fouters Bistro
2A Academy Street
Ayr, Scotland KA7 1HS
phone +44 (0) 1292 261391
fax +44 (0) 1292 619323

Vito's
Burns Statue Square
Ayr, Scotland KA7 1SU
phone +44 (0) 1292 290777
fax +44 (0) 1292 290777
info@vitosayr.co.uk

Brodick Castle
Isle of Arran, Scotland KA27 8HY
phone +44 (0) 1770 302202
www.nts.org.uk

bamburgh (northeast)

Seahouses Tourist Information Centre
Seafield Car Park
Seafield Road
Seahouses (Bamburgh 2.5 m.),
Northumberland NE68 7SW
phone +44 (0) 1665 720 884
fax +44 (0) 1665 721 436
seahousesTIC@beriwck-upon-tweed.gov.uk

Lord Crewe Arms Hotel
Front Street
Bamburgh, Northumberland NE69 7BL
phone +44 (0) 1668 214243

Victoria Hotel
Front Street
Bamburgh, Northumberland NE69 7BP
phone +44 (0) 1668 214 431
fax +44 (0) 1668 214 404

(both hotels also function as restaurants)

Dunstanburgh Castle
Craster
Alnwick, Northumberland NE66 3TT
phone +44 (0) 1665 576231
dunstanburghcastle@nationaltrust.org.uk

Farne Islands
Northumberland
phone +44 (0) 1665 721099
farneislands@nationaltrust.org.uk

barnstaple (west country)

Barnstaple Tourist Information Centre
36 Boutport Street
Barnstaple, Devon EX31 1RX
phone +44 (0) 1271 375000
fax +44 (0) 1271 374037
barnstapletic@visit.org.uk
www.staynorthdevon.co.uk

The Imperial Hotel
Taw Vale Parade
Barnstaple, Devon EX32 8NB
phone +44 (0) 1271 345 861
fax +44 (0) 1271 324 448
reservations@brend-imperial.co.uk

The Royal & Fortescue Hotel
Boutport Street
Barnstaple, Devon EX31 1HG
phone +44 (0) 1271 342 289
fax +44 (0) 1271 340102.
reservations@royalfortescue.co.uk

Zena's Restaurant
Market Street
Barnstaple, Devon
phone +44 (0) 1271 378 844

The Bank (brasserie)
Boutport Street
Barnstaple, Devon
phone +44 (0) 1271 324 446

Chambers Brasserie
The Squame
Barnstaple, Devon
phone +44 (0) 1271 321045

Arlington Court and National Trust
Carriage Collection
Arlington
nr Barnstaple, Devon EX31 4LP
phone +44 (0) 10271 850296
arlingtoncourt@nationaltrust.org.uk

Lundy
Bristol Channel
Devon EX39 2LY
phone +44 (0) 1271 863636
lundy@nationaltrust.org.uk

Watersmeet Gorge
Watersmeet Road
Lynmouth, Devon EX35 6NT
phone +44 (0) 1598 753348
watersmeet@nationaltrust.org.uk

West Exmoor Coast
Heddon Valley
Parracombe
Barnstaple, Devon EX31 4PY
phone +44 (0) 1598 763402
heddonvalley@nationaltrust.org.uk

The Queen's Theatre
Boutport Street
Barnstaple, Devon EX31 1SY
phone +44 (0) 1271 324242

bath (west country)

Bath Tourist Information Centre
Russel Street
Bath, Somerset BA1 1LY
phone +44 (0) 870 444 6442
tourism@bathtourism.co.uk

The Queensbury Hotel
4-7 Russell Street
Bath, Somerset BA1 2QF
phone +44 (0) 1225 447 928
fax +44 (0) 1225 446 065
ahres@compasshotels.co.uk

Dukes Hotel
Great Pulteney Street
Bath, Somerset BA2 4DN
phone +44 (0) 1225 787 960
fax +44 (0) 1225 787 961
info@dukesbath.co.uk

Café du Globe
1a North Parade
Bath, Somerset BA1 1LF
phone +44 (0) 1225 466 437

The Hole in the Wall
16 George Street
Bath, Somerset BA1 2EH
phone +44 (0) 1225 425 242

Sally Lunn's House
4 North Parade Passage
Bath, Somerset BA1 1NX
phone +44 (0) 1225 461 634
www.sallylunns.co.uk

Tilley's Bistro
North Parade Passage
Bath, Somerset BA1 1NX
phone +44 (0) 1225 484 2003
dmott@tilleysbistro.co.uk

American Museum in Britain
Claverton Manor
Bath, Somerset BA2 7BD
phone +44 (0) 1225 460503
info@americanmuseum.org

Holburne Museum of Art
Great Pulteney Street
Bath, Somerset BA2 4DB
phone +44 (0) 1225 466669
www.bath.ac.uk/Holburne/

Museum of Costume
Assembly Rooms
Bennett Street
Bath, Somerset BA1 2QH
phone +44 (0) 1225 477789
www.museumofcostume.co.uk

Roman Baths
Pump Room, Stall Street
Bath, Somerset BA1 1LZ
www.romanbaths.co.uk

Prior Park Landscape Garden
Ralph Allen Drive
Bath, Somerset BA2 5AH
phone +44 (0) 1225 833422
priorpark@nationaltrust.org.uk

Victoria Art Gallery
By Pulteney Bridge
Bath, Somerset BA2 4AT
phone +44 (0) 1225 477233
www.victoriagal.org.uk

Dyrham Park
Dyrham
nr Bath, Gloucestershire SN14 8ER
phone +44 (0) 117 937 2501
dyrhampark@nationaltrust.org.uk

Clevedon Court
Tickenham Road
Clevedon, North Somerset BS21 6QU
phone +44 (0) 1275 872257

Tyntesfield
Wraxall, North Somerset BS48 1NT
phone +44 (0) 844 800 4986
tyntesfield@nationaltrust.org.uk

Theatre Royal
St. Johns Place
Bath, Avon, BA1 1ET
phone +44 (0) 1225 448844
nicky.palmer@theatreroyal.org.uk
www.theatreroyal.org.uk

beaumaris (wales)

Anglesey Tourism Association
phone +44 (0) 845 074 0587
info@angleseytourismassociation.co.uk

**Ye Olde Bulls Head Inn and Loft
Restaurant**
Castle Street
Beaumaris, Anglesey LL58 8AP
phone +44 (0) 1248 810329
info@bullsheadinn.co.uk

Bishopsgate House Hotel and Restaurant
54 Castle Street
Beaumaris, Anglesey LL58 8BB
phone +44 (0) 1248 810302
fax +44 (0) 1248 810166
enquiries@bishopsgatehotel.co.uk

**The Sailors Return Public House,
Restaurant & Accommodation**
Church Street
Beaumaris, Anglesey
phone +44 (0) 1248 811314
fax +44 (0) 1248 811792

Cleifiog B&B
Townsend
Beaumaris, Anglesey
phone +44 (0) 1248811507
www.cleifiogbandb.co.uk

Beaumaris Gaol
Bunkers Hill
Beaumaris, Anglesey LL5 8PE
phone +44 (0) 1248 810921

Plas Newydd
Llanfairpwll, Anglesey LL61 6DQ
phone +44 (0) 1248 714795

Oriel Yns Môn
Rosmeirch
Llangefni, Anglesey LL77 7TQ
phone +44 (0) 1248 724444
www.anglesey.gov.uk/English/culture/index.htm

Penrhyn Castle
Bangor, Gwynedd LL57 8HN
phone +44 (0) 1248 353084
www.nationaltrust.org.uk

berwick–upon–tweed (northeast)

**Berwick-upon-Tweed Tourist Information
Centre**
106 Marygate
Berwick-upon-Tweed, Northumberland
TD15 1BN
phone +44 (0) 1289 330733
fax +44 (0) 1289 330448
tourism@berwick-upon-tweed.gov.uk
www.berwick-upon-tweed.gov.uk

Bridge View
14 Tweed Street
Berwick-upon-Tweed, Northumberland
TD15 1NG
phone +44 (0) 1289 308098
lyndda@tiscali.co.uk
www.bridgeviewberwick.com

The Roxburgh
117 Main Street
Spittal, Berwick-upon-Tweed,
Northumberland TD15 1RP
phone +44 (0) 1289 306266
roxburghhotel@aol.com
www.roxburghguesthouse.co.uk

Sallyport Hotel and Restaurant
1 Sallyport, Off Bridge Street
Berwick-upon-Tweed TD15 1EZ
phone/fax +44 (0) 1289 116796
info@sallyport.co.uk

West Coates
30 Castle Terrace
Berwick-upon-Tweed, Northumberland
TD15 1NZ
phone +44 (0) 1289 309666
karenbrownwestcoates@yahoo.com
www.westcoates.co.uk

The Kings Arms Hotel
Hide Hill
Berwick-upon-Tweed, Northumberland
TD15 1EJ
phone +44 (0) 1289 307454
fax +44 (0) 1289 308867
enquiries@kingsarms-hotel.com

Paxton House
Berwick-upon-Tweed, Northumberland
TD15 1SZ
phone +44 (0) 1289 386291
www.paxtonhouse.com

Maltings Art Centre
Eastern Lane
Berwick Upon Tweed, Northumberland
TD15 1DT
phone +44 (0) 1289 330999
www.maltingsberwick.co.uk

Lindisfarne Castle
Holy Island
Berwick-upon-Tweed, Northumberland
TD15 2SH
phone +44 (0) 1289 389244
lindisfarne@nationaltrust.org.uk

beverley (yorkshire)

Beverley Tourist Information Centre
34 Butcher Row
Beverley, East Yorkshire HU17 0AB
phone +44 (0) 1482 391672
ukinformationcentre.com

The Beverley Arms Hotel
25 North Bar Within
Beverley, East Yorkshire
phone +44 (0) 1482 869 241

Manor House Hotel & Restaurant
Walkington (5 m)
Beverley, East Yorkshire HU17 8RT
phone +44 (0) 1482 881645
fax +44 (0) 1482 866501
info@walkingtonmanorhouse.co.uk
http://www.walkingtonmanorhouse.co.uk

Tickton Grange Hotel & Restaurant
Main Street
Tickton (5 m), East Yorkshire HU17 9SH
phone/fax +44 (0) 1482 866 501
info@the-manor-house.co.uk

bradford–on–avon (west country)

Bradford-on-Avon Tourism Association
50 St Margaret's Street
Bradford-on-Avon, Wiltshire BA15 1DE
phone +44 (0) 1225 865797
fax +44 (0) 1225 868722

Best Western Leigh Park Hotel
Leigh Road West
Bradford-on-Avon, Wiltshire BA15 2RA
phone +44 (0) 1225 864885
fax +44 (0) 1225 862315
info@leighparkhotel.eclipse.co.uk
www.latonahotels.co.uk

Georgian Lodge Hotel
25 Bridge Street
Bradford on Avon, Wiltshire BA15 1BY
phone +44 (0) 1225 862268
fax +44 (0) 1225 862218
georgianlodge@btconnect.com
www.georgianlodgehotel.com

Medlar Tree Restaurant at
Widbrook Grange Hotel
Trowbridge Road
Bradford-on-Avon, Wiltshire BA15 1UH
phone +44 (0) 1225 864750
fax +44 (0) 1225 862890
stay@widbrookgrange.com

The Beehive Real Ale Pub
263 Trowbridge Road
Bradford-on-Avon, Wiltshire BA15 1UA
phone +44 (0) 1225 863 620
www.beehivepub.com

The Courts Garden
Holt, nr Bradford-on-Avon, Wiltshire BA14
6RR
phone +44 (0) 1225 782875
courtsgarden@nationaltrust.org.uk

Westwood Manor
Bradford-on-Avon, Wiltshire BA15 2AF
phone +44 (0) 1225 863374
westwoodmanor@nationaltrust.org.uk

Avebury Stone Circle, Manor, Garden and
Alexander Keiller Museum
High Street
Avebury, Marlborough, Wiltshire SN8 1RF
phone +44 (0) 1672 539250
avebury@nationaltrust.org.uk

Great Chalfield Manor and Garden
nr Melksham, Wiltshire SN12 8NH
phone +44 (0) 1225 782239
greatxchalfieldmanor@nationaltrust.org.uk

Lacock Abbey, Fox Talbot Museum and
Village
Lacock, nr Chippenham, Wiltshire SN15 2LG
phone +44 (0) 1249 730459
lacockabbey@nationaltrust.org.uk

Wiltshire Heritage Museum
41 Long Street
Devizes, Wiltshire SN10 1NS
phone +44 (0) 1380 727369
www.wiltsheritage.or.uk

burford (cotswolds)

Burford Tourist Information Centre
The Brewery, Sheep Street
Burford, Oxfordshire OX18 4LP
phone +44 (0) 1993 823 558
fax +44 (0) 1993 823 590
burford.vic@westoxon.gov.uk

The Bull at Burford Hotel & Restaurant
105 High Street
Burford, Oxfordshire OX18 4RG
phone +44 (0) 1993 822 220
fax +44 (0) 1993 823 243

Inn For All Seasons
The Barringtons
Burford, Oxfordshire OX18 4TN
phone +44 (0) 1451 844 324
fax +44 (0) 1451 844 375

Golden Pheasant Hotel
High Street
Burford, Oxfordshire OX18 4QA
phone +44 (0) 1993 823 151
fax +44 (0) 1993 823 240

Bay Tree Classic
Sheep Street
Burford, Oxfordshire OX18 4LW
phone +44 (0) 1993 822 791
fax +44 (0) 1993 823 008

All of these hotels also operate
as restaurants

Ashdown House
Lambourne
Newbury, West Berkshire RG17 8RE
phone +44 (0) 1494 755569
ashdownhouse@nationaltrust.org.uk

The Buscot and Coleshill Estates
Coleshill Estate Office, Coleshill
Swindon, Wiltshire SN6 7PT
phone +44 (0) 1793 762209
buscotandcoleshill@nationaltrust.org.uk

Buscot Old Parsonage
Buscott
Farringdon, Oxfordshire SN7 8DQ
phone +44 (0) 1793 762209
buscot@nationaltrust.org.uk

Buscot Park
Estate Office, Buscot Park
Farringdon, Oxfordshire SN7 8BU
phone +44 (0) 845 345 3387
estbuscot@aol.com

Great Coxwell Barn
Great Coxwell
Farringdon, Oxfordshire SN7 7LZ
phone +44 (0) 1793 762209
greatcoxwellbarn@nationaltrust.org.uk

Lodge Park and Sherborne Estate
Lodge Park
Aldsworth, Gloucestershire GL54 3PP
phone +44 (0) 1451 844130
lodgepark@nationaltrust.org.uk

bury st edmunds (east anglia)

Tourist Information Centre
6 Angel Hill
Bury St Edmunds, Suffolk IP33 1UZ
phone +44 (0) 1284 764667 / 757083
fax +44 (0) 1284 757 084
tic@stedsbc.gov.uk
http://www.stedmundsbury.gov.uk/

The Angel Hotel
3 Angel Hill
Bury St Edmunds, Suffolk IP33 1LT
phone +44 (0) 1284 714 000
fax +44 (0) 1284 714001
staying@theangel.co.uk

Priory Hotel
Mildenhall Road
Bury St Edmunds, Suffolk IP32 6EH
phone +44 (0) 1284 766 181
fax +44 (0) 1284 767 604
reservations@prioryhotel.co.uk

Ounce House
Northgate St
Bury St Edmunds, Suffolk IP33 1HP
phone +44 (0) 1284 761 779
fax +44 (0) 1284 768 315
enquiries@ouncehouse.co.uk

Maison Bleue
30-31 Churchgate Street
Bury St Edmunds, Suffolk
phone +44 (0) 1284) 760 623
info@maisonbleue.co.uk

Theobalds
68 High St, Ixworth (11 km)
Bury St. Edmunds, Suffolk IP31 2HJ
phone +44 (0) 1359 231 707
http://www.theobaldsrestaurant.co.uk

Manor House Museum
Honey Hill
Bury St Edmunds, Suffolk IP33 1HF
phone +44 (0) 1284 757076
www.stedmundsbury.gov.uk/manorhse.htm

Ickworth House, Park and Gardens
The Rotunda
Horringer
Bury St Edmunds, Suffolk IP29 5QE
phone +44 (0) 1284 735270
ickworth@nationaltrust.org.uk

Theatre Royal
Westgate Street
Bury St Edmunds, Suffolk IP33 1QR
phone +44 (0) 1284 769505
www.theatreroyal.org

buxton (midlands)

Buxton Tourist Information Centre
The Crescent
Buxton, Derbyshire SK17 6BQ
phone +44 (0) 1298 25106
fax +44 (0) 1298 73153

Lee Wood Hotel
13 Manchester Rd
Buxton, Derbyshire SK17 6TQ
phone +44 (0) 1298 23002
fax +44 (0) 1298 23228
leewoodhotel@btinternet.com

Old Hall Hotel
The Square
Buxton, Derbyshire SK17 6BD
phone +44 (0) 1298 22841
fax +44 (0) 1298 72437

Grendon Guest House
Bishops Lane
Buxton, Derbyshire SK17 6UN
phone +44 (0) 1298 78831
fax +44 (0) 1298 79257
grendonguesthouse@hotmail.com

Buxton's Victorian Guest House
3a, Broad Walk
Buxton, Derbyshire SK17 6JE
phone +44 (0) 1298 78759
fax +44(0) 1298 74732
buxtonvictorian@btconnect.com

Columbine
7 Hall Bank
Buxton, Derbyshire SK17 6EW
phone +44 (0) 871 223 9383

Carriages
Newhaven (12 km), Derbyshire SK17 0DU
phone +44 (0) 871 426 4580
http://www.carriagesitalianrestaurant.com

Simply Thai
2-3 Cavendish Circus
Buxton, Derbyshire SK17 6AT
phone +44 (0) 1298 24471

Buxton Opera House
Water Street
Buxton, Derbyshire SK17 6XN
phone +44 (0) 1298 72190

Chatsworth
Bakewell, Derbyshire DE45 1PP
phone +44 (0) 1246 565300
www.chatsworth.org

High Peak Estate
High Peak Estate Office
Edale End
Hope Valley, Derbyshire S33 6RF
phone +44 (0) 1433 670368
highpeakestate@nationaltrust.org.uk

Alderley Edge
c/o Cheshire Countryside Office
Nether Alderley
Macclesfield, Cheshire SK10 4UB
phone +44 (0) 1625 584412
alderleyedge@nationaltrust.org.uk

Hare Hill
Over Alderley
Macclesfield, Cheshire SK10 4QB
phone +44 (0) 1625 584412
harehill@nationaltrust.org.uk

Nether Alderley Mill
Congleton Road
Nether Alderley
Macclesfield, Cheshire SK10 4TW
phone +44 (0) 1625 527468
quarrybankmill@nationaltrust.org.uk

Quarry Bank Mill and Styal Estate
Styal
Wilmslow, Cheshire SK9 4LA
phone +44 (0) 1625 445896
quarrybankmill@nationaltrust.org.uk

Lyme Park
Disley
Stockport, Cheshire SK12 2NX
phone +44 (0) 1663 766492
lymepark@nationaltrust.org.uk

Tatton Park
Knutsford, Cheshire WA16 6QN
phone +44 (0) 1625 374435
tatton@nationaltrust.org.uk

caernarfon (wales)

Caernarfon Tourist Information Centre
Oriel Pendeitsh, Castle Street
Caernarfon, Gwynedd LL55 1ES
phone +44 (0) 1286 672 232
fax +44 (0) 1286 676 476
caernarfon.tic@gwynedd.gov.uk

The Celtic Royal Hotel
Bangor Street
Caernarfon, Gwynedd LL55 1AY
phone +44 (0) 1286 674477
fax +44 (0) 1286 674139
info@celtic-royal.co.uk

The Black Boy Inn
Northgate Street
Caernarfon, Gwynedd LL55 1RW
phone +44 (0) 1286 673604
fax +44 (0) 1286 674955
black@welsh-historic-inns.com

Victoria House B&B
Church Street
Caernarfon, Gwynedd LL55 1SW
phone +44 (0) 1286 678263
Jan@TheVictoriaHouse.co.uk

Plas Tirion Farm
Llanrug
Caernarfon (3 m), Gwynedd LL55 4PY
phone +44 (0) 1286 673 190
fax +44 (0) 1286 671 883
cerid@plas-tirion.co.uk

Pengwern Farm
Saron, Lanwinda
Caernarfon (3 m), Gwynedd LL54 5UH
phone/fax +44 (0) 1286 831500

Floating Restaurant
Slate Quay
Caernarfon, Gwynedd LL55 1SG
phone +44 (0) 1286 672896

Molly's
23-25 Hole In The Wall St
Caernarfon, Gwynedd LL55 1RF
phone +44 (0) 1286 673238

Segontium
Pavilion Hill
Caernarfon, Gwynedd LL55 1AS
phone +44 (0) 1286 675625
segontium@nationaltrust.org.uk
www.segontium.org.uk

Welsh Slate Museum
Gilfach Ddn, Parc Pardarn
Llanberis, Gwynedd LL55 4TY
phone +44 (0) 1286 870630
www.nmgw.ac.uk/wsm

cambridge (east anglia)

The Cambridge Visitor Information Centre
The Old Library, Wheeler Street
Cambridge, Cambridgeshire CB2 3QB
phone +44 (0) 1223 464732/ 871 226 8006

Hotel Felix
Whitehouse Lane, Huntingdon Road
Cambridge, Cambridgeshire CB3 0LX
phone +44 (0) 1223 277 977
fax +44 (0) 1223 277 973
help@hotelfelix.co.uk
http://www.hotelfelix.co.uk

Arundel House Hotel
Chesterton Road
Cambridge, Cambridgeshire CB4 3AN
phone +44 (0) 1223 367 701
fax +44 (0) 1223 367 721
info@arundelhousehotels.co.uk
http://www.arundelhousehotels.co.uk

University Arms Hotel
Regent Street
Cambridge, Cambridgeshire CB2 1AD
phone +44 (0) 1223 351 241

fax +44 (0) 1223 273 037
dua.sales@devere-hotels.com
http://www.devere.co.uk

Browns Restaurant and Bar
23 Trumpington Street
Cambridge, Cambridgeshire CB2 1QA
phone +44 (0) 1223 461 655
http://www.browns-restaurants.com

Midsummer House
Midsummer Common
Cambridge, Cambridgeshire CB4 1HA
phone +44 (0) 1223 369 299
www.midsummerhouse.co.uk

**Riverside Restaurant
at the University Centre**
Granta Place
Cambridge, Cambridgeshire CB2 1RU
phone +44 (0) 1223 337759

22 Chesterton Road
22 Chesterton Road
Cambridge, Cambridgeshire CB4 3AX
phone +44 (0) 1223 351880
fax +44 (0) 1223 323814
davidcarter@restaurant22.co.uk

**Cambridge University Museum
of Archaeology and Anthropology**
Downing Street
Cambridge, Cambridgeshire CB2 3DZ
phone +44 (0) 1223 333516
museum-server.archanth.cam.ac.uk/

Cambridge and County Folk Museum
2-3 Castle Street
Cambridge, Cambridgeshire CB3 0AQ
phone +44 (0) 1223 355159
www.folkmuseum.org.uk

Fitzwilliam Museum
Trumpington Street
Cambridge, Cambridgeshire CB3 0AQ
phone +44 (0) 1223 332900
www.fitzmuseum.cam.ac.uk

Kettle's Yard
Castle Street
Cambridge, Cambridgeshire CB3 0AQ
phone +44 (0) 1223 352124
www.kettle'syard.co.uk

Museum of Classical Archaeology
Sidgwick Avenue
Cambridge, Cambridgeshire CB3 9DA
phone +44 (0) 1223 335153
www.classics.cam.ac.uk/ark.html

Sedgwick Museum of Earth Sciences
Downing Street
Cambridge, Cambridgeshire CB2 3EQ
phone +44 (0) 1223 333456
www.sedgewickmuseum.org

Whipple Museum of the History of Science
Free School Lane
Cambridge, Cambridgeshire CB2 3RH
phone +44 (0) 1223 330906
www.hps.ca.ac.uk/Whipple.html

Imperial War Museum: Duxford
Cambridge, Cambridgeshire CB2 4QR
phone +44 (0) 1223 835000
www.iwm.org.uk/duxford/index.htm

Anglesey Abbey, Gardens and Lode Mill
Quy Road, Lode
Cambridge, Cambridgeshire CB25 9EJ
phone +44 (0) 1223 810080
angleseyabbey@nationaltrust.org.uk

Wicken Fen National Nature Reserve
Lode Lane, Wicken
Ely, Cambridgeshire CB7 5XP
phone +44 (0) 1353 720274
wickenfen@nationaltrust.org.uk

Ely Cathedral
Chapter House, The College
Ely, Cambridgeshire CB7 4DL
phone +44 (0) 1353 667735
receptionist@cathedral.ely.anglican.org

Wimpole Hall and Home Farm
Arrington, Cambridgeshire SGB 0BW
phone +44 (0) 1223 206000
wimpolehall@nationaltrust.org.uk

Cambridge Arts Theatre
6 St Edward's Passage
Cambridge, Cambridgeshire CB2 3PJ
phone +44 (0) 1223 503333
info@cambridgeartstheatre.com

The Corn Exchange
Wheeler Street
Cambridge CB2 3QB
phone +44 (0) 1223 357851
admin.cornex@cambridge.gov.uk

canterbury (southeast)

Canterbury Information Centre
12/13 Sun Street
Canterbury, Kent
phone +44 (0) 1227 378100
accommodation@canterbury.gov.uk

Canterbury Cathedral Lodge
The Precincts
Canterbury, Kent CT1 2EH
phone +44 (0) 1227 865350
fax +44 (0) 1227 865388
stay@canterbury-cathedral.org
www.canterburycathedrallodge.org

ABode Canterbury
30-33 High Street
Canterbury, Kent CT1 2RX
phone +44 (0) 1227 766266
fax +44 (0) 1227 784874
Reservationscanterbury@abodehotels.co.uk
http://www.abodehotels.co.uk

Magnolia House
36 St. Dunstans Terrace
Canterbury, Kent CT2 8AX
phone +44 (0) 1227 765121
fax +44 (0) 1227 765121
info@magnoliahousecanterbury.co.uk
http://www.magnoliahousecanterbury.co.uk

Yorke Lodge
50 London Road
Canterbury, Kent CT2 8LF
phone +44 (0) 1227 451243
fax +44 (0) 1227 462006
enquiries@yorkelodge.com
http://www.yorkelodge.com

Augustine's Restaurant
1-2 Longport
Canterbury, Kent
phone +44 (0) 1227 453063

Cafe Belge
89-90 St. Dunstans Street
Canterbury, Kent CT2 8AD
phone +44 (0) 1227 768222
cafebelge@btinternet.com
www.cafebelge.co.uk

Carmen's of Canterbury
25-26 Sun Street
Canterbury, Kent CT1 2HX
phone +44 (0) 1227 767854
carmensofcanterbury@yahoo.co.uk

Caffe Venezia
60-61 Palace Street
Canterbury, Kent CT1 2DY
phone +44 (0) 1227 787786
www.caffevenezia.co.uk

Manolis Taverna
10 Guildhall Street
Canterbury, Kent CT1 2JQ
phone +44 (0) 1227 769189
www.manolistaverna.co.uk

Canterbury Roman Museum
Longmarket, Butchery Lane
Canterbury, Kent CT1 2JR
phone +44 (0 1227 785 575
museums@canterbury.gov.uk

The Canterbury Tales
St. Margarets Street
Canterbury, Kent CT1 2TG
phone +44 (0) 1227 479227
info@canterburytales.org.uk
www.canterburytales.org.uk

**Museum of Canterbury
with Rupert Bear Museum**
Stour Street
Canterbury, Kent CT1 2NR
phone +44 (0) 1227 475 202
museums@canterbury.gov.uk

Powell-Cotton Museum
Quex House and Gardens
Quex Park
Birchington, Kent CT7 0BH
phone +44 (0) 1843 842168
powell-cotton.museum@virgin.net

The Roman Museum
11a Butchery Lane
Canterbury, Kent CT1 2JR
phone +44 (0) 1227 452747
museums@canterbury.gov.uk
www.canterbury-museums.co.uk

South Foreland Lighthouse
The Front, St Margaret's Bay
Dover, Kent CT15 6HP
phone +44 (0) 1304 852463
southforeland@nationaltrust.org.uk

The White Cliffs of Dover
Langdon Cliffs
Upper Road
Dover, Kent CT16 1HJ
phone +44 (0) 1304 202756
whitecliffs@nationaltrust.org.uk

The Marlowe Theatre
The Friars
Canterbury, Kent CT1 2AS
phone +44 (0) 1227 787787
marlowetheatre@canterbury.gov.uk

cardigan (wales)

Cardigan Tourist Information Centre
Theatr Mwldan, Bath House Road
Cardigan, Pembrokeshire SA43 1JY
phone +44 (0) 1239 613 230
fax +44 (0) 1239 614 853
cardigantic@ceridigion.gov.uk

Hotel Penrallt and Bay Restaurant
Aberporth
Cardigan (5 m), Pembrokeshire SA43 2BS
phone +44 (0) 1239 810227
enquiries@hotelpenrallt.co.uk

Highbury Guest House
Pendre
Cardigan, Pembrokeshire SA43 1JU
phone +44 (0) 1239 613403

Rosehill Farm
Llangoedmor
Cardigan (1.5 m), Pembrokeshire SA43 2LJ
phone +44 (0) 1239 612 019
judy@rosehillfarm.co.uk

The Minted Lamb Restaurant
Morlan Hotel
Aberporth
Cardigan, Pembrokeshire SA43 2EN
phone +44 (0) 1239 811391

Cilgerran Castle
nr Cardigan, Pembrokeshire SA43 2SF
phone +44 (0) 1239 621339
cilgerrancastle@nationaltrust.org.uk

carlisle (lake district & northwest)

Carlisle Visitor Centre
Old Town Hall
Green Market
Carlisle, Cumbria CA3 8JE
phone +44 (0) 1228 625600
Tourism@Carlisle-City.gov.uk

Cumbria Park Hotel
32 Scotland Road
Carlisle, Cumbria CA3 9DG
phone +44 (0) 1228 522887
fax +44 (0) 1228 514796
cumbriaparkhotel@wightcablenorth.net

Number Thirty One
31 Howard Place
Carlisle, Cumbria CA1 1HR
phone +44 (0) 1228 597080
Pruirving@aol.com

Aldingham House
1 Eden Mount
Carlisle, Cumbria CA3 9LZ
phone +44 (0) 1228 522554
fax +44 (0) 1228 522554
enquiries@aldinghamhouse.co.uk

Gallo Rosso
Park House Road
Kingstown
Carlisle, Cumbria CA6 5RS
phone +44 (0) 1228 526037

Tullie House Museum and Art Gallery
Castle Street
Carlisle, Cumbria CA3 8TP
phone +44 (0) 1228 534781
www.tulliehouse.co.uk/index2.htm

Allen Banks and Staward Gorge
Bardon Mill
Hexham, Northumberland NE47 7BU
phone +44 (0) 1434 344218
allenbanks@nationaltrust.org.uk

Hadrian's Wall and Housesteads Fort
Bardon Mill
Hexham, Northumberland NE47 6NN
phone +44 (0) 1434 344363

cheltenham (cotswolds)

Cheltenham Tourist Information Centre
77 Promenade
Cheltenham, Gloucestershire GL50 1PJ
phone +44 (0) 1242 522878
info@cheltenham.gov.uk

The Queen's Hotel
Promenade
Cheltenham, Gloucestershire GL50 1NN
phone +44 (0) 870 40081107
fax +44 (0) 1242 224145
queens@macdonald-hotels.co.uk

Hotel on the Park
38 Evesham Rd
Cheltenham, Gloucestershire GL52 2AH
phone +44 (0) 1242 518 898
fax +44 (0) 1242 511 526
stay@hotelonthepark.com
www.hotelonthepark.com

George Hotel
41-49 St Georges Road
Cheltenham, Gloucestershire GL50 3DZ
phone +44 (0) 1242 235751
fax +44 (0) 1242 224359
hotel@stayatthegeorge.co.uk

Le Champignon Sauvage
24-28 Suffolk Road
Cheltenham, Gloucestershire GL50
phone +44 (0) 1242 573449
fax +44 (0) 1242 254365
mail@lechampignonsauvage.com

Lumiere
Clarence Parade
Cheltenham, Gloucestershire GL50 3PA
phone +44 (0) 1242 222200
dinner@lumiere.cc

Brosh
8 Suffolk Parade
Cheltenham, Gloucestershire GL50 2AB
phone/fax +44 (0) 1242 227277
info@broshrestaurant.co.uk

Cheltenham Art Gallery and Museum
Clarence Street
Cheltenham, Gloucestershire GL50 3JT

phone +44 (0) 1242 237431
www.cheltenham.artgallery,museum

Holst Birthplace Museum
4 Clarence Road
Pittville
Cheltenham, Gloucestershire GL52 2AY
phone +44 (0) 1242 524846

Everyman Theatre
10 Regent St
Cheltenham, Gloucestershire GL50
phone +44 (0) 1242 572573
www.everymantheatre.org.uk

Hailes Abbey
nr Winchcombe
Cheltenham, Gloucestershire GL54 5PB
Phone +44 (0) 1242 602398

Middle Littleton Tithe Barn
Middle Littleton
nr Evesham, Worcestershire WR11 5LN
phone +44 (0) 1905 371006

Winchcombe Folk & Police Museum
High St
Winchcombe, Cheltenham, GL54 5LJ
phone +44 (0) 1242 609151

Winchcombe Railway Museum & Garden
23 Gloucester St
Winchcombe, Cheltenham, GL54 5LX
phone +44 (0) 1242 609305

chester (welsh borders)

Visitor Centre, Town Hall
Northgate Street
Chester, Cheshire CH1 2HS
phone +(44) (0) 1244 402111
fax +(44) (0) 1244 400420
tis@chester.gov.uk

Chester Visitor Centre
Vicar's Lane
Chester, Cheshire CH1 1QX
phone +44 (0) 1244 351609
fax +44 (0) 1244 403188
tis@chester.gov.uk

The Chester Grosvenor and Spa
Eastgate
Chester, Cheshire CH1 1LT
phone +44 (0) 1244 324024
fax +44 (0) 1244 313246
reservations@chestergrosvenor.com
www.chestergrosvenor.co.uk

Mill Hotel & Spa Destination,
Milton Street
Chester, Cheshire CH1 3NF
phone +44 (0) 1244-350035
fax +44 (0) 1244-345635
www.millhotel.com

Chester Town House (B&B)
23 King Street
Chester, Cheshire CH1 2AH
phone +44 (0) 1244 350021
davidbellis@chestertownhouse.co.uk
www.chestertownhouse.co.uk

Aquavitus
58 Watergate Street
Chester, Cheshire CH1 2LA
phone +44 (0) 1244-313721
fax +44 (0) 1244 346266

Bollicini
2 Abbey Green, Rufus Court
Northgate Street
Chester, Cheshire CH1 2JH
phone +44 (0) 1244 329932

Erddig
Wrexham LL13 0YT
phone +44 (0) 1978 355314
erdig@nationaltrust.org.uk

Boat Museum
South Pier Road
Ellesmere Port, Cheshire CH65 4FW
phone +44 (0) 151 355 5017
www.boatmuseum.org.uk

chichester (southeast)

Chichester Tourist Information Centre
29a South Street
Chichester, West Sussex PO19 1AH
phone +44 (0) 1243 775 888
fax +44 (0) 1243 539 449
chitic@chichester.gov.uk

The Ship Hotel
North Street
Chichester, West Sussex PO19 1NH
phone +44 (0) 1243 778000
fax +44 (0) 1243 788000
enquiries@chichester.theplacehotels.co.uk
www.shiphotelchichester.co.uk

Suffolk House Hotel
3 East Row
Chichester, West Sussex PO19 1PD
phone +44 (0) 1243 778 899
admin@suffolk house hotel.co.uk

Comme Ça
67 Broyle Road
Chichester, West Sussex PO19 6BD
phone +44 (0) 1243 788724

The Dining Room at Purchase's
31 North Street
Chichester, West Sussex PO19 1LY
phone +44 (0) 1243 537352
fax +44 (0) 1243 780773
info@thediningroom.biz

Fishbourne Roman Palace
Salthill Road
Fishbourne
Chichester, West Sussex PO19 2QR
phone +44 (0) 1243785859
www.sussexpast.co.uk

Pallant House Gallery
9 North Pallant
Chichester, West Sussex PO19 1TJ
phone +44 (0) 1243 774557
www.pallanthousegallery.com

Petworth House and Park
Petworth, West Sussex GU28 0AE
phone +44 (0) 1798 342207
www.nationaltrust.org.uk/places/petworth

Portsmouth Historic Dockyards
HM Naval Base (P66)
Portsmouth, Hampshire PO1 3NH
phone +44 (0) 23 9286 1533

Royal Naval Submarine Museum
Haslar Jetty Road
Gosport, Hampshire PO12 2AS
phone +44 (0) 2392 510 354
www.rnsubmus.co.uk

Sculpture at Goodwood
Goodwood
Chichester, West Sussex PO18 0QP
phone +44 (0) 1243 538449
www.sculpture.org.uk

Tangmere Military Aviation Museum
Tangmere
Chichester, West Sussex PO20 6ES
phone +44 (0) 1243 775 223
www.tangmere-museum.org.uk

Uppark House and Garden
South Harting
Petersfield, West Sussex GU31 5QR
phone +44 (0) 1730 825857
uppark@nationaltrust.org.uk

Weald and Downland Open Air Museum
Singleton
Chichester, West Sussex PO18 0EU
phone +44 (0) 1243 811348
www.wealddown.co.uk

Chichester Festival Theatre
Wellington Road
Chichester, PO19
phone +44 (0) 1243 784 437
www.cft.org.uk

chipping campden (cotswolds)

Chipping Campden Tourist Information Centre
The Old Police Station, High Street
Chipping Campden, Gloucestershire
GL55 6AB
phone +44 (0) 1386 841206
fax +44 (0) 1386 841681
visitchippingcampden@lineone.net

Cotswold House
The Square
Chipping Camden, Gloucestershire
GL55 6AN
phone +44 (0) 1386 840330
fax +44 (0) 1386 840310
reception@cotswoldhouse.com

Lygon Arms Hotel
High Street
Chipping Campden, Gloucestershire
GL55 6HB
phone +44 (0) 1386 840318
fax +44 (0) 1386 841088
sandra@lygonarms.co.uk

Kings Hotel
The Square
Chipping Campden, Gloucestershire
GL55 6PU
phone +44 (0) 1386 840256
fax +44 (0) 1386 841598
info@kingscamden.co.uk

Hicks'
(at Cotswold House: see above)

Huxleys Restaurant and Bar
High Street
Chipping Campden, Gloucestershire
GL55 6AL
phone +44 (0) 1386 840520

Joel's Restaurant
Island House, High Street
Chipping Campden, Gloucestershire
GL55 6AL
phone +44 (0) 1386 840598

The Fleece Inn
Bretforton
nr Evesham, Worcestershire WR11 7JE
phone +44 (0) 1386 831173
fleeceinn@nationaltrust

Hidcote Manor Garden
Hidcote Bartrim
nr Chipping Campden, Gloucestershire
GL55 6LR
phone +44 (0) 1386 438333
hidcote@nationaltrust.org.uk

Snowshill Manor
Broadway, Worcestershire WR12 7JU
phone +44 (0) 1386 852410
www.nationaltrust.org

chipping norton (cotswolds)

Visitor Information Centre
Market Place
Chipping Norton, Oxfordshire OX7 5NJ
phone +44 (0) 1608 644379

Crown & Cushion Hotel
High Street
Chipping Norton, Oxfordshire OX7 5AD
phone +44 (0) 1608 642533
info@thecrownandcushion.com

The Fox Hotel
Market Place
Chipping Norton, Oxfordshire OX7 5DD
phone +44 (0) 1608642658
the-fox-hotel@talk21.com

The Kings Arms Hotel
18 West Street
Chipping Norton, Oxfordshire OX7 5AA
phone +44 (0) 1608 642668
vivmorris@btconnect.com

The Bell Inn
56 West St
Chipping Norton, Oxfordshire OX7 5ER
phone +44 (0) 1608 642521
sales@thebellpub.co.uk

The Mason's Arms
Banbury Road
Swerford OX7 4AP (8 km)
phone +44 (0) 1608 683212
themasonschef@hotmail.com

Chastleton House
Chastleton
nr Moreton-in-Marsh, Oxfordshire GL56 0SU
phone +44 (0) 1608 674981
chastleton@nationaltrust.org.uk

Farnborough Hall
Farnborough
nr Banbury, Oxfordshire OX17 1DU
phone +44 (0) 1295 690002
farnboroughhall@nationaltrust.org.uk

Upton House and Gardens
nr Banbury, Warwickshire OX15 6HT
phone +44 (0) 1295 670 266
uptonhouse@nationaltrust.org.uk
www.nationaltrust.org.uk

cirencester (cotswolds)

Cirencester Visitor Information Centre
Market Place
Cirencester, Gloucestershire GL7 2NW
phone +44 (0) 1285 654180

The Fleece Hotel
Market Place
Cirencester, Gloucestershire GL7 2NZ
phone +44 (0) 1285 658507
fax +44 (0) 12851017
relax@fleecehotel.co.uk

No 12
12, Park Street
Cirencester, Gloucestershire GL7 2BW
phone +44 (0) 1285 640232
no12cirencester@ukgateway.net

The Old Brewhouse
7 London Road
Cirencester, Gloucestershire GL7 2PU
phone/fax +44 (0) 1285 656099
info@theoldbrewhouse.com

The Old Court Bed & Breakfast
Coxwell Street
Cirencester, Gloucestershire GL7 2BQ
phone +44 (0) 1285 653164
langton@old-court.co.uk
www.old-court.co.uk

The Country Style
The Woolmarket
Cirencester, Gloucestershire GL7 2PR
phone +44 (0) 1285 658078

Gianni
30 Castle Street
Cirencester, Gloucestershire GL7 1QH
phone +44 (0) 1285 643133

Harry Hare's
3 Gosditch Street
Cirencester, Gloucestershire GL7 2AG
phone +44 (0)1285 652 375

Chedworth Roman Villa
Yarnworth, Gloucestershire GL54 3LJ
phone +44 (0) 1242 890256
chedworth@nationaltrust.org.uk

Newark Park
Ozleworth
Wotton-under-Edge, Gloucestershire
GL12 7PZ
phone +44 (0) 1793 817666
newarkpark@nationaltrust.org.uk

Steam - The Museum of the Great Western Railway
Kemble Drive
Swindon, Wiltshire SN2 2TA
phone +44 (0) 1793 466646
www.steam-museum.org.uk

Swindon Art Gallery
Bath Road
Swindon, Wiltshire SN1 4BA
phone +44 (0) 1793 466556

colchester (eastanglia)

Colchester Visitor Centre
1 Queen St
Colchester, Essex CO1 2PG
phone +44 (0) 1206 282920
vic@colchester.gov.uk

The George Hotel
116 High Street
Colchester, Essex CO1 1TD
phone +44 (0) 1206 578494
fax +44 (0) 1206 761732

The Red Lion Hotel
43 High Street
Colchester, Essex CO1 1DJ
phone +44 (0) 1206 577986
fax +44 (0) 1206 578207

The Rose & Crown Hotel
The Oak Room
East Street, East Hill
Colchester, Essex CO2 2TZ
phone +44 (0) 1206 866677
fax +44 (0) 1206 866616
info@rose-and-crown.com

The Lemon Tree
48 St John's Street
Colchester, Essex
phone +44 (0) 1206 767337

The Warehouse Brasserie
12 Chapel Street North
Colchester, Essex CO2 7AT
phone +44 (0) 1206 765656
TheWarehouseBrasserie@hotmail.co.uk

Colchester Castle Museum
Castle Park
Colchester, Essex CO1 1TI
phone +44 (0) 1206 282939
www.colchestermuseums.org.uk

Tymperly's Clock Museum
Trinity Street
Colchester, Essex CO1 1JN
phone +44 (0) 1206 282943
museums@colchester.gov.uk

Bourne Mill
Colchester, Essex CO2 8RT
phone +44 (0) 1206 572422
bournemill@nationaltrust.org.uk

Coggleshall Grange Barn
Grange Hill
Coggleshall, Essex CO6 1RE
phone +44 (0) 1376 562226
coggleshall@nationaltrust.org.uk

Paycocke's
West Street
Coggleshall, Essex CO6 1NS

Flatford: Bridge Cottage
Flatford
East Bergholt, Suffolk CO7 6UL
phone +44 (0) 1206 298260
flatfordbridgeconttage@nationaltrust.org.uk

Rayleigh Mount
Rayleigh, Essex
phone +44 (0) 1284 747500
rayleighmount@nationaltrust.org.uk

**Wolsey Art Gallery
and Christchurch Mansion**
Christchurch Park
Soane Street
Ipswich, Suffolk IP4 2BE
phone +44 (0) 1473 433554
www.ipswich.gov.uk

conwy (wales)

Conwy Tourist Information Centre
Rose Hill St
Conwy
phone +44 (0) 1492 592248
www.conwy.com

**The Castle Hotel and Shakespeare's
Restaurant**
High Street
Conwy LL32 8DB
phone +44 (0) 1492 582800
fax +44 (0) 1492 582300
mail@castlewales.co.uk

Gwynfryn Guest House (B&B)
4 York Place, off Lancaster Square
Conwy LL32 8AB
phone/fax +44 (0) 1492 576733/ (0) 7947
272821
info@gwynfrynbandb.co.uk

The Old Rectory Country House
Llansanffraid Glan
Conwy (2.5 m) LL28 5LF
phone +44 (0) 1492 580611
fax +44 (0) 1492 584555
info@oldrectorycountryhouse.co.uk

Sychnant Pass House
Sychnant Pass Road
Conwy (1.75 m) LL32 8BJ
bre@sychnant-pass-house.co.uk

Amelies
10 High Street
Conwy LL32 8DB
phone +44 (0) 1492 583142

Bistro Conwy
Chapel Street
Conwy LL32 8BP
phone +44 (0) 1492 596326

see also hotels and restaurants in Llandudno

Aberconwy House
Castle Street
Conwy LL32 8AY
phone +44 (0) 1492 592246
aberconwyhouse@nationaltrust

Bodnant Garden
Tal-Cafn
Colwyn Bay
Conwy LL28 5RE
phone +44 (0) 1492 650460
bodnantgarden@nationaltrust.org.uk

Bodelwyddan Castle
Bodelwyddan, Denbighshire LL18 5YA
phone +44 (0) 1745 584 060
www.bodelwyddan-castle.co.uk

Ty Mawr Wybrnant
Penmachno
Betws-y-Coed
Conwy LL25 0HJ
phone +44 (0) 1690 760213
tymawrwybrnant@nationaltrust.org.uk

cowes (isle of wight)

Cowes Tourist Information Centre
9 The Arcade
Cowes, Isle of Wight PO31 7AR
phone +44 (0) 1983 813818
www.islandbreaks.co.uk

Fountain Hotel
High Street
Cowes, Isle of Wight PO31 7AW
phone +44 (0) 1983 292397

New Holmwood Hotel
Queens Road, Egypt Point
Cowes, Isle of Wight PO31 8BW
phone + 64 (0) 1983 292508

Baan Thai Restaurant
10 Bath Road
West Cowes, Isle of Wight PO31 7QN
phone +44 (0) 1983 291917

Cafe Mozart
48 High Street
West Cowes, Isle of Wight PO31 7RR
phone +44 (0) 1983 293681

Duke of York
Mill Hill Road
West Cowes, Isle Of Wight PO31 7BT
phone +44 (0) 1983 295171
fax +44 (0) 1983 295047

Bembridge Windmill
High Street
Bembridge, Isle of Wight PO35 5SQ
phone +44 (0) 1983 873945
bembridgemill@nationaltrust.org.uk

Mottistone Manor Garden
Mottistone, Isle of Wight PO30 4EA
phone +44 (0) 1983 741302
mottistonemanor@nationaltrust.org.uk

The Needles Old Battery and New Battery
West High Down
Alum Bay, Isle of Wight PO39 0JH
phone +44 (0) 1983 754772
needlesoldbattery@nationaltrust.org.uk

Newtown Old Town Hall
Newtown
Newport, Isle of Wight PO30 4PA
phome +44 (0) 1983 531785
oldtownhall@nationaltrust.org.uk

**Derry/Londonderry Tourist Information
Centre**
44 Foyle Street
Derry/Londonderry BT48 6AT
phone +22 (0) 28 71267284
info@derryvisitor.com
www.derryvisitor.com

**City Hotel and Thompson's on the River
Restaurant**
Queens Quay
Derry/Londonderry BT48 7AS
phone +44 (0) 28 7136 5800
fax +44 (0) 281 7136 5801
res@derry-gsh.com

**The Hastings Everglades Hotel
and Satchmo Restaurant**
41 Prehen Road
Derry/Londonderry BT47 2PA
phone +44 (0) 28 71321066
fax +44 (0) 208 7134 9200
info@egh.hastings hotels.com

**Ramada Hotel Da Vinci's Hotel
and Grill Room**
15 Culmore Road
Derry/Londonderry, BT48 8JB
phone +44 (0) 208 7127 9111
fax +44 (0) 7127 9222
info@davincishotel.com

Abbey B&B
4 Abbey Street
Derry/Londonderry, BT48 9DN
phone +44 (0) 28 71 279000
abbey.accom@ntlworld.com

**The Saddler's House
The Merchant's House**
36 Great James Street
Derry/Londonderry BT48 7DB
phone +44 (0) 2871 269691
fax +44 (0) 2871 266913
saddlershouse@btinternet.com

Giant's Causeway
44a Causeway Road
Bushmills, County Antrim BT57 8SU
phone +44 (0) 28 2073 1582

Gray's Printing Press
49 Main Street
Strabane, County Tyrone BT82 8AU
phone +44 (0) 28 7188 0055
grays@nationaltrust.org.uk

Hezlett House
107 Sea Road
Castlerock
Coleraine, County Londonderry BT51 4TW
phone +44 (0) 28 2073 1582
hezletthouse@nationaltrust.org.uk

Mussenden Temple and Downhill Demesne
Mussenden Road
Castlerock, County Londonderry BT51 4RP
phone +44 (0) 28 2073 1582
downhilldemesne@nationaltrust.org.uk

Portstewart Strand
Strand Road
Portsteward, County Londonderry BT55 7PG

Dorchester Tourist Information
Unit 11, Antelope Walk
Dorchester, Dorset DT1
phone +44 (0) 13505 267992
fax +44 (0) 1305 266079

The Casterbridge Hotel
49 High East Street
Dorchester, Dorset
phone +44 (0) 1305 264043

Kings Arms Hotel
30 High East St
Dorchester, Dorset DT1 1HF
phone +44 (0) 1305 265353

La Caverna Restaurant
57 Icen Way
Dorchester, Dorset DT1 1EW
franco@saluci.freeserve.co.uk

Imperial Garden Chinese Restaurant
45 High Street
Dorchester, Dorset DT1 1HU
phone +44 (0) 1305 257471

Judge Jeffreys' Restaurant
6 High West St
Dorchester, Dorset DT1 1UJ
phone +44 (0) 1305 264369

[Thomas] **Hardy's Cottage**
Higher Bockhampton
nr Dorchester, Dorset DT2 8QJ
phone +44 (0) 1305 262366
hardyscottage@nationaltrust.org.uk

Max Gate
Alington Avenue
Dorchester, Dorset DT1 2AB
phone +44 (0) 1305 262538
maxgate@nationaltrust.org.uk

[Vice-Admiral] **Hardy Monument**
Blackdown
Portesham, Dorset
phone +44 (0) 1297 561900
hardymonument@notionaltrust.or.uk

Tourist Information Centre
2 Millennium Place,
Durham DH1 1WA
phone +44 (0) 191 3843720
fax +44 (0) 191 3863015
touristinfo@durhamcity.gov.uk

Farnley Tower
The Avenue
Durham DH1 4DX
phone +44 (0) 191 3750011
fax +44 (0) 1913839694

Cathedral View Town House
212 Gilesgate
Durham DH1 1QN
phone +44 (0) 191 3869566
cathedralview@hotmail.com
www.cathedralview.com

Castle View Guest House
4 Crossgate
Durham DH1 4PS
phone +44 (0) 191 3868852
castleview@hotmail.com

Bistro 21
Aykley Heads House, Aykley Heads
Durham, DH1 5TS
phone +44 (0) 191 3844354

Gourmet Spot
The Avenue
Durham City DH1 4DX
phone +44 (0) 191 3846655
www.gourmet-spot.co.uk

**Treasures of St Cuthbert,
Durham Cathedral**
The College
Durham DH1 3EH
phone +44 (0) 191 386 4266

Oriental Museum
Elvet Hill
Durham DH1 3TH
phone +44 (0) 191 334 5694
www.dur.ac.uk/oriental.museum

**Beamish – the North of England
Open Air Museum**
Beamish
Durham DH9 0RG
phon +44 (0) 191 370 4000
www.beamish.or.uk

Bowes Museum
Newgate
Barnard Castle
Durham DL12 8NP
phone +44 (0) 1833 690606
www.bowesmuseum.org.uk

eastbourne (southeast)

Eastbourne Tourist Information Centre
Cornfield Road
Eastbourne BN21 4QL
phone +44 (0) 871 663 0031
fax +44 (0) 1323 649574
tic@eastbourne.gov.uk
www.visiteastbourne.com

The Grand Hotel
King Edwards Parade
Eastbourne, East Sussex BN21 4EQ
phone +44 (0) 1323 412345
fax +44 (0) 1323 412233

Best Western Lansdowne Hotel
King Edward's Parade
Eastbourne, East Sussex BN21 4EE
phone +44 (0) 1323 725174
fax +44 (0) 1323 739721
reception@landsdowne-hotel.co.uk

Mirrabelle
at Grand Hotel
King Edwards Parade
Eastbourne, East Sussex BN21 4EQ
phone +44 (0) 1323 435066
fax +44 (0) 1323 412233
reservations@grandeastbourne.co.uk

The Hungry Monk Restaurant
Jevington
Polegate, Sussex, BN26 5DF
phone +44 (0) 1323 482178

Alfriston Clergy House
The Tye
Alfriston
Polegate, East Sussex BN26 5TL
phone +44 (0) 1323 870001
alfriston@nationaltrust.org.uk

Batemans
Burwash
Etchingham, East Sussex TN19 7DS
phone +44 (0) 1435 882302
batemans@nationaltrust.org.co.uk

Charleston
Charleston, nr Firle
Lewes, East Sussex BN8 6LL
phone +44 (0) 1323 811626
www.charleston.org.uk

Monk's House
Rodmell
Lewes, East Sussex BN7 3HF
phone +44 (0) 1323 8700001
monkshouse@nationaltrust.org.uk

enniskillen (northern ireland)

Fermanagh Tourist Information Centre
Wellington Road
Enniskillen, County Fermanagh BT74 7EF
phone +44 (0) 28 6632 3110
fax +44 (0) 28 6632 5511
tic@fermanagh.gov.uk

Manor House Country Hotel
Killadeas, County Fermanagh BT94 1NY
(Enniskillen 7 m)
phone +44 (0) 28 6862 2211
fax +44 (0) 28 6862 1545
info@manor-house-hotel.com

Fort Lodge Hotel
72 Forthill Street
Enniskillen, County Fermanagh BT74 6AJ
phone +44 (0) 28 6632 3275
fax +44 (0) 28 6632 0275
hotel@fortlodge.freeserve.co.uk

Mount View Guesthouse
61 Irvinestown Road
Enniskillen, County Fermanagh BT74 6DN
phone +44 (0) 28 6632 3147
fax +44 (0) 28 6632 9611
wendy@mountviewguests.com

4 Hollyhill Road
Enniskillen, County Fermanagh BT74 6DD
phone +44 (0) 28 6632 6026
fax +44 (0) 28 6632 6026
j.mcgovern@swiftsoft.net

**Blakes of the Hollow
with Café Merlot
and Restaurant Number 6**
6 Church Street
Enniskillen, County Fermanagh BT74 6JE
phone +44 (0) 28 6632 0918

Ferndale Country House and Restaurant
Irvinestown Road
Enniskillen, County Fermanagh BT74 4RN
phone +44 (0) 2866 328374
ferndalechandr@gmail.com

Fermanagh County Museum
Enniskillen Castle Barracks
Enniskillen, County Fermanagh BT74 7HL
phone +44 (0) 28 6632 5000

**Royal Inniskilling Fusiliers Regimental
Museum**
The Castle
Enniskillen, County Fermanagh BT74 7HL
phone +44 (0) 28 6632 3142

Florence Court
Enniskillen, County Fermanagh BT92 1DB
phone +44 (0) 28 6634 8249
florencecourt@nationaltrust.org.uk

exeter (west country)

Exeter Tourist Information Centre
Paris Street
Exeter, Devon EX1 1NN
phone +44 (0) 1392 265 700

ABode Exeter
The Royal Clarence
Cathedral Yard
Exeter, Devon EX1 1HD
phone +44 (0) 1392 319 955
reservationsexeter@abodehotels.co.uk

Queens Court Hotel
6-8 Bystock Terrace
Exeter, Devon EX4 4HY
phone +44 (0) 1392 272 709
enquiries@queenscourt-hotel.co.uk
www.queenscourt-hotel.co.uk

The Edwardian
30-32 Heavitree Road
Exeter, Devon EX1 2LQ
phone +44 (0) 1392 276102
fax +44 (0) 1392 253 393

Cat in the Hat
29 Magdalen Road
St Leonards
Exeter, Devon EX2 4TA
phone +44 (0) 1392 211 700

Gino's Restaurant
Bartholomew Street East
Exeter, Devon
phone +44 (0) 01392 493 636
www.ginosrestaurant.co.uk

Michael Caines Restaurant
Royal Clarence Hotel
Cathedral Yard
Exeter, Devon EX1 1HD
phone +44 (0) 1392 223 638

**Royal Albert Memorial Museum
and Art Gallery**
Queen Street
Exeter, Devon EX4 3RX
phone +44 (0) 1392 665858

Topsham Museum
25, The Strand
Topsham
Exeter, Devon EX3 0AX
phone +44 (0) 1392 873244
museum@topsham.org.uk

Castle Drogo
Drewsteignton
nr Exeter, Devon EX6 6PB
phone +44 (0) 1647 433306
castledrogo@nationaltrust.org.uk

Killerton
Broadclyst
Exeter, Devon EX5 3LE
phone +44 (0) 1392 881345
killerton@nationaltrust.org.uk

Killerton – Budlake Old Post Office Room
Broadclyst
Exeter, Devon EX5 3LW
phone +44 (0) 1392 881690

Killerton: Marker's Cottage
Broadclyst
Exeter, Devon EX5 3HR
phone +44 (0) 1392 461 546
markerscottage@nationaltrust.org.uk

A La Ronde
Summer Lane
Exmouth, Devon EX8 5BD
phone +44 (0) 1395 265514
alaronde@nationaltrust.org.uk

Bradley
Newton Abbott, Devon TQ12 6BN
Bradley@nationaltrust.org.uk

The Church House
Widecombe in the Moor
Newton Abbot, Devon TQ13 7TA
phone +44 (0) 1364 621321
churchhouse@nationaltrust.org.uk

Knightshayes Court
Bolham
Tiverton, Devon EX16 7RQ
phone +44 (0) 1884 254665
knightshayes@nationaltrust.org.uk

**Branscombe – The Old Bakery,
Mill and Forge**
Branscombe
Seaton, Devon EX12
phone +44 (0) 1392 881691

Coleton Fishacre
Brownstone Road
Kingswear, Devon TQ 0ED
phone +44 (0) 1803 752466
coletonfishacre@nationaltrust.org.uk

Compton Castle
Marldon
Paignton, Devon TQ3 1TA
phone +44 (0) 1803843235
comptoncastle@nationaltrust.org.uk

Greenway Garden
Greenway Road
Galmpton
nr Brixham, Devon TQ5 0ES
phone +44 (0)1803 842382

Loughwood Meeting House
Dalwood
Axminster, Devon EX13 7DU
phone +44 (0) 1392 881691
loughwood@nationaltrust.org.uk

Lydford Gorge
The Stables, Lydford Gorge, Lydford
nr Okehampton, Devon EX20 4BH

Shute Barton
Shute
nr Axminster, Devon EX13 7PT
phone +44 (0) 1297 34692

Tiverton Castle
Park Hill
Tiverton, Devon EX16 6RP
phone +44 (0) 1884 253 200 / 255 200
tiverton.castle@ukf.net

Tiverton Museum
Beck's Square
Tiverton, Devon EX16 6PJ
phone +44 (0) 1884 256295
enquiries@tivertonmuseum.org.uk

Exeter Northcott Theatre
Stocker Road
Exeter, Devon EX4 4QB
phone +44 (0) 1392 493 493
info@exeternorthcott.co.uk

gloucester (cotswolds)

Gloucester Tourist Information Centre
28 Southgate Street
Gloucester GL1 2DP
phone +44 (0) 1452 396572.
tourism@gloucester.gov.uk

Edward Hotel
88-92 London Rd
Gloucester GL1 3PG
phone +44 (0) 1452 525865
booking line +44 (0) 845 4566399

New County Hotel
44 Southgate St
Gloucester GL1 2DU
phone +44 (0) 1452 307 000

The New Inn
16 Northgate St
Gloucester GL1 1SF
phone +44 (0) 1452 522 177
booking line +44 (0) 845 45 66 399

The Wharf House
Over, Gloucester
phone +44 (0) 1452 332 900
fax +44 (0) 1452 332 901

Jewel in the Crown
88-90 Westgate Street
Gloucester
Phone +44 (0) 1452 310 366
fax +44 (0) 1452 332 288
farid.uddin@hot-toast.com

Waterside Grill
Fosters on the docks, Kimberley Warehouse
Gloucester
phone +44 (0) 1452 300 990
fax (0) 1452 382 157

Ashleworth Tithe Barn
Ashleworth, Gloucestershire GL19 4JA
phone +44 (0) 1452 814213
ashleworth@nationaltrust.org.uk

Little Fleece Bookshop
Painswick, Gloucestershire GL6 6QQ
phone +44 (0) 1452 812264
littlefleece@nationaltrust.org.uk

Westbury Court Garden
Westbury-on-Severn, Gloucestershire GL14 1PD
phone +44 (0) 1452 760461
westburycourt@nationaltrust.org.uk

Woodchester Park
Nympsfield
nr Stroud, Gloucestershire
phone +44 (0) 1452 814213
woodchesterpark@nationaltrust.org.uk

guildford (southeast)

Tourist Information Centre
14 Tunsgate
Guildford, Surrey GU1 3QT
phone +44 (0) 1483 444333
fax +44 (0) 1483 302046
tic@guildford.gov.uk

Angel Posting House and Livery
91 High Street
Guildford, Surrey GU1 3DPBN26 5DF
phone +44 (0) 1323 482 178
fax +44 (0) 1483 533 770
www.angel postinghouse.com

Olivetto Ristorante & Wine Bar
124 High Street
Tunsgate
Guildford, Surrey GU1 3HQ
phone +44 (0) 1483 563277

Al Vicolo
1-5 Swan Lane
Guildford, Surrey GU1 4EQ
phone +44 (0) 1483 50 63 06

Clandon Park
West Clandon
Guildford, Surrey GU4 7RQ
phone +44 (0) 1483 222482
clandonpark@nationaltrust.org.uk

Hatchlands Park
East Clandon
Guildford Park, Surrey GU4 7RT
phone +44 (0) 1483 222482
hatchlands@nationaltrust.org.uk

Watts Gallery
Down Lane
Compton
Guildford, Surrey GU3 1DQ
phone +44 (0) 1483 810235

Boxhill
The Old Fort
Box Hill Road
Box Hill, Surrey KT20 7LB
phone +44 (0) 1306 885502
boxhill@nationaltrust.org.uk

Claremont Landscape Garden
Portsmouth Road
Esher, Surrey KT10 9JG
phone +44 (0) 1372 487806
Claremont@nationaltrust.org.uk

Hampton Court Palace
East Molesey, Surrey KT8 9AU
phone +44 (0) 870 752 7777
www.hrp.org.uk/webcode/Hampton_home.asp

The Homewood
Portsmouth Road
Esher, Surrey KT10 9JL
phone +44 (0) 1372 476424
thehomewood@nationaltrust.org.uk

**Hindhead Commons
and The Devil's Punchbowl Café**
London Road
Hindhead, Surrey GU26 6AB
hindhead@nationaltrust.org.uk

Leith Hill
c/o Mark Cottage
Leith Hill Lane
Holmbury St Mary
Dorking, Surrey RH5 6LY
phone +44 (0) 1306 711777
leithhill@nationaltrust.org.uk

Oakhurst Cottage
Hambledon
nr Godalming, Surrey GU8 4HF
phone +44 (0) 1483 208477
oakhurstcottage@nationaltrust.org.uk

Polesden Lacey
Great Bookham
nr Dorking, Surrey RH5 6BD
phone +44 (0) 1372 452048
polesdenlacey@nationaltrust.org.uk

**River Wey and Godalming Navigations
and Dapdune Wharf**
Navigations Office and Dapdune Wharf
Wharf Road
Guildford, Surrey GU1 4RR
phone +44 (0) 1483 561389
riverwey@nationaltrust.org.uk

Winkworth Arboretum
Hascombe Road
Godalming, Surrey GU8 4AD
phone +44 (0) 1483 208477
winkworth arboretum@nationaltrust.org.uk

The Witley Centre
Witley
Godalming, Surrey GU8 5QA
phone +44 (0) 1428 683207
witleycentre@nationaltrust.org.uk

harrogate (yorkshire)

Tourist Information Centre
Royal Baths
Crescent Road
Harrogate, North Yorkshire HG1 2RR
phone +44 (0) 1423 537 300
fax +44 (0) 1423 537 305
tic@harrogate.gov.uk

Belmont B&B
86 Kings Road
Harrogate, North Yorkshire HG1 5JX
phone +44 (0) 1423 528 086
mobile +44 (0) 7950 342 584

Hotel Du Vin
Prospect Place
West Park
Harrogate, North Yorkshire HG1 1LB
phone +44 (0) 1423 85 6800
fax +44 (0) 1423 856 801
info@harrogate.hotelduvin.com

Grants
Swan Road
Harrogate, North Yorkshire HG1 2SS
phone +44 (0) 1423 560666
Fax +44 (0) 1423 502550
enquiries@grantshotel-harrogate.com

Alexa House
26 Ripon Road
Harrogate, North Yorkshire HG1 2JJ
phone +44 (0) 1423 501988
fax +44 (0) 1423 504086
enquires@alexa-house.co.uk
http://www.tiscover.co.uk/alexahouse

Orchid Restaurant
28 Swan Road
Harrogate, North Yorkshire HG1 2SE
phone +44 (0) 1423 560 425
fax +44 (0) 1423 530967
info@orchidrestaurant.co.uk

Quantro Restaurant
3 Royal Parade
Harrogate, North Yorkshire HG1 2SZ
phone +44 (0) 1423 503034
info@quantro.co.uk

Courtyard Restaurant
1 Montpellier Mews
Montpellier Street
Harrogate, North Yorkshire
phone +44 (0)1423 530 708

Sasso
8-10 Princes Square
Harrogate, North Yorkshire HG1 1LX
phone/fax +44 (0) 1243 508 838

Brimham Rocks
Summerbridge
Harrogate, North Yorkshire HG3 4DW
phone +44 (0) 1423 780688
brimhamrocks@nationaltrust.org.uk

Harewood House
Leeds, West Yorkshire LS17 9LQ
phone +44 (0) 113 218 1010
www.harewood.org

hastings (southeast)

Hastings Information Centre
Queen's Square
Priory Meadow
Hastings, East Sussex
phone +44 (0) 1424 781111
Fax +44 (0) 1424 781186
hic@1066.net

Royal Victoria Hotel
Marina
St Leonards on Sea
Hastings, East Sussex TN38 0BD
phone +44 (0) 1424 445544
fax +44 (0) 1424 721995
reception@royalvichotel.co.uk

The Tower House Hotel
28 Tower Road West
St. Leonards-on-Sea, East Sussex TN38 0RG
phone +44 (0) 1424 427217
fax +44 (0) 1424 430165
reservations@towerhousehotel.com

Maggie's fish and chips
Above the fish market
Rock-a-Nore Road, Old Town
Hastings, East Sussex TN34 3DW
phone 44 (0) 1424 430205

Pomegranate
50 George Street, Old Town
Hastings, East Sussex TN34 3EA
phone +44 (0) 1424 429221

St. Clement's
3 Mercatoria
St. Leonards-on-Sea, East Sussex TN38 0EB
phone +44 (0) 1424 200355

haworth (yorkshire)

Haworth Tourist Information Centre
2/4 West Lane
Haworth, West Yorkshire BD22 8EF
phone +44 (0) 1535 642 329/ 645 864
fax +44 (0) 1535 647 721
haworth@ytbtic.co.uk

Aitches
11 West Lane
Haworth, West Yorkshire BD22 8DU
phone +44 (0) 1535 642501
aitches@talk21.com

Haworth Old Hall
Sun Street
Haworth, West Yorkshire BD22 8BP
phone +44 (0) 1535 642709
fax +44 (0) 1535 647857
haworth.oldhall@.co.uk

Hill Top Farmhouse
Haworth Moor, West Yorkshire BD22 0EL
phone +44 (0) 1536 643524

Weaver's Restaurant
15 West Lane
Haworth, West Yorkshire BD22 8DU
phone +44 (0) 1535 643822
fax +44 (0) 1535 644832
weaversinhaworth@aol.com

Brontë Parsonage Museum
Church Street
Haworth
Keighley, West Yorkshire BD22 8DR
phone +44 (0) 1535 642323

Cliffe Castle Museum
Spring Gardens Lane
Keighley, West Yorkshire BD20 6LH
phone +44 (0) 1535 618230

Hardcastle Crags
Hollin Hall
Crimsworth Dean
Hebden Bridge, West Yorkshire HX7 7AP
phone +44 (0) 1422 844518
hardcastlecrags@nationaltrust.org.uk

East Riddlesden Hall
Bradford Road
Keighly, West Yorkshire BD20 5EL
phone +44 (0) 1535 607075
eastriddlesen@nationaltrust.org.uk

Gawthorpe Hall
Padiham
nr Burnley, Lancashire BB12 8UA
phone +44 (0) 1282 771004
gawthorpehall@nationaltrust.org.uk

helmsley (yorkshire)

Helmsley Tourist Information Centre
Helmsley Castle Visitor Centre
Castlegate
Helmsley, North Yorkshire YO62 5AB
phone +44 (0) 1439 770173
fax +44 (0) 1439 771 116
helmsley.tic@english-heritage.org.uk

The Black Swan Hotel
Rutland Room Restaurant
Market Place
Helmsley, North Yorkshire YO62 5BJ
phone +44 (0) 118 971 4700

Feversham Arms Hotel
1 High Street
Helmsley, North Yorkshire YO62 5AG

The Pheasant Hotel
Harome
Helmsley (2.5 miles), North Yorkshire
YO62 5JG
phone +44 (0) 1439 771241
fax +44 (0) 1439 771744
reservations@thepheasanthotel.com
www.thepheasanthotel.com

Beck Isle Museum of Rural Life
Bridge Street
Pickering, North Yorkshire YO18 8DU
phone +44 (0) 1751 473653

Nunnington Hall
Nunnington
nr York, North Yorkshire YO62 5UY
phone +44 (0) 1439 748283
nunningtonhall@nationaltrust.org.uk

Rievaulx Terrace and Temples
Rievaulx
Helmsley, North Yorkshire YO62 5LJ
phone +44 (0) 1439798340 / 793840
rievaulxterrace@nationaltrust.org.uk

helston (west country)

Lizard Peninsula Tourism Association
phone +44 (0) 1326 281481
www.lizard-peninsula.co.uk

Lyndale Cottage Guest House
4 Greenbank, Meneage Road
Helston, Cornwall TR13 8JA

phone +44 (0) 1326 561082
fax +44 (0) 1326 565813
enquiries@lyndalecottage.co.uk
www.lyndlecottage.co.uk

Roslyn Cottage
Trewennack
Helston, Cornwall TR13 0PQ
phone +44 (0) 1326 573581
roslyncottage@hotmail.com
www.cornwall-online.co.uk/roslyn-cottage

Seefar Guest House
Peverell Terrace
Porthleven, Cornwall TR13 9DZ
phone +44 (0) 1326 573778
seefar@talk21.com
www.cornwall-online.co.uk/seefar

Morleys Restaurant
The Mews, 4 Wendron St
Helston, Cornwall TR13 8PS
phone +44 (0) 1326 564433

The Lugger Restaurant
Harbour Head, Porthleven
Helston, Cornwall TR13 9JA
phone +44 (0) 1326 562761

Critchards Seafood Restaurant
Harbourside, Porthleven
Helston, Cornwall TR13 9JA
phone +44 (0) 1326 562 407

Godolphin
Godolphin Cross
Helston, Cornwall TR13 9RE
phone +44 (0) 1736 762479
godolphin@nationaltrust.org.uk

Penrose Estate: Gunwalloe and Loo Pool
nr Helston, Cornwall
phone +44 (0) 1326 561407
southwestcornwall@nationaltrust.org.uk

Glendurgan Garden
Mawnan Smith
nr Falmouth, Cornwall TR11 5JZ
phone +44 (0 1326 250906
glendurgan@nationaltrust.org.uk

The Lizard and Kynance Cove
Cornwall
phone +44 (0) 1326 561407
lizard@nationaltrust.org.uk

hereford (welsh borders)

Hereford Tourist Information Centre
1 King Street
Hereford, Herefordshire HR4 9BW
phone +44 (0) 1432 268430

Castle House
Castle Street
Hereford, Herefordshire HR1 2NW
phone +44 (0) 1432 356321
fax +44 (0) 1432 365909
info@castlehse.co.uk

Aylestone Court Hotel
2 Aylestone Hill
Hereford, Herefordshire HR1 1HS
phone +44 (0) 1432 341891
fax +44 (0) 1432 267691

Floodgates Brasserie
Left Bank Village
Bridge Street
Hereford, Herefordshire HR4 9DG
phone +44 (0) 871 4264710
www.leftbank.co.uk

The Weir
Swainshill
nr Hereford, Herefordshire HR4 7QF
phone +44 (0) 1981 590509
theweir@nationaltrust.org.uk

inverness scottish (highlands and islands)

Inverness Tourist Information Centre
Castle Wynd
Inverness, Highland IV2 3BJ
phone +44 (0) 1463 234353
fax +44 (0) 1463 710609
info@visitscotland.com

Rocpool Reserve
Culduthel Road
Inverness, Highland IV2 4AG
phone +44 (0) 1463 240089
fax +44 (0) 1463 248431
info@rocpool.com

Glendruidh House Hotel
Druid Glen
Old Edinburgh Road South
Inverness, Highland IV2 6AR
phone +44 (0) 1463 226499
fax +44 (0) 1463 710745
info@coZZee-neSSie-bed.co.uk

Glenmoriston Town House
and Abstract Restaurant
20 Ness Bank
Inverness, Highland IV2 4SF
phone +44 (0) 1463 223 777
fax +44 (0) 1463 712 378
reception@glenmoristontownhouse.com

Ballifeary Guest House
10 Ballifeary Road
Inverness, Highland IV3 5PJ
phone +44 (0) 1463 235572
fax +44 (0) 1463 717583
info@ballifearyguesthouse.co.uk

Moyness House
6 Bruce Gardens
Inverness, Highland IV3 5EN
phone/fax +44 (0) 1463 233836
info@moyness.co.uk

Cafe 1
75 Castle St
Inverness, Highland IV2 3EA
phone +44 (0) 1463 226200
info@cafe1.net

Inverness Museum
Castle Wynd
Inverness, Highland IV2 3EB
phone +44 (0) 1463 237114
Inverness.museum@highland.gov.uk

kendal (lake district and northwest)

Tourist Information Centre
Town Hall, Highgate
Kendal, Cumbria LA9 4DL
phone +44 (0) 1539 725758
kendaltic@southlakeland.gov.uk

Riverside Hotel
Beezon Road, Stramongate Bridge
Kendal, Cumbria LA9 6EL
phone +44 (0) 1539 734861
info@riversidekendal.co.uk

Headlands Hotel
53 Milnthorpe Road
Kendal, Cumbria LA9 5QG
phone +44 (0) 1539 732464

Arthouse B&B
84 Shap Road
Kendal, Cumbria LA9 6DP
phone +44 (0) 1539 741503

Balcony House Guest House
82 Shap Road
Kendal, Cumbria LA9 6DP
phone +44 (0) 1539 731402

The Punch Bowl Inn and Restaurant
Crosthwaite
Lyth Valley, Cumbria LA8 8HR
phone +44 (0) 15395 68237
info@the-punchbowl.co.uk

The New Moon Restaurant
129 Highgate
Kendal, Cumbria LA9 4EN
phone +44 (0) 1539 729254
info@newmoonrestaurant.co.uk

Abbot Hall
Kirkland
Kendal, Cumbria LA9 5AL
phone +44 (0) 1539 722464
www.abbothall.org.uk

Sizergh Castle and Garden
Sizergh
nr Kendal, Cumbria LA8 8AE
phone +44 (0) 15395 60951
sizergh@nationaltrust.org.uk

keswick (lake district and northwest)

Keswick Tourist Information Centre
Moot Hall
Keswick, Cumbria CA12 5JS
phone +44 (0) 17687 72645
keswicktic@lake-district.gov.uk

Kings Arms Hotel
Main Street
Keswick, Cumbria CA12 5PE
phone +44 (0) 17687 72083
fax +44 (0) 17687 75550
info@kingsarmskeswick.co.uk

The Skiddaw Hotel
Main Street
Keswick, Cumbria CA12 5BN
phone +44 (0) 1768 772071 l
fax +44 (0) 1768 774850
reservations@skiddawhotel.co.uk

Lairbeck Hotel
Vicarage Hill
Keswick, Cumbria CA12 5QB
phone +44 (0) 17687 73373
fax +44 (0) 8716 612552
info@lairbeckhotel-keswick.co.uk

Claremont House
Chestnut Hill
Keswick, Cumbria CA12 4LT
phone +44 (0) 17687 72089
claremonthouse@btinternet.com

Morrel's Restaurant and Rooms
34 Lake Road
Keswick, Cumbria CA12 5DQ
phone +44 (0) 17687 72666
info@morrels.co.uk

Borrowdale
Bowe Barn
Borrowdale Road
Keswick, Cumbria CA12 5UP
phone +44 (0) 17687 74649
borrowdale@nationaltrust.org.uk

Buttermere and Ennerdale
Unit 16
Leaconsfield Industrial Estate
Cleator Moor, Cumbria CA25 5QB
phone +44 (0) 1946 816940
buttermere@nationaltrust.org.uk

Wordsworth House
Main Street
Cockermouth, Cumbria CA13 9RX
phone +44 (0) 1900 820884
wordsworthhouse@nationaltrust.org.uk

kingston–upon–hull (yorkshire)

Hull Tourist Information Centre
1 Paragon Street
Hull, East Yorkshire HU1 3NA
phone +44 (0) 1482 223 559
tourist.information@hullcc.gov.uk

The Kingston Theatre Hotel
1-2 Kingston Square
Kingston-upon-Hull, East Yorkshire HU2 8DA
phone +44 (0) 1482 225828
fax +44 (0) 1482 587969
www.kingstontheatrehotel.com

Holiday Inn Hull Marina
Castle Street
Hull, East Yorkshire HU1 2BX
phone +44 (0) 870 4009043
www.holidayinn.co.uk

The Two Rivers Restaurant at The Deep
(Friday and Saturday evenings
reservations required)
Waterfront
Hull, East Yorkshire
phone +44 (0) 1482 382883
tworivers@thedeep.co.uk

Ayutthaya Thai
47 Jameson Street
Hull HU1 3JA
phone +44 (0) 1482 219544

Ferens Art Gallery
Queen Victoria Square
Hull, East Yorkshire HU1 3RA
phone +44 (0) 1482 613902
www.hullcc.gov.uk/museums

Hull and East Riding Museum
36 High Street
Hull, East Yorkshire HU1 1PS
phone +44 (0) 1482 613902
www.hullcc.gov.uk/museums

Hull Maritime Museum
Queen Victoria Square
Hull, East Yorkshire HU1 2AA
phone +44 (0) 1482 610610
www.hullcc.gov.uk/museums/maritime/index.php

Maister House
160 High Street
Hull, East Yorkshire HU1 1NL
phone +44 (0) 1723 870423
maisterhouse@nationaltrust.org.uk

University of Hull Art Collection
The University
Cottingham Road
Hull, Humberside HU6 7RX

Wilberforce House Museum
25 High Street
Hull, East Yorkshire HU1 1NQ
phone +44 (0) 1482 613902

knighton (wales)

Knighton Tourist Information Centre
Offas Dyke Centre, West Street
Knighton, Powys LD7 1EN
phone +44 (0) 1547 529424
Fax +44 (0) 1547 529242
oda.offasdyke@demon.co.uk

The Knighton Hotel
Broad Street
Knighton, Powys LD7 1BL
phone +44 (0) 1547 502530

The Fleece House Guest House
Market Street
Knighton, Powys LD7 1BB
phone +44 (0) 1547 520168
info@fleecehouse.co.uk

Milebrook House
Ludlow Road, Milebrook
Knighton (1.5 m), Powys LD7 1LT
phone +44 (0) 1547 528632
fax +44 (0) 1547 520509
hotel@milebrook.kc3ltd.co.uk

Horse & Jockey Inn
Wylcwm Place
Knighton, Powys LD7 1AE
phone +44 (0) 1547 520062
www.thehorseandjockeyinn.co.uk

lancaster (lake district and northwest)

Lancaster Tourist Information Centre
29 Castle Hill
Lancaster, Lancashire LA1 1YN
phone +44 (0) 1524 32878
lancastertic@lancaster.gov.uk

**Lancaster House Hotel
and Foodworks Restaurant**
Green Lane
Ellel
Lancaster, Lancashire LA1 4GJ
phone +44 (0) 1524 844822
fax +44 (0) 1524 844766
crs.lancaster@elhmail.co.uk

The Sun Hotel and Bar
63 Church Street
Lancaster, Lancashire LA1 1ET
phone +44 (0) 1524 66006
info@thesunhotelandbar.co.uk

Edenbreck House B&B
Sunnyside Lane
Lancaster, Lancashire LA1 5ED
phone +44 (0) 1524 32464/ (0) 7833705971
edenbreckhouse@aol.com

Wagon and Horses B&B
27 St Georges Quay
Lancaster, Lancashire LA1 1RD
phone +44 (0) 1524 846094
wagon-and-horses@supernet.com

The Borough
3 Dalton Square
Lancaster, Lancashire LA1 3PR
phone +44 (0) 1524 64170

Etna
22 New Street
Lancaster, Lancashire LA1 1EG
phone +44 (0) 1524 69551

Quite Simply French
27a St Georges Quay
Lancaster, Lancashire LA1 1RD
phone +44 (0) 1524 843199

Ruskin Library
University of Lancaster
Lancaster, Lancashire LA1 4YH
phone +44 (0) 1524 593587
Ruskin.library@lancaster.ac.uk

lavenham (east anglia)

Lavenham Tourist Information Centre
Lady Street
Lavenham, Suffolk CO10 9RA
phone +44 (0) 1787 248207
fax +44 (0) 1787 249459
lavenhamtic@babergh.gov.uk
http://www.babergh-south-suffolk.gov.uk/

Angel Hotel
Market Place
Lavenham, Suffolk CO10 9QZ
phone +44 (0) 1787 247 388
fax +44 (0) 1787 248 344
angellav@aol.com

Lavenham Priory
Water Street
Lavenham, Suffolk CO10 9RW
phone +44 (0) 1787 247 404
fax +44 (0) 1787 248 472
mail@lavenhampriory.co.uk

Great House Hotel
Market Place
Lavenham, Suffolk CO10 9QZ
phone +44 (0) 1787 247 431
fax +44 (0) 1787 248 007
info@greathouse.co.uk

The Swan
High Street
Lavenham, Suffolk CO10 9QA
phone +44 (0) 1787 247 477
fax +44 (o)1787 248 286
info@theswanatlavenham.co.uk

Restaurants
All four listed hotels also function
as restaurants. You need look no further

Gainsborough's House
46 Gainsborough Street
Sudbury, Suffolk CO10 2EU
phone +44 (0) 1787 372958
www.gainsborough.org

The Guildhall of Corpus Christi
Market Place
Lavenham, Suffolk CO10 9QZ
phone +44 (0) 1787 247646
lavenhamguildhall@nationaltrust.org.uk

Melford Hall
Long Melford
Sudbury, Suffolk CO10 9AA
phone +44 (0) 1787 376395
melford@nationaltrust.org.uk

Thorington Hall
Stoke by Nayland, Suffolk CO6 4SS
phone +44 (0) 1284 747500

lerwick (highlands and islands)

Lerwick Tourist Information Centre
Market Cross
Lerwick, Shetland ZE1 0LU
phone +44 (0) 8701 999440
fax +44 (0) 1595 695807
info@visitshetland.com

Kveldsro House Hotel
Greenfield Place
Lerwick, Shetland ZE1 0AQ
phone +44 (0) 1595 692195
fax +44 (0) 1595 696595
reception@kveldsrohotel.co.uk

Lerwick Hotel
15 South Road
Lerwick, Shetland UK ZE1 0RB
phone +44 (0) 1595 692166
fax +44 (0) 1595 694419
reception@lerwickhotel.co.uk

Glen Orchy Guest House
20 Knab Rd
Lerwick, Shetland ZE1 0AX
phone/fax +44 (0) 159 692031
glenorchyhouse@virgin.net

Monty's Bistro and Deli
5 Mounthooly Street
Lerwick, Shetland
phone +44 (0) 1595 696655

The Maryfield House Hotel and Restaurant
Bressay (a short ferry ride from Lerwick)
phone +44 (0) 1595 820207

Shetland Museum
Lower Hillhead
Lerwick, Shetland ZE1 0EL
phone +44 (0) 1595 695057
museum@sic.shetland.gov.uk

lincoln (midlands)

Tourist Information
9 Castle Hill
Lincoln, Lincolnshire LN1 3AA
phone +44 (0) 1522 873 800
fax +44 (0) 1522 541 447 / 541 452
tourism@lincoln.gov.uk

Bailhouse & Mews B&B
34 Bailgate
Lincoln, Lincolnshire LN1 3AP
phone +44 (0) 1522 520 883
fax +44 (0) 1522 521 829
info@bailhouse.co.uk
http://bailhouse.co.uk/contact-the-
bailhouse.html

Hillcrest Hotel
Lincoln, Lincolnshire LN2 5RT
phone +44 (0) 1522 510 182
fax +44 (0) 1522 538 009
reservations@hillcrest-hotel.com

Minster Lodge
3 Church Lane
Lincoln, Lincolnshire LN2 1QJ
phone +44 (0) 1522 513220
fax +44 (0) 1522 513220

Browns Pie Shop
33 Steep Hill
Lincoln, Lincolnshire LN21LU
phone +44 (0) 1522 527330

The Jews House Restaurant
(vegetarian)
15 The Strait
Lincoln, Lincolnshire LN21JD
phone +44 (0) 1522 524 851

The Old Bakery Restaurant
26-28 Burton Rd
Lincoln, Lincolnshire LN1 3LB
phone +44 (0) 1522 576057
www.theold-bakery.co.uk

Usher Gallery, Lincoln
Lindum Road
Lincoln, Lincolnshire LN2 1NN
phone +44 (0) 1522 527980
www.lincolnshire.gov.uk/Usher.htm

Clumber Park
The Estate Office
Clumber park
Worksop, Nottinghamshire S80 3AZ
phone +44 (0) 1909 544917
clumberpark@nationaltrust.org.uk

Mr Straw's House
7 Blyth Grove
Worksop, Nottinghamshire S81 0JG
phone +44 (0) 1909 482380
mrstrawshouse@nationaltrust.org.uk

Tattershall Castle
Tattershall, Lincolnshire LN4 4LR
phone +44 (0) 1526 342543
tattershallcastle@nationaltrust.org.uk

The Workhouse, Southwell
Upton Road
Southwell, Nottinghamshire NG25 0PT
phone +44 (0) 1636 817250
theworkhouse@nationaltrust.org.uk

linlithgow (scottish lowlands)

Linlithgow Tourist Information Centre
Burgh Halls, The Cross
Linlithgow (April-October)
phone +44 (0) 8452 255121

Champany Inn and Restaurants
Champany
Linlithgow EH49 7LU
phone +44 (0) 1506 834532
fax +44 (0) 1506 834302
reception@champany.com

Arden Country House
Belsyde Country Estate
Linlithgow EH49 6QE
phone +44 (0) 1506 670172
fax +44 (0) 1506 670172
information@ardencountryhouse.com

West Port Hotel
18-20 West Port
Linlithgow EH49 7AZ
phone +44 (0) 1506 847456
fax +44 (0) 1506 846455
info@removeme.maclay.co.uk

Livingston's Restaurant
52 High Street
Linlithgow EH49 7AE
phone +44 (0) 1506 846565
fax +44 (0) 1506 846565
contact@livingstons-restaurant.co.uk

New Lanark
South Lanarkshire ML11 9DB
phone +44 (0) 1555 661345
www.newlanark.org

Dean Gallery
Belford Road
Edinburgh, Lothian EH4 3DS
phone +44 (0) 131 624 6200
www.nationalgalleries.org

**Raymond Russell Collection of Early
Keyboard Instruments**
St Cecilia's Hall
Niddry Street
Cowgate, Edinburgh, Lothian EH1 1LJ
phone +44 (0) 131 650 2805

Scottish National Gallery of Modern Art
Bedford Road
Edinburgh, Lothian EH4 3DR
phone +44 (0) 131 624 6200
www.nationalgalleries.org

Scottish National Portrait Gallery
1 Queen Street
Edinburgh, Lothian EH2 1JO
phone +44 (0) 131 332 2266
www.natgalscot.ac.uk

Talbot Rice Gallery
University of Edinburgh
Old College
South Bridge
Edinburgh, Lothian EH8 9YL
phone +44 (0) 131 650 2211

Palace of Holyroodhouse
Edinburgh, Lothian EH8 8DX
phone +44 (0) 131 556 5100
www.royal.gov.uk

Museum of Scotland
Chambers Street
Edinburgh, Lothian EH1 1JF
phone +44 (0) 131 225 7534
www.nms.ac.uk

National Gallery of Scotland
The Mound
Edinburgh, Lothian EH2 2EL
phone +44 (0) 131 624 6200

Burrell Collection
Pollok Country Park
2060 Pollokshaws Road
Glasgow, Strathclyde G43 1AT
phone +44 (0) 141 287 2550
www.glasgowmuseims.com

Glasgow Museum and Art Gallery
Argyle Street
Glasgow, Strathclyde G3 8AG
phone +44 (0) 141 287 2699
www.glasgowmuseums.com

**St Mungo Museum
of Religious Life and Art**
2 Castle Street
Glasgow, Strathclyde G4 0RH
phone +44 (0) 141 552 4744
www.glasgowmuseums.com

Gallery of Modern Art
Royal Exchange Square
Glasgow, Strathclyde G1 3AH
phone +44 (0) 141 229 1996
www.glasgowmuseums.com

**Hunterian Art Gallery
and the Mackintosh House**
University of Glasgow
Glasgow, Strathclyde G12 8QQ
phone +44 (0) 141 330 4221
www.gla.ac.uk/Museum

Hunterian Museum
University Avenue
University of Glasgow
Glasgow, Strathclyde G12 8QQ
phone +44 (0) 141 339 8855
www.gla.ac.uk/Museum

Museum of Transport
1 Bunhouse Road
Glasgow
Strathclyde G3 8DP
phone +44 (0) 141 287 2720
www.glasgowmuseums.com

People's Palace
Glasgow Green
Glasgow, Strathclyde G40 1AT
phone +44 (0) 141 554 0223
www.glasgowmuseums.com

Pollok House
Pollok Country Park
2060 Pollokshaws Road
Glasgow, Strathclyfe G43 1AT
phone +44 (0) 141 616 6410
www.glasgowmuseums.com

llandrindod wells (wales)

Llandrindod Wells Tourist Information Centre
Old Town Hall
Memorial Gardens
Llandrindod Wells, Powys LD1 5DL
phone +44 (0) 1597 822600
fax +44 (0) 1597 829164
llandtic@powys.gov.uk

The Metropole Hotel and Radnor Restaurant
Temple Street
Llandrindod Wells, Powys LD1 5DY
phone +44 (0) 1597 823 700
fax +44 (0) 1597 824 828

Greylands
High Street
Llandrindod Wells, Powys LD1 6AG
phone +44 (0) 1597 822253
greylands@btinternet.com

Guidfa House
Crossgates
Llandrindod Wells, Powys LD1 6RF
phone +44 (0) 1597 851241
fax +44 (0) 1597 851836
guidfa@globalnet.co.uk

Rhydithon Guest House
Dyffryn Road
Llandrindod Wells, Powys
phone/fax +44 (0) 1597 822624

Llanerch Inn and Restaurant
Llanerch Lane
Llandrindod Wells, Powys LD1 6BG
phone +44 (0) 1597 822086
fax +44 (0) 1597 824618

llandudno (wales)

Llandudno Tourist Information Centre
1-2 Chapel Street
Llandudno, Gwynedd LL30 2YU
phone +44 (0) 1492 876413
fax +44 (0) 1492 872722
llandudno@nwtic.com

Bodysgallen Hall Hotel, Restaurant and Spa
Llandudno, Gwynedd LL30 1RS
phone +44 (0) 1492 584466
fax +44 (0) 1492 582519
(from USA fax toll free on 800 260 8338)

Dunoon Hotel
Gloddaeth Avenue
Llandudno, Gwynedd LL30 2DW
phone +44 (0) 1492 860787
fax +44 (0) 1492 860031
reservations@dunoonhotel.co.uk

St. Tudno Hotel & Terrace Restaurant
North Parade, Promenade
Llandudno, Gwynedd LL30 2LP
phone +44 (0) 1492 874411
fax +44 (0) 1492 860407
sttudnohotel@btinternet.com

Sefton Court Hotel
49 Church Walks
Llandudno, Gwynedd LL30 2HL
phone +44 (0) 1492 875235
fax +44 (0) 1492 875235
information@seftoncourt-hotel.co.uk

Candles
Premier House, 29 Lloyd St
Llandudno, Gwynedd LL30 2UU
phone +44 (0) 1492 874422

Martins Restaurant
11 Mostyn Ave
Llandudno, Gwynedd LL30 1YS
phone +44 (0) 1492 870070

Osborne House Café Grill
17 North Parade
Llandudno, Gwynedd LL30 2LP
phone +44 (0) 1492 860330
sales@osbornehouse.com.
(see also hotels and restaurants in Conwy)

llangollen (wales)

Llangollen Tourist Information Centre Y Chapel
Castle Street
Llangollen, Denbighshire LL20 8NU
phone +44 (0) 1978 860828
fax +44 (0) 1978 861563
llangollen@nwtic.com

Bryn Howel Hotel
Trevor
Llangollen (2 m), Denbighshire LL20 7UW
phone +44 (0) 1978 860 331
fax +44 (0) 1978 860 119
reception@brynhowel.com

Gales Wine Bar, Restaurant and Guest House
18 Bridge Street
Llangollen, Denbighshire LL20 8PF
phone +44 (0) 1978 860089
fax +44 (0) 1978 861313
Rgale@galesofllangollen.co.uk

Hillcrest Guest House
Hill Street
Llangollen, Denbighshire LL20 8EU
phone/fax +44 (0) 1978 860208
enquiry@hillcrest-guesthouse.com

Oakmere Guest House
Hill Street
Llangollen, Denbighshire LL20 8HS
phone +44 (0) 1978 861126
fax +44 (0) 1978 860208
OakmereGH@aol.com

The Corn Mill
Dee Lane
Llangollen, Denbighshire LL20 8PN
phone +44 (0) 1978 869555
fax +44 (0) 1978 869930
corn.mill@brunningandprice.co.uk

The Gallery
15 Chapel St
Llangollen, Denbighshire LL20 8NN
phone +44 (0) 1978 860076

Chirk Castle
Chirk
Wrexham, Clwyd LL14 5AF
phone +44 (0) 1691 777701
chirkcastle@nationaltrust.org.uk

ludlow (welsh borders)

Ludlow Visitor Information Centre
Castle Street
Ludlow, Shropshire SY8 1AS
phone +44 (0) 1584 875053
fax +44 (0) 1584 877931

The Feathers Hotel
The Bull Ring
Ludlow, Shropshire SY8 1AA
phone +44 (0) 1584 875261
fax +44 (0) 1584 876030
enquiries@feathersatludlow.co.uk

Overton Grange Hotel
Old Hereford Road
Ludlow, Shropshire SY8 4AD
phone +44 (0) 1584 873500
fax +44 (0) 1584 873500
info@overtongrangehotel.com

The Bull Hotel
14 The Bull Ring
Ludlow, Shropshire SY8 1AD
phone +44 (0) 1584 873611
fax +44 (0) 1584 873666
info@bull-ludlow.co.uk

Hibiscus Restaurant
17 Corve Street
Ludlow, Shropshire SY8 1DA
phone +44 (0) 1584 872325
www.hibiscusrestaurant.co.uk

Acton Scott Historic Working Museum
Wenlock Lodge
Acton Scott
Church Stretton, Shropshire SY6 6QN
phone +44 (0) 1694 781306
www.shropshireonline.gov.uk/museums.nsf

Carding Mill Valley and the Shropshire Hills
Chalet Pavillion
Carding Mill Valley
Church Stretton, Shropshire SY6 6JG
phone +44 (0) 1694 723068

Berrington Hall
nr Leominster, Herefordshire HR6 0DW
phone +44 (0) 1568 615721
berrington@nationaltrust.org.uk

Croft Castle and Parkland
Yarpole
nr Leominster, Herefordshire HR6 9PW
phone +44 (0) 1568 780141
croftcastle@nationaltrust.org.uk

Kinver Edge and the Rock Houses
The Warden's Lodge
Comber Road
Kinver

nr Stourbridge, Staffordshire DY7 6HU
phone +44 (0) 1384 872553
kinveredge@nationaltrust.org.uk

masham (yorkshire)

Masham Tourist Information Centre
Mashamshire Community Office
Little Market Place
Masham, North Yorkshire HG4 4DY
phone +44 (0) 1765 680 200
fax +44 (0) 1765 680 209
mashammco@fsmail.net

Swinton Park Hotel
Masham, North Yorkshire HG4 4JH
phone +44 (0) 1765 680900
(toll free from USA) 1866 8103039
fax +44 (0) 1765 680901
enquiries@swintonpark.com

Bank Villa Guest House
Masham, North Yorkshire, HG4 4DB
phone +44 (0) 1765 689605
fax +44 (0) 1765 688545
bankvilla@btopenworld.com

Vennel's Restaurant
7 Silver Street
Masham, North Yorkshire HG4 4DX
phone +44 (0) 1765 689000
info@vennelsrestaurant.co.uk

matlock (midlands)

Tourist Information Centre
Crown Squame
Matlock, Derbyshire DE4 3AT
phone +44 (0) 1629 583388
fax +44 (0) 1629 584131
matlockinfo@derbyshiredales.gov.uk

Riber Hall
Riber Village
Matlock, Derbyshire DE4 5JU
phone +44 (0) 1629 582 795
fax +44 (0) 1629 580 475
info@riber-hall.co.uk
http://www.riber-hall.co.uk/

The Old Lock-Up
North End, Wirksworth
Matlock, Derbyshire DE4 4FG
phone +44 (0) 1629 826272
fax +44 (0) 1629 826272
wheeler@theoldlockup.co.uk

Country Cottage Restaurant
69 Matlock Green
Matlock, Derbyshire DE4 3BT
phone +44 (0) 1629 584600

Alison House
Intake Lane, Cromford
Matlock, Derbyshire DE4 3RH
phone +44 (0) 1629 822 211
alisonhouse@tochh.org.uk

The County and Station
258-260 Dale Road, A6
Matlock Bath
Matlock, Derbyshire, DE4 3NT
phone +44 (0) 1629 580802
information@countyandstation.co.uk

The Druid Inn
Main Street
Birchover, Derbyshire DE4 2BL
phone +44 (0) 1629 650 302

Hardwick Hall and Stainsby Mill
Hardwick Estate
Doe Lea, Derbyshire S44 5QJ
phone +44 (0) 1246 850430
hardwickhall@nationaltrust.org.uk
stainsbymill@nationaltrust.org.uk

Ilam Park
Ilam
Ashbourne, Derbyshire DE6 2AZ
phone +44 (0) 1335 350503
ilampark@nationaltrust.org.uk

Keddleston Hall
Quarndon
Derby, Derbyshire DE22 5JH
phone +44 (0) 1332 842191
www.nationaltrust.org

Longshaw Estate
nr Sheffield, Derbyshire S11 7TZ
phone +44 (0) 1433 637904
longshaw@nationaltrust.org.uk

The Old Manor
Norbury
Ashbourne, Derbyshire DE6 2ED
phone +44 (0) 1283 585337
oldmanor@nationaltrust.co

Sudbury Hall and the National Trust
Museum of Childhood
Sudbury
nr Uttoxeter, Derbyshire DE6 5HT
phone +44 (0) 1283 585305
sudburyhalnationaltrust.org.uk

Winster Market House
Main Street
Winster
nr Matlock, Derbyshire DE4 2DJ
phone +44 (0) 1335 350503
winstermarkethouse@nationaltrust.org.uk

melrose (scottish lowlands)

Melrose Tourist Information Centre
Abbey House, Abbey Street
Melrose, Roxburghshire, Scotland TD6 9LG
phone +44 (0) 870 6080404
fax +44 (0) 1750 21886
bordersinfo@visitsscotland.com
www.melrose.bordernet.co.uk

Braidwood
Buccleuch Street
Melrose, Roxburghshire, Scotland TD6 9LD
phone +44 (0) 1896 822488
fax +44 (0) 1896 822148
enquiries@braidwoodmelrose.co.uk
www.braidwoodmelrose.co.uk

Burts Hotel
Melrose, Roxburghshire, Scotland TD6 9PN
phone +44 (0) 1896 822285
fax +44 (0) 1896 822870
reservations@burtshotel.co.uk

George and Abbotsford Hotel
High Street
Melrose, Roxburghshire, Scotland TD6 9PD
phone +44 (0) 1896 822308
fax +44 (0) 1896 823363
enquiries@georgeandabbotsford.co.uk
www.georgeandabbotsford.co.uk

The Townhouse
Market Square
Melrose, Roxburghshire, Scotland TD6 9PQ
phone +44 (0) 1896 822645
fax +44 (0) 1896 823474

Hoebridge Inn
Gattonside
Melrose, Roxburghshire, Scotland TD6 9LZ
phone +44 (0) 1896 823082

Marmions Brasserie
Buccleuch Street
Melrose, Roxburghshire, Scotland TD6 9LB
phone +44 (0) 1896 822 245

Abbotsford
Melrose, Roxburghshire, Scotland TD6 9BQ
phone +44 (0) 1896 752 043
enquiries@scottsabbotsford.co.uk
www.scottsabbotsford.co.uk

minehead (west country)

Minehead Tourist Information Centre
17 Friday Street
Minehead, Somerset TA24 5UB
phone +44 (0) 1643 702 624
fax +44 (0) 1643 707166
info@mineheadtic.co.uk

Glendower House
30-32 Tregonwell Road
Minehead, Somerset TA24 5DU
phone +44 (0) 1643 707 144
booking line +44 (0) 845 45 66 399

The Langbury
Blue Anchor Bay
Minehead, Somerset TA24 6LB
phone +44 (0) 1643 821375
booking line (0) 845 45 66 399

Yarn Market Hotel
25-33 High Street
Dunster, Somerset TA24 6SF
phone +44 (0) 1643 821 425

Cobblestones
24 High St
Dunster, Minehead, Somerset TA24 6SG
phone +44 (0) 871 2073804

Hathaways
6-8 West St
Dunster, Minehead, Somerset TA24 6SN
phone +44 (0) 871 2075510

Mullions
43 The Avenue
Minehead, Somerset TA24 5AY
phone +44 (0) 871 2075876

The Old Harbour House Restaurant
Quay St
Minehead, Somerset TA24 5UJ
phone +44 (0) 871 2075977

Coleridge Cottage
35 Lime Street
Nether Stowey
Bridgewater, Somerset TA5 1NQ
phone +44 (0) 1278 732662

Dunster Castle
Dunster
nr Minehead, Somerset TA24 6SL
phone +44 (0) 1643 823004
dunstercastle@nationaltrust.org.uk

Dunster Working Watermill
Mill Lane
Dunster
nr Minehead, Somerset TA24 6SW
phone +44 (0) 1643 821759

Holnicote Estate
Selworthy
Minehead, Somerset TA24 8TJ
phone +44 (0) 1643 362452

norwich (east anglia)

Tourist Information Office
The Forum
Millenium Plain
Norwich, Norfolk NR2 1TF
phone +44 (0) 1603 727 927
fax +44 (0) 1603 765 389
tourism@norwich.gov.uk

Annesley House Hotel
6 Newmarket Rd
Norwich, Norfolk NR2 2LA
phone +44 (0) 1603 624 553
fax +44 (0) 1603 621 577
annesleyhouse@bestwestern.co.uk
www.bw-annesleyhouse.co.uk

Beeches Hotel
and Victorian Gardens
2-6 Earlham Road
Norwich, Norfolk NR2 3DB
phone +44 (0) 1603 621 167
fax +44 (0) 1603
beeches@mjbhotels.com

Beaufort Lodge
62 Earlham Road
Norwich, Norfolk NR2 3DF
phone +44 (0) 1603 627 928
fax +44 (0) 1603 440 712
beaufortlodge@aol.com

Adlards Restaurant
79-79a Upper St. Giles St
Norwich, Norfolk NR2 1AB
phone +444 (0) 1603 633 522
bookings @adlards.co.uk
www.adlards.co.uk

By Appointment
25-29 St Georges Street
Norwich, Norfolk NR3 1AB
phone/fax +44 (0) 1603 630 730

St. Benedicts Restaurant
9 St. Benedicts St
Norwich, Norfolk NR2 4PE
phone +44 (0) 1603 765 377
fax +44 (0) 1603 624 541

Tatler's
21 Tombland
Norwich, Norfolk NR3 1RF
phone +44 (0) 1603-766-670
fax +44 (0) 1603 766 625
infor@tatlers.com

Norwich Castle Museum
Norwich, Norfolk NR1 3JU
phone +44 (0) 1603 493625
www.norfolk.go.uk/tourism/museums/
museums.htm

Sainsbury Centre for Visual Arts
University of East Anglia
Norwich, Norfolk NR4 7TJ
phone +44 (0) 1603 593199
www.uea.ac.uk/scva/

Blakeney National Nature Reserve
Norfolk Coast Office, Friary Farm, Cley Road
Blakeney, Norfolk NR257NW
phone +44 (0) 1263 740241
blakeneypoint@nationaltrust.org.uk

Blickling Hall, Gardens and Park
Blickling, Norfolk NR11 6NF
phone +44 (0) 1263 738030
blickling@nationaltrust.org.uk

Felbrigg Hall, Garden and Park
Fellbrig
nr Cromer, Norfolk NR11 8PR
phone +44 (0) 1263 83744
fellbrig@nationaltrust.org.uk

Horsey Windpump
Horsey, Norfolk NR29 4EF
phone +44 (0) 1263 740241

Sheringham Park
Visitor centre, Wood Farm
Upper Sheringham, Norfolk NR26 8TL
phone +44 (0) 1263 820550
sheringhampark@nationaltrust.org.uk

oban (highlands and islands)

Oban Tourist Information Centre
Argyll Square
Oban, Argyll, Scotland PA34 4AN
phone +44 (0) 1631 563122
fax +44 (0) 1631 564273
info@oban.org.uk

The Barriemore Hotel
Corran Esplanade
Oban, Argyll, Scotland PA34 5AQ
phone +44 (0) 1631 566356
fax +44 (0) 1631 571084
reception@barriemore-hotel.co.uk

The Manor House Hotel
Gallanach Road
Oban, Argyll, Scotland PA34 4LS
phone +44 (0) 1631 562087
fax +44 (0) 1631 563053
nfo@manorhouseoban.com

Oban Caledonian Hotel
Queen's Park Place
Oban, Argyll, Scotland PA34 5RT
phone +44 (0) 1631 563133
fax +44 (0) 1631 562998
reservations@freedomglen.co.uk

Glenburnie Hotel
Esplanade
Oban, Argyll, Scotland PA34 5AQ
phone +44 (0) 1631 562089
fax +44 (0) 1631 562089
graham.strachan@btinternet.com

Boxtree Restaurant
108 George Street
Oban, Argyll, Scotland PA34 5NT
phone +44 (0) 1631 563542

Coast
104 George Street
Oban, Argyll, Scotland PA34 5NT
phone +44 (0) 1631 569900
nicola@coastoban.co.uk

Oban Distillery
Stafford Street
Oban, Argyll PA34 5NH
phone +44 (0) 1631 572004

Iona
Isle of Iona PA76
phone +44 (0) 1463 232034
http://www.nts.org.uk

oxford (midlands)

Oxford Information Centre
15-16 Broad Street
Oxford, Oxfordshire OX1 3AS
phone +44 (0) 1685 726 871
tic@oxford.gov.uk

Burlington House B&B
374 Banbury Road
Oxford, Oxfordshire OX2 7PP
phone +44 (0) 1865 513 513
www.burlington-house.co.uk

The Old Bank Hotel
92-94 High Street
Oxford, Oxfordshire OX1 4BN
phone +44 (0) 1865 799599
www.oldbank-hotel.co.uk

Malmaison
3 Oxford Castle
Oxford, Oxfordshire OX1 1AY
phone +44 (0) 1865 268 400
fax +44 (0) 1865 268 402
oxford@malmaison.com

Savannah
17 Park End Street
Oxford, Oxfordshire OX1 1HU
phone +44 (0) 1865 793 793
www.savannah.co.uk

Livebait
16 Turl Street
Oxford, Oxfordshire OX1 3DH
phone +44 (0) 1865 324 930

Rosamund The Fair
Castlemill Boatyard
Oxford, Oxfordshire OX2 6BX
phone +44 (0) 1865 553370

Le Petit Blanc
71-72 Walton Street
Oxford, Oxfordshire OX2 6AG
phone +44 (0) 1865 510999

Cherwell Boathouse Restaurant
Bardwell Road
Oxford, Oxfordshire OX2 6ST
phone +44 (0) 1865 552746

Ashmolean Museum
Beaumont Street
Oxford, Oxfordshire OX1 2PH
phone +44 (0) 1865 278000
fax +44 (0)1865 278018
www.ashmolean.org/index.php

Bate Collection of Musical Instruments
Faculty of Music
St Aldate's
Oxford, Oxfordshire OX1 1DB
phone +44 (0) 1865 276128
www.bate.ox.ac.uk/index.html

Christ Church Picture Gallery
Christ Church
Oxford, Oxfordshire OX1 1DP
phone +44 (0)1865 276172
www.chch.ox.ac.uk

Museum of the History of Science
Broad Street
Oxford, Oxfordshire OX1 3AZ
phone +44 (0) 1865 277280
fax +44 (0) 1865 277288
www.mhs.ox.ac.uk/index.htm

Pitt Rivers Museum
South Parks Road
Oxford, Oxfordshire OX1 3PP
phone +44 (0) 1865 270927
www.prm.ox.ac.uk

University of Oxford Botanic Garden
Rose Lane
Oxford, Oxfordshire OX1 4AZ
phone +44 (0) 1865 286690
postmaster@botanic-garden.ox.ac.uk
botanic-garden.ox.ac.uk

Priory Cottages
1 Mill Street
Steventon
Abingdon, Oxfordshire OX13 6SP
phone +44 (0) 1793 762209
priorycottages@nationaltrust.org.uk

Oxford Playhouse
11-12 Beaumont St
Oxford, Oxfordshire OX1 2LW
phone +44 (0) 1865 305305
www.oxfordplayhouse.com

penrith (lake district and northwest)

Penrith Tourist Information Centre
Robinson's School
Middlegate
Penrith, Cumbria CA11 7PT
phone +44 (0) 1768 867466
fax +44 1768 891754
pen.tic@eden.gov.uk

George Hotel
Devonshire Street
Penrith, Cumbria CA11 7SU
phone +44 (0) 1768 862696
fax +44 (0) 1768 868223
georgehotel@lakedistricthotels.net
www.lakedistricthotels.net/georgehotel

Crosby Bed and Breakfast
93 Lowther Street
Penrith, Cumbria CA11 7UW
phone +44 (0) 1768 890339
stay@crosbybandb.co.uk

Roundthorn Country House
Beacon Edge
Penrith, Cumbria CA11 8SJ
phone +44 (0) 1768 863952
fax +44 (0) 1768 864100
info@roundthorn.co.uk

Norcroft Guest House
Graham Street
Penrith, Cumbria CA11 9LQ
phone +44 (0) 1768 862 365
fax +44 (0) 1768 210425
info@norcroft-guesthouse.co.uk

Passepartout Restaurant
51-52 Castlegate
Penrith, Cumbria CA11 7HY
phone +44 (0) 1768 865852

Ristorante Dolce-Vita
Bishops Yard
Penrith, Cumbria CA11 7XU
phone +44 (0) 1768-891998

Villa Bianca: The Grand Cottage
Corney Square
Penrith, Cumbria CA11 7PX
phone +44 (0) 1768 210826

Costas Tapas Bar & Spanish Restaurant
9 Queen St
Penrith, Cumbria CA11 7XF
phone +44 (0) 1768 895550

Acorn Bank Garden and Watermill
Temple Sowerby
nr Penrith, Cumbria CA10 1SP
phone +44 (0) 17683 61893

Ullswater and Aira Force
Tower Buildings
Watermillock
Penrith, Cumbria CA11 0JS
phone +44 (0) 17684 82067
ullswater@nationaltrust.org.uk

penzance (west country)

Penzance Tourist Information Office
Station Road
Penzance, Cornwall
phone +44 (01) 736-362 207

Chy-An-Mor Hotel
15 Regent Terrace
Penzance, Cornwall TR18 4DW
phone +44 (0) 1736-363 441
fax +44 (0) 1736 363 441
reception@chyanmor.co.uk

Estoril Hotel
46 Morrab Road
Penzance, Cornwall
phone +44 (0) 1736-362 468
fax +44 (0) 1736 367 471
reception@estorilhotel.co.uk

Hotel Penzance
Britons Hill
Penzance, Cornwall TR18 3AE
phone +44 (0) 1736 363117
fax +44 (0) 1736 350970
enquiries@hotelpenzance.com

Abbey Restaurant
Abbey Street
Penzance, Cornwall TR18 4AR
phone +44 (0) 1736-330 680

The Lime Tree
16 Chapel Street
Penzance, Cornwall TR18 4AW
phone +44 (0) 1736-332 555
info@the-lime-tree.co.uk
www.the-lime-tree.co.uk/

Bakehouse Restaurant
Old Bakehouse Lane
Chapel Street
Penzance, Cornwall TR18-4AE
phone +44 (0) 1736-331 331
info@bakehouserestaurant.co.uk

Barbara Hepworth Museum and Sculpture Garden
Barnoon Hill
St Ives, Cornwall TR26 1AD
phone +44 (0) 1736 796226

Cornish Mines and Engines
Pool
nr Redruth, Cornwall TR15 3NP
phone +44 (0) 1209 315027
cornishmines@nationaltrust.org.uk

Godrevy Cliffs and Coves
Gwithian
nr Hayle, Cornwall
phone +44 (0) 1872 552412

Levant Mine and Beam Engine
Trewellard
Pendeen
nr St Just, Cornwall TR19 7SX
phone +44 (0) 1736 786156
levant@nationaltrust.org.uk

Penlee House Gallery and Museum
Morrab Road
Penzance, Cornwall TR18 4HE
phone +44 (0) 1736 363625
www.penleehouse.org.uk

St Michael's Mount
Marazion
nr Penzance, Cornwall TR17 OHS
phone +44 (0) 1736 710507

Trengwainton Garden
Madron
nr Penzance, Cornwall TR20 8RZ
phone +44 (0) 1736 363148
trengwainton@nationaltrust.org.uk

The Minack Theatre
Porthcurno
Penzance, Cornwall TR19 6JU
phone +44 (0) 1736 810181/471
info@minack.com

perth (scottish lowlands)

Perth Tourist Information Centre
Lower City Mills
West Mill Street
Perth, Perthshire PH1 5QP
phone +44 (0) 1738 450600
fax +44 (0) 1738 444863
perthtic@perthshire.co.uk

Huntingtower Hotel
Crieff Road
Perth, Perthshire PH1 3JT
phone +44 (0) 1738 583771
fax +44 (0) 1738 583777
reservations@huntingtowerhotel.co.uk

**Parklands Hotel, Acanthus and No. 1
The Bank Restaurants**
2 St Leonard's Bank
Perth, Perthshire PH2 8EB
phone +44 (0) 1738 622451
fax +44 (0) 1738 622046
info@theparklandshotel.com

Beechgrove Guest House
Dundee Road
Perth, Perthshire PH2 7AQ
phone +44 (0) 1738 636147
fax +44 (0) 1738 636147
beechgroveg.h@sol.co.uk

Kinnaird Guest House
5 Marshall Place
Perth, Perthshire PH2 8AH
phone +44 (0) 1738 628021
info@kinnaird-guesthouse.co.uk

63 Tay Street Restaurant
63 Tay Street
Perth, Perthshire PH2 8NN
phone +44 (0) 1738 441451
fax +44 (0) 1738 441461
info@63taystreet.com

Deans @ Let's Eat Restaurant
77-79 Kinnoull Street
Perth, Perthshire PH1 5EZ
phone +44 (0) 1738 643377
fax +44 (0) 1738 621464
deans@letseatperth.co.uk

Fergusson Gallery
Marshall Place
Perth, Tayside, Perthshire PH2 GNU
phone +44 (0) 1738 441944
www.pkc.gov.uk/ah/fergussongallery.htm

Huntingtower Castle
Perth, Perthshire PH1 3JR
phone +44 (0) 1738 627231
http://www.historic-scotland.gov.uk

Perth Museum and Art Gallery
George Street
Perth, Tayside, Perthshire PH1 5LB
phone +44 (0) 1738 632488

Scone Palace
Perth, Perthshire PH2 6BD
phone +44 (0) 1738 552300
visits@scone-palace.co.uk
http://www.scone-palace.co.uk

pitlochry (highlands and islands)

Pitlochry Tourist Information Centre
22 Atholl Road
Pitlochry, Perthshire PH16 5BX
phone +44 (0) 1796 472215
pitlochrytic@perthshire.co.uk

Green Park
Clunie Bridge Road
Pitlochry, Perthshire PH16 5JY
phone +44 (0) 1796 473248
fax +44 (0) 1796 473520
bookings@thegreenpark.co.uk

Pine Trees Hotel
Strathview Terrace
Pitlochry, Perthshire PH16 5QR
phone +44 (0) 1796 472121
info@pinetreeshotel.co.uk

Craigatin House and Courtyard B&B
165 Atholl Road
Pitlochry, Perthshire PH16 5QL
phone +44 (0) 1796 472478
fax +44 (0) 1796 470167
enquiries@craigatinhouse.co.uk

Knockendarroch House
Higher Oakfield
Pitlochry, Perthshire PH16 5HT
phone +44 (0) 1796 473473
fax +44 (0) 1796 474068
bookings@knockendarroch.co.uk

Torrdarach House
Golf Course Road
Pitlochry, Perthshire PH16 5AU
phone +44 (0) 1796 472136
fax +44 (0) 1796 473733
www.smoothound.co.uk

The Old Armoury
Armoury Road
Pitlochry, Perthshire PH16 5AP
phone +44 (0) 1796 474281
fax +44 (0) 1796 473157
info@theoldarmouryrestaurant.com

The Loft Restaurant
Golf Course Road, Bridge of Tilt
Pitlochry (5.6 m), Perthshire PH18 5TG
phone +44 (0) 1796 481377

Pitlochry Festival Theatre
Port-Na-Craig
Pitlochry, Perthshire PH16 5DR
phone +44 (0) 1796 484 600
www.pitlochry.org.uk

poole (west country)

Poole Welcome Centre
Poole Tourism
Enefco House, Poole Quay
Poole, Dorset BH15 1HJ
phone +44 (0) 1202 253 253
info@pooletourism.com

Grovefield Manor Hotel
18 Pinewood Road
Branksome Park
Poole, Dorset BH13 6JS
phone +44 (0) 1202 766 798
www.grovefield Manor.com

Harbour Heights
Haven Road
Sandbanks
Poole, Dorset BH13 7LW
phone +44 (0) 1202 707 272
fax +44 (0) 1202 708 594
enquiries@harbourheights.net
www.fjbhotels.co.uk

Haven Hotel & La Roche Restaurant
Banks Road
Sandbanks
Poole, Dorset BH13 7QL
phone +44 (0) 1202 707 333
fax +44 (0) 1202 708 796
reservations@havenhotel.co.uk
sales@havenhotel.co.uk
www.fjbhotels.co.uk

Mansion House
Thames Street
Poole, Dorset BH15 1JN
phone +44 (0) 1202 685666
fax +44 (0) 1202 665 709
enquiries@themansionhouse.co.uk
www.themansionhouse.co.uk

Alcatraz
40-42 Poole High Street
Poole, Dorset BH15 1BT
phone +44 (0) 1202 660244
office@alcatraz.co.uk

Basilica
73 Seamoor Road
Westborne
Bournemouth, Dorset BH4 9AE
phone +44 (0) 1202 757 722
jonathan@basilica.biz

Da Vincis Warehouse
Poole Quay
Poole, Dorset BH15 1HJ
phone +44 (0) 1202 677 238
onfo@davincis.co.uk

Isabels
32 Station Road
Parkstone, Dorset BH14 8UD
phone +44 (0) 1202 747 885

Brownsea Island
Poole, Dorset BH13 7EE
phone +44 (0) 1202 707744
brownseaisland@nationaltrust.org.uk

Clouds Hill
Warehan, Dorset BH20 7NQ
phone +44 (0) 1929 405616

Kingston Lacy
Wimborne Minster, Dorset BH21 4EA
phone +44 (0) 1202 883402
kingstonlacy@nationaltrust.org.uk

Corfe Castle
The Square
Corfe Castle
Wareham, Dorset BH20 5EZ
+44 (0) 1929 481294
corfecastle@nationaltrust.org.uk

Russell-Cotes Art Gallery and Museum
East Cliff
Bournemouth, Dorset BH1 3AA
phone +44 (0) 1202 451800

Studland Beach and Nature Reserve
Purbeck Estate Office
Studland
Swanage, Dorset BH19 3AX
phone +44 (0) 1929 450259
studlandbeach@nationaltrust

ripon (yorkshire)

Ripon Tourist Information Centre
Minster Road
Ripon, North Yorkshire HG4 1QT
phone +44 (0) 1765 604625/
(0) 1423 537300
fax +44 (0) 1765 604625
ripontic@harrogate.gov.uk

Old Deanery Hotel and Restaurant
Minster Road
Ripon, North Yorkshire HG4 1QS
phone +44 (0) 1765 600003
fax +44 (0) 1765 694127
reception@theolddeanery.co.uk

Best Western Ripon Spa Hotel
Park Street
Ripon, North Yorkshire HG4 2BU
phone +44 (0) 1765 602172
fax +44 (0) 1765 690770
spahotel@bronco.co.uk

Mallard Grange B&B
Aldfield, Nr Fountains Abbey
Ripon, North Yorkshire HG4 3BE
phone +44 (0) 1765 620242
fax +44 (0) 1765 620242
maggie@mallardgrange.co.uk

Lockwoods
83 North Street
Ripon, North Yorkshire HG4 1DP
phone/fax +44 (0) 1765 607555
info@lockwoodsrestaurant.co.uk

**Fountains Abbey and
Studley Royal Water Garden**
Fountains
Ripon, North Yorkshire HG4 3DY
phone +44 (0) 1765 608888
fountainsenquiries@nationaltrust.org.uk

rochester (southeast)

Rochester Tourist Information Centre
95 High Street
Rochester, Kent ME1 1LX
phone +44 (0) 1634 843666
or +44 (0) 1634 338105
fax +44 (0) 1634 847891
visitor.centre@medway.gov.uk

Bridgewood Manor
Bridgewood Roundabout, Kent ME5 9AX
phone +44 (0) 1634 201333
fax +44 (0) 1634 201330
reservationsbm@marstonhotels.com

Cosgroves Restaurant
146 High St
Rochester, Kent
phone +44 (0) 1634 844993

Elizabeths of Eastgate
154 High St
Rochester, Kent ME1 1ER
phone +44 (0) 1634 843472
www.elizabethsofeastgate.co.uk

Topes Restaurant
60 High St
Rochester, Kent
phone +44 (0) 1634 845270
www.topesrestaurant.com

Owletts
The Street
Cobham
Gravesend, Kent DA12 3AP
phone +44 (0) 1372 453401
owlets@nationaltrust.org.uk

St John's Jerusalem
Sutton-at-Hone
Dartford, Kent DA4 9HQ
phone +44 (0) 1732 810378
stjohnsjerusalem@nationaltrust.org.uk

rye (southeast)

Rye Tourist Information Centre
The Heritage Centre Strand Quay
Rye, East Sussex TN31 7AY
phone +44 (0) 1797 226696
fax +44 (0) 1797 223460
ryetic@rother.gov.uk
www.visitrye.co.uk/

The George In Rye
98 High St
Rye, East Sussex TN31 7JT
phone +44 (0) 1797 222114
fax +44 (0) 1797 224 065
http://thegeorgeinrye.com

Rye Lodge Hotel
Hilders Cliff
Rye, East Sussex TN31 7LD
phone +44 (0) 1797 223838
fax (0) 1797 223585
info@ryelodge.co.uk

The Hope Anchor
Watch Bell Street
Rye, East Sussex, TN31 7HA
phone +44 (0) 1797 222 216
http://www.thehopeanchor.co.uk/

Fish Cafe
Tower Street
Rye, East Sussex TN31 7AT
phone +44 (0) 1797 222 226
http://www.thefishcafe.com

Mermaid Inn
Mermaid Street
Rye, East Sussex TN31 7EY
phone +44 (0) 1797 426 5567
http://www.mermaidinn.com

Lamb House
West Street
Rye, East Sussex TN31 7ES
phone +44 (0) 1580 762334
http://www.nationaltrust.org.uk/main/w-vh/w-visits/w-findaplace/w-lambhouse/

Smallhythe Place
Smallhythe
Tenterden, Kent TN30 7NG
phone +44 (0) 1580 762334
smallhytheplace@nationaltrust.org.uk

salisbury (west country)

Salisbury Tourist Information
Centre Fish Row
Salisbury, Wiltshire SP1 1EJ
phone +44 (0) 1722 334 956
visitorinfo@salisbury.gov.uk

White Hart Hotel
1, St. John Street
Salisbury, Wiltshire SP1 2SD
phone +44 (0) 1722/327476
fax +44 (0) 1722/412761
H6616@accor.com

Grassmere House
70 Harnham Road
Salisbury, Wiltshire SP2 8JN
phone +44 (0) 1722 338 388
fax +44 (0) 1722 333710

The Old Mill Hotel and Restaurant
Town Path
Salisbury, Wiltshire SP2 8EU
phone +44 (0) 1722 327517

The Legacy Rose and Crown Hotel
Harnham Road
Salisbury, Wiltshire SP2 8JQ
phone +44 (0) 870 832 9946
fax (0) 870 832 9947

The Lemon Tree
90 Crane St
Salisbury, Wiltshire SP1 2QD
phone +44 (0) 1722 333471
info@thelemontree.co.uk

The Haunch of Venison
1 Minster Street
Salisbury, Wiltshire SP1 1TB
phone +44 (0) 1722 411 313
fax +44 (0) 1722 341 774
oneminsterst@aol.com

Mompesson House
The Close
Salisbury, Wiltshire SP1 2EL
phone +44 (0) 1722 420980

Philipps House and Dinton Park
Dinton
Salisbury, Wiltshire SP3 5HH
phone +44 (0) 1722 716663
philippshouse@nationaltrust.org.uk

Salisbury and South Wiltshire Museum
The King's House
65 The Close
Salisbury, Wiltshire SP1 2EN
phone +44 (0) 1722 332151
www.salisburymuseum.org.uk

Little Clarendon
Dinton
Salisbury, Wiltshire SP3 5DZ
phone +44 (0) 1985 843600
littleclarendon@nationaltrust.org.uk

Stonehenge Landscape
3-4 Stonehenge Cottages
King Barrows
Amesbury, Wiltshire SP4 7DD
phone +44 (0) 1980 664780
stonehenge@nationaltrust.org.uk

Wilton House
Wilton
Salisbury, Wiltshire SP2 0BJ
phone +44 (0) 1722 746720
www.wiltonhouse.co.uk

scarborough (yorkshire)

Scarborough Harbourside Tourist Information Centre
Scarboroughm North Yorkshire YO11 1PP
phone +44 (0) 1723 383637
fax +44 (0) 1723 507302
Tourismbureau@scarborough.gov.uk

Mansion House Hotel
45 Esplanade
South Cliff
Scarborough, North Yorkshire YO11 2AJ
phone +44 (0) 1723 373930
fax +44 (0) 870 7578468
jonathan@mansionhousehotel.com

The Royal Hotel
St. Nicholas Street
Scarborough, North Yorkshire YO11 2HE
phone +44 (0) 1723 364 333
info@englishrosehotels.co.uk

Lanterna Ristorante
33 Queen Street
Scarborough, North Yorkshire
phone +44 (0) 1723 363616
info@giorgioalessio.co.uk
www.lanterna-ristorante.co.uk

Pepper's Restaurant
11 York Place
Scarborough, North Yorkshire YO11 2NP
phone +44 (0) 1723 500642
peppers.restaurant@virgin.net

Stephen Joseph Theatre
Westborough
Scarborough, North Yorkshire YO11 1JW
phone +44 (0) 1723 370541
enquiries@sjt.uk.com

Bridestones, Crosscliff and Blakey Topping
c/o Peakside
Ravenscar
Scarborough, North Yorkshire YO13 0NE
phone +44 (0) 1723 870423
bridestones@nationaltrust.org.uk

sherborne (west country)

Tourist Information Centre
3 Tilton Court
Digby Road
Sherborne, Dorset DT9 3NL
phone +44 (0) 1935 815 341
sherborne.tic@westdorset-dc.gov.uk

The Eastbury Hotel and Restaurant
Long Street
Sherborne, Dorset DT9 3BY
phone +44 (0) 1935 813 131
fax +44 (0) 1935 817 296
paul@theeastburyhotel.co.uk
www.theeastburyhotel.co.uk

The Sherborne Hotel
Horsecastles Lane
Sherborne, Dorset DT9 6BB
phone +44 (0) 1935 813191
fax +44 (0) 1935 816 493
info@sherbornehotel.co.uk

The Bakehouse B&B
1 Acreman Street
Sherborne, Dorset DT9 3NU
phone/fax +44 (0) 1935 817 969
antiquemalcolm@aol.com
www.bakehouse.me.uk

The Pheasants B&B
24 Greenhill
Sherborne, Dorset DT9 4EW
phone +44 (0) 1935 815 252

The Green
3 The Green
Sherborne, Dorset DT9 3HY
phone +44 (0) 1935 813821

Barrington Court
nr Ilminster, Somerset TA19 0NQ
phone +44 (0) 1460 242614
http://www.nationaltrust.org.uk/main/w-vh/w-visits/w-findaplace/w-barringtoncourt/

Fleet Air Arm Museum
Royal Naval Air Station
Yeovilton
Yeovil, Somerset BA22 8HT
phone +44 (0) 1935 840565
www.fleetairarm.com

Montacute House
Montacute, Somerset TA15 6XP
phone +44 (0) 1935 823289
montacute@ntrust.org.uk

Stoke-sub-Hamdon Priory
North Street
Stoke-sub-Hamdon, Somerset TA4 6QP
phone +44 (0) 1935 823289
www.nationaltrust.org.uk/main/w-vh/w-visits/w-findaplace/w-stokesubhamdonpriory/

Stourhead
Stourhead Estate Office
Stourton
Warminster, Wiltshire BA 12 6QD
phone +44 (0) 1747 841152
stourhead@nationaltrust.org.uk

Tintinhull Garden
Farm Street
Tintinhull
Yeovil, Somerset BA22 8PZ
phone +44 (0) 1935 823289
tintinhull@nationaltrust.org.uk

Treasurer's House
Martock, Somerset TA12 6JL
phone +44 (0) 1935 825015
treasurersmartock@nationaltrust.org.uk

shrewsbury (welsh borders)

Shrewsbury Visitor Information Centre
The Music Hall, The Square
Shrewsbury, Shropshire SY1 1LH
phone +44 (0) 1743 281 200
fax +44 (0) 1743 218 213
tic@shrewsburytourism.co.uk

Prince Rupert Hotel
Butcher Row
Shrewsbury, Shropshire SY1 1UQ
phone +44 (0) 1743 499955
fax +44 (0) 1743 357306
post@prince-rupert-hotel.co.uk

Catherine of Aragon Suite
The Old House
20 Dogpole
Shrewsbury, Shropshire SY1 1ES
phone +44 (0) 1743 271 092
fax +44 (0) 1743 465 006
enquiries@aragonsuite.co.uk

Tudor House
2 Fish Street
Shrewsbury, Shropshire SY1 1UR
phone/fax +44 (0) 1743 351 735
enquire@tudorhouseshrewsbury.co.uk

The Armoury Pub
Victoria Quay, Victoria Avenue, Welsh Bridge
Shrewsbury, Shropshire SY1 1HH
phone +44 (0) 1743 340 525
fax +44 (0) 1743 340 526
armoury@brunningandprice.co.uk
www.armoury-shrewsbury.co.uk

The Bellstone Brasserie
Shrewsbury, Shropshire SY1 1HU
phone +44 (0) 1743 242 100
admin@bellstone-hotel.co.uk
www.bellstone-hotel.co.uk

Chambers Restaurant & Bar
Church Street
Shrewsbury, Shropshire SY1 1UQ
phone +44 (0) 1743 233 818
post@prince-rupert-hotel.co.uk
www.prince-rupert-hotel.co.uk

Attingham Park
Shrewsbury, Shropshire SY4 4TP
phone +44 (0) 1743 708123
attingham@nationaltrust.org.uk

Attingham Park Estate: Cronkhill
Shrewsbury, Shropshire @Y5 6JP
phone +44 (0) 1743 708123
cronkhil@nationaltrust.org.uk

Town Walls Tower
Shrewsbury, Shropshire SY1 1TN
phone +44 (0) 1743 708162
townwallstower@nationaltrust.org.uk

Benthal Hall
Brosely, Shropshire TF12 5RX
phone +44 (0) 1952 882159
benthal@nationaltrust.org.uk

Dudmaston
Quatt
nr Bridgnorth, Shropshire WV15 6QN
phone +44 (0) 1746 780866
dudmaston@nationaltrust.org.uk

Ironbridge Gorge Museums
Iron Bridge
Telford, Shropshire TF8 7AW
phone +44 (0) 1952 432166
www.ironbridge.org.uk

Powis Castle and Garden
Welshpool, Powis SY2 8RF
phone +44 (0) 1938 551944
powiscastle@nationaltrust.or.uk

Sunnycroft
200 Holyhead Road
Wellington
Telford, Shropshire TF1 2DR

southwold (east anglia)

Southwold Tourist Information Centre
69 High Street
Southwold, Suffolk, IP18 6DS
phone +44 (0) 1502 724729
fax +44 (0) 1502 722978
southwold.tic@waveney.gov.uk

The Crown Hotel
High Street
Southwold, Suffolk IP18 6DP
phone +44 (0) 1502 722 275
fax +44 (0) 1502 727263
crown.hotel@adnams.co.uk
www.adnamshotels.co.uk

Northcliffe Guest House
20 North Parade
Southwold, Suffolk IP18 6LT
phone +44 (0) 1502 724074
fax +44 (0) 1502 722218
www.southwold.blythweb.co.uk/northcliff

The Swan Hotel
Market Place
Southwold, Suffolk IP18 6EG
phone +44 (0) 1502 722186
fax +44 (0) 1502 724800
swan.hotel@adnams.co.uk
www.adnamshotels.co.uk

Sole Bay Inn
East Green
Southwold, Suffolk
phone +44 (0) 1502 723 736

The Queen's Head
The Street, Bramfield
Halesworth, Suffolk IP19 9HT
phone +44 (0) 1986 784 214
fax +44 (0) 1986 784797
enquiries@queensheadbramfield.co.uk

Blyth Hotel
Station Road
Southwold, Suffolk, IP18 6AY
phone +44 (0) 1502 722632
reception@blythhotel.com
www.blythhotel.com

Southwold Museum
9-11 Victoria treet
Southwold, Suffolk 1PH 6HZ
phone +44 (0) 1502 722437
www.southwoldmuseum.org

Dunwich Heath
Coastal Centre and Beach
Dunwich, Suffolk IP17 3DJ
phone +44 (0) 1728 648501
dunwichheath@nationaltrust.org.uk

Dunwich Museum
St James' Street
Dunwich, Suffolk IP7 3EA
phone +44 (0) 1728 648796

Lowestoft Maritime Museum
Whapload Road
Lowestoft, Suffolk NR32 1XG
phone +44 (0) 1502 561963
www.aboutnorfolksuffolk.co.uk/Lowestoft_ma
ritime.htm

st albans (southeast)

Town Hall
Market Place
St Albans, Hertfordshire
phone +44 (0) 1727 864 511
tic@stalbans.gov.uk

St Michael's Manor
Fishpool Street
St Albans, Hertfordshire AL3 4RY
phone +44 (0) 1727 864444
fax +44 (0) 1727 848909
www.stmichaelsmanor.com

Sopwell House Hotel
Cottonmill Lane, Sopwell
St Albans, Hertfordshire AL1 2HQ
phone +44 (0) 1727 864477
fax +44 (0) 1727 844741/845636
enquiries@sopwellhouse.co.uk

Darcys Restaurant
2 Hatfield Road
St. Albans, Hertfordshire AL1 3RP
phone +44 (0) 1727 730 777
fax +44 (0) 1727 730 666
info@darcysrestaurant.co.uk

Museum of St Albans
Hatfield Road
St Albans, Hertfordshire AL1 3RR
phone +44 (0) 1727 819340
www.stalbansmuseums.org.co.uk

Verulamium Museum
St Michael's
St Albans, Hertfordshire AL3 4S
phone +44 (0) 1727 751810
www.stalbansmuseums.org.uk

Ashridge Estate
Visitor Centre
Moneybury Hill
Ringstall
Berkhamstead, Hertfordshire HP4 1LX
phone +44 (0) 1494 755557
ashridge@nationaltrust.org.uk

Shaw's Corner
Ayot St Lawrence
nr Welwyn, Hertfordshire AL6 9BX
phone +44 (0) 1438 829221
shawscorner@nationaltrust.org.uk

Whipsnade Tree Cathedral
Trustees c/o Chapel Farm
Whipsnade
Dunstable, Bedfordshire LU6 2LL

st andrews (scottish lowlands)

St Andrews Tourist Information Centre
70 Market Street
St Andrews, Fife KY16 9NU
phone +44 (0) 1334 472021
standrewstic@kftb.ossian.net

Rufflets Country House Hotel and Garden Restaurant
Strathkinness Low Road
St Andrews, Fife KY16 9TX
phone +44 (0) 1334 472594
reservations@rufflets.co.uk

Scores Hotel and Restaurant
76 The Scores
St Andrews, Fife KY16 9BB
phone +44 (0) 1334 472451
fax +44 (0) 1334 4739471
reception@scoreshotel.co.uk

Aslar Guest House
120 North Street
St Andrews, Fife KY16 9AF
phone +44 (0) 1334 473460
enquiries@aslar.com

18 Queens Terrace
St Andrews, Fife KY16 9QF
phone +44 (0) 1334 478849
fax +44 (0) 1334 470 283
stay@18queensterrace.com

The Seafood Restaurant St Andrews
Bruce Embankment
St Andrews, Fife KY16 9AB
phone +44 (0) 1334 479475
fax +44 (0) 1334 479476
reservestandrews@theseafoodrestaurant.com

Discovery Museum
Discovery Quay
Dundee, Tayside DD1 4XA
phone +44 (0) 1382 309060
fax +44 (0) 1382 225891
www.rrsdiscovery.com

McManus Galleries and Museum
Albert Square
Dundee, Tayside DD1 1DA
phone +44 (0) 1382 432084
www.mcmanus.co.uk

Fife Folk Museum
High Street
Ceres
nr Cupar, Fife KY15 5NF
phone +44 (0) 1334 828180
www.fifefolkmuseum.co.uk

st davids (wales)

St Davids National Park Visitor Centre
1 High Street
St Davids, Pembrokeshire SA62 6SAW
phone +44 (0) 1437 720 392
enquiries@stdavids.pembrokeshirecoast.org.uk

The Old Cross Hotel and Restaurant
Cross Squame
St Davids, Pembrokeshire SA62 6SP
phone +44 (0) 1437720387
fax +44 (0) 1437 720394
enquiries@oldcrosshotel.co.uk

Warpool Court Hotel
St Davids, Pembrokeshire SA62 6BN
phone +44 (0) 1437 720300
fax +44 (0) 1437 720676
info@warpool courthotel.com

Ramsey House B&B
Lower Moor
St Davids, Pembrokeshire SA62 6RP
phone +44 (0) 1437 720321
fax +44 (0) 1437 720025
info@ramseyhouse.co.uk

The Waterings B&B
Anchor Drive
High Street
St Davids, Pembrokeshire SA62 6QH
phone +44 (0) 1437 720876
enquiries@waterings.co.uk

CWTCH (cottage)
22 High Street
St Davids, Pembrokeshire SA62 6SD
phone +44 (0) 1437 720491
fax +44 (0) 1437 720491
info@cwtchrestaurant.co.uk

Morgan's Restaurant
20 Nun Street
St Davids, Pembrokeshire SA62 6NT
phone/fax +44 (0) 1437 720508
eat@morgans-restaurant.co.uk

The Artramont Arms Village Pub
Croes-Goch (6 m), Pembrokeshire
phone +44 (0) 1348 831309
artramont@artramontarms.co.uk
www.artramontarms.co.uk

St David's Visitor Centre and Shop
Captains House, High Street
St David's, Haverford West, Pembrokeshire
SA62 6SD
phone +44 (0) 1437 720385
stdavids@nationaltrust.org.uk

stamford (midlands)

Stamford Tourist Information Centre
Stamford Arts Centre
27 St Mary's Street
Stamford, Lincolnshire PE9 2DL
phone+44 (0) 1780 755611
fax +44 (0) 1780 755611
stamfordtic@skdc.com

The Crown Hotel
6 All Saints Place
Stamford, Lincolnshire PE9 2A
phone +44 (0) 1780 763 136
fax +44 (0) 1780 756 111
reservations@thecrownhotelstamford.co.uk
www.thecrownhotelstamford.co.uk

Stamford Lodge Guest House
66 Scotgate
Stamford, Lincolnshire PE9 2YB
phone +44 (0) 1780 482 932

The George of Stamford
71 St Martins
Stamford, Lincolnshire PE9 2LB
phone +44 (0) 1780 750750/750700
fax + (0) 1780 750701
reservations@georgehotelofstamford.com

Jim's Yard
3 Ironmonger St
St Martin's
Stamford, Lincolnshire PE9 2LB
phone +44 (0) 1780 756080
fax +44 (0) 1780 480848
jim@jimsyard.biz

**Oak Panelled Dining Room
at The George Hotel**
71 St Martins
Stamford, Lincolnshire PE9 2LB
phone +44 (0) 1780 750750

Restaurant at The Garden House Hotel
High Street, St Martins
Stamford, Lincolnshire PE9 2LP
phone +44 (0) 1780 763359

Ascott House and Gardens
Estate Office
Wing
nr Leighton Buzzard, Bedfordshire LU7 0PS
phone +44 (0) 1296 688242
fax +44 (0) 1296 681904
info@ascottestate.co.uk
www.ascottestate.co.uk/

Belton House
Grantham, Lincolnshire NG32 2LS
phone +44 (0) 1476 566116
belton@nationaltrust.org.uk

Lyveden New Bield
near Oundle, Northamptonshire PEB 5AT
phone +44 (0) 1 832 205358
lyvedennewbield@nationaltrust.org.uk

Woolsthorpe Manor
Water Lane
Woolsthorpe by Colsterworth, Lincolnshire
NG33 5PD
phone +44 (0) 1476 860338
woolsthorpemanor@nationaltrust.org.uk

stirling (scottish lowlands)

Stirling Tourist Information Centre
41 Dunbarton Road
Stirling, Stirlingshire FK8 2QQ
phone +44 (0) 8707 200614
fax +44 (0) 1324 638440
stirlingtic@aillst.ossian.net

**Stirling Highland Hotel
and Scholars Restaurant**
Spittal Street
Stirling, Stirlingshire FK8 1DU
phone +44 (0) 1786 272727
fax +44 (0) 1786 272829
stirlingreservations@paramount-hotels.co.uk

Park Lodge Hotel
32 Park Terrace
Stirling, Stirlingshire FK8 2JS
phone +44 (0) 1786 474862
fax +44 (0) 1786 449748
info@parklodge.net

Number 10 B&B
Gladstone Place
Stirling, Stirlingshire FK8 2NN
phone/fax +44 (0) 1786 472681
cameron-10@tinyonline.co.uk

West Plean House
Denny Road
Stirling, Stirlingshire FK7 8HA
phone +44 (0) 1786 812208
fax +44 (0) 1786 480550
info@westpleanhouse.com

Stirling Castle
Castle Wynd
Stirling, Stirlingshire FK8 1EJ
phone +44 (0) 1786 450000
http://www.historic-scotland.gov.uk

Stirling Smith Art Gallery and Museum
Dumbarton Road
Stirling, Stirlingshire FK8 2RQ
phone +44 (0) 1786 471917
www.smithartgallery.demon.co.uk

stoke—on—trent (midlands)

Stoke-on-Trent Tourist Information Centre
Victoria Hall
Cultural Quarter
Stoke-on-Trent, Staffordshire ST1 3AD
phone +44 (0) 1782 236000 F
fax +44 (0) 1782 236005
stoke.tic@stoke.gov.uk

North Stafford Hotel
Station Road
Stoke on Trent, Staffordshire ST4 2AE
phone +44 (0) 1782 744477

Best Western Stoke-on-Trent Moat House
Etruria Hall
Festival Way
Stoke on Trent, Staffordshire ST1 5BQ
phone +44 (0) 1782 609988

Ivory
13A Brunswick Street
Stok on Trent, Staffordshire ST5 1HF
phone +44 (0) 1782 710580

Portofino Stoke
61 Stoke Road
38-40 Marsh Street South, ST1 1JD
Stoke On Trent, Staffordshire ST4 2QN
phone +44 (0) 1782 209444

Corkys
405 London Road
Stoke On Trent, Staffordshire ST4 5AW
phone +44 (0) 178 2413421

The Plough Inn
147 Etruria Road
Stoke On Trent, Staffordshire ST1 5NS
phone +44 (0) 1782 269445

Gladstone Pottery Museum
Uttoxeter Road
Longton
Stoke-on-Trent, Staffordshire ST3 1PQ
phone +44 (0) 1782 319232
www.stoke.gov.uk/Gladstone

Potteries Museum and Art Gallery
Bethesda Street
Hanley
Stoke-on-Trent, Staffordshire ST1 3DW
phone +44 (0) 1782 232323
www.stoke.gove.uk/museums/pmag

Spode Museum
Spode Works
Church Street
Stoke-on-Trent, Staffordshire ST4 1BX
phone +44 (0) 1782 744011
www.spode.co.uk

Biddulph Grange Garden
Grange Road
Biddulph, Staffordshire ST8 7SD
phone +44 (0) 1782 517999
biddulphgrange@nationaltrust.org.uk

Little Moreton Hall
Congleton, Cheshire CW12 4SD
phone +44 (0) 1260 272018
littlemoretonhall@nationaltrust.org.uk

Shugborough Estate
Milford
nr Stafford, Staffordshire ST17 0XB
phone +44 (0) 1889 881388
shugborough.promotions@staffordshire.gov.uk

stornoway (highlands and islands)

Stornoway Tourist Information Centre
26 Cromwell Street
Stornoway, Isle of Lewis HS1 2DD
phone +44 (0) 1851 703088
fax +44 (0) 1851 705244

Cabarfeidh Hotel and Restaurant
Manor Park, Perceval Road South
Stornoway, Isle of Lewis HS1 2EU
phone +44 (0) 1851 702604
cabarfeidh@calahotels.com

Royal Hotel and Boatshed Restaurant
Cromwell Street
Stornoway, Isle of Lewis HS1 2DG
phone +44 (0) 1851 702109
royal@calahotels.com

Hebridean Guest House
61 Bayhead Street
Stornoway, Isle of Lewis HS1 2DZ
phone +44 (0) 1851 702268
fax +44 (0) 1851 701791
hebgh@sol.co.uk

Park Guest House and Restaurant
30 James Street
Stornoway, Isle of Lewis HS1 2QN
phone +44 (0) 1851 702485
fax +44 (0) 1851 703482

Museum nan Eilean
Francis Street
Stornoway, Isle of Lewis HS1 2NF
phone +44 (0) 1851 709266
rlanghorne@cne-siar.gov.uk

Stratford-upon-Avon Tourist Information Centre
Bridgefoot
Stratford-upon-Avon, Warwickshire CV37 6GW
phone +44 (0) 870 1607930
fax +44 (0) 1789 295262
stratfordtic@shakespeare-country.co.uk

Shakespeare Hotel
Chapel St
Stratford-upon-Avon, Warwickshire CV37 6ER
phone +44 (0) 870 4008182
shakespearehotel.net

The Falcon Hotel
Chapel Street
Stratford-upon-Avon, Warwickshire CV37 6HA
phone +44 (0) 870 8329905
fax +44 (0) 870 8329906
res-falcon@legacy-hotels.co.uk

Courtland Hotel
12 Guild Street
Stratford-upon-Avon, Warwickshire CV37 6RE
phone +44 (0) 1789 292401
fax +44 (0) 1789 292737
info@courtlandhotel.co.uk

Alveston Manor
Clopton Bridge
Stratford-upon-Avon, Warwickshire CV37 7HP
phone +44 (0) 870 4008181
fax +44 (0) 178 9414095
sales.alvestonmanor@macdonald-hotels.co.uk

Malbec Restaurant
6 Union Street
Stratford-upon-Avon, Warwickshire CV37 6QT
phone/fax +44 (0) 1789 269106
eatmalbec@aol.com

Lambs
12 Sheep Street
Stratford upon Avon, Warwickshire CV37 6EF
phone +44 (0) 1789 292554
fax +44 (0) 1789 293372
eat@lambsrestaurant.co.uk

The Manor Grill
Clopton Bridge
Stratford-upon-Avon, Warwickshire CV37 7HP
phone +44 (0) 870 4008181
fax +44 (0) 178 9414095
sales.alvestonmanor@macdonald-hotels.co.uk

Harvard House
High Street
Stratford-upon-Avon, Warwickshire CV37 6HB
phone +44 (0) 1789 204 507

Royal Shakespeare Theatre
The Courtyard Theatre
Southern Lane
Stratford-upon-Avon, Warwickshire CV37 6BB
phone +44 (0) 1789 403444
ticketqueries@rsc.org.uk

The Shakespeare Birthplace Trust
[for all the Shakespeare properties]
Shakespeare Centre, Henley Street
Stratford upon Avon, Warwickshire CV37 6QW
phone +44 (0) 1789 204016
info@shakespeare.org.uk
www.shakespeare.org.uk

Charlecote Park
Warwick, Warwickshire CV35 9ER
phone +44 (0) 1789 470277
charlecotepark@nationaltrust.org.uk

Coughton Court
nr Alcester, Warwickshire B49 5JA
phone +44 (0) 1789 762435
coughtoncourt@nationaltrust.org.uk

Kinwarton Dovecote
Kinwarton
nr Alcester, Warwickshire B49 6HB
phone +44 (0) 1789 400777
kinwartondovecote@nationaltrust.org.uk

stromness (highlands and islands)

Stromness Tourist Information Centre
Ferry Terminal
Pier Head
Stromness, Orkney, Shetland KW16 1BH
phone +44 (0) 1856 850716
fax +44 (0) 1856 850777
stromness@visitorkney.com

**The Royal Hotel
and Haven Restaurant**
Stromness, Orkney KW16 3BS
phone +44 (0) 1856 850342
enquiries@royalhotel.biz

**The Stromness Hotel
and Scapa Flow Restaurant**
The Pierhead
Stromness, Orkney, Shetland KW16 3AA
phone +44 (0) 1856 850298
info@stromnesshotel.com

The Ferry Inn and Restaurant
John Street
Stromness, Orkney, Shetland KW16 3AA
phone +22 01856 850280
fax +22 01856 851332
adrian@ferryinn.com

Hamnavoe Restaurant
35 Graham Place
Stromness, Orkney, Shetland KW16 3BY
phone +44 01856 850606

Stromness Museum
52 Alfred Street
Stromness, Orkney, Shetland KW16 3DF
phone +44 (0) 1856 850025
www.orkney.org/museums/stromness.htm

The Italian Chapel
Lambholm
Orkney, Shetland KW17
phone +44 (0) 1856 781268
http://www.churchesinscotland.co.uk

Pier Art Centre
Victoria Street
Orkney, Shetland KW16 3AA
phone +44 (0) 1856 850209

St Magnus Cathedral
Church Of Scotland
Broad Street
Kirkwall, Orkney, Shetland KW15
phone +44 (0) 1856 874894
www.churchofscotland.org.uk/

Skara Brae
Sandwick, Orkney, Shetland KW16 3LR
phone +44 (0) 1856 841815
http://www.historic-scotland.gov.uk

swaffham (east anglia)

Swaffham Tourist Information Centre
The Shambles, Market Place
Swaffham, Norfolk PE37 7AB
phone +44 (0)1760 722255
fax +44 (0) 1760 723410
swaffham@eetb.infoMap

Lydney House
Norwich Road
Swaffham, Norfolk PE37 7QS
freephone 0800 980 2460
fax +44 (0) 1760 721410
rooms@lydney-house.demon.co.uk

The George Hotel
Station Street
Swaffham, Norfolk PE37 7LJ
phone +44 (0) 1760 721 238
fax +44 (0) 1760 725333
georgehotel@bestwestern.co.uk
http://www.bw-georgeswaffham.co.uk

Strattons Hotel
4 Ash Close
Swaffham, Norfolk
phone +44 01760 723845
fax +44 01760 720458
enquiries@strattonshotel.com
www.strattonshotel.com

These three hotels also function as
restaurants. Other places worth trying are:

Albert Victor
Stocks Green
Castle Acre, Norfolk, PE32 2AE
phone +44 01760 755213
www.albertvictor.net

The Market Cross Restaurant
15 Market Place
Swaffham, Norfolk PE37 7AB
phone +44 01760 724260

The Olde Windmill Inn
Great Cressingham
near Swaffham, Norfolk
phone +44 (0)1760 756 232
fax +44 (0) 1760 756 400
halls232@aol.com
www.windmillinn-greatcressingham.com

Brancaster
Brancaster Millennium Activity Centre
Dial House
Brancaster Staithe, Norfolk PE318BW
phone +44 (0) 1485 210719

Houghton Hall
King's Lynn, Norfolk PE31 6UE
phone +44 (0)1485 528569
www.houghtonhall.com

St George's Guildhall and Arts Centre
29 King Street
King's Lynn, Norfolk PE30 1HA
phone +44 (0) 1553 765565
stgeorgesguildhall@nationaltrust.org.uk

Oxburgh Hall, Garden and Estate
Oxburgh, Norfolk PE33 9PS
phone +44 (0) 1366 328258
oxburghhall@nationaltrust.org.uk

Peckover House and Garden
North Brink
Wisbech, Cambridgeshire PE13 1JR
phone +44 (0) 1945 583463
peckover@nationaltrust.org.uk

tenby (wales)

Tenby Tourist Information Centre
Unit 2 The Gateway Complex
Tenby, Pembrokeshire SA70 7LT
phone +44 01834 842 402
fax +44 01834 845 439
tenby.tic@pembrokeshire.gov.uk

The Broadmead Hotel
Heywood Lane
Tenby, Pembrokeshire SA70 8DA
phone +44 (0) 1834 842641
fax +44 (0) 1834 84575

Fourcroft Hotel
North Beach
Tenby, Pembrokeshire SA70 8AP
phone +44 (0) 1834 842 886
fax +44 (0) 1834 842 888
stay@fourcroft-hotel.co.uk

Glenholme B&B
Picton Terrace
Tenby, Pembrokeshire SA70 7DR
phone +44 (0) 1834 843909

Glenthorne Guest House
9 Deer Park
Tenby, Pembrokeshire SA70 7LE
phone +44 (0) 1834 842300
glenthorneguesthouse@tiscali.co.uk

The Mews Bistro
Upper Frog Street
Tenby, Pembrokeshire SA70 7JD
phone +44 (0) 1834 844068

Plantagenet House Restaurant & Bar
Quay Hill, Tudor Square
Tenby, Pembrokeshire SA70 7BX
phone +44 (0) 1834 842350
fax +44 (0) 1834 943915

The Reef Cafe
Vernon House
St. Julians Street
Tenby, Pembrokeshire SA70 7AS
phone +44 (0) 1834 845258

Tudor Merchant's House
Quay Hill
Tenby, Pembrokeshire SA70 7BX
phone +44 (0) 1834 842279
tudormerchantshouse@nationaltrust.org.uk

Colby Woodland Garden
Armroth
Narberth, Pembrokeshire SA67 8PP
phone +44 (0) 1834 811885
Colby@nationaltrust,org.uk

Stackpole Estate
Old Home Farm Yard
Stackpole
nr Pembroke, Pembrokeshire SA71 5DQ
phone +44 (0) 1646 661359
stackpole@nationaltrust.or.uk

tewkesbury (cotswolds)

Tewkesbury Tourist Information Centre
The Museum
64 Barton Street
Tewkesbury, Gloucestershire GL20 5PX
phone +44 (0) 1684 295027
fax +44 (0) 1684 292277
tewkesburytic@tewkesbury.gov.uk
www.visitcotswoldsandsevernvale.gov.uk/

Jessop House Hotel
65 Church Street
Tewkesbury, Gloucestershire GL20 5RZ
phone +44 (0) 1684 292017
fax +44 (0) 1684 273076
bookings@jessophousehotel.com
www.jessophousehotel.com

Tewkesbury Park Hotel and Restaurant
Lincoln Green Lane
Tewkesbury, Gloucestershire GL20 7DN
phone +44 (0) 1684 295405
fax +44 (0) 1684 292386
tewkesburypark@corushotels.com
www.tewkesburypark.co.uk

Malvern View Guest House
1 St Mary's Road
Tewkesbury, Gloucestershire GL20 5SE
phone +44 (0) 1684 292776

The Bell Hotel Restaurant
52 Church Street
Tewkesbury, Gloucestershire
phone +44 (0) 1684 293293

The Bay Tree
78 Church Street
Tewkesbury, Gloucestershire GL20 5RX
phone +44 (0) 1684 290357

Bredon Barn
Bredon
nr Tewkesbury, Worcestershire GL20 6EU
phone +44 (0) 1451 844752
bredonbarn@nationaltrust.org.uk

tobermory (highlands and islands)

Tobermory Tourist Information Centre
Main Street
Tobermory, Isle of Mull, Strathclyde,
Scotland, PA75 6NU
phone +44 (0) 8707 200 625
fax +44 (0) 1688 302145
www.tobermory.co.uk

**Tobermory Hotel
and Water's Edge Restaurant**
53 Main Street
Obermory, Isle of Mull, Argyll PA75 6NT
phone +44 (0) 1688 302091
fax +44 (0) 1688 302254
tobhotel@tinyworld.co.uk

Highland Cottage Hotel and Restaurant
(booking essential)
Breadalbane Street
Tobermory, Isle of Mull PA75 6PD
phone +44 (0) 1688 302030
davidandjo@highlandcottage.co.uk

Ptarmigan House Guest House
The Fairways
Tobermory, Isle of Mull PA75 6PS
phone +44 (0) 1688 302863
ptarmiganhouse@hotmail.co.uk

Brockville B&B
Raeric Road
Tobermory, Isle of Mull PA75 6RS.
phone/fax +44 (0) 1688 302741
helen@brockville-tobermory.co.uk

The Anchorage Restaurant
Main Street
Tobermory, Isle of Mull
phone +44 (0) 1688 302313

Mull Theatre
Royal Buildings
Main Street
Tobermory, Isle of Mull PA75 6NU
phone +44 (0) 1688 302828

Duart Castle
Sir Lachlan MacLean
Lochdon, Isle of Mull, Argyll PA64 6AP
phone +44 (0) 1680 812309
http://www.duartcastle.com

truro (west country)

The Tourist Information Centre
Municipal Buildings
Boscawen Street
Truro, Cornwall
phone +44 (0) 1872 274555
fax (0) 1872 263031
tic@truro.gov.uk

Brookdale Hotel
Tregolls Road
Truro, Cornwall TR1 1JZ
phone +44 (0) 1872 273 513
fax+440(1) 872 272 400
www.hotelstruro.com

Carlton Hotel
49 Falmouth Road
Truro, Cornwall TR1 2HL
phone +44 (0) 1872 272 450
fax+44 (0) 1872 223 938
reception@carltonhotel.co.uk
www.carltonhotel.co.uk

Royal Hotel
Lemon Street
Truro, Cornwall TR1 2QB
phone +44 (0) 1872 270345
fax (0) 1872 242453
reception@royalhotelcornwall.co.uk
www.royalhotelcornwall.co.uk

Zafiro's
3 New Bridge Street
Truro, Cornwall TR1 2AA
phone +44 (0) 1872 223163

Indaba Fish
Tabernacle Street
Truro, Cornwall TR1-4EJ
phone +44 (0) 1872 274700
www.indaba-truro.co.uk
info@indaba-truro.co.uk

Stingi Lulu's
Royal Cornwall Museum, River Street
Truro, Cornwall TR1 2SJ
phone +44 (0) 1872 262300
www.stingilulus.com
info@stingilulu.com

Carbonara Ristorante Italiano
13 NewBridge Street
Truro, Cornwall TR1-2AA
phone +44 (0) 1872 223008
www.carbonararistorante.com

Tabbs
85 Kenwynn Street
Truro, Cornwall TR1 3BZ
phone +44 (0) 1872 262110
www.tabbs.co.uk
info@tabbs.co.uk

Royal Cornwall Museum
River Street
Truro, Cornwall TR1 2SJ
phone +44 (0) 1872 272205

Boscastle
Cornwall
phone +44 (0) 1840 250353
boscastle@nationaltrust.org.uk

Eden Project
Bodelva
St Austell, Cornwall PL24 2SG
phone +44 (0) 1726 811911
www.edenproject.com

Lanhydrock
Bodmin, Cornwall PL30 5AD
phone +44 (0) 1208 265950
lanhydrock@nationaltrust.org.uk

National Maritime Museum, Cornwall
Discovery Quay
Falmouth, Cornwall TR11 3SA
phone +44 (0) 1326 313388
www.nmmc.co.uk

St Anthony Head
Roseland peninsula, Cornwall
phone+44 (0) 1872 862945
stanthonyhead@nationaltrust.org.uk

Tintagel Old Post Office
Fore Street
Tintagel, Cornwall PL34 0DB
phone +44 (0) 1840 770024
tintageloldpo@nationaltrust.org.uk

Trelissick Garden
Feock
nr Truro, Cornwall TR3 6QL
phone +44 (0) 1872 862090
trelissick@nationaltrust.org.uk

Trerice
Kestle Mill
nr Newquay, Cornwall TR8 4PG
phone +44 (0) 1637 875404
trerice@nationaltrust.org.uk

tunbridge wells (southeast)

Royal Tunbridge Wells Tourist Information Centre
The Old Fish Market
The Pantiles
Royal Tunbridge Wells, Kent TN2 5TN
phone +44 (0) 1892 515675
fax +44 (0) 1892 1892 534660
touristinformationcentre@tunbridgewells.gov.uk

The Royal Wells Hotel
Mount Ephraim
Tunbridge Wells, Kent TN4 8BE
phone +44 (0) 1892 511188
fax +44 (0) 1892 511908
info@royalwells.co.uk
www.royalwells.co.uk

Smart & Simple Hotels
54 London Road
Tunbridge Wells, Kent TN1 1DS
phone +44 (0) 1892 525580

Signor Franco's
5a, High St
Tunbridge Wells, Kent TN1 1UL
phone +44 (0) 1892 549199

Thackeray's
85 London Road
Tunbridge Wells, Kent TN1 1EA
phone +44 (0) 1892 511921
reservations@thackerays-restaurant.co.uk.

Bistro at Hotel du Vin
Crescent Road
Tunbridge Wells, Kent, TN1 2LY
phone +44 (0) 1892 526455

Knole
Sevenoaks, Kent TN15 0RP
phone +44 (0) 1732 450608
www.nationaltrust.org.uk

Bodiam Castle
Bodiam
nr Robertsbridge, East Sussex TN32 5UA
phone +44 (0) 1580 830196
bodiamcastle@nationaltrust.org.uk

Chartwell
Mapleton Road
Westerham, Kent TN16 1PS
phone +44 (0) 1732 866368
chartwell@nationaltrust.org.uk

Emmetts Garden
Idle Hill
Sevenoaks, Kent TN14 6AY
phon +44 (0) 1732 751509
emmetts@nationaltrust.org.uk

Ightham Mote
Mote Road
Ivy Hatch
Sevenoaks, Kent TN15 0NT
phone +44 (0) 1732 811145
ighthammote@nationaltrust.org.uk

Nymans Estate
Handcross
nr Haywards Heath, West Sussex RH17 6EB
phone +44 (0) 1444 405250
nymans@nationaltrust.org.uk

Old Soar Manor
Plaxtol
Borough Green, Kent TN15 0QX
phone +44 (0) 1732 811145
oldsoarmanor@nationaltrust.org.uk

Quebec House
Quebec Square
Westerham, Kent TN16 1TD
phone +44 (0) 1732 866368
quebechouse@nationaltrust.org.uk

Scotney Castle
Lamberhurst
Tunbridge Wells, Kent TN3 8JN
phone +44 (0) 1892 898
scotneycastle@nationaltrust.org.uk

Sheffield Park Garden
Sheffield Park, East Sussex TN22 3QX
phone +44 (0) 1825 790231
sheffieldpark@nationaltrust.org.uk

Sissinghurst Castle Garden
Sissinghurst
nr Cranbrook, Kent TN17 2AB
phone +44 (0) 1580 710701
sissinghurst@nationaltrust.org.uk

Standen
West Hoathly Road
East Grinstead, West Sussex RH19 4NE
phone +44 (0) 1342 323029
standen@nationaltrust.org.uk

Wakehurst Place
Ardingly
nr Haywards Heath, West Sussex RH17 6TN
phone +44 (0) 1444 894066
wakehurst@kew.org

warwick (midlands)

Warwick Tourist Information Centre
Court House
Jury Street
Warwick, Warwickshire CV34 4EW
phone +44 (0) 1926 492212
fax +44 (0) 1926 494837
touristinfo@warwick-uk.co.uk

Old Fourpenny Shop Hotel
27-29 Crompton Street
Warwick, Warwickshire CV34 6HJ
phone +44 (0) 1926 491360
fax +44 (0) 1926 411892
fourpennyshop@aol.com

Charter House B&B
87-91 West Street
Warwick, Warwickshire CV34 6AH
phone +44 (0) 1926 1926 496965
fax +44 (0) 1926 411892

Park Cottage B&B
113 West Street
Warwick, Warwickshire CV34 6AH
phone +44 (0) 1926 410319
fax +44 (0) 1926 497994
janet@parkcottagewarwick.co.uk

Saffron
21 Market St
Warwick, CV34 4DE
phone +44 (0) 1926 402061

Art Kitchen
7 Swan Street
Warwick, Warwickshire CV34 4BJ
phone +44 (0) 1926 494303
fax (0) 1926 494304
reservations@theartkitchen.com

Prym's Restaurant
48 Brook Street
Warwick, Warwickshire CV34 4BL
phone +44 (0) 1926 493504
fax +44 (0) 1926 493504

Baddesley Clinton
Rising Lane
Baddesly Clinton Village
Knowle
Solihull, West Midlands B93 0DQ
phone +44 (0) 1564 783294

Canons Ashby House
Canons Ashby, Northamptonshire NN11 3SD
phone +44 (0) 1327 860044
canonsashby@nationaltrust.org.uk

Packwood House
Lapworth
Solihull, West Midlands B94 6AT
phone +44 (0) 1564 783294
packwood@nationaltrust.org.uk

wells (west country)

Wells Tourist Information Centre
Town Hall
Market Place
Wells, Somerset BA5 2RB
phone +44 (0) 1749 672 552
fax +44 (0) 1749 670869
touristinfo@wells.gov.uk.

Swan Hotel
Sadler Street
Wells, Somerset BA5 2RX
phone +44 (0) 1749 836300
fax +44 (0) 1749 836301
info@swanhotelwells.co.u

Beryl (B & B)
Hawkers Lane
Wells, Somerset BA5 3JP
phone +44 (0) 1749 678738
fax +44 (0) 1749 670508
stay@beryl-wells.co.uk
www.beryl-wells.co.uk

Glencot House
Glencot Lane
Wookey Hol (2.5 km)
Wells, Somerset BA5 1BH
phone +44 (0) 1749 677160
fax (0) 1749 670210
relax@glencotehouse.co.uk

Anton's Bistrot
Market Place
Wells, Somerset
phone +44 (0) 1749 673 457

The Old Spot
12 Sadler Street
Wells, Somerset
phone +44 (0) 1749 689 099

Fyne Court Nature Reserve
Broomfield
Bridgwater, Somerset TA5 2EQ
phone +44 (0) 1823 652400
fynecourt@nationaltrust.org.uk

Glastonbury Tor
nr Glastonbury, Somerset
phone +44 (0) 1985 843600
glastonburytor@nationaltrust.org.uk

King John's Hunting Lodge
The Square
Axbridge, Somerset BS26 2AP
phone +44 (0) 1934 732012
kingjohns@nationaltrust.org.uk

Lytes Cary Manor
nr Charlton Mackrell
Somerton, Somerset TA11 7HU
phone +44 (0) 1458 224471
lytescarymanor@nationaltrust.org.uk

Priest's House
Muchelney
Langport, Somerset TA10 0DQ
phone +44 (0) 1458 253771

Stembridge Tower Mill
High Ham, Somerset TA10 9dj
phone +44 (0) 1935 823289
stembridgemill@nationaltrust.org.uk

whitby (yorkshire)

Whitby Tourist Information Centre
Langbourne Road
Whitby, North Yorkshire YO21 1YN
phone +44 (0) 1723 383637
fax +44 (0) 1723 507302

Bagdale Hall
1 Bagdale
Whitby, North Yorkshire YO21 1QL
phone +44 (0) 1947 602958
fax +44 (0) 1947 820714
bagdale@btconnect.com
www.bagdale.co.uk

Corra Lynn
28 Crescent Avenue
Whitby, North Yorkshire YO21 3EW
phone +44 (0) 1947 602214
selly.sellwood@btopenworld.com

Netherby House Hotel
90 Coach Road
Sleights
Whitby (3 miles), North Yorkshire YO22 5EQ
phone +44 (0) 1947 810211
info@netherby-house.co.uk
www.netherby-house.co.uk

Green's
13 Bridge Street
Whitby, North Yorkshire YO22 4BG
phone +44 (0) 1947 600284
info@greensofwhitby.com

Trenchers
New Quay Road
Whitby, North Yorkshire, YO21 1DH
phone +44 (0) 1947 603212
enquiries@trenchersrestaurant.co.uk

The Magpie Café
14 Pier Road
Whitby, North Yorkshire YO21 3PU
phone +44 (0) 1947 602058

Quayside
7 Pier Road
Whitby, North Yorkshire YO21 3PU
phone +44 (0) 1947 825346

Sutcliffe Gallery
1 Flowergate
Whitby, North Yorkshire YO21 3BA
phone +44 (0) 1947 602239
www.sutcliffe-gallery.co .uk

Captain Cook Memorial Museum
Grape Lane
Whitby, North Yorkshire YO22 4BA
phone +44 (0) 1947 601900
www.cookmuseumwhitby.co.uk

Ormesby Hall
Church Lane
Ormesby
nr Middleborough, Redcar & Cleveland TS7 9AS
phone +44 (0) 1642 324188
ormesbyhall@nationaltrust.org.uk
http://www.nationaltrust.org.uk/main/w-vh/w-visits/w-findaplace/w-ormesbyhall/

Roseberry Topping
Newton-under-Roseberry, North Yorkshire
phone +44 (0) 1642 328901
roseberrytopping@nationaltrust.org.uk

winchester (southeast)

Tourist Information Centre
Winchester Guildhall
High Street
Winchester, Hampshire SO23 9GH
phone +44 (0) 1962 840 500
fax +44 (0) 1962 850 348
www.visitwinchester.co.uk

Hotel du Vin and Bistro
Southgate Street
Winchester, Hampshire SO23 9EF
phone +44 (0) 1962 841414
fax +44 (0) 1962 842458
info@winchester.hotelduvin.com

Winchester Royal Hotel
St. Peter Street
Winchester, Hampshire SO23 8BS
phone +44 (0) 1962 840840
fax +44 (0) 1962) 841582
winchester.royal@forestdale.com

The Old Vine
8 Great Minster Street
Winchester, Hampshire SO23 9HA
phone +44 (0) 1962 854616

Pappagallo Italian Restaurant
1 City Road
Winchester, Hampshire SO23 8SD
phone +449 (0) 1962 841107
fax +44 (0) 1962 742467

Winchester City Mill
Bridge Street
Winchester, Hampshire S23 0EJ
phone +44 (0) 1962 870057
winchestercitymill@nationaltrust.org.uk

Hinton Ampner
Bramdean, Hampshire SO24 0LA
phone +44 (0) 1962 771305
hintonampner@nationaltrust.org.uk

**Mottisfont Abbey Garden,
House and Estate**
Mottisfont
nr Romsey, Hampshire SO51 0LP
phone +44 (0) 1794 341220
mottisfontabbey@nationaltrust.org.uk

Sandham Memorial Chapel
Harts Lane
Burghclere
nr Newbury, Hampshire RG20 9JT
phone +44 (0) 1635 278394
sandham@nationaltrust.org.uk

The Vyne
Sherborne St John
Basingstoke, Hampshire RG24 9HL
phone +44 (0) 1256 883858
thevyne@nationaltrust.org.uk

windsor (southeast)

Royal Windsor Information Centre
24 High St
Windsor, Berkshire SL4 1LH
phone +44 (0) 1753 743900
www.windsor.gov.uk

The Royal Adelaide Hotel
46 Kings Road
Windsor, Berkshire SL4 2AG
phone +44 (0) 1753 863916
fax +44 (0) 1753 830682
royaladelaide@meridianleisure.com

Clarence Hotel
9 Clarence Road
Windsor, Berkshire SL4 5AE
phone +44 (0) 1753 864436
fax +44 (0) 1753 857060
enquiries@clarence-hotel.co.uk

The Crooked House of Windsor
51 High Street
Windsor, Berkshire SL4 1LR
phone/fax +44 (0) 1753 857 534
manager@crooked-house.com

Bel and The Dragon
Thames Street
Windsor, Berkshire SL4 1PQ
phone +44 (0) 1753 866056
fax +44 (0) 1753 865707

Browns Restaurant and Bar
Barry Avenue, The Promenade
Windsor, Berkshire SL4 1QX
phone +44 (0) 1753 831 976

Windsor Castle
Windsor, Berkshire SL4 1NJ
phone +44 (0) 20 7766 7304
www.royal.gov.uk/output/Page557.asp

Runnymede
Runnymede Estate Office
North Lodge
Windsor Road
Old Windsor, Berkshire SL4 2JL
phone +44 (0) 1784 432891
Runnymede@nationaltrust.org.uk

Stanley Spencer Gallery
High Street
Cookham-on-Thames, Berkshire SL6 9SJ
phone +44 (0) 1628 471885
www.stanley Spencer.org

woodstock (midlands)

Woodstock Tourist Information Centre
Oxfordshire Museum
Park Street
Woodstock, Oxfordshire OX20 1SN
phone +44 (0) 1993 813 276
fax +44 (0) 1993 813 632
woodstock.vic@westoxon.gov.uk

Bear Hotel & Restaurant
Park Street
Woodstock, Oxfordshire OX20 1SZ
phone +44 (0) 870 400 8202
fax +44 (0) 1993 813 380

The Feathers Hotel and Restaurant
Market Street
Woodstock, Oxfordshire OX20 1SX
phone +44 (0) 1993 812291
fax +44 (0) 1993 813158
reception@feathers.co.uk

The Kings Arms Hotel & Restaurant
19 Market Street
Woodstock, Oxfordshire OX20 1SU
phone +44 (0)1993 813636
fax +44 (0) 1993 813737

Woodstock Arms Gastropub
Market Street
Woodstock, Oxfordshire OX20 1SX
phone +44 (0) 1993 811251

Blenheim Palace
Woodstock, Oxfordshire OX20 1PX
phone +44 (0) 800 602080
www.blenheimpalace.com

worcester (midlands)

Worcester Tourist Information Centre
The Guildhall
High Street
Worcester, Worcestershire WR1 2EY
phone +44 (0) 1905 726311/722480
fax +44 (0) 1905 722481
touristinfo@cityofworcester.gov.uk

Gables B&B
166 Bromyard Road,
Worcester, Worcestershire WR2 5EE
phone/fax +44 (0) 1905 425488

Burgage House B&B
4 College Precincts
Worcester, Worcestershire WR1 2LG
phone +44 (0) 1905 25396
louise.newsholme@googlemail.com

Barrington House B&B
204 Henwick Road,
Worcester, Worcestershire WR2 5PF
phone +44 (0) 1905 422965
vfilleul@hotmail.co.uk

Welland House B&B
43 Bromyard Road, St Johns
Worcester, Worcestershire WR2 5BZ
phone +44 (0) 1905 421 924
worcbnb@aol.com

The Glasshouse Restaurant
Dansebury House, Sidbury
Worcester, Worcestershire WR1 2HU
phone +44 (0) 1905 611 120
eat@theglasshouse.co.uk

The Old Rectifying House
North Parade
Worcester, Worcestershire WR1 3NN
phone +44 (0) 1905 619 622

Saffrons Bistro
15 New Street
Worcester, Worcestershire WR1 2DP
phone +44 (0) 1905 610 505
nick@saffronsworcester.wanadoo.co.uk

Elgar Birthplace Museum
Crown East Lane
Lower Broadheath, Worcestershire WR2 6RH
phone +44 (0) 1905 333224
www.elgarmuseum.org

Brockhampton Estate
Greenfields
Bringsty
nr Bromyard, Herefordshire WR6 5TB
phone +44 (0) 1885 488099
brockhampton@nationaltrust.org.uk
*http://www.nationaltrust.org.uk/main/w-vh/w-
visits/w-findaplace/w-brockhamptonestate/*

Croome Park
Croome D'Abitot, Worcestershire WR8 9DW
phone +44 (0) 1905 371006
croomepark@nationaltrust.org.uk
*http://www.nationaltrust.org.uk/main/w-vh/w-
visits/w-findaplace/w-croomepark/*

The Greyfriars
Friar Street
Worcester, Worcestershire WR1 2LZ
phone +44 (0) 1905 23571
greyfriars@nationaltrust.org.uk
*http://www.nationaltrust.org.uk/main/w-vh/w-
visits/w-findaplace/w-thegreyfriars/*

Hanbury Hall
School Road
Hanbury
Droitwich Spa, Worcestershire WR9 7EA
phone +44 (0) 1527 821214
*http://www.nationaltrust.org.uk/main/w-vh/w-
visits/w-findaplace/w-hanburyhall/*

Hawford Dovecote
Hawford, Worcesterahire WR3 7SG
phone +44 (0) 1527 821214
hawforddovecote@nationaltrust.org.uk
*http://www.nationaltrust.org.uk/main/w-vh/w-
visits/w-findaplace/w-hawforddovecote/*

Wichenford Dovecote
Wichenford
nr Worcester, Worcestershire
phone +44 (0) 1527 821214
wichenforddovecote@nationaltrust.org.co
*http://www.nationaltrust.org.uk/main/w-vh/w-
visits/w-findaplace/w-wichenforddovecote/*

york (yorkshire)

York Tourist Information Centre
St. Leonards Place
York, North Yorkshire YO1 7HB
phone +44 (0) 1904 550 099
tourism@yorkvic.co.uk
www.visityork.org

Ashberry House
103 The Mount
York, North Yorkshire YO24 1AX
phone +44 (0) 1904 550 099
tourism@yorkvic.co.uk

Dean Court Hotel
Duncombe Place
York, North Yorkshire YO1 7EF
phone +44 (0) 1904 550 099
tourism@yorkvic.co.uk
www.deancourt-york.co.uk

The Grange Hotel
1 Clifton
York, North Yorkshire YO30 6AA
phone +44 (0) 1904 550 099
tourism@yorkvic.co.uk
www.grangehotel.co.uk

Minster Hotel
60 Bootham
York, North Yorkshire YO30 7BZ
phone +44 (0) 1904 621 267
fax +44 (0) 1904 654 719
info@yorkminsterhotel.co.uk
www.yorkminsterhotel.co.uk

The Windmill
Hull Road
Dunnington, York (4 miles), North Yorkshire
YO19 5LP
phone +44 (0) 1904 481898
fax +44 (0) 1904 488480

Delrio's
10 Blossom Street
York, North Yorkshire YO24 1AE
phone +44 (0) 1904 622 695
info@delriosrestaurant.com
www.delriosrestaurant.com

Four High Petergate Bistro
4 High Petergate
York, North Yorkshire YO1 7EH
phone +44 (0) 1904 658516
enquiries@fourhighpetergate.co.uk
www.fourhighpetergate.co.uk

Gourmet Burger Kitchen
2 Lendal
York, North Yorkshire YO1 8AQ
phone +44 (0) 1904 639537

Hotel du Vin Bistro
89 The Mount
York, North Yorkshire YO24 1AX
phone +44 (0) 1904 557350

The Olive Tree
10 Tower Street
York, North Yorkshire YO1 9SA
phone +44 (0) 1904 624433
info@theolivetreeyork.co.uk
www.theolivetreeyork.co.uk

Beningbrough Hall
Beningbrough
York, North Yorkshire YO30 1DD
phone +44 (0 1904 470666
www.nationaktrust.org.uk

Castle Howard
York, North Yorkshire YO60 7DA
phone +44 (0) 1653 648444
www.castle howard.co.uk

Goddards Garden
27 Tadcaster Road
York, North Yorkshire YO24 166
phone +44 (0) 1904 702021
goddardsgarden@nationaltrust.org.uk

Jorvik Viking Centre
Coppergate
York, North Yorkshire YO1 1NT
phone +44 (0) 1904 643211
www.jorvik-viking-centre.co.uk

National Railway Museum
Leeman Road
York, North Yorkshire YO26 4XJ
www.nrm.org.uk

Treasurer's House
Chapter Street
York, North Yorkshire Y01 2JD
www.nationaltrust.org

Yorkshire Museum
Museum Gardens
York, North Yorkshire YO1 7FR
phone +44 (0) 1904 7FR
www.york.yorkshire.museum

Yorkshire Coast
Peakside
Ravenscar
Scarborough, North Yorkshire YO13 0NE
phone +44 (0) 1723 870423
yorkshirecoast@nationaltrust.org.uk

SUGGESTED READING

ART AND ARCHITECTURE

Girouard, Mark. *Life in the English Country House: A Social and Architectural History*. New Haven and London: Yale University Press, 1978.
The English Town. New Haven and London: Yale University Press, 1990.
Pevsner, Nikolaus. *The Cathedrals of England*. Two volumes, London: Viking, 1985.

CULTURE AND HISTORY

Ayto, John, and Crofton, Ian. *Brewer's Britain & Ireland: The History, Culture, Folklore and Etymology of 7500 Places in these Islands*. London: Weidenfeld & Nicolson, 2005.
Fisher, Mark. *Britain's Best Museums and Galleries*. London: Penguin Books, 2004.
Mosley, Charlotte (ed.). *The Mitfords: Letters between Six Sisters*. London: Fourth Estate, 2007.
Schama, Simon. *A History of Britain*. Three volumes, London: BBC Books, 2000.

LITERATURE

Austen, Jane. *Persuasion*. London: Penguin Classics.
Chaucer, Geoffrey. *The Canterbury Tales*. Trans. Neville Coghill. London: Penguin Classics (many reprintings).
Dickens, Charles. *Great Expectations*. London: Penguin Classics (many reprintings).
Golding, William. *The Spire*. London: Faber and Faber, 1964.
Shakespeare, William. *The Complete Works*. Eds. Stanley Wells and Gary Taylor. Oxford: Oxford University Press 1988 (many reprintings).
Marsh, Kate (ed.). *Writers and Their Houses: A Guide to the Writers' Houses of England, Scotland, Wales and Ireland: Essays by Modern Writers*. London: Hamish Hamilton, 1993.

TRAVEL

Barnes, David. *The Companion Guide to Wales*. Woodbridge: Companion Guides, 2005.
Bryson, Bill. *Notes from a Small Island*. London: Doubleday, 1995
Lehane, Brendan. *The Companion Guide to Ireland*. London: Collins, 1985.
Youngson, A.J. *The Companion Guide to Edinburgh and the Scottish Borders*. Woodbridge: Companion Guides, 2000.

PHOTOGRAPHY CREDITS

All the pictures in this book are by **Wojtek Buss** except the following:

127, 203, 208, 209, 211, 212, 213, 220, 221, 234, 235 Tips
210 Tips / Anne Montfort / Photononstop
202 Tips / Andrea Pistolesi
126 Tips / Petra Wegner

Wojtek Buss was born in 1963 and grew up on the Baltic coast. In 1987, he settled in France and began to specialize in travel photography. He has worked successfully for agencies including Cedri, Rapho, and Hoa-Qui (Eyedea). In recent years, he has concentrated on the architectural traditions of western and eastern Europe, and today much of his work is focused on journalism and prints. His photographs have been shown all over the world, from Paris to Barcelona, London, and New York.

First published in the United States of America in 2008
by Rizzoli International Publications, Inc.
300 Park Avenue South
New York, NY 10010
www.rizzoliusa.com

Production: Colophon srl, Venice, Italy

Editorial Direction: Andrea Grandese

Editor in Chief: Rosanna Alberti

Layout: Colophon, Venice

Design Concept: Stephen Fay

2008 2009 2010 2011 2012 2013 2014 2015 / 10 9 8 7 6 5 4 3 2 1

Printed in China

ISBN-13: 978-0-8478-3050-3

Library of Congress Control Number: 2008924558